Ride the Frontier

Ride the Frontier

*Exploring the Myth
of the American West on Screen*

Flavia Brizio-Skov

McFarland & Company, Inc., Publishers
Jefferson, North Carolina

This book has undergone peer review.

LIBRARY OF CONGRESS CATALOGUING-IN-PUBLICATION DATA

Names: Brizio-Skov, Flavia, author.
Title: Ride the frontier : exploring the myth of the American West on screen / Flavia Brizio-Skov.
Description: Jefferson, North Carolina : McFarland & Company, Inc., Publishers, 2021 | Includes bibliographical references and index.
Identifiers: LCCN 2020051550 | ISBN 9781476683065 (paperback : acid free paper) ∞
ISBN 9781476641911 (ebook)
Subjects: LCSH: Western films—History and criticism. | West (U.S.)—In motion pictures.
Classification: LCC PN1995.9.W4 .B75 2021 | DDC 791.43/65878—dc23
LC record available at https://lccn.loc.gov/2020051550

BRITISH LIBRARY CATALOGUING DATA ARE AVAILABLE

ISBN (print) 978-1-4766-8306-5
ISBN (ebook) 978-1-4766-4191-1

© 2021 Flavia Brizio-Skov. All rights reserved

No part of this book may be reproduced or transmitted in any form or by any means, electronic or mechanical, including photocopying or recording, or by any information storage and retrieval system, without permission in writing from the publisher.

Front cover image © 2021 Shutterstock/Silky

Printed in the United States of America

McFarland & Company, Inc., Publishers
 Box 611, Jefferson, North Carolina 28640
 www.mcfarlandpub.com

A David
e Esmeralda

A mio padre, mia madre, e a Vico in memoriam

Table of Contents

Acknowledgments   ix
Introduction: Why the Western?   1

1. Transnational Adaptation, Transculturation and Indigenization: Dashiell Hammett's *Red Harvest*, Carlo Goldoni's *The Servant of Two Masters*, Akira Kurosawa's *Yojimbo* and Sergio Leone's *A Fistful of Dollars*   13
    Prologue   13
    The National   16
    The Origins: Local and Translocal   22
    The Transnational   26
    Conclusion   42

2. Celluloid Indians, 1950s Westerns and the Termination Act: *Broken Arrow, White Feather, The Battle of Apache Pass, Devil's Doorway, The Last Wagon* and *The Last Hunt*   45
    Prologue   45
    Broken Arrow *(1950)*   52
    White Feather *(1955) and* The Battle of Apache Pass *(1952)*   57
    Devil's Doorway *(1950)*   59
    The Last Wagon *(1956)*   67
    The Last Hunt *(1956)*   74
    Conclusion   79

3. Heroines in Western Films? Mikhail Bakhtin's "Dialogic Imagination" in *Shane, High Noon* and *Westward the Women*   84
    Monoglossia: The Submissive Woman and Shane *(1953)*   89
    Heteroglossia: The Transgressive Woman and High Noon *(1952)*   93
    X-glossia: Transformational Women and Westward the Women *(1951)*   100

Table of Contents

4. Hybridity and (De)Construction of Femininity
   and Masculinity in *Rancho Notorious, Johnny Guitar*
   and *Duel in the Sun*   109
   - Rancho Notorious: *The Filmic Text (1952)*   111
   - Johnny Guitar: *Paratext*   121
   - Johnny Guitar: *Peritext and the Novel (1953)*   123
   - Johnny Guitar: *The Filmic Text (1954)*   127
   - Duel in the Sun *(1946): Paratext*   136
   - Duel in the Sun: *The Novel (1944)*   139
   - Duel in the Sun: *The Filmic Text (1946)*   141
   - *Patriarchy and Failed Masculinities*   143
   - *Patriarchy and Failed Femininities*   146
   - *Capitalism and Patriotism*   149

5. New Paths of the Western in the Third Millennium:
   The Lone Ranger, Yesterday and Today   152
   - *The Western Genre Today*   152
   - *Enter* The Lone Ranger: *Prologue*   155
   - The Lone Ranger *Yesterday or How the West Was Conquered*   156
   - The Lone Ranger *(2013): Paratext*   161
   - The Lone Ranger *Today or How the West Was Lost*   164

Chapter Notes   177

Bibliography   225

Index   233

Acknowledgments

I am indebted to the College of Arts and Science of the University of Tennessee for giving me the opportunity to commit two academic years to writing while serving as a Resident Fellow at the University of Tennessee Humanities Center. The fellowship was a rich and productive time that allowed me to dedicate myself entirely to my research and to bring my project to fruition. The opportunities afforded by the fellowships of the Humanities Center are truly central to the goals of the University Regents to elevate the University of Tennessee system into one of the top 25 public university systems in the country. I would like to acknowledge the importance that such research opportunities provide for faculty members to complete large projects.

Huge thanks are also due to my colleagues who have read, commented, and discussed my writings with acumen and understanding, sharing with me their knowledge and scholarship. I have cherished their comments. They are friends and scholars from all over the world, united by the same love for literature, cinema, and writing. I want to specifically acknowledge Tom Heffernan, Frank Burke, Flavia Laviosa, Mark Pietralunga, Anthony Tamburri, Ben Lawton, Paolo Russo, Susanna Delfino, Fernando Fasce, Maria José de Lancastre, and Rocco Morano. To them, and to many others not mentioned here, you have my personal and professional gratitude.

I want to express my thanks to my husband, David, an engineer in the Diplomatic Corps, who has a wonderful command of English and always commented on my writing with incredible insight and intelligence.

Last, but assuredly, not least, I thank, Gary Mitchem, senior editor at McFarland, who, based on my experience with the editorial universe acquired through many book projects, stands out as a rare exception.

Acknowledgments

Extremely knowledgeable, Gary gave freely of his time and was readily available at all junctures in the publishing process. I would like to thank another editor as well: my personal editor, Ed Miller, who helped me prepare this, and an earlier manuscript, with a dedication and passion that is hard to find.

Introduction: Why the Western?

As long as I can remember, when a rider with a cowboy hat, six-shooter, and spurs or a Native American wearing a headdress appears in the movie frame, I have been glued to the screen. I am not sure if this fascination derives from the spectacle, the vast expanse of the immense prairies, or from the wilderness. I am from Europe where such spaces never existed, but they have always had a special allure for me.

Of one thing I am sure, for me as for millions of other viewers who still love Western films, the "Wild West" has always represented the exotic, the mythical. This charm originated with historian Frederick Jackson Turner's theory of the frontier, pulp fiction, dime novels, Frederic Remington's paintings ... and especially with a cinema that since its inception has created a fictional land in which (white) justice always triumphs and heroes/heroines are for the most part invincible.[1] In fact, the "Wild West" as portrayed in movies never existed. It has always been a fantasy, but one so powerful, so fascinating, that it has survived on the screen to this day, more than a century after the U.S. Census of 1890 declared that the days of the American frontier were over.[2]

Nowadays the myth lives on, even though production of Western movies is much smaller than it was during the golden age of the genre, the 1940s and the 1950s.[3] In the third millennium, in a global digital world in which technological progress is constantly affecting, changing our lives, and shrinking the number of moviegoers, Westerns have continued to be made: *The Missing* (2003, dir. Tommy Lee Jones), *Once Upon a Time in Mexico* (2003, dir. Robert Rodriguez), *Open Range* (2003, dir. Kevin Costner), *The Proposition* (2005, dir. John Hillcoat), *Bandidas* (2006, dir. Walter Hill), *Seraphim Falls* (2006, dir. David Von Ancken), *3:10 to Yuma* (2007, dir. James Mangold), *The Assassination*

Introduction: Why the Western?

of Jesse James by the Coward Robert Ford (2007, dir. Andrew Dominik), *Sukiyaki Western Django* (2007, dir. Takashi Miike), *Appaloosa* (2008, dir. Ed Harris), *The Good, the Bad, the Weird* (2008, dir. Jee-woon Kim), *Jonah Hex* (2010, dir. Jimmy Hayward), *True Grit* (2010, dir. Joel and Ethan Coen), *The Warrior's Way* (2010, dir. Sigmoo Lee), *Cowboys and Aliens* (2011, dirs. Aaron and Tyler Berk), *Meek's Cutoff* (2011 dir. Kelly Reichardt), *Rango* (2011, dir. Gore Verbinski), *Django Unchained* (2012, dir. Quentin Tarantino), *The Lone Ranger* (2013, dir. Gore Verbinski), *The Homesman* (2014, dir. Tommy Lee Jones), *The Salvation* (2014, dir. Kristian Levring), *Slow West* (2015, dir. John Maclean), *The Hateful Eight* (2015, dir. Quentin Tarantino), *The Revenant* (2015, dir. Alejandro Inarritu), *Bone Tomahawk* (2015, dir. S. Craig Zahler), *Jane Got a Gun* (2016, dir. Gavin O'Connor), *The Magnificent Seven* (2016, dir. Antoine Fuqua), *Hostiles* (2017, dir. Scott Cooper), and *Woman Walks Ahead* (2018, dir. Susanna White).[4]

As Paryz and Leo affirm, "After 2000, it would be difficult to point out such breakthrough moments as the releases of Costner's [*Dances with Wolves*, 1990] and Eastwood's [*Unforgiven*, 1992] films in the early 1990s...."[5] For Paryz and Leo, the Western "will not recover its previous status," even if it will remain a culturally valid form of film art.[6]

The Westerns of the third millennium have so far shown an infusion of new stylistic and narrative solutions into old themes as in the case of remakes (*3:10 to Yuma, The Magnificent Seven, True Grit*). There has been a cross-pollination with other genres like horror (*The Quick and the Undead, Western Zombie*) and science fiction (*Rango, Cowboys and Aliens*) and hybridity between spaghetti Western and Southern slavery themes (*Django Unchained*).[7] Transplantation and citation of spaghetti Westerns, mixed with martial arts, and parody, created cross-cultural adaptations in South-Asian productions (*Sukiyaki Western Django, The Good, the Bad, the Weird*). Many films reworked the "revenge story" (*The Salvation*), some centering it on a heroine (*True Grit, Jane Got a Gun, Bandidas*). *Appaloosa* functioned as a reverse mirror of *Unforgiven*, being focused on "forgiveness" and subverting traditional patriarchal values. *The Hateful Eight*, through astonishing camera work and a masterful, but claustrophobic *mise-en-scène*, created a narrative in which the old formula is reduced to one item, violence—a violence that causes total destruction, leaving no survivors. So far, Tarantino is the only director who has made a Western populated exclusively by hateful characters, all of whom deserve to die.[8]

Introduction: Why the Western?

While the film output is scaled down, although still alive, in recent years, research on the Western has proliferated. I am not talking about the works of scholars who are considered the staple of the genre—the pioneers whose books jumpstarted the research on Western cinema. Many volumes have appeared in the last two decades that explore interesting themes that branched into transnational, cultural, and popular theories, superseding the original structuralist/semiotic, and *auteur*-oriented studies of the past.[9] Early critical studies of the Western opened up the terms of a debate about the meaning of the Western, its relationship to both its time setting and the time of its production, establishing the boundaries of the cinematic genre, and situating it in a complex relation with contemporary culture, ideology, and history. Acknowledging such a vast scholarship, this study concentrates instead on the body of critical works that have appeared in the third millennium, using David Lusted's *The Western* as an ideal jumping off point, as it already provides a useful overview of the critical literature on the subject up to the year 2000.[10]

A sample of the latest endeavors in the field includes: Jeremy Byman, *Showdown at High Noon* (2004); Stanley Corkin, *Cowboys as Cold Warriors* (2004); John E. O'Connor, *Hollywood's West* (2005); Stephen McVeigh, *The American Western* (2007); Patrick McGee, *From Shane to Kill Bill: Rethinking the Western* (2007); Neil Campbell, *The Rhizomatic West: Representing the American West in a Transnational, Global, Media Age* (2008); Robert B. Pippin, *Hollywood Westerns and American Myth* (2010); Jennifer L. McMahon and B. Steve Csaki (eds.), *The Philosophy of the Western* (2010); Austin Fisher, *Radical Frontiers in the Spaghetti Western* (2011); Mary Lea Bandy and Kevin Stoehr, *Ride, Boldly Ride* (2012); Thomas Klein, Ivo Ritzer and Peter Schulze (eds.), *Crossing Frontiers: Intercultural Perspectives on the Western* (2012); Cynthia J. Miller and A. Bowdoin Van Riper (eds.), *Undead in the West: Vampires, Mummies, Zombies, and Ghosts on the Cinematic Frontier* (2012); Sue Matheson (ed.), *Love in Western Film and Television* (2013); Andrew Patrick Nelson (ed.), *Contemporary Westerns: Film and Television Since 1990* (2013); Neill Campbell, *Post-Westerns—Cinema, Region, West* (2013); Cynthia J. Miller and A. Bowdoin Van Riper (eds.), *International Westerns: Re-Locating the Frontier* (2013); Pawel Goral, *Cold War Rivalry and the Perception of the American West* (2014); Mary Ellen Higgins, Rita Keresztesi, and Dana Oscherwitz (eds.), *The Western in the Global South* (2015); Marek Paryz and Jihn

Introduction: Why the Western?

R. Leo (eds.), *The Post-2000 Film Western: Contexts, Transnationality, Hybridity* (2015); Andrew Patrick Nelson, *Still in the Saddle* (2015); Richard Aquila, *The Sagebrush Trail* (2015); Matthew Carter, *Myth of the Western* (2015); Lee Broughton, *Euro-Western* (2016); Scott F. Stoddard (ed.), *The New Western—Critical Essays on the Genre Since 9/11* (2016); Austin Fisher (ed.), *Spaghetti Westerns at the Crossroads: Studies in Relocation, Transition and Appropriation* (2016); Sue Matheson (ed.) *A Fistful of Icons* (2017); Iain Robert Smith, *The Hollywood Meme* (2017).[11]

Even a cursory browsing of the above titles reveals how, in recent scholarship, the West as a space has been refocused outside the canonical conceptual grids of the empire—that is, national identity, epic conquest, Turner's Frontier, and Manifest Destiny. Less and less it is seen as "epic" space—settled, enclosed, and internally coherent, fixed in time and etched in memory—rather than a "meeting place, the location of the intersections of particular bundles of activity spaces, of connections and interrelations, of influences and movements."[12] The brilliant attempt by Neil Campbell to reconstitute the American West within the critical discourses of Arjun Appadurai, Deleuze and Guattari, Paul Giles, Derrida, Paul Gilroy, and James Clifford among others, has opened up new territories of exploration: the West has become "rhizomatic," that is a cultural space of disparate cultures, the site of a clash of different races whereby American identities should no longer be shaped according to restricted *local* parameters.[13] Campbell de-territorializes the West and displaces static myths, thinking of the American West as a site of interference, interaction that is constantly expanding. These "lines of flight" produce the rhizomatic West. Instead of a coherent national narrative, Campbell sees multiple voices entering into mutual relations of dialogue, parody, contestation, and the West as a place where centripetal and centrifugal forces intersect, compelling us to consider what lies outside the mapped grid, and the porous borders between the inside and the outside. Turner's idea of the frontier as a single line that leads to one destination characterized by nationhood, union, and a fixed identity, basically the conceptual grid of the "establishment," has been "de-framed" so we can now scrutinize from the outside the ideologies, practices, texts and official mythologies.[14]

According to Campbell, it is necessary to move away from the old utopia of unity, away from the "obsession with 'roots,' 'place,' and nationhood and to reposition the West within a more transnational,

Introduction: Why the Western?

global matrix."[15] Venturing beyond national and nationalistic perspectives offers ways of shifting toward a post–Western perspective "where the 'post' signifies the 'going beyond' and 'after' the established and 'taken-for-granted' notions of the West as a fixed and settled phenomenon."[16] Moreover, Campbell remarks, "the straight line (road, frontier, grid, linear history and narrative, monologue) is disrupted by the trope of crossing (dialogue, diaspora, rhizome…)"[17] in a revisionary process full of 'untidy elements in a story of hybridization and intermixture that inevitably disappoints the desire for cultural and therefore racial purity.'"[18] It is inside these parameters that many of the studies mentioned above and my present work articulate themselves critically. Campbell, Bakhtin and others have opened up a discourse that allows us to look back at the cultural artifacts of the past under a new light. With this in mind, I traced the transnational trajectory of a "meme" that migrated and replicated itself in different forms and across boundaries: the transcultural genesis of Leone's *A Fistful of Dollars* (Chapter 1).[19] Following Iain Robert Smith's lead, I explored the complex dynamics underpinning the circulation of cinema, to see what precisely happens when an American model, in our case the Western, is appropriated and reworked by multiple cultures, highlighting the interstitial and porous nature of each culture and how, nevertheless, every culture maintains a certain specificity, overcoming models of dominance or resistance.[20]

Chapter 1, in fact, traces from the bottom up the development of *A Fistful of Dollars* as a paradigmatic case of transnational adaptation, transculturation, and indigenization, examining the different popular texts—filmic and literary—involved in the process: namely, Dashiell Hammett's *Red Harvest*, Carlo Goldoni's *The Servant of Two Masters* and Akira Kurosawa's *Yojimbo*. I isolate the national from the transnational, the local from the translocal, aware that "the local always has to be seen against the background of the global,"[21] and without forgetting specific cultural, economic contexts and ideological backgrounds. The study of the hybridization process that gave rise to the first Italian spaghetti Western becomes a point of departure and not of arrival in the critical investigation.

In order to further deconstruct the hegemonic grid and the myth of the "melting pot," Chapter 2 unpacks a group of 1950s Westerns that claimed to be "historically based narrations." While silencing the "Other" and reifying the image of cavalry and of the communities involved, these films appear as "protectors" of the "vanishing Americans," trying, on

Introduction: Why the Western?

one level, to appease their audience and, on another, burying deeply inside their narrations any thorny issues related to acts of extermination. The so called "pro–Indian" cycle of the 1950s isolates a "model" that gets repeated over and over very successfully and is exemplified by three films—*Broken Arrow* (1950), *The Battle of Apache Pass* (1952) and *White Feather* (1955)—that projected on screen a consolatory image of the Indians. By pinning these three prototypical titles against three films of the same period—*Devil's Doorway* (1950), *The Last Wagon* (1956) and *The Last Hunt* (1956)—that sympathetically and more sincerely portrayed on screen the tragic dilemma of Native Americans, trapped as they were between the "Termination Act" and forced assimilation, the civil rights struggle and preservation of their heritage, my analysis demonstrates that the American public was not ready to accept a truly pro–Indian message. In fact, while movies that contained hidden hegemonic and paternalistic sub-texts were extremely successful with critics and public alike, the three "liberal" Westerns mentioned above received vehement reviews and failed at the box-office. The bulk of the pro–Indian cycle embodies more the dream of a harmonious possible coexistence between Indians and whites than an indictment of social discrimination. Most of these films propose complete assimilation to the white ways as a solution to the "Indian problem," together with total acceptance of white expansionism and peaceful reservation existence. *Devil's Doorway*, *The Last Wagon* and *The Last Hunt*, on the other hand, try to extend justice and equality to the "Other," offering a more liberal racial perspective through filmic texts about intolerance toward the Indian.

Bakhtin's *The Dialogic Imagination* has been a helpful guide to placing Chapter 3 "outside" the narrative discourse of many filmic texts (i.e., outside the male hegemonic point of view), so as to step out of the "ideal reader's position" to assume the role of the rebellious archeologist who digs out the discourse of the Other to give voice to white and racialized women alike. Going against the grain of much scholarship, I contend that heroines do populate the Western genre. The crux of the problem is that for the longest time women in Westerns have been viewed through the wrong lens, which tended to focus either on the male hero or on the main plotline to the point that female characters have often gone unnoticed. Bakhtin speaks of "monoglossic discourse" as the language of authority, the utterance whose function is to re-inscribe cultural myths of power and their representation; on the

Introduction: Why the Western?

other hand, heteroglossia challenges the dominant ideology and permits a multiplicity of voices. Furthermore, x-glossia is the moment of transformation in which a new identity is created that transcends the binary opposition of heteroglossia (i.e., self vs. authoritative voice) or the impositions of the language of power (monoglossia). X-glossia is the creation of something new, of new identities, and in it the word and the intention of the self and of the Other are transcended. Using Bakhtin as a magnifier, I therefore look at discourse as a bearer of gendered identification, analyzing *Shane* and *High Noon* as examples respectively of monoglossia and heteroglossia and *Westward the Women*—a film almost forgotten by critics—as a rare example of x-glossia. It goes without saying that in the case of heteroglossia and x-glossia we have heroines, independent female characters who are, as much as the male heroes, in charge of their own destiny.

Building on this, Chapter 4 examines hybridity as the coexistence of antagonistic discourses inside a narrative body that blends different cinematic genres, whose "lines of flight" create centripetal and centrifugal forces inside the same text—tangled lines that, by taking us "off the map," open the door to new meanings and transfuse "new blood" into "old fabric." As Campbell suggests, by removing oneself from the dominant center one can "glimpse alternative, critical, transformative, 'virtual' (unthought/unseen) perspectives that help reshape and question persistent grids of representation."[22]

Three Hollywood classic Westerns of the postwar era succeed in different ways in constructing an unusual image both of femininity and masculinity: *Duel in the Sun* (1946), *Rancho Notorious* (1952), and *Johnny Guitar* (1954) all hybridize Western with melodrama to project on screen "the collective drives, conscious and unconscious, of the American [contemporary] woman."[23] The adherence to the male order oscillates between rebellion and resiliency and sometimes results in total refusal, producing interesting results such as heroines stealing away the leading roles from the male characters. Moral order is hardly ever restored, and violence brings punishment, but rarely a positive solution. The happy ending is non-existent, and trauma gets added to the formula. The heroes, like the female protagonists, are usually tortured individuals consumed by harrowing desires often unacceptable by society. These characters are either prisoners of masculinity models coded in contradictory terms or victims of passions they cannot restrain. Both the heroes and the heroines suffer a crisis and a change of

Introduction: Why the Western?

identity that often cannot be reconciled and, therefore, push them along a doomed trajectory.

While in melodramas there is a romantic triangle, some betrayals and, at the end, a resolution that offers an example of redemption and moral rectitude, these films subvert the model. Here the excessive emotions externalized through violent actions are the expression of anger at different manifestations of injustice. These films address various notions of class, gender, racial issues, and social inequality. As a result, they create femininities and masculinities along very different lines from the ones of more traditional Westerns (e.g., *Shane*, *The Searchers*). These male and female protagonists do not conform. In the best scenario, they are marginalized from society (*Johnny Guitar*), and in the worst cases (*Rancho Notorious*, *Duel in the Sun*), they plunge into unlawfulness and destruction. These films are not failed Westerns as some critics have claimed; they are hybrids that have exceeded the boundaries of the Western genre, smuggling into it romance and melodrama, altering the archetypal formula of good versus evil with incursions into psychology, class, domination and race. For what is most significant in melodrama, according to Jonna Eagle, is the "ability to produce the terms of morality, precisely at the level of feeling, to articulate morality as and through feelings. ... It is the merger of morality and sensation that makes melodrama such an efficacious mode of representation—the conjunction of a visceral, affectively rich address with the project of excavating the signifiers of good and evil...."[24]

Chapter 5 sets forth with an overview of the critical discussion around the Western genre as a trajectory of films that started as horse operas in the silent era, acquired more complexity in the 1930s, became "classic" and peaked in the 1950s and early 1960s and then started to decline. Against this evolutionist approach are critics like Steve Neale who affirms that genres are, "processes ... dominated by repetition, but ... also marked fundamentally by difference, variation and changes."[25] In order to determine whether the Westerns of the third millennium constitute a legacy of the past or a radical shift from it, Chapter 5 compares two versions of an extremely popular model: *The Lone Ranger*. Started as a radio show aired in the 1930s, *The Lone Ranger* became a TV series in the 1950s, acquiring a tremendous popularity that lasted into the 1960s. In 2013, Gore Verbinski directed a new version of *The Lone Ranger* based on the original texts. The exorbitant cost of the film and its equally enormous lack of popularity among critics and viewers alike convinced me

Introduction: Why the Western?

to pursue a thorough comparison between the original and the hypertext. The results of my analysis prove that the film is not a remake, but a permutation/transformation of the original seminal texts.[26]

Verbinski's film is a special "adaptation" in the sense that it happens inside the same culture and not across different ones. I believe that the word "remake," in this instance, does not fit the film, because we face a hypertext in which "a unit of culture ... spreads and replicates, transforming itself to fit with whatever new habitat it finds itself in" and the third millennium is certainly a new habitat in which to situate the old story, being populated by a new audience and by new ideologies or lack of.[27] The new version contains a comic exuberance that the older version lacked, presenting a rhythmic orchestration of actions, violence, and strange realities that make it difficult to decide if the narration commands the events or if the action rules the narration. The end of the film resists narrative closure and opens up many possibilities. At the incipit of the film, we meet old Tonto in a sort of Wild West museum. The frontier is obviously over and can only be remembered in a diorama; like the bison and the grizzly, the Native American is a specimen of a species so endangered that it gets exhibited in a museum setting. Starting from this premise that the Indian is a vanishing breed, it is comforting to see that, in the end, the narration has empowered Tonto, liberating him from the strictures of the stereotypical characterization of the original so much that he has stopped being someone who succumbs to servitude and submission. In fact, he manages to go back where he belongs. Re-imagining the Lone Ranger story along different lines than the source has allowed the film to offer the viewers alternative forms of consciousness in addressing Native Americans.

Ride the Frontier locates itself at the intersection of Italian and American cinema studies, cultural theories, and film criticism. For this reason, it is a hybrid that does not fit into a definite niche but, rather, extends rhizomatically into multiple areas. For readers and scholars who are wondering if there is a common theme in this book, I can say that there is indeed one, and it could be summarized as looking at the past with new eyes, or, as Campbell puts it, "Ask different questions that force us to 'look again' ideologically at what we have taken for granted."[28] Chronologically, there is more cohesion than might appear at first: most of the films I analyzed belong to the golden age of the Western genre, that is the 1940s and the early 1950s, the only incursion into the present being Verbinski's *The Lone Ranger*, whose model, however, reached

Introduction: Why the Western?

maximum popularity in the 1950s with the televisual series. Thematically, this volume is kept together by the desire to fill some of the many gaps that I have found in the studies of the genre. I was motivated by the desire to show that the spaghetti Westerns are not a sub-genre, a spin-off or the ugly duckling of the American Western. On the contrary, they are a "variation" that has profoundly affected (and still does affect) the history of the Western production worldwide.[29]

Celluloid Indians have been sporadically studied; it was time to look into the very popular and successful pro–Indian filmic cycle of the 1950s, produced during one of the more complex periods in the history of the United States, to see what kind of discrepancy existed between what we see on screen and what happened in society to Native Americans. It was time to see how much reification, hiding, and silencing was involved in the filmic narrations after the Indians stopped appearing on screen as "hollering savages" and became more defined characters. It was time to discover which texts had the courage to reverberate, transposed in a fictional past, the contemporary situation of the Native Americans.[30]

In the classic Westerns,[31] the woman is normally depicted as a center of civilization. She is often the one who changes the hero's destiny, so in the end, instead of roaming the prairie looking for adventures, he will be absorbed into the community and, as a family man, he will contribute to progress. However, in many Westerns she remains a marginal character who waits around for the hero to come back or needs to be rescued from a dangerous situation; she is hardly ever in charge of her own destiny. The marginality of female characters, the fact that they don't often influence the action, usually pushed forward by the male hero, has convinced some critics that the Western is indeed a masculine genre, in which women are marginalized.[32] Nevertheless, through the notion of Bakhtin's dialogic imagination one realizes that it is indeed possible to find heroines also in the classic Western era.

Some of the films analyzed here (namely, *Rancho Notorious*, *Johnny Guitar*, *Duel in the Sun*) received lukewarm critical reception at the time of release but, over time, became cult movies. Deconstructing these "bad Westerns" is a way to bring to the surface the hidden subtexts (oppression of patriarchy, race, women's roles, and power dynamics in society) that exist under the main narrations. These were considered flawed products, Westerns that had too much, or too little of the "right ingredients"; however, they turned out to be melodramas that

Introduction: Why the Western?

mix trauma, class oppression, sexual liberation, passion, and injustice together in, iconographically speaking, glamorous and alluring "packages" that still fascinate the viewer.

Finally, Disney's *The Lone Ranger* was an interesting case study of a film with an excellent pedigree—being made by the same team that worked on the celebrated *Pirates of the Caribbean* franchise—that became unpopular among public and critics alike. As per Shelley Armitage, perhaps only the baby boomers were familiar with the subject, whereas children and juveniles—the typical Disney audiences of today—were not familiar enough with the story of the Lone Ranger and his sidekick Tonto.[33] To dig into the text to discover the possible causes of this failure was an intriguing proposition that ultimately evidenced how the film was in fact carefully put together, and managed to subvert the traditional linear narration of many Westerns. Verbinski, in fact, "liberates" Tonto from bondage, and delivers a time-image text; his film is an original Western that is too complex and too sophisticated for the average viewer, and constitutes a "model," or at least, an inspiration for future production, and certainly is a "variation" worth studying.[34]

In *Ride the Frontier* I explore many filmic texts that, using Campbell's words, "participate in many of the formal, thematic, and topic discourses of the classic, established Western, while not belonging entirely within its borders."[35] It becomes evident that genre is understood here as a process, full of variations, modifications, and changes, as Neale asserts, but also, in a Derridean sense, as a process of "contamination, a law of impurity ... a sort of participating without belonging—a taking part in without being part of..." because genres are always rhizomatic.[36]

1

Transnational Adaptation, Transculturation and Indigenization

Dashiell Hammett's Red Harvest, *Carlo Goldoni's* The Servant of Two Masters, *Akira Kurosawa's* Yojimbo *and Sergio Leone's* A Fistful of Dollars

Prologue

All films are national in the sense that they are the product of a specific culture and a certain language. Nonetheless, the industry's mission of disseminating films all over the world for profit makes any film into a transnational product destined to travel beyond the borders of its country of origin. We could assume, therefore, that all films are in some sense transnational in nature; in fact, recently this idea has been backed up by the debate about what constitutes a "nation." Nation as a monolithic entity made up of people having the same customs and culture, speaking the same language, and living within the same geographical borders has been proven to be an obsolete concept because all nations seem to be composed of a polyphony of social and ethnic voices within heteroglot cultures. As Shohat and Stam affirm:

> Any definition of nationality, then, must see it as partly discursive in nature, must take class, gender, and sexuality into account, must allow for racial differences and cultural heterogeneity, and must be dynamic, seeing "the nation" as an evolving, imaginary construct rather than an original essence.[1]

1. Transnational Adaptation, Transculturation, Indigenization

Things get complicated even further because cinema is also part of popular culture. In the past, the term "mass culture" recalled the Frankfurt School and the oppressive culture of capitalist consumerism, as "culture fed to the people"; whereas, "popular culture" evoked Gramsci and a culture "produced by and for the people."[2] Nowadays, according to some critics, it is impossible to make such a distinction because mass and popular culture are imbricated and "popular culture is now fully enmeshed in transnational globalized techno-culture."[3]

The term transnational originated in the historical field in the late 1990s when Ian Tyrrell's seminal essay "What Is Transnational History?" changed the course of the academic discipline, claiming that studying the history of a nation from inside its borders is outmoded because the study of history concerns the movements of peoples, ideas, technologies, and institutions across national boundaries.[4]

The study of cross-national influences and the focus on the relationship between nation and factors beyond the nation spilled over into many other fields, especially into cinematic studies. Today, transnational refers to the impossibility of assigning a fixed national identity to much cinema, to the dissolution of any stable connection between film's place of production and the nationality of its makers and performers.[5] As Ezra and Rowden observe:

> The global circulation of money, commodities, information, and human beings is giving rise to films whose aesthetic and narrative dynamics, and even the modes of emotional identification they elicit, reflect the impact of advanced capitalism and new media technologies as components of an increasingly interconnected world-system. [...] The concept of transnationalism enables us to better understand the changing ways in which the contemporary world is being imagined by an increasing number of filmmakers across genres as a global system rather than as a collection of more or less autonomous nations.[6]

The increased circulation of films has been made possible by technologies such as videos, DVD, digital media, and international film festivals as well as geopolitical events like the end of the Cold War with the fall of the Berlin Wall, the birth of the European Union and so on. Therefore, "transnational cinema arises in the interstices between the local and the global,"[7] taking into account issues of power, hegemony, migration, exile, political asylum, terrorism, tourism, class, race, gender, sexuality, minorities, diasporic identities, technology and all the other "post-" prefixes (post-industrialism, postmodernism, postcolonialism, post-capitalism).

Prologue

The film industry, however, has long operated on a transnational basis. Since the 1920s films have been made as co-productions, using the resources and experiences of different nations, and very often directors have been nomadic, going from one production base to another.[8] Furthermore, cinema has always been transnational when it comes to distribution and reception. The meaning that an audience reads into a film is dependent on the "indigenous" culture of the viewers, with outcomes that, according to Higson, can range from cultural imperialism to liberating effects or re-interpretations along indigenous frames of reference.[9]

This chapter, therefore, will map the itinerary of a specific text from its literary origin to its filmic renditions, and will demonstrate how "transnational and national" mutate and undergo hybridization, changing from novel to screen, and emigrating from one nation to another. To this purpose, Sergio Leone's *A Fistful of Dollars* (1964) is a paradigmatic case study, released as it was at a time when studies of European cinema focused mostly on historically specific national movements such as Italian Neorealism, French *Nouvelle Vague*, German Expressionism, or on individual *auteurs* and art cinema (Rossellini, Godard, Bergman, Resnais), considered at the time as the only artistic expressions of a national cinema worthy of consideration.[10]

In the complex debate about national and transnational cinema, the study of international remakes is a promising method to map the field with some accuracy.[11] Remakes or adaptations in all their variations, from novel to screen, from film to film, from play to screen, and so on, imply a process of transculturation, re-appropriation, reinterpretation and permutation.[12] As Linda Hutcheon points out, adaptation "… is repetition, but without replication, bringing together the comfort of the ritual and recognition with the delight of surprise and novelty … it involves both memory and change, persistence and variation."[13]

One of the best known cases of transnational adaptation occurred between Akira Kurosawa's *Yojimbo* (1961) and Sergio Leone's *A Fistful of Dollars* (1964).[14] The (uncredited) inspiration for the Japanese film was a detective story, *Red Harvest* (1929), by Dashiell Hammett (1894–1961). The prototext, thus, emigrated from the Unites States to Japan and then to Italy, transitioning across genres. Tracing the history of this prototext will prove not only that cinema is transnational, but also that "cultural formations are invariably hybrid and impure."[15] At the beginning of the 1960s, the classic American Western was still a commodity

1. Transnational Adaptation, Transculturation, Indigenization

exported across national boundaries by the powerful Hollywood distribution machinery, even though no longer in numbers as high as in the 1940s and 1950s. Leone (1929–1989), a profound *connoisseur* of classic Westerns and an admirer of the genre, "transported" the American Western into an Italian frame of reference that jettisoned the ideological foundation of the original, modified it, imbued it with a different value system and redistributed it worldwide very successfully. The revolutionary, iconoclastic, violent and rebellious message of the first spaghetti Western gave rise to a new type of Western.[16] The influence of classic Hollywood Westerns on Leone's films is undeniable, but by the time his trilogy was distributed worldwide he became an established icon of world cinema and his films, in turn, became models for American Western directors.[17]

The National

The Italian Cinematic Scene

The first center-left government of Italy was created in 1963. The Christian-Democrat Party that had ruled the Ministry of Tourism and Entertainment with a conservative grip since 1948 lost its absolute majority. At the Rome Experimental Center for Cinematography, the Venice Film Festival, and at the Italian Radio and Television (RAI), more open-minded people started changing the decision-making process.[18] In 1962, Parliament modified the existing censorship law provision: the new commissions consisted of cinema experts designated by representatives of the various cinematic sectors of the film industry, not only magistrates and ministry officials chosen by the government until then.[19] In this more relaxed atmosphere, the Italian cinema of the 1960s thrived: comedy Italian Style became more sexually daring, the spaghetti Western more violent, the *Mondo* documentaries more explicit. The "economic boom" of the early 1960s launched an unprecedented process of modernization, introduced all classes to mass consumption, and changed the social and economic fiber of the whole nation. As a matter of fact, this actualized a process that should have happened at the end of World War II, but was delayed for different reasons: the destruction of the infrastructure of the country during the conflict, the permanence of old-guard fascist mentality in the juridical, legislative,

The National

and administrative branches of the government, and the onset of the Cold War that split the country into ideologically opposed political camps, the Communists on one side and the Christian Democrats and the Catholic Church on the other.[20]

Despite the complex socio-political situation, the 1960s is considered the period of maximum splendor in the Italian cinematic industry (see Brunetta 2003, Bondanella 2009). Fellini's *La dolce vita* (1960) was number one at the box office. Antonioni's *L'avventura* won the Palme d'Or at the Cannes Film Festival (1961). Visconti's *Rocco e i suoi fratelli* (1960) and De Sica's *La ciociara* (1960), like the films of other renowned directors (Pasolini, Germi, Rosi, Zurlini, Petri, Bertolucci, Ferreri, Maselli, Bellocchio, De Seta, Olmi, Cavani), were successfully received by the public and critics. In the realm of genre cinema, Comedy Italian Style debunked taboos and flaws of the *italiano medio*[21] by satirizing their habits, greed, and lack of integrity, and became enormously popular, thanks to directors like Monicelli, Risi, Comencini, Germi, Zampa, Lattuada, Sordi, Scola, and Salce, whose films constituted the core of a vast and successful production of *commedie amare*.[22] *Auteur* films and Comedy Italian Style distinguished Italian cinema from Hollywood by the use of the nation's particular language and cultural themes.[23] However, the success enjoyed throughout the 1960s and until the late 1970s is also linked to other types of popular genres such as *peplum*, horror, and spaghetti Western, to mention the biggest productions. These genres, however, would not all fall easily into the category of national cinema.[24]

The Hybrid Genres

Since the 1920s, Italy has had a long history of "American cultural colonization"; from the time of Rudolph Valentino, the national market has been dominated by Hollywood imports. The impact of a brief hiatus between 1938 and 1945, during which foreign films (except German films) disappeared from the Italian screen, was quickly lost amid the large backlog of American films that the Allied Forces dumped on the national circuit from 1945 on.[25] As is now commonly recognized, the dominance of American cinema in the immediate postwar era was motivated by geopolitical and ideological reasons: Italy was in the center of the Mediterranean and had a strong Communist Party. The Americans helped the Christian Democrats gain power to prevent any possible

1. Transnational Adaptation, Transculturation, Indigenization

defection towards Communism, and poured a lot of money into Italian reconstruction via the Marshall Plan, thus gaining, in exchange, a strategic place in the Mediterranean. During the Cold War, it became imperative to promote, against the Soviet model, the superiority of the "American way of life" through culture. Cinema, together with other economic and political venues, was an ideal vehicle to achieve such a goal.[26]

In the postwar era, American runaway companies came to Italy to reinvest funds blocked by the Italian government.[27] Italian state funds and the American dollars turned Cinecittà in the 1950s into "Hollywood on the Tiber."[28] The first production was *Quo Vadis?* (Mervyn LeRoy, 1951), an historical epic filmed entirely in the Italian studios. LeRoy's movie was followed by many others, including *Ben-Hur* (William Wyler, 1959) and *Cleopatra* (Joseph Mankiewicz, 1963). The historical epic had been an asset of Italian national cinema since the silent era (*Cabiria*, directed by Pastrone, 1914), had been popular during Fascism, (*Scipione l'Africano*, directed by Carmine Gallone, 1937) and even after the war (*Fabiola*, directed by Blasetti, 1948). Throughout the 1950s and until 1963, Italian directors realized that they could recycle set materials and found footage left over by the American productions, using their inventiveness to create low-budget historical and mythological films. Their commercial operation created a genre called *peplum*. As D'Amelio points out, *peplum* was an example of transnational cinema, wherein American body builders were hired to play the Hercules/Maciste/Ursus/Sansone protagonist, and contributed greatly to the Americanization of Italian culture, consolidating the ideal of American superiority, and celebrating over and over the white male hero who, through superior strength, defeats injustice.[29] If we exclude their cinematic roots, the sandal-and-sword epics were less an example of national cinema than of transnational cinema, or, more precisely, of a national cinema that "Americanizes" itself. Such self–Americanization is also made apparent by the widespread practice of Anglicizing cast names, so that the public would believe they were watching a Hollywood production instead of a low-budget Italian film.

Even though the spaghetti Western can be easily associated with the *peplum* and considered a similar case of American self-colonization, the two popular genres need to be kept separate. The *peplum*'s ideological message could be summarized by the famous sentence from *The Leopard*, "If we want things to stay as they are, things will have to change," a statement that underlines the conservative message of these sandal films in which the hero routinely rescues people from the bad ruler so that the good ruler can be reinstated.[30] The mythological epic "formula" is used to favor the status quo, in the hope that the Italians would continue to vote for the party in power (the Christian Democrats) away from any possible leftist persuasion.[31] The case of the spaghetti Western is different. The Italian Western constitutes a special case of hybridity, being the heir of a more complex and modern vision of the world in which the American hegemonic message gets absorbed, de-constructed and spewed out as something else.

Sergio Leone

Thanks to a monumental biography by Sir Christopher Frayling, titled *Sergio Leone: Something to Do About Death*, we have gained vast knowledge of the Italian director.[32] The volume not only offers an enormous amount of accurate and detailed information about the socio-political climate of the time, the cinematic industry, and the Italian and American filmmakers who came in contact with Leone, it is also an *homage* to a cinematic genius and an act of love toward an admired friend. In 1946 young Leone started as a runner on the sets of films by established directors of the pre-war period—Mario Camerini (Leone's godfather), Carmine Gallone, and Mario Bonnard, all friends of Leone's father.[33] Between 1946 and 1956 Leone was assistant director for Luigi Comencini, Mario Soldati, Aldo Fabrizi, and Steno, collaborating also on various screenplays. He was also second-unit director in various colossal epics—*Quo Vadis?* (Mervyn LeRoy, 1951), *Helen of Troy* (Robert Wise/Raoul Walsh, 1956), *Ben-Hur* (William Wyler, 1959)—and had the opportunity to work with some of the filmmakers of his favorite Westerns: William Wyler (*The Westerner*, 1940; *The Big Country*, 1958) and Raoul Walsh (*The Big Trail*, 1930; *They Died with Their Boots On*, 1941; *Pursued*, 1947; *Colorado Territory*, 1949). In 1958 he was second-unit director on Fred Zinnemann's *The Nun's Story* (1959), filming the Congo sequences. Leone was also thrilled to work with the director of *High Noon* (Zinnemann, 1952).

From 1948 to 1959, Leone worked on about 50 films, learning, as he claimed in an interview, "what not to do when directing."[34] As a well-known and highly-paid assistant director, he was somebody who could manage large crowds on the set and could also direct complex

1. Transnational Adaptation, Transculturation, Indigenization

second-unit action sequences like the chariot-race in *Ben-Hur*, sea battles between triremes, explosions on galleys, and so on.[35] In 1959 Leone helped Bonnard on the set of *The Last Days of Pompeii*, an Italian-Spanish-West German co-production shot in the countryside of Andalusia, the Spanish locations that Leone would use later on for his Westerns. When Bonnard got sick, Leone took over the film (uncredited) and called in a group of young collaborators; these were Sergio Corbucci, Duccio Tessari, Enzo Barboni and Franco Giraldi, the future founding fathers of the spaghetti Westerns.[36] The success of *Pompeii* gave Leone the opportunity to direct his first feature film, a *peplum* titled *The Colossus of Rhodes* (1959).

The *Colossus* was a costume film in which irony and the nonchalant attitude of the protagonist (Rory Calhoun) subverted completely the image created by the muscular protagonists of mainstream *pepla*. The attitude of the hero had more in common with Eastwood's future *persona* in the Western trilogy than with the sandal-and-sword epics of the time. The visual imagination of Leone in the construction of the thirty-meter-high colossus in the battle and earthquake scenes turned the movie into a box office success. The film harvested 657 million lire on the national circuit, making Leone a much sought-after filmmaker.

Surprisingly enough, in 1961, instead of directing his own film, Leone accepted work again as second-unit director for Robert Aldrich in *Sodom and Gomorrah*, perhaps, as Frayling suggests, to have the opportunity to meet the maker of famous Westerns like *Apache* (1954), *Vera Cruz* (1954), and *The Last Sunset* (1961). The collaboration did not work out well. Leone, however, directed a spectacular sequence, the charge of the Helamites in the Moroccan desert that was praised by the critics, combining "helicopter shots, a specially dug runway, a camera-car in the thick of the action, and close-ups of hooves, faces, spears, all edited in accelerating rhythm."[37] Then, in 1963 Leone saw *Yojimbo* by Akira Kurosawa and, as his wife said in an interview, had a passionate response to the film: "You know, the original story of *Yojimbo* comes from an American novel [*Red Harvest*], and it would be wonderful to take it back to where it originally came from."[38] Leone was immediately struck by the idea of turning the samurai film into a Western. He worked, as Frayling reports, on the "adaptation," making a transcript of the dialogue of *Yojimbo* translated from Japanese, retaining only the basic structure of Kurosawa's film.[39]

The story of the gestation of *A Fistful of Dollars*—the shoestring

The National

budget, the fact that his was a second production to be shot with the props left behind by *Bullets Don't Argue* by Mario Caiano, also filmed in Spain, the tormented search for a protagonist, and so forth—is thoroughly documented and does not need to be rehashed here.[40] The movie was released in Italy in August 1964, but was distributed in the USA only in 1967 because Leone's distributer, Jolly Film, "forgot" to secure remake rights and to pay Kurosawa's studio, Toho Film, $10,000. The litigation went on for years and eventually was resolved in favor of Kurosawa, who earned quite a sum out of *A Fistful of Dollars* distribution rights in the Far East. The lawyers of Jolly Film built their defense by citing Carlo Goldoni's eighteenth-century play, *The Servant of Two Masters*, as the inspiration of Leone's film.

Although Hollywood's output of Westerns decreased in the 1960s, Spain and West Germany had produced some successful films and had built in Tabernas (Almeria, Spain) the sort of Mexican-looking sets from which the spaghetti Western would profit a couple of years down the road. In 1962, the Germans produced a Western that had been very successful. *The Treasure of the Silver Lake*, by Harald Reinl, was the first of a series of films (the "Winnetou Westerns") loosely based on Karl May's 19th century novels. *The Treasure*, filmed in Yugoslavia, had lots of action sequences and stunts with former Tarzan, Lex Barker, as Shatterhand. The box office success of this series encouraged the Italian producers to make Westerns, especially because the *pepla* were losing their attraction with the public at the time. Before Leone's *A Fistful of Dollars* was released, Italians had already made some Westerns, but they were low quality remakes of American classic Westerns, often characterized by long and repeated sequences of the same riders galloping up and down the same Yugoslavian or Italian canyons, with poorly put together scripts that reworked without any sparks the vendetta theme, the good versus evil, the treasure hunt, and so on.[41]

It is common knowledge that, by and large, most of the Italian Westerns that followed Leone's *A Fistful of Dollars* were also co-productions, usually Italian-Spanish-German or Yugoslavian, and Italian directors like Leone had to operate in a transnational environment. They had to hire actors from different countries, shoot abroad, and often re-dub the soundtracks in various languages. As with the *peplum* genre, Italian directors preferred to hire imported American actors in leading roles, and they and the whole cast appeared in the credits under English pseudonyms so that the movie could be passed off as an American

1. Transnational Adaptation, Transculturation, Indigenization

production. In view of the "Anglo-Saxon coating" that was applied to the Italian Westerns, one question arises: What is left of the national? Where is the "Italianness," if there is one, of the spaghetti Western? Because Leone is the creator of the Italian Western, the one who initiated the cycle that was "copied" many times over for a decade, we need to look at *A Fistful of Dollars* as a prototype, a movie that once dissected can shed light on the national-transnational dichotomy of the Spaghetti Western. However, before studying the prototype, we must look at the complex history of the origin of the first spaghetti Western, considering that *A Fistful of Dollars* was "transcoded" by Leone from Kurosawa's *Yojimbo* (1961) who derived his script (uncredited) from Dashiell Hammett's *Red Harvest* (1929). Leone, on the other hand, claimed that his inspiration for *A Fistful of Dollars* was Carlo Goldoni's play, *The Servant of Two Masters* (1753). As a consequence, we need to look into all the prototexts.

The Origins: Local and Translocal

Dashiell Hammett's *Red Harvest* (1929)

Red Harvest is the story of an American private detective who, during a Prohibition-era investigation, goes to Personville, a small Midwestern mining town ruled by criminals. The town is so plagued by corruption that it is referred to as "Poisonville"[42] in the novel. The male protagonist is identified as "the Continental Op" or simply "the Op," because he is an operative who is employed by a Continental Detective Agency based in San Francisco. The Op arrives in a place where he knows nobody, and nobody knows him; he does not make friends, and he does not seem to be friendly, even with the two fellow operatives from his agency. The reader finds out very little about him in the narration, except that he is a loner and a "man with no name." When he arrives in Personville, he learns that the person who hired him has been assassinated, but he does not leave; instead, he starts fighting corruption and battling crime. The archetypal plot of good versus evil swings between the detective story and the thriller, between irony and melodrama when "a man-hunter locates a *pharmako*s and gets rid of him."[43] According to Northrop Frye, the triumph of "moral virtue over villainy" in melodrama implies the idealization of those virtues by the audiences.[44] In the case of

The Origins: Local and Translocal

Hammett's novel, we deal with a manhunter who, in his relentless pursuit of justice, makes it difficult for the audience to idealize his quest. As Frye explains, "we read a murder story [gangster story, in this case] with a strong sense of the unreality of the villainy involved" regarding them "as a kind of ironic game."[45] It is precisely because we do not take these crimes seriously that we, as readers, derive pleasure in these stories. It is indeed difficult for the reader of Hammett's novel to take the protagonist seriously because he proceeds in his pursuit of reforming a community wracked with violence and unrest in a rather unorthodox way. He stirs things up and turns the bad people loose on each other. To do this, he does not shy away from lying and cheating. The old Machiavellian saying, "the end justifies the means," could not be more appropriate for describing his *modus operandi*. Most of the time the Op functions outside the boundary of the law. What keeps him from slipping completely into unlawfulness is the fact that he has to answer to his boss, the "Old Man" in San Francisco, who seems to represent some form of law and order to which he eventually has to conform.

In sum, the detective is a sort of rogue operative who fights against a society populated by corrupted capitalists, wicked police, crooked politicians, and a variety of gangsters: gamblers, assassins, smugglers, and bootleggers. Along the way he shoots two men in self-defense, but feels no regret because he acknowledges the necessity of cruelty in his job, even if he sometimes feels compassion for the men undone by their human frailty (see the painful death of Reno Starkey). His sympathy, however, is never verbalized and his emotions are never revealed. The reader has access to his inner thoughts and emotions only through brief glimpses. The private eye is a manipulative, skillful individual, who uses people for what are essentially his ends. He is an agent of justice and a vigilante fueled by a sense of mission and his own sense of vindication—meaning that the ones who try to do him wrong, like Chief of Police Noonan, deserve to die, and the Op makes sure they do. Upon his arrival in town, he starts off by tackling the toughest and smartest opponent (Max Thayler "Whisper"). At first, he clears the gangster of a murder accusation, then he proceeds to frame him for a murder he did not commit. The novel features several killings, but most of them occur "offstage" and are recalled by some of the characters after the fact. The Op is not troubled by violence. He accepts it as a natural consequence of the state of things, and he knows he has to play dirty in order to survive. The novel ends with the hero accomplishing his task without having to

1. Transnational Adaptation, Transculturation, Indigenization

resort to a shoot-out because the remaining criminals eliminate each other.

To conclude, our hero is a wisecracker with a peculiar sense of humor, and he uses his linguistic agility (slang, underworld idioms, colorful insults) as a way to challenge any authority. He sports an attitude, he does not speak much, and he is rather surgical in his way of communicating with friends and foes alike. Unlike Dinah Brand, the only female character in the novel—a totally mercenary "fallen woman" whose only goal in life is to pursue money and wealth—the hero is not interested in any monetary acquisition; once the agency fee gets paid, he is satisfied. Morally, the protagonist is more an anti-hero than a hero: he stirs things up and proceeds to consciously ruin people, causing their deaths, and, in so doing, he appears to share some of the rueful qualities of the villains. Toward the end, however, he realizes that he has been "poisoned by Poisonville," and to make amends, he passes the baton to one of his colleagues and to the new police force. They will tie up the loose ends, and, hopefully, defeat crime using more orthodox ways.

The title of the novel itself is symbolic. The Op indeed gets a bloody harvest, and by the time he is finished with his mission the town has been painted red by the blood spilled in the streets by the criminal factions destroying one another, thanks to the skillful meddling of the hero. The protagonist is a sort of Grim Reaper, who leaves a trail of blood behind wherever he goes.[46]

Carlo Goldoni's *The Servant of Two Masters* (*Il servitore di due padroni*, 1745)

The Servant of Two Masters (1745) is a comedy written by Carlo Goldoni (Venice, 1707–1793) that relies on the *commedia dell'arte* stock roles.[47] At the time, playwrights used to write a simple *canovaccio* (general outline) from which each actor could improvise *impromptu* with *lazzi* (word play), pantomime, acrobatic skills, and so on. By writing well-constructed comedies with credible characters set in a realistic environment (usually contemporary Venice), Goldoni managed to initiate a theatrical tradition *a-la-Molière* in Italy, and saved comedy from stereotyping and regurgitating the *commedia dell'arte* routines.

In the Preface to the first edition of *The Servant*, the playwright calls his work a *commedia giocosa* (playful comedy) in view of the "little joke" or "game" by Truffaldino, the servant of the title, constituting the greater

The Origins: Local and Translocal

part of it. Goldoni proceeds to inform the reader that his comedy has been purged of all the coarse improprieties of the *commedia* and that Truffaldino is a stock character that is both stupid and cunning, "stupid by the things he does without thinking, oblivious to their possible consequences, but extremely cunning, when prompted by self-interest or malice, which is the true character, traditionally, of the peasant."[48] Because Truffaldino is never called by his name in the play, but only referred to as "my servant," a "comedy of errors" (waiting tables in two rooms simultaneously, mixing the contents of the two masters' trunks) develops among the characters and, as a consequence, the servant succeeds in juggling two masters who are unaware they share the services of the same person with various tragicomic outcomes such as duels, suicide attempts and confrontations.

Truffaldino (from the Italian *truffare*, to cheat) carries in the root of his name the trait that distinguishes his character. He is a small-time cheater who would say anything in order to avoid a thrashing by his masters. He lies because he is poor and perpetually in pursuit of food to fill his belly; he "creates" people and situations out of his imagination in order to reach his humble goals, a few coins more and a meal. However, it must be pointed out that the protagonists of the comedy are two couples of lovers, not Truffaldino. The servant, however, is in many ways the "propeller" of the story. Without his selfish machinations the lovers would never meet, the conflicts would never be resolved, and the true identities never discovered.

In spite of the above, it would be hard to claim that Carlo Goldonis' 18th century play, *The Servant of Two Masters*, could have been an inspiration for Leone's first Western. The idea of mentioning Goldoni's play might have been a brilliant attempt at building a defense in the legal contention with Kurosawa's studio, Toho films, but it would be difficult to consider the play anything other than a distant source of inspiration.[49] Goldoni's servant carries a personality trait that appears throughout Italian cultural history from antiquity (Plautus) to modern times (Comedy Italian Style of the 1960s): the art of getting by. The poor guy who uses his wits to make ends meet is a classic trope: he is not bad, but not totally good, and he is a coward who avoids any confrontation. He is often funny and *simpatico*, but totally unreliable. He is a jack of all trades, but not particularly skillful at anything. He avoids hard work as much as possible, relying on his art of getting by to survive. In Goldoni's play, while it is obvious that the servant is indeed alternating between

1. Transnational Adaptation, Transculturation, Indigenization

two masters, that is the two couples, he is meddling not to destroy them, but to make a living.

It seems that with Goldoni's servant we are in a zone very distant from the one in which *Red Harvest*'s detective operates. The Op is obsessed by his mission, he is a voluntary *deus ex-machina* of destruction, and he is skillful and determined. Both Hammett's novel and Goldoni's play are steeped in their respective national traditions. The first is a hard-boiled detective story, a literary genre invented by Hammett, Raymond Chandler and other American writers who, in the '20s and '30s, based their works on gangsters, Prohibition, organized crime and tough-as-nails private eyes and policemen. The detective fiction with the gangster movies and the Westerns are expressions of a well-defined national identity. Goldoni's body of work also conveys the traditions of his society, 18th century Venice, with its social classes, customs and mores. Both Goldoni and Hammett could be grouped under the label of national popular culture. However, the differences between the detective and the servant are striking. The detective is an anti-hero full of courage and determination, while the servant is a sort of *miles gloriosus* without "art nor part" who avoids any conflict; the former lies to achieve his goals, the latter lies to get by.[50] It is evident that the protagonists of *Yojimbo* and *Fistful* have a lot more in common with the Op than with Truffaldino.

The Transnational

From America to Japan: Akira Kurosawa's *Yojimbo* (*The Bodyguard*, 1961)

Akira Kurosawa (1910–1998) states in interviews that the inspiration for his samurai film, *Yojimbo* (1961), was Dashiell Hammett's novel *Red Harvest*.[51] According to Linda Hutcheon, adaptation is "both an interpretative and a creative act; it is storytelling as both rereading and re-relating."[52] Adaptation is, then, repetition with variation. A transcultural adaptation occurs when a text travels from one culture to another; often a change of language is involved together with a change of place and/or time period. For example, Akira Kurosawa's *Throne of Blood* (1957) is a Japanese film adaptation of Shakespeare's *Macbeth*. *The Magnificent Seven* (1960) is a Hollywood remake of Kurosawa's *Seven*

The Transnational

Samurai (1954).⁵³ When the original story migrates and is inserted in a different context, a different society and culture, change is inevitable, and with it, corresponding modifications of the political valence or the meaning of the story. As Hutcheon puts it, a *transculturation* and *indigenization* of the original text occurs. Moving from page to screen and therefore carrying out a form of translation, adaptation, re-writing and permutation, *Red Harvest* crossed borders to become a Japanese film. Kurosawa's film is indeed a clever operation in which the detective/gangster story is "lifted" from the American hard-boiled fiction genre and "grafted" onto the Japanese *jidaigeki* genre (period films/samurai films) very successfully.⁵⁴ This transfer—even if the novel is uncredited—allowed the director to create an equivalent in his own culture, succeeding in making a brilliant transculturation and indigenization of the borrowed material.

Kurosawa's operation is not an adaptation, but a transcoding of Dashiell Hammett's *Red Harvest*; the director managed to preserve the original, transforming the American gangsters of the 1920s into Japanese gamblers/thugs of the end of the Edo period (1603–1868). From an ideological point of view, Hammett's novel is an implied critique of the corruption of America in the Prohibition era and a critique of the way in which big capital squashed organized labor. Hammett was writing about his time. Kurosawa's film seems to talk about a distant past, but, in fact, is a comment on the Japanese society of the 1950s. In a village plagued by corrupted policemen, government officials, greedy (silk and *sake*) merchants, gamblers and thugs, arrives a wandering samurai (Toshiro Mifune). He has to keep himself afloat in a world without balance: the old *shogunate* system of military rulers and feudal lord has collapsed, and he has no lord to fight for anymore. He is a wandering soul whose existence is driven by destiny, as exemplified at the beginning of the film by a stick thrown in the air at a crossroads to decide the path to take. However, Kurosawa's film is not talking about the dissolution of the lord/samurai/feudal system in Japan, but about the crisis of values of a nation that was first brought to the verge of destruction by militarism; then, following the defeat of World War II, it went through a fast process of modernization, especially during the American occupation (1945–1952). As a result, in the late 1950s Japan was a country in which old-fashioned values were competing with consumerism and capitalism, and money was becoming the supreme goal. Hammett's critique of America is implied; Kurosawa goes a step forward in showing how his

1. Transnational Adaptation, Transculturation, Indigenization

characters are driven by greed and how, in turn, greed drives them to destruction.

In *Red Harvest* the point of view is only the prerogative of the detective (the Op); in *Yojimbo* the point of view is split between the samurai and the tavern owner, Gonji. Gonji functions as the moral compass of the story who, from the setup to the midpoint, counterbalances the supposed amorality of the samurai. In spite of the newly-created character of Gonji, the focus of the film remains, as in the novel, on the protagonist's deeds and vicissitudes until his final success. Like Hammett's Op, the samurai succeeds in the end, but he is not as lucky as the private eye because in order to attain victory he must face alone the last standing clan in a brutal and uneven confrontation that not only involves sword fighting, but even a firearm. The Gonji character and the episodes narrating the saving of the woman and her family from the criminal clan, the brutal beating of the samurai, the farmer's son's story and the arrival of the government officials do not appear in Hammett's novel; they are all Kurosawa's additions. In short, through these added episodes the filmmaker gives his film a moral center. In *Red Harvest*, the cynicism of the Op never falters: if anything, he is even more cynical and cruel by the end, so much so that he has to leave because he thinks that the town has poisoned him. Whereas Hammett's protagonist remains cynical, the samurai reveals his honesty through his good deeds from the midpoint (i.e., the rescue of the woman) on.

Yojimbo is an action film peppered with several bloody sword fights, but it is also a morality play. To this end, Kurosawa frames the story between two events that do not exist in the novel. The first occurs in the initial sequences of the film. The samurai, on his way to a village, meets a farmer who is quarrelling with his son in the countryside because the young man wants to join a gambling clan; the boy claims that he prefers a life of crime and money to a life of honesty, poverty and hard work. Eventually, the samurai will spare the young man's life and tell him to go back to his father's farm, declaring that it is better to live a long life in poverty than a short life in crime.[55] The emphasis that Kurosawa puts on ethical issues is clear, especially if we keep in mind Gonji's constant nagging of the samurai. The *sake* vendor repeatedly complains about the present decadence of the village, and constantly encourages the samurai to leave a place in which murder and prevarication rule. When Sanjuro says to Gonji that he is staying because the town is full of men who are better off dead than alive, the vendor assumes that his

The Transnational

decision is fueled by greed. Furthermore, the grumpy keeper starts to be nice to the samurai only when he discovers that the swordsman has freed the woman from bondage and, therefore, has proven himself not as greedy and selfish as he might have appeared at first.

In transcoding the original into his samurai film, Kurosawa has preserved the theme of the original story, the proverbial fight between good and evil, and the main characters. Nevertheless, he turned the protagonist from a sleuth to a masterless samurai (*ronin*). The plot order is kept linear in the film as in the novel. The director, however, does not follow the rule of "adapting by cutting." On the contrary, he proceeds to "adapt by adding" new elements to the story. The *incipit* and the end are kept as in the original story, but the filmmaker creates the innkeeper character (*sake* vendor), and adds four other episodes from scratch (the woman's rescue, the farmer's son's story, the beating of the protagonist, and the bribing of the officials). Kurosawa does not cut parts of the novel as is traditionally done, but adds to it, using these episodes to prove his point. The saving of the woman brings about the savage torturing of the samurai who refuses to reveal the location of the family he has liberated. The protagonist is in reality a very moral and honest individual who sacrifices himself for the others, even if he claims that he is there to cause the clash of the two clans in order to get money for himself. In this sense he is very different from the Op who does not perform any good deeds while dispensing justice.

The division of the novel in chapters is respected by Kurosawa, who separates the various episodes on the screen by wipes and fades to black, a transition technique that clearly divides the story in distinct parts. The wipes create a theatrical effect, giving the viewer the impression of watching a play on stage with curtains closing. On top of that, the criminal gangs are made up of grotesque individuals who, when confronting one another, step back and forward in a sort of balletic dance, seemingly dominated by the desire to kill, and the fear of annihilation. These ritualistic movements give the audience the impression that the hired assassins move like actors on a stage. The theatricality is also emphasized by the fact that the diegetic space consists of a stretch of road inside the village where Gonji's tavern is and where the houses of the two rival clans sit at the opposite sides of a rectangular area. Throughout the film, the innkeeper and the samurai watch what is going on in the village from the windows and, thanks to the use of a deep-focus lens, the viewer has access to what happens outside as well. This opening and closing of

1. Transnational Adaptation, Transculturation, Indigenization

shutters has the effect of curtains, determining the beginning and ending of each sequence.

The samurai uses violence to clean up the corrupt village, selling his bodyguard skills to one or the other clan in a continuous alternation that triggers havoc; then, he leaves after having "purified" the environment or, as he ironically puts it, when the town is "very quiet," meaning that, with the exception of the *sake* vendor and the coffin maker, everybody is dead.

The wisecrack attitude of the Op is also a trait of the samurai's character; he talks very little and never reveals his real name. In the novel, "Op," short for operative, is not a real name; in the film the samurai is nameless, but when asked, he invents a name on the spot and, noticing a field out of the window, he calls himself "thirty-year-old mulberry field (*Sanjuro Kawabaki*)." Disguising playfully his own identity is a sign of not taking himself too seriously. For the same reason he never presents himself as a defender of social justice, he simply does what he does best, sword fighting. Like the detective, the bodyguard sports a sort of black humor. He tells the coffin maker to prepare three coffins, then he proceeds to kill three thugs and severs the arm of a fourth one. Finally, after looking back at the latter, he adds "make it four." His "very quiet town" comment at the end of the film is also very funny, and very cynical. His friend, the innkeeper, has been wishing to live in a tranquil town since the moment the samurai met him. In the end, amid great devastation, with dead bodies of criminals strewn everywhere in the street, and the clan houses on fire, the samurai tells Gonji that now the town is "quiet again" as he wished.

Turning from telling to showing, music becomes crucial. Instead of period genre music played by traditional Japanese instruments, Kurosawa opted for contemporary modern music, subverting the traditional genre formula. The beautiful soundtrack arranged by Sato Masaru, renowned composer and Kurosawa's long-time collaborator, utilizes cheerful tunes to accompany the sequences in which the samurai slaughters the thugs, and quick and happy marching tempos when the samurai steps into dangerous confrontations.

This creates a contrast between the filmic sequences and the responses that the score elicits in the audience with ironic effects; the juxtaposition of the soundtrack and the wisecracking of the samurai adds a black humor flavor to the film. Kurosawa also introduces realistic sound effects, like the sound of a sword slashing human flesh. The

The Transnational

Yojimbo (The Bodyguard, 1961). Directed by Akira Kurosawa. Toshiro Mifune (as Sanjuro Kuwabatake, the samurai) shows no mercy killing the village thugs (Photofest).

samurai does not use the sword in ritualistic movements. He is swift and violent, limbs are cut and shown on the screen, and blood gushes from the wounds. When Sanjuro enters the village, a dog passes by holding a human hand in his mouth, an omen of the carnage that will follow. Even in the final confrontation between Sanjuro and the Ushitora clan the jazzy twangs add suspense to the sequence, but also a certain playfulness.[56]

Yojimbo means bodyguard in Japanese, and the irony is evident even in the title. The samurai pretends to be a bodyguard and sells himself as such to the clans, but, in fact, he is the opposite. He does not want to defend the "lords of the village"; he wants to kill them. He cynically and cleverly explains to the *sake* vendor that in this world, with certain bodyguards around, the employers should watch their backs. Kurosawa uses a variety of camera shots in re-focusing the themes, the characters and the plot from the page to the screen. In the first part of the movie, he uses low-angle medium close-ups of Sanjuro, making the

1. Transnational Adaptation, Transculturation, Indigenization

samurai the viewer's focusing point because his upper body occupies the screen. Later, the filmmaker employs a deep-focus lens and we experience a wider space that encompasses the village, the houses, the street with the characters and, as a result, a whole community, even if a faulty one. In the process, Kurosawa also exploits superbly the compositional possibilities of the wide-screen format.

In short, the director manages to re-contextualize *Red Harvest* and he does it so successfully that he achieves a form of transculturation.[57] As Hutcheon reminds us, genres set up audience expectations. As a consequence, choosing to transcode a text into a film has a lot to do with the choice of genre. Kurosawa accomplishes a "Japanization" of the hard-boiled fiction, choosing a samurai film instead of a gangster sub-genre like the *yakuza*, obtaining enormous success with his daring choice.[58] If it is undeniable that Hammett's theme is indeed archetypal and universal (good against evil), Kurosawa's operation managed to reset the original story into his own culture, and, at the same time, he innovated the formula of the *jidaigeki* genre by altering its conventions. He created a cynical, ironic, wisecracking, anti-hero who goes against the rigid formula of the traditional samurai films and who does not commit *hara-kiri* in the end, but results victorious by choosing violence over *Bushido* (the code of honor). Substituting realistic violence with the elegant handling of the sword through choreographed movements as in the samurai filmic tradition, the director made the audience realize how artificial the *jidaigeki* was. Kurosawa's transposition stands on its own, separate from the palimpsest, brings surprise and novelty to the original (variation), and revolutionizes the Japanese filmic period genre, thus starting a new samurai filmic trend.[59]

From Japan to Italy: Leone's *A Fistful of Dollars* (*Per un pugno di dollari*, 1964)

Eleftheriotis argues that spaghetti Westerns are hybrid forms because they are the products of "cultural interaction and exchange" between the American Western genre and Italian cinema, between Hollywood and a European national cinema. We could not agree more with the critic; we need, however, to point out the textual specificities of Leone's westerns, first at the level of production in relation to industry and the market, national and international, and, then at the level of aesthetics, in relation to the textual practices that distinguish his film from the American Western. Finally, it is essential to determine what happens to national identity when it gets reworked through the formula of the American genre.[60] As mentioned, the Italian film industry flourished throughout the 1960s: Italian films dominated the domestic market and box office figures were higher than in all other European countries. The strong American involvement in film production in Italy had allowed Italian distributors to gain access to the world market, so much so that in 1964 co-productions accounted for 153 out of 270 total Italian films.[61]

As Hutcheon contends, "adaptation is how stories evolve and mutate to fit times and different places....."[62] In the case of Leone's first film we have a typical case of hybridization and permutation; therefore, we need to consider Leone's reworking of *Yojimbo* as an endeavor *sui generis*. While Kurosawa embedded Hammett's narrative into an indigenous genre, the samurai film, Leone transferred Sanjuro's story into a foreign genre, the Western. This approach was not a novelty: Kurosawa's *The Seven Samurai* (1954) had been translated into *The Magnificent Seven* in 1960 by John Sturges with very fortunate results.[63] We assume that Leone, a profound *connoisseur* of American cinema, must have been aware of Sturges' film. Furthermore, as Yoshimoto remarks, the traditional samurai films (*jidaigeki*) and the Western had a lot in common:

> Both genres, set in important periods of Japanese and American national histories, feature armed heroes—samurai and gamblers, cowboys and gunmen—whose violence plays the essential role in the narrative development and resolution. The Western and *jidaigeki* heroes are often social outsiders who restore order or help people fighting against villains while being fully aware that their virtuous action does not allow them to reintegrate themselves in a renewed social order. And, *jidaigeki* is not a pure Japanese genre.[64]

Yoshimoto, like Anderson in a 1973 article, affirms that Hollywood cinema, which started a successful cycle in the 1920s with films such as *The Mark of Zorro* (Fred Niblo, 1920), featuring Douglas Fairbanks as a swashbuckling hero, spawned imitations in the Japanese film industry.[65] Hollywood filmic conventions, however, were assimilated into Japanese culture and transformed to a point that the samurai films became a Japanese genre.

The source of the affinity can be found in the similarities of historical situations in both nations. The Western looks at a period of

1. Transnational Adaptation, Transculturation, Indigenization

transition in American history, mostly between 1860 and 1890, when westward expansion and the idea of "Manifest Destiny" were coming to a close. The frontier ceased to exist as such in 1890 and the railroad had, by then, reached the Pacific Coast. The same is true for Japan. The samurai films register the crisis of passage from an agrarian society to a modern and urban one, a difficult transitional moment in Japanese history that took place between the end of the 19th century and the 1950s, even though the samurai films are usually set in feudal times (1185–1867). The similarities between the two genres are emphasized by Anderson when he claims that, like the American Western, the *jidaigeki* is "a uniquely national film genre that has reinforced a national myth; it has dramatized the nation's fundamentalist code of ethics as nostalgic allegory."[66] However, the action in the samurai films is restricted to small towns and villages surrounded by farmland, which involves a spatial restriction, the spectacle of vast landscapes, open ranges, green valleys, and rocky mountains that connoted the American Western having disappeared.[67]

Clearly the comparison between the Western and the traditional samurai films holds when one refers to American Westerns made before Leone's *A Fistful of Dollars* (1964) and samurai films made before Kurosawa's *Yojimbo*. If, on the one hand, it is undeniable that Kurosawa altered the conventions of the latter thus uprooting the genre, the same is true for Leone's western. Leone extrapolated the story of *Yojimbo*, transferred it into the American Western, then proceeded to alter the classic formula by *mediterraneanizing* it. In 1963, after having watched *Yojimbo* in Rome, Leone started to work at a *Moviola* to translate the dialogue of the film from Japanese into Italian "in order to be sure not to repeat a single word."[68] Leone claimed that he undressed Kurosawa's characters of their samurai masks and redressed them as cowboys, "to make them cross the ocean and return to their place of origin," in other words, back to the America of Dashiell Hammett.[69] There would be no problem with his statement if *A Fistful of Dollars* were just a remake of the Japanese film, similar to, for example, *Last Man Standing* (Walter Hill, 1996).[70] But Leone's film does not fit the bill. Leone took the narrative of *Yojimbo*, transferred it into a foreign genre and went on to modify the basic formula on which that very genre was based. Leone subverted the Western formula the same way as Kurosawa subverted the *jidaigeki*, something that Walter Hill's film did not achieve.

A Fistful of Dollars, therefore, is not a remake, but a sophisticated operation in which Leone Italianized the iconography of the Western.

The Transnational

At the level of *mise-en-scène*, he changed the landscape and the look of the hero. At the level of genre, Leone altered the genre formula, voiding it of the moral and cultural values that are the foundation of American identity. The Italian director, while keeping the plot line of the Japanese film, eliminated some events and characters and altered the relevance of other characters and events, subverting the moral stand of the Western formula and the iconography significantly. To a certain extent, Leone simplified the storyline: The merchants affiliated with the criminal clans disappear, together with the more layered structure of Japanese society. In *A Fistful of Dollars* corruption is circumscribed to two factions: the liquor smuggler bandits (i.e., the Mexican Rojos brothers Ramon, Miguel and Esteban), and the Baxters, a family of Yankee gun smugglers whose leader, John Baxter, happens to be the local sheriff. In *Yojimbo*'s, Hansuke, the meddling, corrupted, greedy officer of the town, disappears, while in the Italian film, coffin maker Piripero and saloon keeper Silvanito acquire more screen time and become more relevant from the very beginning.[71] The cantina owner threatens the Rojos with a gun to save the son of Marisol, Ramon's kept woman, and in the end he shoots Esteban Rojo to save the gringo's life. Marisol also becomes crucial to the development of the story; in fact, the Stranger meets her upon his arrival in town and her liberation sets in motion the brutal beating of the protagonist and his final revenge.[72]

On the whole, the plot remains the same as in Kurosawa's film: a man with no name/stranger/gringo/*pistolero* (Clint Eastwood) happens upon the Mexican village of San Miguel that looks like a cemetery and is not far from the U.S. border. The stranger comes across a dead body sitting on a horse with a sign reading: "Adios, amigo!" He also finds a crazy bell ringer who talks about killing, money and death, and a lot of women dressed in black, before stopping at a well. While drinking, he witnesses a puzzling scene: the beating of a small child and a man by some thugs, while a beautiful woman watches from a window. When the gringo gets into town he is ridiculed by the Baxter's thugs and meets Silvanito, who explains to him why the town looks so lifeless. Like Sanjuro, he is interested in offering his gun for hire to both clans in order to make money, and to pit them against each other to accomplish his ploy.

All the ingredients (storyline, characters, happy end), except the *mise-en-scène* and the weapon of the protagonist, in this case a six-shooter instead of a sword, have remained the same. However, the elimination of the chance encounter between the samurai and the

1. Transnational Adaptation, Transculturation, Indigenization

A Fistful of Dollars (*Per un pugno di dollari,* United Artists, 1964). Directed by Sergio Leone. Clint Eastwood as Joe, the gunslinger, and José Calvo as Silvanito, the saloon owner, discussing the two criminal gangs that rule the village (Photofest).

farmer's son in the opening sequence of the Japanese film alters completely the equation between the two filmic texts. By creating the episode of a son who chooses a life of crime over the hard-working life of his father, Kurosawa shows a critical crux.[73] The moralizing, almost didactic tone of the episode gives Kurosawa's film a different ideological spin. Kurosawa criticizes the greed brought about by capitalism at the expense of more traditional moral values. The samurai might be interested in making money, but he is even more interested in cleansing the town and, in order to succeed, he pretends to be selling himself as a bodyguard. The violence of the samurai is justified because it is a moralizing force; he is therefore, like the Op, an avenging angel sent to purge the town of men who are better off dead than alive. From this perspective, Kurosawa seems to share John Ford's strong ethical sense of what is right and wrong. The great classic Westerns from *Stagecoach* to *Shane*, from *High Noon* to *The Searchers* all exhibit this unchallenged sense of justice. There is good and bad, and bad characters are doomed because justice always prevails eventually.

The Transnational

The concern with the evils of modernity remains at the core of *Yojimbo*, because Kurosawa frames Sanjuro's story inside the departure of the farmer's son from home and his eventual return to the family. In so doing, the Japanese filmmaker prevents the destruction of the family unit and reaffirms the validity of the farmer's (and his wife's) values: hard work, sacrifice and honesty as opposed to greed brought about by modernity. On the other hand, Leone has accepted modernity and its evils as inevitable; the war against greed and injustice cannot be won on a large scale, but some battles can be won by some super-human individuals like the "man with no name." Leone's protagonist, while pursuing his capitalist dream, can correct a few wrongs along the way. The Italian filmmaker's westerns are like adult fables in which injustice can be defeated thanks to the exceptional skills of a man who uses violence to change, almost unintentionally and momentarily, his diegetic world. The Italian Western is charged with an anarchic and rebellious force that is missing in the Japanese counterpart.

It is at the ideological level that Leone achieves transculturation. The signs so important in the American Western get stripped of their significance. The *mise-en-scène* becomes a collection of props. The link between the Western and the historical events, the message, the myth of progress and democracy and the regeneration through violence are stripped away. The archetype of good versus evil remains but gets redirected; here the hero kills the bad guys because he wants money and deep down he hates a corrupt, violent system that can be opposed only with violence. Here is where Leone imbued the film with an outlook that was the result of his era and culture. Kurosawa and Leone were born twenty years apart. Kurosawa was already an adult during the militarization of Japan that preceded the onset of World War II. A descendant of a samurai family line, he had by 1961 witnessed enough change in Japanese society to realize that something important had been lost during its rapid industrialization and modernization process. His filmography is based, as many critics point out, on the importance of the individual, his moral fiber and his humanitarian values.[74] By 1963, Leone was a young man who had survived the Fascist dictatorship and World War II practically unscathed, and, after building his career in the 1950s, was witnessing the rapid changes in a country that was becoming a modern and industrialized nation following the bleak years of the reconstruction. His world was becoming more affluent, but was transforming itself into a capitalist jungle with money as the supreme goal, where many of

1. Transnational Adaptation, Transculturation, Indigenization

the ideals of the Resistance, such as constructing a more equitable and just society for everybody, had been lost.

Leone's jettisoning the farmer's son episode from his film eliminates any ethical pretense. For the Italian director, San Miguel is a micro-capitalist society where everybody would accept one "boss" as the norm ("Every town has a boss" says the gringo), but in this case we have one too many bosses and, therefore, the competing economic interests create havoc and destruction. Leone's gunfighter embraces capitalism. In fact, the gringo sees this situation as a possible source of profit. Unlike the samurai, the gunman does not want to destroy the clans because they are evil; he destroys them to make money, since their destruction will bring him wealth. When Consuelo Baxter tells the gringo that he will soon be rich, implying that he seems to be always in the right place at the right time, he replies that there is nothing wrong with getting rich. When he gets hired by the Rojos clan, he warns them that he does not "work cheap." If we add to this, what he says to Silvanito, "there is money to be made in a place like this"—i.e., two bosses in competition leave space for a third party to throw a wrench in their doings—it is evident that, unlike the samurai, the "man with no name" has a pretty detailed acceptance of how modern society works: professionalism, information, money, competing business. Unlike the samurai, he will walk out of town with gold in his pocket. Sanjuro leaves after having committed a good deed (liberating the town) as poor as before, whereas the stranger will leave after having committed a good deed (liberating the town and finding the government loot) with lots of money in his pocket.

The gringo, however, does not like prevarication, he hates bullies, and he clearly favors the oppressed. As a result, he uses violence to eliminate the cutthroats. On the one hand, we could consider the gringo an "immoral" individual, and certainly his goal is less noble than the samurai's. On the other hand, he also performs some good deeds; he liberates Marisol and her family, gives them some money, endures torture because of this, and rescues his friend Silvanito. Like the Op and the samurai, he is an avenging angel, but he is an angel with a penchant for gold; by the time he leaves San Miguel, he is a rich man, but not greedy or stupid enough to steal the government loot. When the officials arrive to retrieve the stolen gold, he will not be around to answer questions because he will be long gone, leaving the village "nice and clean," but ready to go to the dogs again. Leone's Westerns always project a rather

The Transnational

cynical view of the world: corruption, greed and a lot of injustice. The moral universe of the classic American Western could not be any more distant. In Leone's West, violence does not regenerate anybody. Progress and history are manipulated by big capital and government, and his protagonists live in a dangerous everlasting "present."

With *Yojimbo*, Kurosawa subverted the conventions of the samurai genre showing realistic violence, negating the bushido code of honor via the happy end, and using modern music in the sound track. Leone subverted a foreign genre by altering the role of violence. In the classic American Western, the cowboy hero resorts to violence only when there is no other way out (usually relegating the explosion of violence in the showdown at the end of the movie), in the Italian Western the anti-heroes resort to violence all the time.[75] Furthermore, they have made violence into a profession, and they have perfected their weapon skills to a point that they are unbeatable. That is why they are often bounty hunters, or exceptional gunfighters. Unlike the John Wayne–style hero who would never trick the bad guys, the Italian gunmen do not follow such ethical behavior, but tend to use "whatever works" to achieve their goal.[76] While the classic cowboys were, in most cases, reacting to adverse situations, these new *pistoleros* are pro-active. They look for violent situations and often create conflicts. They are not on a mission. At most, they think that the ways of the world can be temporarily modified. Basically, they have lost the faith in "progress and a better society" that animated the heroes of classic westerns. The Indians have been defeated (in fact, they have disappeared altogether from the Italian screen). Progress has arrived and it does not look appealing at all. Justice has not yet been achieved.

The gunslingers of Leone's trilogy are outsiders who have no desire to integrate themselves into society, and who do not particularly like their world, dominated as it is by injustice, violence and corruption. They have figured out that money is a necessity, and they have accepted the rules of capitalism, but they do not like the way things work. So, as soon as they have a chance, they use violence to undermine the unjust microcosm they inhabit, but they harbor no illusions. Leone's films are indeed "fables for adults"[77]; fables because they reconstruct a mythical land that never existed, but was borrowed by another mythical place, the American Western genre, that long before had created a Far West that existed only on screen and had nothing to do with the real geographical or historical entity. These are fables for adults because, in spite of

1. Transnational Adaptation, Transculturation, Indigenization

the happy endings, they are pervaded by a sense of pessimism and disillusionment for a world that is what it is and will never change. In this world, especially in Leone's *Duck, You Sucker!* (*Giù la testa!*, 1971), there is empathy for the oppressed. There is a powerful urge to rebel against the oppressors, the necessity of matching violence with violence. However, the end of *Duck, You Sucker!* contains a cautionary tale: the Revolution appears as a double-edged sword for correcting wrongs.

If ideologically, the cynical vision of the world that transpires from Leone's *A Fistful of Dollars* can have a direct correlation with the director's own outlook on life because of his Italian upbringing and his living in a country that was undergoing an accelerated process of modernization and industrialization while, at the same time, exhibiting signs of the conflict and contradiction that were soon going to explode during the students' and workers' rebellion of 1968, Leone's lasting contribution to the Western has to be found especially in the unusual iconography of his films. Because of budget and production constraints, *A Fistful of Dollars* was filmed in the Spanish desert area of Almeria where the landscape supposedly recalled Arizona or New Mexico, a setting appropriate for the filmic village of San Miguel as a Mexican border town.[78] The aridity of the landscape, the Mediterranean architecture that looks like adobe style, the dark features of the characters, especially of the stunt men and the heavies, who were either Spaniards hired on location or Italians, contributed to make the film look like an unusual kind of Western. All these factors, instead of weighing negatively on the production of the film, helped Leone to colonize the American Western through the *mediterraneanization* of the *mise-en-scène*. Also the anti-hero is not immune from the subversion. He does not wear a white hat and ride an immaculate stallion like the classic cowboy; he is unshaven and wanders into town riding a mule. He chews on a cigarillo even when he speaks, thus slurring his diction, and sports a nonchalant attitude that together with his slow movements make him look like a big, dangerous cat ready to pounce, but otherwise too lazy to do much else, recalling the stereotypical image of the "lazy Mediterranean" rather than the energetic Anglo-Saxon.[79]

In colonizing the Western genre, Leone also imbued it with Catholic symbols typical of his own culture. In *A Fistful of Dollars*, *Yojimbo*'s little Japanese temple becomes a little church with bells and a bell ringer; the gringo, like a reincarnated avenging angel during the final duel, seems to be crucified in a Christ-like position by the bullets, before

The Transnational

A Fistful of Dollars (Per un pugno di dollari, **United Artists, 1964). Directed by Sergio Leone. Clint Eastwood as Joe, the gunslinger, gets ready to dispatch the Baxter thugs (Photofest).**

undergoing a complete resurrection. The black-and-white photography of the samurai film with the dark Japanese wooden structures and the village road swept by wind and gray dust is transformed into a place where the white of the stucco houses reflects the light of a blinding sun, and bright colors abound everywhere in the sparsely populated village.

Three large-scale massacres are presented, two of which along the Rio Bravo river. One is executed with gusto by Ramon Rojo (Gian Maria Volontè) with a machine gun; the other occurs off-screen and is shown via indirection in a shot of a pile of dead bodies in a wagon. The third massacre is the elimination of the Baxter clan, executed again with great pleasure by the Rojos and their henchmen who mow down the surrendering smugglers when they rush out of a house in flames. Leone's protagonist also contributes to the body count; he exterminates the thugs at Marisol's house to liberate her, and he kills all the Rojos in the final duel. The episode of the torturing of the gringo is more realistic and a lot more sadistic than in *Yojimbo.* Suspense is added to every confrontation by a special choice of camera shots. A multiplicity of shot/reverse shots, deep-focus shots, and close-ups prolong the suspense, provoking anxiety in the viewer. Extreme close-ups of the gringo's face, squinting eyes, grinning smile, fingers on the trigger, his gun, his hand, his boots,

1. Transnational Adaptation, Transculturation, Indigenization

alternate with extreme close-ups of the faces of his opponents, their hands, their eyes ... until finally the hero's six-gun fires a few rounds and the henchmen fall dead. The combination of extreme close-ups together with the musical theme (prolonged twangs of electric guitar) recurring throughout the film and accompanying the protagonist's violent deeds keep the viewer on edge. The soundtrack, arranged by Ennio Morricone, mixes virtuoso whistling, with guitar and choral arrangements by Alessandro Alessandroni, trumpet (*deguello*-style) by Michele Lacerenza, choir singing by I Cantori Moderni (soprano Edda dell'Orso) and whip cracking, clinking spurs, and rifle blasts. As Dario Argento stated in an interview about Leone's first film, "...This was a Western we dreamed of seeing—the historical Western was not so inventive, not so crazy, not so stylish, not so violent."[80]

Conclusion

With *A Fistful of Dollars*, Leone managed to create a transcultural translation of the Japanese film, a *domestication* of the American genre, and finally succeeded in giving birth to the spaghetti Western, which was neither a spin-off of the American Western nor a sub-genre, but a new development of the Western genre. Afterward the American Western would never be the same and the classic Western would be considered almost defunct. Both filmmakers preserve in their filmic rendition the man-hunter that battles evil at the center of their narration. Both films, in transferring the story from Hammett's novel to the screen, have kept Northrop Frye's archetype intact.[81] The audience enjoys the deeds of the "hero" in his unstoppable path, with one difference—in *Yojimbo* Sanjuro is an example of moral virtue with which we can identify, while in *A Fistful of Dollars* it is more difficult to identify with the Stranger because his self-righteousness approaches at times that of the lynching mob, as Frye suggests.

Eleftheriotis writes, "the Italianness of the spaghetti Western does not reside in hidden national cultural references, plots, themes and underlying value system, but in the very ability ... to weaken (if not erase) the national as its referent."[82] We disagree with the above statement because Leone mirrored in his film the contemporary modern values (the ones of the newly industrialized Italy) together with the reservations, doubts and misgivings that the Economic Miracle brought

Conclusion

about. The Italian filmmaker did not erase the Italian identity, instead he projected a modern identity that was no longer specific to Italy, but one that was becoming common to many Western nations. By the 1960s, Italy, like many other European countries, was highly industrialized: consumerism and capitalism were widespread, but faith in institutions was fading away. This cynical way of looking at the world was no longer unique. If it is true that at the iconic level the disentangling of "the hero of the spaghetti Western from the context of the American cultural and historical specificity" creates a place from which the viewer can experience the Wild West without buying into the American myth, it is also true that by that time very few people in the world were buying into such a myth anyway.[83] In the United States the civil rights movement showed that the exploitation of minorities and Native Americans (the celluloid Indians of so many Hollywood productions) had to stop. The rebellion of the minorities spurred a much overdue re-reading of the American frontier that eventually de-mythicized the dream of Manifest Destiny.[84] The Vietnam War, the Black Panthers, and the counter-culture movements started shaking the general faith in a system that was "working for everybody," showing how the capitalist dream was working only for some, usually the white and the rich. The distribution in the U.S. market of *A Fistful of Dollars* in 1967 coincided with an international situation in which rebellious tendencies were brewing in Europe as in the Unites States. The faith in a democracy in which justice always prevails and the institutions are honest was crumbling in many countries.

As Martinez suggests, retold stories "build bridges across cultures and then proceed to burn them while retaining some memory of the connection."[85] *A Fistful of Dollars* is, therefore, a permutation, a story retold across borders, translated into an indigenous culture, one that produced a new "narrative" despite the presumed connection with what had gone before. The resonance between the spaghetti Western and films like *The Wild Bunch* (Peckinpah, 1969), *Two Mules for Sister Sara* (Don Siegel, 1970), *High Plains Drifter* (Eastwood, 1973), *The Outlaw Josey Wales* (Eastwood, 1976) and the revisionist Westerns that followed is evident.

In conclusion, Leone's gunman in *A Fistful of Dollars* embodies the contradictions of postmodern man, somebody who hates wrongs, sees the flaws in the system but, at the same time, knows that he cannot change it. Leone's protagonists embody a multiplicity of facets: They are anarchic and rebellious; they are capitalistic (they cherish money);

1. Transnational Adaptation, Transculturation, Indigenization

they are violent when need be; and they do not want to conform because they are outsiders. It is this hybridity that has made them so appealing. Leone's Westerns have been crossing borders, going back to America and to Japan and they have been enormously successful at the box office all over the globe. The polysemic nature of Spaghetti Westerns allowed them to appeal to multiple audiences and to cross trans-genre boundaries. It is clear that Leone changed the Western in a way that was appreciated by multiple and diverse audiences and that the most varied viewers found in his filmic stories "something" with which they could identify.[86] Leone with *A Fistful of Dollars* imported the American model (the Western), re-appropriated the translocal (*Yojimbo*) and transformed it into the local at the level of aesthetics, then proceeded to strip off the ideological valence of the model, infusing into it the doubts and cynicism of a society in transition between consumerism and industrialization. The icons of the American Western are present in Leone's film. The denotation is clear. All the props are there, even if different from the American Western, but, at the level of connotation, the social and cultural associations linked to the signs have disappeared. They have been deprived of the social context they originally had. It is at the level of discourse in a Foucaltian way that *A Fistful of Dollars* becomes transnational, because the preferred message among the many encoded in the text creates a particular understanding of the world that was not only Italian, but was becoming globalized. The commercial success of the film in Italy and abroad proves that the viewers at consumption, in decoding the film from their ideological perspectives, took away the preferred meaning.

2

Celluloid Indians, 1950s Westerns and the Termination Act

Broken Arrow, White Feather,
The Battle of Apache Pass,
Devil's Doorway, The Last Wagon
and The Last Hunt

Prologue

André Bazin and Pauline Kael were among the first critics to appreciate the Western genre. Their critiques combine intuition and synthesis, originality and depth. Bazin can be considered a true pioneer in that he was the first to define the Western as the American genre *par excellence*, and that without the cinematic rendition of the conquest of the West, the Frontier would have been left behind and confined to the realm of paper. Instead, thanks to cinema, the West has acquired an aesthetic dimension, acquiring a status of legend and myth, thus becoming the founding epic of a nation.[1] Bazin examined the evolution of the genre and defined the postwar production as one "that would be ashamed to be just itself and looks for some additional interest to justify its existence—an aesthetic, sociological, moral, psychological, political, or erotic interest"; he also identified the Second World War as the factor that triggered such complexity,[2] and went on to call this postwar cinematic phenomenon "super–Western." Bazin's categories have been accepted, disputed, and redone, but they still form the critical foundation of the genre, of what today we call "classic Western." However, the intuitions of the French critic go beyond these categorizations. He

2. Celluloid Indians, 1950s Westerns and the Termination Act

speaks highly of the Western of the 1950s and especially of Anthony Mann's films, claiming that there is something special about the films of this period, something novelistic about them.[3] It is exactly the urge to define that "something novelistic" isolated by Bazin that motivates the analysis of some of the 1950s Westerns presented in this chapter.

There is general consensus on considering John Ford the founding father of the classic Western, with many important films to his credit such as *Stagecoach, Rio Grande, The Man Who Shot Liberty Valance, The Searchers* to cite a few; the sheer volume of the themes examined in his productions and the breadth of his vision would suffice to support this view. In the case of Anthony Mann's Westerns, however, the viewer gets struck by something else; the modernity of Mann's films leaves us in awe, the violence troubles us. Almost fifty years later, the viewer is drawn into a cinematic world that seems to precede that of Sam Peckinpah and has little in common with much of the production of the other filmmakers of the 1950s.

As Richard Slotkin observes, in the 20th century:

> Movies became the most important of the mass media for the creation of public myths: the body of stories and symbols, part fiction, part history, through which Americans defined themselves as a national culture. Films genres [the creation of the Hollywood studios] were not only categories of production; they also roughly corresponded to key strains or elements in public myths. Myth is a way of thinking about and understanding the historical moment in which one lives—not an analytical, but a symbolic or poetic way of thinking, in which the telling of the story or fable provides an effective way of looking at things. Thus, the studio-era Western addressed the beliefs and concerns arising from the nation's obsession with growth, progress, the conquest of nature, and the necessity of violence. ... Although each genre was responsive to the concerns of the era that produced it, as those concerns changed, the genres were also adapted. And these modifications of genre corresponded to changes in public myth.... So, to understand the ways in which film genres develop and change is to open a window on the forces that shape America's national ideology, our way of looking at the world.[4]

Slotkin's words outline clearly the subtle connection between cinema, myth-making and ideology. The cultural loop between what the public thinks and likes, and the orientation of the studio production is a given—considerable amounts of money invested in a commercial product must guarantee success at the box office—but other variables enter into this equation. These include issues related to national identity, national space, integration, contamination, attempts to reclaim America as a white Anglo-Saxon Protestant monoculture, considerations about

Prologue

race and gender. When dealing with the Western genre, the first question to address is, what does it mean to be American? The preoccupation with this question is the foundation of the majority of the classic Westerns as it involves the re-writing of history in fictional cinematic terms.

The classic Westerns are movies often governed by racist, imperialist and conflict-oriented ideological agendas. They usually delineate an American identity that goes from the populist to the hegemonic, an identity based on the myth of progress and democracy. Such an identity, however, is frequently built on a very conservative notion of national identity. In the Western the representation of "Cowboys versus Indians" usually attempts to reclaim national identities against foreign influence, the "Other." According to Steve Neale, immediately after the end of World War II, movies like *Duel in the Sun* (dir. King Vidor, 1946), *Daughter of the West* (dir. Harold Daniels, 1949), *The Cowboy and the Indians* (dir. John English, 1949), *Ranger of the Cherokee Strip* (dir. Philip Ford, 1949), prepared the ground for the cycle of pro–Indian Westerns of the following decade.[5] In 1950, the enormous success of *Broken Arrow* (dir. Delmer Daves) opened the flood gate to the cycle: *Across the Wide Missouri* (dir. William Wellman, 1951); *The Big Sky* (dir. Howard Hawks, 1952); *Rose of Cimarron* (dir. Harry Keller, 1952); *The Battle of Apache Pass* (dir. George Sherman, 1952); *Hiawatha* (dir. Kurt Neumann, 1952); *Navajo* (dir. Norman Foster, 1952); *Hondo* (dir. John Farrow, 1953); *Broken Lance* (dir. Edward Dmytryk, 1954); *Taza, Son of Cochise* (dir. Douglas Sirk, 1954); *Apache* (dir. Robert Aldrich, 1954), *Drum Beat* (dir. Delmer Daves, 1954); *The Half-Breed* (dir. Stuart Gilmore, 1952); *Apache Woman* (dir. Roger Corman, 1955); *White Feather* (dir. Robert D. Webb, 1955); *The Vanishing American* (dir. Joseph Kane, 1955); *Santa Fe Passage* (dir. William Witney, 1955); *Dakota Incident* (dir. Lewis R. Foster, 1956); *Walk the Proud Land* (dir. Jesse Hibbs, 1956); *The White Squaw* (dir. Ray Nazarro, 1956); *The Last Wagon* (dir. Delmer Daves, 1956); *The Last Hunt* (dir. Richard Brooks, 1956); *Yellowstone Kelly* (dir. Gordon Douglas, 1959); *Last Train from Gun Hill* (dir. John Sturges, 1959); *Flaming Star* (dir. Don Siegel, 1960); *Oklahoma Territory* (dir. Eduard L. Cahn, 1960); *The Unforgiven* (dir. John Huston, 1960).[6]

Within such a large number of titles, one should resist the temptation to divide them into A and B movies, or works by more or less famous directors, or categorize them according to their success at the box office. Instead, it would be more revealing to investigate why, in the postwar period, Hollywood produced these "sympathetic" films. The reason

2. Celluloid Indians, 1950s Westerns and the Termination Act

behind the emergence of this cycle of films has to be found within the historical context. The Second World War and the related war efforts caused social upheavals and displaced a large number of people in the nation. During the conflict, the Office of War Information waged a strong ideological campaign, promoting tolerance, freedom and justice against the evil empires of Nazi Germany and Japan. A branch of the agency, the Motion Picture Bureau, advised studios against "any representation of minorities that might be harmful to the national image of a racial brotherhood."[7] After the war, however, when the minority veterans came home, they ended up in a country still marred by contradictions, institutionalized racism and discrimination. They found a country engulfed in the Cold War, whose fear of Communism had spawned the House Un-American Activities Committee (1938–69) and the investigation of 6.6 million persons between March 1947 and December 1952. The Committee blacklisted a large number of film industry writers, screenwriters, directors, producers, actors, composers and so forth who were known or alleged to have been members of the American Communist Party and whose careers were destroyed.[8]

Fear of Communism pushed the Truman administration to promote the Marshall Plan to prevent Europe from falling under Soviet influence. In spite of the witch-hunt climate, the election of Truman somehow favored the growth of more liberal attitudes towards minorities.[9] Hollywood registered the climate and, in these years, a whole wave of social problem films about the African-Americans, the Japanese, the Jews, etc., were produced.[10] The fact that most minorities fought gallantly during the conflict had convinced most of mainstream Americans that the minorities proved themselves and deserved equal treatment.[11] Many Hollywood liberals (directors, scriptwriters and producers) who were later blacklisted worked on the pro–Indian cycle: Dudley Nichols (*The Big Sky*), Edward Dmytryk (*Broken Lance*), Ben Maddow and John Huston (*The Unforgiven*), Richard Brooks (*The Last Hunt*), Samuel Fuller (*Run of the Arrow*), Douglas Sirk (*Taza, Son of Cochise*), and Albert Maltz who wrote the script of *Broken Arrow*, but was fronted by Michael Blankfort.[12]

Traditionally the pro–Indian cycle has been seen as a trope in which the Indians could be replaced by the African-Americans or other minorities.[13] Many scholars have looked at this cycle as an allegory that hints at the condition of every minority: the blacks, still segregated after the Second World War; the Japanese confined into camps

Prologue

during the conflict; the Jews, the Puerto-Ricans and so forth. Steve Neale, instead, claims that the movies of this cycle, especially Anthony Mann's *Devil's Doorway*, address specifically the Native American condition. We could not agree more with Neale's position, because when we deal with the Western genre, we cannot forget the key role of the Indians.[14]

We need to keep in mind that the Western is a genre in which the "redskins" have played an essential part from the beginning. Since the time of the horse operas the "red men" have often played the part of the bad guys in the Western formula.[15] This role is derived from the myth of the Frontier, i.e., the epic struggle that the white pioneers endured in order to conquer the wilderness and the Indians. The Indians, therefore, are an intrinsic part of the myth. Many years after the official closing of the Frontier as formulated by Turner (1890), the end of the Great Depression and the New Deal, and with the onset of more liberal attitudes in the postwar era, the realization that the "Indian Problem" was a social problem that needed to be addressed finally reverberated into the Western genre. It would take at least another twenty years before the American public was ready to accept a revisionist reading of the epic conquest of the West. The pro–Indian cycle of the 1950s, however, paved the road for the success of later movies such as *Little Big Man* (dir. Arthur Penn, 1970) or *Dances with Wolves* (dir. Kevin Costner, 1990), and elaborated on the debate that was taking place at the time in American society, albeit in fictional terms.

The story of the Native Americans goes hand in hand with the story of the filmic Indians. The Native Americans had fought *en masse* in the world conflict, distinguishing themselves, but upon their return they did not get equitable treatment re-entering civilian life.[16] In 1919, Native American veterans were awarded citizenship in gratitude for their service in World War I, and in 1924 citizenship was extended to all Native Americans. In 1887, the Dawes Act had tied the acquisition of citizenship to the acquisition of individual allotments of land and to the abandonment of traditional tribal loyalties, customs and ways of life. Between the 1920s and the 1950s ambivalent shifts in attitude among the liberals favored at times Indian assimilation and, at other times, tribalism, traditional values and different ways of life over assimilation.[17] In the postwar period many Native American veterans no longer wanted to return to the poverty and regulations associated with reservation life and preferred to integrate themselves into mainstream

2. Celluloid Indians, 1950s Westerns and the Termination Act

society. At that time, even the more conservative political forces in the nation were advocating the integration of Native Americans into society.[18]

The key words were freeing the Indians, so the Termination Act that came after a very heated national debate ended up being a way of jettisoning any federal responsibilities toward the Indian nations. It was a way of solving the problem and, once again, divesting Native Americans of their last pieces of land. Undoubtedly, the Indian problem was a very complex one, encapsulated as it was in a difficult era. In 1947, the Truman administration started a civil rights program and desegregation was ordered for the military in 1948, but it took more than a decade to be enforced.[19] However, civil rights politics affected Native Americans differently than the other minorities. As some historians have pointed out, Native Americans never considered themselves segregated because they never sought out integration into white society in the first place.[20] In the middle of the civil rights struggle, paradoxically, the Indian nations were facing forced assimilation thanks to the Termination Act. The "Termination Act: House Joint Resolution 490" was introduced by Representative Reva Beck Bosone in July 1950. Beginning that year, Congress terminated 389 Treaties it had ratified with indigenous nations. It proposed Termination as a way to help the federal budget. Liberal elements supported the act because it favored assimilation. The Cold War and the proliferation of nuclear weapons created a great demand for uranium, much of which had been found in Indian lands. Conservative forces favored Termination as a way of furthering the interests of corporate mining because copper, essential for telegraph lines and electronics, had been found in Indian lands.[21]

Hollywood, as always, picked up on the hot social debate and tried to ease it out through its cinematic output. With its ability to speak to the present while recounting the past, the Western was the perfect ideological vehicle to do the job. It is important to note that setting events in the past can have other interesting consequences. As Fitzgerald points out, placing painful information in the past, also called "re-temporalization," is a way of *distancing* embarrassing events from the present. Situating the events around 1880 in the filmic and televisual *Broken Arrow* is a way to show that "crimes perpetuated against them [American Indians] are a thing of the past and that it is too late to do anything about them … a way of pushing the Indians into a mythical realm, which in 1956

Prologue

served to distract the public from actual problems of the time, which mainstream viewers most likely preferred to avoid and would continue to haunt and embarrass U.S. leaders in the international arena—issues such as structural racism, poverty and termination."[22]

The pro–Indian films produced in the 1950s deal with a more balanced idea of justice and exhibit a form of primeval consciousness of the "others as human beings." They somehow reflect the attitude of the liberal white society that, at the time, was enraged by reservation living conditions and policies, and was favoring the assimilation of the Native Americans into society. The majority of the films of this cycle succeed in offering a rehabilitation of the "red man" who ceases to be the menacing presence of before. In spite of this effort, however, the white cowboy/hero/protagonist of the cycle remains the only one who, in the end, saves the day.[23]

In *Broken Arrow* (Delmer Daves, 1950) or in *Run of the Arrow* (Samuel Fuller, 1950), the filmic story juxtaposes "Good Indians" with "Bad Indians" making sure that the good Indians are the ones that are friends with the hero and the good white men, are peaceful, and are striving for assimilation into white culture.[24] The pro–Indian films show a paternalistic attitude that becomes evident in the way they deal with miscegenation.[25] In these movies, sudden plot twists are employed to avoid the problem of miscegenation; often the female Indian married to the white cowboy/hero dies. Even if it is true that the Westerns of this cycle do acknowledge the existence of the "Other" with a certain respect, these films are incapable of surmounting the obstacle posed by race contamination. In most of these films the death of the Indian maiden solves the thorny problem of her racial difference, her future functioning in a white society, and her mix-race progeny.[26]

There is no doubt that the cycle of the 1950s constituted an improvement on the traditional image of the "Indian as savage" found in many classic Westerns. Even La Farge's Association on [Native] American Affairs welcomed the more positive and rehabilitating message of *Broken Arrow*.[27] Most films of this cycle favor co-existence, mutual respect, and tolerance, but, if we dig deeper into these filmic texts, we are bound to discover a more troubling truth—underneath the main narrative level, sub-text hides a less sympathetic discourse. In order to undo such hegemonic messages, we need to analyze the love story subplot as a key to deconstructing the main narratives. In many of these films the Indian princess succumbs to the charm and superior

2. Celluloid Indians, 1950s Westerns and the Termination Act

intelligence of the white hero. The Indian maid needs to be possessed, and therefore colonized, in order to stop being a threat to the male protagonist, and, in the end, she must die so any problems of integration, assimilation and miscegenation are avoided, and the hero can continue to roam the prairie looking for new adventures.

Unlike many classic Westerns centered on conflict and violence, the cycle promotes more peaceful, diplomatic resolutions that come down to two options—assimilation or reservation life. Thus, the history of the Native American genocide gets erased via filmic stories that, even if superficially celebrating the "Other" as equal, in reality reify the role of the American cavalry, passing it off as a benevolent entity that, impotent in front of the relentless march of progress, tries to protect the Indians from extinction via peace treaties and reservation life. In general, these films are well constructed and full of action, with alluring plots, and, often, a good director at the helm, but they are not novelistic; a brief analysis of the prototype of the cycle—the one that opened the flood gate to this production, thanks to its enormous success—will expose the hidden imperialist agenda of these Westerns.

Broken Arrow *(1950)*

The very successful and much celebrated *Broken Arrow* (1950) was produced by Julian Blaustein for 20th Century–Fox—under the auspices of legendary Hollywood mogul Darryl Zanuck—directed by a skillful filmmaker, Delmer Daves, and based on a script by Michael Blankfort, liberally adapted from the novel, *Blood Brothers* (1947), by Elliott Arnold. The film had all the right cards to be a great success and, in fact, it did become a hit.[28]

The protagonist of *Broken Arrow* is a white male cowboy/hero, Tom Jeffords (James Stewart), who ends up acting as link between the white community and the Apaches in the Arizona Territory of 1870. He becomes friends with Cochise (Jeff Chandler) and makes a yearned-for peace treaty possible. Jeffords comes to know the Apaches, discovers their humanity, overcomes his hate for them, starts respecting them, and, finally, convinces Cochise and U.S. Army General Oliver O. Howard to put an end to their hostilities. Jeffords is definitely a better human being than many of his fellow countrymen. He is courageous and honorable, and exceptionally smart: before meeting Cochise he learns the

Broken Arrow *(1950)*

Broken Arrow **(20th Century–Fox, 1950). Directed by Delmer Daves, with James Stewart as Tom Jeffords, and Jeff Candler as Chief Cochise. The medium shot underlines the fact that the two men are equally heroic, courageous and honest (Photofest).**

Apache language to perfection. Cochise (who is a noble savage, i.e., a great leader and a wise warrior) is up there with Jeffords in fairness, honesty and courage. He is often photographed from low angles so that he appears morally superior compared to the other characters. The white community and the Indian community, however, are both plagued by bad apples; ultra-racist white men on one side and Geronimo and his renegade warriors on the other will stop at nothing in order to continue the bloodshed.[29]

Parallel to this central plotline—i.e., Jeffords and Cochise seeking reasonable solutions—is the love story between the cowboy and the Indian princess, Sonseeahray (played by 16-year-old Debra Paget). It is the love story that upsets the balance of the narrative and obfuscates the equality-between-races theme at which the main narrative supposedly aims. The first time we encounter Sonseeahray, she is presented as the "White-Painted Lady, Mother of Life," a sort of goddess

2. Celluloid Indians, 1950s Westerns and the Termination Act

with healing and purifying powers. Her elaborate attire, her beauty and her innocence make her appear as Mother Earth, the symbol of a virgin land waiting to be conquered by the heroic white man, the embodiment of Manifest Destiny.[30] Furthermore, Sonseeahray chooses to marry Jeffords over another very valorous Apache warrior, and in doing so she somehow vouches for the superior charm of the white male, whose masculinity is apparently irresistible. In claiming the white hero, she proves to be eager to integrate into Jeffords's world and to abandon her native land. The combination of these two factors unveils the imperialist discourse hidden in the filmic text. The Indian princess has to be, on the one hand, possessed and colonized, so that her existence, seen as a potential threat to white society, can be neutralized, but, on the other hand, she has to die so any future contamination of the white race is avoided.

Certainly, Jeffords is able to stop the cruel killings between the

Broken Arrow (20th Century–Fox, 1950). Directed by Delmer Daves. From front left: Jeff Chandler as Cochise, Debra Paget as Sonseeahray, James Stewart as Tom Jeffords, and Mickey Kuhn as cowboy Bob Slade. Tom, with Indian princess Sonseeahray and Chief Cochise, learns about the evil deeds of a bunch of white people (Photofest).

Broken Arrow *(1950)*

whites and the Indians, but who gains from the treaty he successfully negotiates? The treaty helps the American government: with peace, the U.S. mail service will be able to run through the territory previously controlled by the Apaches, and the settlers will be able to advance. Cochise agrees to be confined to a corner of Arizona, so he and his people will be residing on a smaller part of the territory. Both factors will benefit the white community that will speed up on its path towards progress, expansion, and civilization.

The viewer, at this point, realizes that the arrow that Cochise breaks to sanction the treaty will have to be broken many more times because a whole series of treaties will follow over the years, and, eventually, the Apaches will be confined into an area so small that they will be brought to the verge of starvation.[31] The imperialistic meta-narrative becomes even more evident when both Jeffords and General Howard claim that the treaty will be everlasting, because it will be signed by the "big chief of the white tribe, President Grant." A totally self-serving answer that defuses what really happened in history.[32]

From an historical point of view, the movie is totally inaccurate, in spite of the authoritative voice-over of Tom Jeffords who, in the opening, claims that these are the "facts as they really happened." The whole story is narrated *a posteriori* by Tom to emphasize the historicity of the events as lived. The voice over of Jeffords in the opening of the film mentions that the Indians would speak in English so the viewer can understand them. In this way director Delmer Daves avoided using a made-up language, and managed to show respect for the Indians who appear as intelligent human beings, not as ignorant savages. Daves also did not want stars for the main characters. Except for James Stewart as Tom Jeffords, he picked then relatively unknown actors Jeff Chandler as Cochise, and young Debra Paget as Sonseeahray. Production notes indicate that Fox delved into ethnographical sources to portray Apache culture like the social dance, jewels, attires, etc. However, many historians attacked the wedding ceremony in which Jeffords and Sonseeahray become "blood brothers" as a Hollywood fantasy. The ceremony, in our opinion, was created to emphasize visually the merging of two different cultures and the possible coexistence of two different races.[33]

It is true that Cochise, Tom Jeffords and General Howard existed, and that Cochise and Howard signed a treaty in 1872, but the verisimilitude stops here. It being understood that a film, like any other fictional

2. Celluloid Indians, 1950s Westerns and the Termination Act

work, can only reverberate reality, in this case it is clear that the events are recounted in a manner to stir the viewer toward a happy, complacent, honorable view of American history.[34] *Broken Arrow* does an excellent job in communicating a pro–Indian attitude that sugar-coats the imperialist aims of a society that, even in the 1950s, was still unable to come to terms with its injustice. Ideologically, *Broken Arrow* proposes peace treaties and reservation life as the best possible solution to the Native American problem. Geronimo, the rogue Apache chief, who does not accept the treaty is portrayed as a renegade warmonger who ambushes innocent white people.[35] In fact, Geronimo is the only one in the filmic story who sees through the white men and rejects their fake promises and peace treaties, a wise choice that history will prove correct.

Another aspect of the film that looks sugar-coated is the Indian camp setting. The Apache camp is portrayed as an idyllic heaven, with beautiful meadows, sparkling brooks, gorgeous wickiups, white horses, etc. The Apache nation seems immune to the dangers of the encroaching civilization. The Indian camp is surrounded by cavalry, gangs of white, aggressive land and gold prospectors, mail system riders, hunters, settlers and more, all of whom are preying on their territory, but somehow the camp manages to insulate itself from reality.

Broken Arrow is a well-made film, an enjoyable Hollywood product, peppered with daring dialogues stating harsh truths, but the events are presented as they *could* have happened in a world without prejudice, greed, and racism. Land is at the core of the story, but the solution offered is a diplomatic one, and not a violent one as in many classic Westerns. The film was very successful among viewers and critics alike, not so much because it managed to project an honorable image of the Indians, but because it implicitly celebrated the intrinsic fair play, honesty and superiority of the Euro-American society. The movie was selling a revised edition of the frontier myth at a time when Americans, who had won a war against Fascism, had to show to the world that they were indeed the liberators who firmly believed in Democracy. How could the country that liberated Auschwitz harbor discrimination toward a different race? Acknowledging the heroic accomplishments of the Native American veterans in the war, mainstream society was trying to come to terms with its past, but it was still too early to see it as it really was. In this ideological frame of mind, a film like *Broken Arrow* fitted perfectly.

White Feather *(1955) and*
The Battle of Apache Pass *(1952)*

Released five years after the success of *Broken Arrow*, *White Feather* (1955) was another pro–Indian film. Directed by Robert D. Webb from a screenplay by Delmer Daves (with Leo Townsend), the film tells the story of a cowboy, Josh Tanner (Robert Wagner) who comes to the Cheyenne country, becomes friend with Little Dog (Jeffrey Hunter)—the son of Chief Broken Hand—marries his sister, Appearing Day (Debra Paget), and works as a link between the Fort Laramie cavalry captain and the Cheyenne chief. A peace treaty gets signed and hostilities are avoided. In short, the main plot device of *White Feather* is almost a copycat of *Broken Arrow*'s: However, Tanner is luckier than Jeffords (in *Broken Arrow*) because his wife does not die, but gets fully integrated into the white world. The one who dies is Little Dog who refuses to leave his homeland, and goes down fighting alone against a cavalry unit.

The story projects a very sympathetic view of the Indians, their displacement, their loss of freedom and land. Both the cavalry captain and the cowboy-hero grow fond of the Indians, and feel for their unfortunate situation. The Indian point of view is also explored. The film on the whole has impressive shots of riders, but it is a bit too melodramatic as most films of the pro–Indian cycle are. It sugar-coats the demise of the Indian civilization, assuming that, at this point in history, it was inevitable (see the crowds of eager gold and land prospectors and homesteaders waiting for the treaty to be signed so they can plunge on the Indian land). Except for a few haters, the majority of the white characters are sympathetic with the Indian cause, even if they do nothing to change the situation. The demise of the Indians (destined to reservation life) is an inevitable fate accepted by everybody.

As in *Broken Arrow*, we have the voice over of Josh Tanner in the opening of the film claiming that the events narrated are as they really happened; so the viewer is supposed to consider the filmic fiction as a slice of history. The same voice, at the end of the film, informs us that Chief Broken Hand lived long enough to see his grandchild enter West Point. In this way, we are relieved to know that the displacement of the Indians, in spite of its troubling beginning, eventually ended up promoting their integration and assimilation into American society and, in the long run, worked for the best. Like *Broken Arrow*, the movie gives another rendition of history as it *could* have happened, but did not.

2. Celluloid Indians, 1950s Westerns and the Termination Act

In 1952, George Sherman directed *The Battle of Apache Pass*, a lesser known but well made pro–Indian Western that is a sort of prequel to *Broken Arrow*. The narrative combines two historical events. In 1862, Cochise was falsely accused of having kidnapped a white boy, and when he went to parley he was ambushed by Lieutenant George Bascom who tried to imprison him. Cochise managed to escape, but some of his people were captured and executed. In 1862, Cochise trapped the cavalry in the canyon of Apache Pass, and for the next ten years he waged a guerrilla-style war against the encroaching white civilization. Cochise continued his raids until 1872 when, facilitated by Tom Jeffords, he finally signed the peace treaty with General Howard. Sherman's film fictionally recounts what happened to Cochise in the years before the signing of the peace treaty, and justifies his continuing battle against the white settlers, illustrating the reasons behind his behavior. It goes without saying that the historical events are changed, and enhanced by including into the mix marauding Indians led by Geronimo (Jay Silverheels) who conspires with a greedy, white Indian agent who wants to exploit Apache land in order to promote the interests of powerful capitalists from back East. He is helped in his schemes by a dishonest Indian scout (Jack Elan). The two evil factions succeed in triggering war between the peaceful Apaches, led by Cochise, and Major Jim Colton, head of the cavalry outpost and friend of the Indian chief.

The filmic story is sympathetic to the Indians—the confrontations and the acts of retaliations on both sides are inevitable—but Cochise is portrayed as a noble warrior and a sincere man who has been unjustly betrayed. However, besides the racist and greedy whites who get killed in the end, the cavalry comes out smelling like roses. Major Colton is a pure soul who admires Cochise and wants to protect the Apaches from the "blessings of civilization." In the battle of Apache Pass, Major Colton uses cannons against Cochise warriors only as a last resort to avoid the annihilation of his soldiers. In fact, the supremacy of the cavalry weaponry is recognized by the Apaches, who retreat. Cochise leaves for his mountain hideout, but not before telling his friend Colton that eventually he will be back when the bad blood between the Apaches and the whites will be forgotten. As in *Broken Arrow*, the film creates a version of history as it *could* have happened and succeeds in cleansing the history of the U.S. Cavalry. Historically, the cavalry during the Indian wars did not shy from using tricks to capture and eliminate powerful opponents; see, for example, what happened, to Cochise's father in law, Mangas Colorada.[36]

Devil's Doorway *(1950)*

In the pro–Indian cycle of the 1950s three lesser known Westerns stand out: *Devil's Doorway, The Last Wagon* and *The Last Hunt*. The pessimism informing the ideological agenda of these films strikes an emotional chord in viewers, affecting them in a Deleuzean way, being truly novelistic in the sense intended by Bazin, and therefore, deserving a thorough examination.

Devil's Doorway (1950, Anthony Mann) presents a narrative that goes against the grain and stands out as an exception, not only within the pro–Indian cycle, but also within Anthony Mann's filmic productions.[37] The main protagonist of the film is a Shoshone Indian who has a potentially romantic interest in a white woman who helps him as a lawyer. The traditional duo, white cowboy and Indian maiden, is reversed. Here we have an Indian man and a white woman, both struggling to be accepted by the white society in which they live, one because of the color of his skin, the other because of her gender, being a female in a traditional male profession. The male protagonist is also a decorated hero of the Civil War who comes home to his profitable Wyoming cattle ranch after the end of the conflict in 1865. The fact that the cowboy-hero is a Native American is not unusual—in this cycle there are other examples of films whose hero is an Indian. What is surprising is the fact that this hero, Lance Poole (Robert Taylor), is an Indian who has somehow crossed the racial and economic boundaries of his minority group: He considers himself American, has fought a war, is liked by the white community (at least upon his first arrival in town), and owns a very successful and vast cattle ranch (Sweet Meadows). Poole seems to be, at the beginning of the film, the embodiment of the successful integration of the "Other." As the film progresses, however, we witness the inescapable disintegration of Poole's initial status and identity, because the white community does not permit the existence of a successful minority.

As we know, the model of the classic Western is always based on three entities: the hero, the community, and the bad guys. In *Devil's Doorway* the hero is an Indian. The communities are two, the Shoshone Indians who live peacefully in Sweet Meadows, and the white people

2. Celluloid Indians, 1950s Westerns and the Termination Act

Devil's Doorway (MGM, 1950). Directed by Anthony Mann. Robert Taylor as Lance Poole sports his blue Union uniform coat, having just arrived home from the war as a decorated soldier (Photofest).

who live in the nearby town, Medicine Bow. The bad guys enlist a lawyer, Verne Coolan (Louis Calhern), who leads the town community, and is bent on the Indians' destruction. There is also another community of outsiders, the sheep herders, invited by Coolan to take possession of Poole's vast ranch under false premises. The fact that some of the

Devil's Doorway *(1950)*

white folks at the beginning of the film are friendly with Poole does not prevent them in the five-year course of the story from enforcing racial laws (no whiskey served to Indians), or the government's unjust laws (no ownership of land for Indians), and, in the final confrontation, to take the side of the settlers against Poole's Indians.

The protagonist, Poole, like any classic Western hero, must indeed vindicate a wrong, defend his land and use violence to solve the problem, because the situation is such that he cannot do otherwise. We are facing two unusual camps: Poole and the Shoshone Indians (the good guys) on one side; on the other, Coolan, the townsfolk and the sheep herders (the bad bunch).[38] In *Devil's Doorway*, the turning upside down of the Western formula (the Indians as good guys) includes also the inverted roles played by Poole and Orrie, male Indian and white woman instead of the white male and Indian maiden seen in the majority of the pro–Indian movies of the 1950s.

Here we have a white guy, Coolan, who is the bad guy, and a community that seems to be uncertain about what to do, but ends up being manipulated by the villain, who, on the other hand, is helped in the implementation of his racism by the government's unjust laws.

The point of view of the film is aligned with Poole's. This way, while the story unfolds on the screen towards its very pessimistic and tragic end, issues related to race, ethnicity and miscegenation acquire more and more evidence for the viewer. Before analyzing the film in detail, we would like to point out that this film sticks out like a sore thumb within the Western genre production. First of all, it is a Hollywood film made by a renowned director that ends with the death of the hero, something almost unheard of in the classic Western tradition. Secondly, the movie is very political. The events unfolding on the screen create a situation for the "Others" with no way out. There is no hope for the Indians because their annihilation is actively sought by the white community. Paradoxically, the extinction of the Indians will contribute to the survival of the white community: the sheep herders will be able to live and prosper in Poole's valley. As a consequence, the existential journey of Poole as an exemplary "Other" follows a path that goes from Americanization (decorated army sergeant, major/ranch owner) via Indianization (back to his roots), to savagery (battle) and finally to death (extinction). The message of the film denies the Indians any possible integration into mainstream society, and shows how they have been divested of their civil and human rights.

2. Celluloid Indians, 1950s Westerns and the Termination Act

At the opening of the film, Poole is warned by his father about the situation. The old man claims that the white men hate them and that Poole, now that the war is over, will be again an "Indian." Poole is very proud of his acquired American identity, however, and does not believe him. Stylistically the change in Poole's perception is registered via the stripping of his Americanism. At the beginning of the film he dresses like a cowboy, insists that his father should speak English, and is proud of being a wealthy cattle owner (he deposits $18,000 in the local bank). Little by little, going through the various unfortunate legal battles he undertakes to maintain ownership of his land, he starts wearing Indian jewels, a head band, and long hair. His Indianization takes over, because the law of the country for which he has fought does not recognize him as a citizen and, therefore, destroys his American identity.

Devil's Doorway is a striking film not only for its content, but also for its iconography. Guy Trosper's clever script is combined with John Alton's splendid photography. The choice of filming in black and white, instead of color, has enhanced the use of *chiaroscuro* techniques, a style familiar to Alton who had worked with Anthony Mann's previous *noir* films like *T-Men* (1947), *Raw Deal* (1948) and *Border Incident* (1949). Gorgeous landscape shots of Poole's sunny valley contrast with the claustrophobic and darker interior shots of Poole's farm, Orrie's house (Poole's female lawyer) and the town saloon. Most of the interior shots frame major confrontations between the characters and show only the partially illuminated faces of the actors, creating an ominous and foreboding atmosphere. *Devil's Doorway* should be considered a *noir*-Western not only for its iconography, black and white photography, and the use of *chiaroscuro*, but also for its content: a doom story of Indian eradication.[39]

At the beginning of the film, the welcoming drink offered to Poole in the town saloon by Zeke (Poole's father's hunting friend) and Scotty (the saloon owner) is filmed from the point of view of an almost invisible bar customer. In the corner of the screen only his hat, hand and glass are visible. The identity of this mysterious character is revealed later on when we discover he is the Indian hater, lawyer and schemer Coolan. The camera is positioned behind him and, as a result, the spectator observes the welcoming reception with a sense of apprehension, wondering if this character is friend or foe. The identity of Coolan is revealed in a medium shot only when he intervenes in the conversation, uttering racially disparaging remarks against Poole's Medal of Honor.

Devil's Doorway *(1950)*

At this point we realize that not everybody is happy about the Indian's return. When Poole leaves the saloon, even his friend Zeke expresses uncertainty about Poole's successful future.

Orrie Masters (Paula Raymond), the female lawyer who helps Poole in his legal battles and has an undeclared romantic interest in him, functions as the link between Poole and the white community. Despite her well-meaning efforts, Orrie is incapable of understanding Poole's reality. She is a white lawyer who believes in the essential justice of the American legal system without realizing that the system works only for whites. There is attraction between Poole and Orrie, but the possibility of a cross-racial romance is negated. The fear of miscegenation, as a consequence, is averted. On the other end the absence of a full-blown romance does not surprise in a film that denies to its hero any possibility of survival. On the verge of kissing each other, but restraining themselves at the last minute from doing it, Poole, with far-sightedness, says to Orrie: "Don't cry Orrie, a hundred years from now it might have worked."

As a consequence, she cannot comprehend why Poole, when facing the invasion of his valley by the settlers and their sheep, decides, against her advice, not to compromise. Poole is not willing to share his vast ranch with anybody,

Devil's Doorway (MGM, 1950). Directed by Anthony Mann. Paula Raymond as Orrie Masters, the lawyer, and Robert Taylor as Lance Poole on the verge of kissing. Poole is dressed in his Indian regalia, having been progressively stripped of his American identity (**Photofest**).

2. Celluloid Indians, 1950s Westerns and the Termination Act

because the valley has become a refuge against bigotry and a place where not only Poole's Indians can live in peace, but also where the Shoshone Indians who escaped from the horrors of reservation life can find a home.[40] Orrie is blinded by her faith in the law, and does not seem to be able to see that Poole, after being refused a drink in the saloon, denied ownership of his land, and having witnessed so much injustice, has let his Indian nature come to the fore.[41] His attachment to the land has also come to the surface with the rediscovery of his roots. The movie makes a point in showing that, for an Indian, the land is not just a piece of property to exploit, but a home, the tie to his ancestry, the link to mother earth, and the reason of his existence. The loss of land is equivalent to the loss of identity, as Poole's father affirms before dying: "An Indian without land loses his very soul." Because the loss of identity is equivalent to death, Poole chooses the proverbial last stand, enacting a clever and furious battle plan that includes dynamite and causes a carnage among riders, posse, and sheep.[42]

Poole opts for the open conflict because he is powerless in front of white racism, white laws and white greed (the townsfolk want his land). He realizes that the law does not apply to him because of the color of his skin, something that Orrie cannot see. It is precisely his desire for justice that drives him to fight and, as a result, to succumb. It is obvious that Poole does not want assimilation, but rather he wants to be king on his land; he wants to be accepted as an Indian-American with the same rights of the Euro-Americans. Poole's pessimistic final words uttered to a cavalry officer before dying, "we're all gone," more than Orrie's final statement, "it would be too bad if we ever forget," remind the viewer that there is no place for the Indians and no land for them, only reservation camps, where, in fact, the Shoshone women and children, the only survivors of the massacre, will return at the end. When Poole dies, he falls out of the frame dressed in Indian regalia with the Medal of Honor on his chest on his cavalry uniform, signaling that the establishment has finally succeeded in destroying both his identities.

The land motif that is pivotal in *Devil's Doorway* is also central to the history of the Frontier. The land conquest was the primary motivation for the immigration of millions of Europeans who came to America dreaming of owing a piece of land, and who believed in the creation of a more prosperous and better life for themselves. As Jacquelyn Kilpatrick points out, the hard work that the settlers put in the land gave them the moral right to claim the land as theirs. The land was the "fruit

Devil's Doorway *(1950)*

of their physical labor" and therefore they believed it belonged to them. The settlers, moreover, had a utilitarian view of the land, so they firmly believed that the unused land was wasted.[43] The concept of land as property is one of the fundamental ideas that connotes the differences between Euro-American and Native American cultures. Native Americans did not have individual ownership of land, so their claims to the land were ignored, the land was seen as empty, especially since many native tribes were nomadic, and did not have permanent dwellings. Since land was imperative to the westward expansion of the settlers, and the land was indeed occupied by different people, it became necessary to justify the white expansion ideologically, and so the frontier became the white man's struggle for bringing "civilization, progress, democracy" to the West.[44] *Devil's Doorway* does a good job in showing the motivations behind the legal theft of Indians' land and the deadly ramifications of such expropriation, while implicitly advocating for tribal sovereignty.

The *Devil's Doorway* story boldly shows that the only good Indian is indeed a dead Indian.[45] In the film both Poole's attempts to assimilate (military service/decorated hero/wealthy rancher) and the option of reservation life fail (Shoshone Indians prefer to die rather than go back to the reservation). It is evident that the land claim issue that is at the base of the conflict refers, we can infer, to the Termination Act. According to this law, Native American tribes were going to be compensated for the past wrongs once and for all through the setting up of an Indian Claims Commission (1946). The Indians were encouraged to leave the reservations and relocate into cities, and the federal services previously granted to the Indian communities were to be terminated. The Act negated any sovereignty of the Indian Nations. The federal government was setting the Indians free. However, unlike other minorities such as the African-Americans, for which desegregation and assimilation were two important goals in the fight for civil rights in the postwar era, integration for Native Americans often meant the disintegration of their identity. *Devil's Doorway* does a good job in showing the viewer how important the land, his valley, is for Poole and how the root of his Indian identity is intertwined with nature, the mountains, and the valley where multiple generations of his ancestors have lived before.[46] The connection between land and identity is evident when Poole speaks of his land in the feminine, as if it were a woman for whom he has tender feelings. While Coolan also is enchanted by the beauty of Poole's valley, he sees only its utilitarian aspect, mentioning that it has a watering hole

2. Celluloid Indians, 1950s Westerns and the Termination Act

so large that a clipper could float in it, grass always green, no cold winds, and is a paradise of profit for any cattle/sheep owner.[47]

The film script sets the story at the end of the Civil War, but the affinities between the social problems of Poole's Indians and the situation of the Native Americans at the end of World War II force us to conclude that compensation, relocation and assimilation did not work for Lance Poole in the film, as they did not work for most Native Americans in the 1950s. After watching the film, one is left to ponder on unresolved issues like Indian Nations' sovereignty, ethnic identity, and cultural pluralism. If we take popular genre cinema as one of the mechanisms a society uses to give voice to its worries about its future at a time when democratic institutions seem to be less stable—and this was certainly the position of America at the onset of the Cold War—then, *Devil's Doorway* makes a radical and unusual (for its sincerity) statement about our past, while addressing the present. It is evident that the film aims at pointing out the failure of the Reservation system and the Termination policies. At the end of the film, the expansionist dream of the white community does succeed, but the price to pay for white progress, democracy and civilization is prejudice, injustice and greed. As Slotkin states, Anthony Mann's film is radical in its depiction of racial politics and innovative in its manipulation of the genre formula.[48]

The return-from-the-war theme is common to many Westerns, the most famous example being *The Searchers*; however, the reverberations between what happens to Poole after the war and what happened to thousands of Native Americans at the end of the second world conflict are worth pointing out.[49] The connections between the events of the filmic story and history are not casual. Poole comes back at the end of the Civil War as a decorated war hero. In the postwar era, a multitude of Native American veterans received high military honors for their heroism. Sixty thousand Native Americans joined the war effort; twenty-five thousand were in combat units and the rest in industry that supported the conflict. Like Poole, the Native Americans distinguished themselves as great fighters, but, when they came back, they found themselves trapped between the laws of the Bureau of Indian Affairs and the Termination Act.[50] After the initial moment of glory bestowed on them by the various communities and the government, many Native American veterans did not survive in civilian life any better than Poole did on screen.[51]

Because the Western film is a type of collective dream of an ideal space in which justice triumphs at any price, the viewer is shocked when this does not happen in *Devil's Doorway*. The film negates one of the fundamental features of the classic model. As a consequence, the four terms that characterize the myth of the frontier in the genre—battle, success, progress and democracy—get deconstructed. Success, progress and democracy are not present because the good guys die in the end, and their death implies the negation of any possible future progress or success. Ironically, the three terms, if they could be claimed by anybody, would be claimed by the bad guys, because it is the white society that will continue to take advantage of the land robbed from the Indians. The absence of the happy ending is unusual for a Hollywood production (MGM), but it functions well in reminding the viewer of the precarious status of the Native Americans within American society.[52]

The Last Wagon *(1956)*

The Last Wagon was directed by Delmer Daves who also contributed to the screenplay together with James Edward Grant and Gwen Bagni (writer of the original story). The film is set in 1873 Arizona and stands out for its magnificent scenery, beautifully photographed by Wilfred M. Cline on location in Sedona, Arizona (Oak Creek Canyon and Red Rock Crossing). Like *Devil's Doorway,* the film subverts the classic Western formula. The hero is not a cowboy, but a white man who has Indianized himself to the point of being called Comanche Todd; he has been raised by the Comanche, and, in the course of the story, we discover that he has chosen the Comanche set of ideas and beliefs over the whites? By Indianizing himself, he has opted for the wilderness over civilization, wickiups over houses and forests over towns.

In spite of his white skin and blue eyes, the protagonist has to be considered an Indian. The story, rather cleverly, combines three classic Western tropes: revenge, chase, and journey to salvation. The journey, both moral and physical, is the one of the small group of characters who are forced to gravitate around the protagonist as the only survivors of a wagon train massacre. The group of six youngsters constitutes a microcosm that is representative of American society.

Three other larger groups of communities are looming at the periphery of the story. They could be considered marginal for the limited screen time they get, but they are essential in propelling the action

2. Celluloid Indians, 1950s Westerns and the Termination Act

forward. At the beginning of the film, we encounter a wagon train of Christian pioneers and, at the end, a courtroom crowd, a group made up of cavalrymen, Indians and white settlers. The warring Apaches are the third group, whose presence we are reminded of mostly by smoke signals, drumming, sporadic appearances, and the trail of dead bodies they leave behind. The Apaches remain, for the most part, a presence lurking in the wilderness. None of the Apaches is developed into a character; they are a ghost community. We learn that they are retaliating against the pioneers because the whites have massacred more than one hundred Indian women and children. However, their point of view is filtered through Todd's interpretation of the Apache signs (dance, native chanting, smoke signals, music).

The story of *The Last Wagon* cleverly avoids the Indian camp story, the sheriff-town story, the cavalry-fort story, and the trapper story, focusing instead on a journey of a group of survivors through the wilderness. Cinematographically the film opens with a very exciting man-hunt sequence. The scene alternates between extreme high shots and low shots of five men running between gigantic red buttes and deep canyons, dominated by a bright blue sky and an imposing panorama (filmed from a high bluff) of endless valleys and mountains extending to the horizon. The chase sequence is spectacularly filmed, with crane shots and panning shots that dwarf the horses and the humans who appear as insignificant entities in comparison to the majesty of nature. At first, a long shot shows a rider being killed as he approaches a river, filmed with the camera positioned behind the shooter; a subsequent panning movement to the left reveals a man in buckskins with a rifle in his hands, and a very menacing expression on his face. When the credits start rolling, the viewers finds themselves *in medias res*, without knowing who is friend or foe. When the chase resumes, we realize that three men are in pursuit of the buckskin-wearing character.

The latter manages to kill two riders before being subdued by the third one, Sheriff Bull Harper (George Mathews), who proceeds to drag him like an animal, chain him to a tree, and deny him any water and food. Up to this point, we do not know anything about the buckskin-wearing character.

It is only when Harper meets a wagon train of pioneers that we learn that the prisoner is Comanche Todd, who is the killer of Harper's three brothers and is going to be taken to Tucson to be hanged. We do not know Comanche Todd's side of the story until later; we learn only

The Last Wagon *(1956)*

The Last Wagon (20th Century–Fox, 1956). Directed by Delmer Daves. Richard Widmark as Comanche Todd displays his superior fighting skills in the initial sequence of the film (Photofest).

that Todd is a white man who has chosen Indians over his own kind, and according to the lawman, "...any 'Injun-lovin' white who chooses Comanche against his own kind is no good." Somehow, the abuses that Harper commits trigger different reactions in the pioneers who, in the end, intervene to prevent the torturing of Todd. They drop a hatchet near him, accidentally causing the demise of the sheriff, who promptly gets killed by Todd.

The killing of Sheriff Harper concludes what we could call the prologue to the story, the part that sets the stage for the developing of the following events. In the night, six of the youngsters decide to take a secret swim, and leave the wagons. Upon their return they discover that everybody in the camp has been tortured, killed, and burned by the Apaches. The only survivor is Todd who is lying at the bottom of a ravine chained to a wheel of a wagon, miraculously alive. It is here that the main part of the story begins.

2. Celluloid Indians, 1950s Westerns and the Termination Act

The six youngsters who survived the massacre resemble a scaled down American society: Jenny (Felicia Farr) and Billy (Tommy Rettig) are humane, goodhearted and sympathetic to Todd; Jolie (Susan Kohner) is half Indian and is suffering discrimination by her own white half-sister Valinda (Stephanie Griffin), an arch-racist, whose sentiments are shared by another young man, Ridge (Nick Adams); the third male, Clint, is instead more moderate in his mistrust of Todd. In the course of the story, Todd manages to change the way the youngsters feel about the Indians. Jolie will learn to be proud of her heritage, Jenny will fall in love with Todd. Billy will choose him as a father-figure. Clint will become more pro–Indian. Valinda will learn that discrimination is wrong. Ridge will scale down his hate of the "Other." The change occurs because the six characters, deprived of the original pioneer community, must rely on Todd for their survival in the hostile territory. Todd becomes the leader who saves them thanks to his Indian skills, courage, and honesty. In the end he manages to take his party, and a small detail of cavalrymen, to safety out of the Apache territory, using a decoy (dynamite) to scare off the attacking Apaches.

The group's return to civilization drives the third and last part of the film, in which the salvation of the group brings about the possible death sentence of Todd, who faces a murder charge for having killed the Harper brothers. The last part of the movie takes place in a courtroom, and the trial, presided over by General Howard, the same "Bible-Reading Howard" we have already encountered in *Broken Arrow*. The sparring dialogue between the general and Todd is the most interesting part of the film. In this exchange, two opposite visions of the world collide and clash against each other.

On one side, we have the Bible-reading general who believes in God, justice and the authority of the military; on the other, we have Todd who believes in Comanche justice. It is at this point that we finally get a detailed narration of the reasons behind Todd's killing of the Harpers; the Harpers had murdered his wife and his two sons. Todd claims that he has killed, but also the general has killed. The general replies that there is a difference between killing in war and in peace. Todd retorts that Comanche only kill their enemies (as he did), while the general and the Americans also kill their friends, bringing up, as an example, the Civil War. Todd states that he no longer considers himself white, since his family was exterminated by the four white men, so, while the general might be bound by the regulation of the white law, and might

The Last Wagon *(1956)*

believe that no individual should take the law into his own hands, he is a Comanche and, therefore, follows different laws. Todd is also convinced that a jury made of white men would have never hung four white men for killing an Indian squaw and two Comanche boys. When the general responds, "Murder is murder," implying that he would have condemned the Harpers because the color of the skin does not matter to him, Todd responds that this is exactly what he did, he executed them. Finally, Todd affirms that what matters is justice, and justice is justice everywhere even "…in places where they give medals for killing Indians like out here. Medals like the ones you are wearing!"

At this point, Jenny jumps up, and, to defuse their confrontation, channels the discussion in a more positive direction, reminding everybody about the lives—six youngsters and sixteen cavalry soldiers—Todd saved from the Apaches. With a surprising change of mind, the general seems to forget Todd's scathing remarks, and proceeds to sentence him to be married to Jenny, saving his neck from the rope.

In the overall economy of a film so stylishly shot, well-acted, and spiced with clever dialogues, the happy ending feels a bit too far-fetched. It is hard to believe that Comanche Todd, after having accused the white establishment of giving medals for killing Indians, having seriously put in doubt the possibility of a fair trial in the murder case of an Indian maid and two Indian boys, and expressing qualms about the fairness of the whole judicial system, would have been let go free. However, the film remains pretty innovative in spite of complying with Hollywood happy ending standards.

The movie proposes the Indian point of view of the protagonist as the winning one. In the beginning, the deeply religious pioneers are humane, but refuse to listen to Comanche Todd's version of the events. When it comes to killing, they listen only to Sheriff Harper's side of the story, offering a pretty myopic view of the world, confined into rigid parameters that clearly exclude the "Others." Todd, on the other hand, saves all the youngsters including the ones who, like Valinda and Ridge, claim to hate Indians, show in their actions a profound distrust of him, and, at a certain point, even threaten with their behavior the survival of the whole group.

The love story between Todd and Jenny is also very daring considering the moral standards of the 1950s. Todd likes Jenny from the beginning, but it is she who chooses to spend the night under the stars with him. It is she who boldly defends Todd in front of the general during the

2. Celluloid Indians, 1950s Westerns and the Termination Act

The Last Wagon (20th Century–Fox, 1956). Directed by Delmer Daves. Shown along the front, from right: Richard Widmark as Comanche Todd, Felicia Farr as Jenny, Tommy Rettig as Billy, Susan Kohner as Jolie Normand, Stephanie Griffin as Valinda Normand, Ray Stricklyn as Clint and Nick Adams as Ridge. In a court of law, the young survivors try to save Todd from the rope (Photofest).

trial, affecting the outcome of the sentence. Todd makes his move on Jenny talking about the beauty of living in nature, dwelling in a wickiup, having the sky as a roof ... and he succeeds in defeating Jenny's defense of the white way of living: house, school, town. Faith in God and the Law is also challenged all along by Todd who believes in the Comanche version of paradise (the dead go to the High Ground) and in a sort of simplified version of justice guided by an the eye-for-an-eye principle.

The film subverts the Western formula because the Indian gets the white girl, and the mixed couple chooses the wilderness over civilization. Like Ringo and Dallas at the end of John Ford's *Stagecoach*, Jenny and Todd also are saved from the "blessings of civilizations," but they not only decide to abandon the community, they even resolve to live the Indian way. With this move, the staples of the Western genre—success, progress, and democracy—and the superiority of the white civilization

The Last Wagon *(1956)*

are negated. Todd wins the battle with the Apaches using a trick to prevent the bloodshed in order to save the whites and himself. But his victory does not open the gate to progress and democracy. The benefits of his victory are limited to the people involved. This is a Western in which the community (the six youngsters) is changed for the better by the deeds of an Indian, and the bad guys are in reality four white men, the Harpers. The Apaches cannot be included in the bad guys group because they are doing what is done in war—they retaliate for an attack on their land against their people.

Ultimately, *The Last Wagon* succeeds in creating a filmic story that celebrates the Indian way as superior, debunking the myth of the frontier and praising the validity of living "beyond the frontier." Of course, the celebration of the wilderness recalls other myths: namely, the garden of Eden and the "noble savage" of Jean-Jacques Rousseau, and James Fennimore Cooper's novels. However, when framing this celebration within the historical context under scrutiny, the return to the wilderness in 1956 was a way to reject both assimilation and reservation life as viable options for the Native Americans, and a way of proposing a third way, no matter how difficult it might have appeared by then. It was a way to hope for a return to Nature as a better way of living, as a place still immune from the evils of civilization. The film re-validates the Indian ways thanks to a hero who chooses the "Other" over his own kind many years before Lieutenant Dunbar of *Dances with Wolves* (1990) was going to make the same choice.

While *Devil's Doorway* indicates that the Native Americans, after having lost their land to the white man, are finished. *The Last Wagon*, more optimistically, recognizes the superiority of the Indian way and proposes a return to Nature away from civilization, favoring a sort of reverse frontier course, in spite of its practical impossibility. Both films, if analyzed against the historical-ideological-social background in which they were conceived, oppose Reservation and Assimilation as options for the Native Americans; their implied critique looks at the outcome of white civilization, deconstructing the myth of the Frontier. The conquest of the wilderness has displaced a people, destroyed them in order to create towns ruled by discriminating laws, populated by racist bigots and dominated by a pervasive desire to acquire land, accumulate wealth, and exploit resources in an endless cycle called progress, but could be easily labeled as capitalism. A world in which the bad guys often get the upper hand.

2. Celluloid Indians, 1950s Westerns and the Termination Act

The Last Hunt *(1956)*

The Last Hunt (1956) is another film that moves away from civilization, focusing, thematically and cinematographically, on the wilderness. *The Last Hunt* was filmed in Custer State Park in South Dakota. The director, Richard Brooks, was permitted to film the annual required thinning (done by expert government riflemen) of the largest buffalo herd existing in America. This is why the sequences that show the killing of the animals are chilling. One by one the bisons are systematically shot down, while they are peacefully grazing in the meadows, in a merciless slaughter that is justified, apparently, because the territory now allowed to these animals, who once roamed the Great Plains freely in millions, is so small it can accommodate only a limited number of animals. The opening credits of the movie tell us that in 1853 there were six million buffaloes in America, thirty years later, in 1883, when the filmic story takes place, there were only three thousand buffaloes left. Brooks,[53] who also wrote the script based on Milton Lott's novel with the same title, set the movie in 1883 South Dakota at the time in which the wild buffalo was on the verge of extinction. The indiscriminate killing was a way for the white hunters to make money while, at the same time, deprive the Indians of their primary source of sustenance.

The film recounts a hunt that is the last in the sense that the animals are almost gone from the plains, hunted mercilessly into oblivion. The filmic hunt is also the last endeavor of the two protagonists: Charlie Gilson (Robert Taylor, casted against type) and Sandy McKenzie (Stewart Granger).[54] In their pursuit, they are helped by two skinners, old Woodfoot (Lloyd Nolan), and a young "half-breed," Jimmy O'Brien (Russ Tamblyn). As in *The Last Wagon*, communities do not play a central role on screen. They are important for the development of the events, but they exist at the margins of the main events taking place. One community resides in the town, which is shown through a sequence of shots that focus on the general store, the main street, and the saloon. These shots help the viewer define what kind of townsfolk live there. In one of the opening scenes, the store keeper suggests to young Jimmy to get out of his reservation clothes, get a haircut and dress like a white man if he wants to get a job in town, suggesting that, in spite of his red hair, he could pass for white.

Jimmy does undergo such transformation, only to be beaten and robbed by the saloon thugs who, before leaving him unconscious in the

The Last Hunt *(1956)*

street, call him "stinkin' Indian," demonstrating that the nature of their hatred cannot be neutralized by Jimmy's assimilation efforts.[55] When one of the hunters, Sandy (who is sympathetic towards the Indians), goes to town to sell the buffalo skins, he gets drawn into a fight when he reacts to the general racist remarks of the barman and the saloon girl.

The remaining community is made up of the Indians of the Reservation, a group of people reduced to suffer from starvation and cold, whose lives depend on government aids. These Indians no longer resemble the proud warriors they once were when roaming the plains and hunting the buffaloes. They now look like street beggars. The core of the story takes place in the plains and in the base camp where the five main characters—the two hunters, the two skinners and an Indian maiden (Debra Paget)—interact.

The film opens with an establishing low-angle shot of a herd of running buffaloes, followed by an impressive sequence of close-ups of a stampede. It is here that we encounter the two protagonists, Charlie and Sandy, in a sequence that establishes the differences between the two men. Charlie is a man who enjoys killing and considers violence a natural state. Sandy does not like killing, but the destruction of his cattle by the buffalo stampede forces him to become Charlie's hunting partner. Charlie is a complex character, unkind, maniacal, psychotic, but also terribly alone, who feels persecuted by everything and everybody; in him self-hate is transformed into hatred for mankind and becomes a self-destructing force. He is a killer; even worse, he enjoys killing. He mercilessly kills the Indians who stole his mules, he cajoles Jimmy's Indian friend into a duel in order to shoot him with pleasure, and he murders Woodfoot after the skinner tries to stop him (with an unloaded gun) from chasing Sandy. After having shot an entire herd of buffaloes, we observe Charlie walking around, amid so much devastation, beaming with satisfaction, power and a sense of accomplishment. He seems to relate to the "Others," Indians or whites, only through violence. He despises equally animals and humans, stating that "Indians are not even human," and that "killin's like ... like the only real proof you're alive." Considering the Western formula, he fits the bad guy label, even if his personality is full of nuances; he shows friendship and respect for Sandy, and he saves his life at the beginning of the film.

Sandy on the other hand, is humane, sympathetic towards the Indians and, even if he kills the buffaloes because he needs the money, he is

2. Celluloid Indians, 1950s Westerns and the Termination Act

The Last Hunt (MGM, 1956). Directed by Richard Brooks. From left: Lloyd Nolan as Woodfoot, Robert Taylor as Charles Gilson, Stewart Granger as Sandy McKenzie; background: Russ Tamblyn as Jimmy O'Brian. Angry hunter Gilson disagrees with wise skinner Woodfoot at the camp (Photofest).

affected by the slaughter, and refuses to shoot the white buffalo sacred to the Indians. Sandy has grown up in close contact with the Indians who taught him how to hunt, to ride and to live. He has great respect for them, and speaks their language. He treats them as equals, as opposed to Charlie, who treats them as slaves. He tolerates Charlie and tries to understand him, until two major causes of conflict arise: the killing of the Indian boy and the mistreating of the Indian maiden. When Charlie refuses to let Jimmy take the mortally wounded Indian boy back to his people, Sandy confronts Charlie with a knife, and when Charlie hits the Indian woman, he threatens to kill him if he harms her again. Sandy has a sense of justice and, in the course of the story, becomes more and more helpful toward the underdogs.

While Sandy becomes more and more humane, Charlie becomes more and more delusional.[56] He mistakes the thundering noise of a storm for running buffaloes, chases buffaloes that are not there and thinks that the Indian girl is "his woman" even though he has forced

The Last Hunt *(1956)*

himself on her since capturing her. Sandy, on the other hand, treats Jimmy as a son, offers to take the Indian girl back to the reservation, and then volunteers to go back to town in a blizzard to get food and cattle for the starving Indians, knowing very well that Charlie is waiting to kill him. The relationship of the two men with the Indian woman is revelatory of their opposite personalities. Charlie treats the woman as his property, as a sexual object. Sandy is gentle with her, speaks her language, falls for her, and discovers that the child she takes care of is not hers. The woman does not like Charlie, but she stays because her people are starving in the reservation, and the child needs food to survive. The Indian maiden gives voice to the natives' condition, revealing that her people, being confined to the reservation, are reduced to thieving to survive or starving after the white man has exterminated the buffaloes, and that the white man is now destroying their religion by killing the last of the white buffaloes. The mental and physical annihilation of a race could not be depicted more perfectly.

The Last Hunt (MGM, 1956). Directed by Richard Brooks. Hunter Sandy McKenzie (Stewart Granger) talks to the Indian prisoner (Debra Paget), showing compassion and understanding for the girl (Photofest).

2. Celluloid Indians, 1950s Westerns and the Termination Act

Inside the Western dichotomy of good versus evil, Charlie and the townsfolk would have to be in the latter camp, while Sandy, the Indians, and the two skinners should be included in the first. By the end of the movie, the conscience-stricken Sandy becomes more proactive in his anti-racist attitude. Woodfoot, the Cassandra voice of the group, predicts that in the long run the killing of the buffaloes affects the hunter because he becomes "spooked" and "killing crazy," and, eventually, goes out of his mind—something that indeed happens to Charlie. Jimmy, the young man of mixed-race, so eager to assimilate himself and live among the whites at the beginning, in the end is ready to go back to his people, choosing the reservation over the town as a place in which, it seems, a more decent breed of people live.

The film ends with the death of Charlie, who, waiting to confront Sandy in a duel, freezes to death with the gun in his hand. Before dying, Charlie manages to kill and skin one more buffalo to keep himself warm during the blizzard, but not even the buffalo skin can protect him from the forces of Nature. In the final shot we see in the distance Sandy and the Indian woman riding away safely towards the Reservation, while the camera pans to the left, above the spot where Charlie's frozen body lies, revealing the tree with the white buffalo skin that was used by Jimmy for the Indian boy's burial. The seemingly invincible killer has finally succumbed, clearly showing that Nature has won their last confrontation.

The Last Hunt concentrates on a microcosm of five characters, who, unlike the ones of *The Last Wagon*, do not represent a scaled down image of American society. With the exception of Charlie, the two whites (Sandy and Woodfoot), the Indian woman and the "half-breed" are the embodiment of an illuminated minority, a diverse group whose survival is threatened by the presence of racist and maladjusted individuals like Charlie and the townsfolk. The violent interaction of Charlie with the group negates the celebrated "regeneration through violence" of the Frontier myth. The necessity of violence, the essential quality of Charlie, does not regenerate anybody: his slaughter of the buffaloes destroys the environment and his killing of the Indians and Woodfoot looks like senseless murder. The final result of his violence is annihilation. The violent interaction of Charlie with the animal world also debunks the other component of the myth of the Frontier, the conquest of the wilderness.

Conquering the wilderness, killing the buffaloes and displacing the Indians was done in the name of progress, but what constitutes this progress? In 1883, when Native Americans and buffaloes were vanishing

Conclusion

quickly, towns were finally growing, and they often harbored individuals such as Charlie, or bigots full of hatred like the townsfolk. No wonder that, in the end, Sandy, the surviving white protagonist, chooses Indian life over civilization and Jimmy, with his mixed-heritage, and the Indian maiden as his companions. The film is a study of hatred and violence that courageously criticizes America's racial intolerance toward the "Other," and denounces the conquest of the wilderness as an ecological disaster and the displacement of the native peoples as genocide.

Conclusion

The bulk of the pro–Indian Westerns of the 1950s embody more the dream of a harmonious possible coexistence between Indians and whites than an indictment of social discrimination.[57] Most of these films assume that the solution of the Indian problem comes through complete assimilation to the white ways, acceptance of the expansionist white society, and, as a consequence, peaceful reservation life. *Devil's Doorway, The Last Wagon* and *The Last Hunt* on the other hand try to extend justice and equality to the "Other," offering a more liberal racial perspective trough filmic stories about frontier intolerance. They show the Indians as victims of white man's inexorable progress, and, at the same time, show disenchantment with the white community.[58]

If the above three films can be considered an exception to the rule, and the jump starter of a national conscience that was going to develop fully only a couple of decades later, it is certain that the cycle in its totality came out when the congressional inquiries of Hollywood's alleged un–American activities were rampant, and therefore overt criticism of racial intolerance would have incurred considerable risk. The Western, setting its stories in a distant past, traditionally escaped the radar of political and moral censorship (Hays Code), and when it did not happen, it was usually only penalized for the use of brutality; but the elimination, through editing, of the incriminated frames usually solved the problem in the majority of the cases, without disturbing the overall filmic construction.[59]

John H. Lenihan summarizes the traditional image of the celluloid Indian effectively:

> The American film industry, from the earliest years of Western filmmaking, had inherited the nineteenth-century ambivalence toward the Indian. At worst, the

2. Celluloid Indians, 1950s Westerns and the Termination Act

> Indian was considered a brute savage and represented the antithesis of civilized respectability and Christian virtue. His seemingly innate brutality, as evinced by violent resistance to pioneer expansion, served to justify his extinction. At best, he was natural man living the free, primitive life, until civilization intruded upon his Garden of Eden and rendered him tragically obsolete. His proud refusal to adapt to civilized ways, together with his childlike susceptibility to liquor and his weakness in the face of a superior military force, spelled his doom as Lord of the North American continent.[60]

Lenihan considers the idea of progress central to the genre as well:

> Westerns have traditionally idealized a progressive America in which the interests of the individual are identified and reconciled with those of the larger society. The hero fought either Indians to establish peace or outlaws to restore law and order for the good of the community. The community in turn acknowledged its gratitude and respect for the hero as he rode into the sunset or settled within its fold.[61]

In a nutshell, Lenihan outlines the fundamental characteristic of the classic Western genre. The Indian seen as a noble savage or as enemy is always doomed to extinction in the majority of the films, and the heroes, if they are not fighting the Indians, are fighting the outlaws. In both cases, violence is fundamental to the genre.

The pro–Indian cycle of the 1950s indeed tried to offer a diplomatic alternative to the Indian conflict that is the at the core of so many Westerns, but they came up with Reservation or Assimilation as solutions. When the national sentiment about Native Americans changed after World War II, the motion picture industry began to offer different representations of ethnic people, so the bloodthirsty Indians became noble savages, condemned by an unjust destiny, and filmmakers rushed to give to the public what they wanted.[62] Only the novelistic Westerns (to use Bazin's definition) escaped the constrictions of the genre and for this they were penalized; they did not do well at the box-office because the public and the critics were still grappling with too many racial prejudices to fully appreciate their sincere approach.[63]

Finally, one must consider the different factors that came into play in motion pictures. Since the silent era, non–Indian actors were generally cast as Indian characters, and misrepresentation of Native American ethnography permeates the history of the Western genre at least up to *Dances with Wolves* in 1990.[64] Native Americans were given a bad hand in history and, unfortunately, also in films. The image of the "evil savage," as Vine Deloria points out, was conceived in order to deny the Indians the status of human beings, so dispossession and extermination

Conclusion

could be justified morally and legally.[65] While the Indians were simply "other" culturally and religiously, such a difference was construed by whites as intrinsic inferiority and, as a consequence, the Indian was viewed as a noble savage, cruel, innocent and courageous, but doomed.[66] Additionally, the American Indians in movies were forced to act the part the white directors had in mind, so they played the role of "savages" or "nobles" perpetuating the inaccuracies.[67] As Michael Valdez Moses argues, the portrayals of Native Americans in the Hollywood Western, "whether idealized or demonized, served a variety of often contradictory and mutable ideological and cultural aims, chief among them the critique of perceived defects and shortcomings of modern American society."[68]

The image of the cinematic Indian has been criticized fiercely by scholars like Vine Deloria and others who railed against the use of white actors with painted faces who spoke broken English or made-up languages, uttered monosyllabic sounds (ugh), and made the Indian appear as inferior.[69] The critique extends also to the ways of life portrayed in the majority of the Westerns: The filmic Indians live in wickiups and wear feathery war bonnets, moccasins, breastplates, breechclout, head bands, face and body painting and fringe pants. They dance to drum beats, and no matter to which tribes or nations they belong, they are modeled on the Great Plains Indians (Blackfoot, Arapaho, Cheyenne, Comanche, Kiowa, Crow, Sioux).

According to O'Connor, language elements, cultural beliefs, and religious rituals of one tribe have been attributed to others and often invented on the set.[70] The Plains Indians ended up becoming the quintessential celluloid Indians because they were dashing horsemen and fighters, their territory was the last to be conquered by the white man and they did put up a resistance. It was the Lakota, Northern Cheyenne and Arapaho Indians led by Crazy Horse who defeated Lieutenant Colonel George Armstrong Custer and the 7th Cavalry Regiment in the Battle of Little Bighorn in 1876.[71] The military resistance of Apache, Comanche, Navajo and Sioux to the occupation of Indian territory by whites was significant. The Indian Wars west of the Mississippi spanned more than fifty years in the 19th century. As the authors of *The Only Good Indian…. The Hollywood Gospel* remind us: "By using whites to portray Indians and by exploiting Native Americans from different tribes to play at being Indians from other tribes, Hollywood denied the Native American his individual identity."[72]

2. Celluloid Indians, 1950s Westerns and the Termination Act

This stereotyping is clearly symptomatic of a general lack of respect toward the rich cultural diversity of the many Indian nations that populated North America. There is no doubt that the choice of white actors (usually under contract with a Hollywood Studio) for the Indian main roles—that is, Cochise, Geronimo and other Indian leading characters—is due to the fact that producers and directors were using stars to attract the public to guarantee a good box-office return. The relatively small numbers of Native American actors may have been another restrictive factor.[73] Producers knew that the audiences did not generally know the difference between a Sioux and a Cheyenne, thus they would certainly not know the variation in tribal traditions or clothing, and, despite the lack of accuracy, the film would be popular anyhow.[74]

However, as John Price suggests, it is difficult to dismiss the stereotyping of the Indians as unimportant because "millions of people the world over have acquired their beliefs about North American Indians through motion pictures."[75] Stereotyping, as Price affirms, soothed the guilty conscience of the nation, as time and again it was shown how the white, European, Christian men conquered the forces of barbarism and paganism.[76] The filmic image of the Indian in most classic Westerns presents evil, hollering savages attacking white settlers, cavalry details and so forth.[77] The pro–Indian cycle of the 1950s changed that image, using the noble savage, the honorable and courageous, but doomed figure; the Indian becomes the vanishing American ready to disappear into reservation or assimilation. Clearly, the celluloid Indian was modeled according to the ideological changes that occurred all along in white popular consciousness. In this sense, whereas the novelistic Westerns studied above constitute an exception, ideologically speaking, at the level of story content, they do fall into the old stereotyping trap when it comes to the use of white actors with painted faces, the inaccurate depiction of rites, and the assemblage of native weapons and attires belonging to different tribes.[78]

It is also worth noticing that in the many Hollywood productions in which multitudes of Native Americans were used as hollering savages and as spectacular riders/stuntmen in the wagon chase, the attack of the fort or the showdown—in all those action sequences that made the genre popular and exciting over the decades—the names of these extras seldom appear in the film credits.[79] On top of that, in the majority of the classic Westerns the nation or tribe to which the extras belong is hardly ever mentioned in the screen credits.[80] Even if it is true that

Conclusion

the Hollywood film industry was created by Euro-American pioneers who certainly believed, at least in the beginning, in Manifest Destiny, we would hope to see in the future more accuracy in the filmic representation of the Indian customs and cultures in movies; we hope that ethnological accuracy will go hand in hand with ideological discourse. We do welcome the use of Native American actors, way of life accuracy and respect for the other cultures; however, we want to underline that it is the projected image of the celluloid Indian on the whole that needs to be corrected.

The Hollywood Indian was and remains a figment of white fantasy and, as a consequence, his correction—while we wait for a much desirable filmic reconstruction of the Indian experience made by Native Americans—can be generated only inside the fictional universe that produced it. Verisimilitude of customs, real idioms and use of Native American actors even if welcomed, need to be combined with a continuous re-writing of history.[81] We also believe that the use of white actors who "indianize" themselves, as in *The Last Wagon* and in many later Westerns, is one way of revisiting the image of the filmic Indian as an attempt to understand the "Other" and perceive him not as a savage, but as a threatened individual who defends his people and his country, provided it is done using accurate knowledge of the Native American traditions.[82] As we all know, history is written by the victors and it is they who need to re-write it. Hollywood altered history and used it in the classic Western films to legitimize the march of progress and civilization, finding in the Indian the ideal enemy. In the pro–Indian cycle of the 1950s the movie picture industry projected a more (superficially) sympathetic filmic image, attempting to accommodate a better perspective of the Native Americans who in the postwar were starting to occupy more space in the imagination of the viewers. In the 1950s only three films, *Devil's Doorway*, *The Last Hunt* and *The Last Wagon*, managed to go against the grain and reverberate on screen the contemporary situation of the Native Americans nation, albeit without subverting all the stereotypes.

3

Heroines in Western Films?
Mikhail Bakhtin's "Dialogic Imagination" in Shane, High Noon and Westward the Women

After the 1970s, filmic production of Westerns declined. A resurgence in the 1990s brought films like *Dances with Wolves* (Kevin Costner, 1990), *Unforgiven* (Clint Eastwood, 1992), *The Ballad of Little Jo* (Maggie Greenwald, 1993), *Bad Girls* (Jonathan Kaplan, 1994), *The Quick and the Dead* (Sam Raimi, 1995), and so forth. However, since then, Westerns have appeared less frequently.[1] As a consequence, the examination of the representation of women in the Western genre has remained anchored to the conventional female roles of the classic Hollywood period (1930–1960) that also constitutes the bulk of the production.[2] Even if from the 1990s on, feminist movies like *The Ballad of Little Jo* and other revisionist Westerns garnered positive reviews, these films were not so high profile, so important or so many in number as to counterbalance the classic production. Because the Western formula is based on a conflict and on its violent resolution as a result of the hero's action, most Westerns exhibit a male protagonist.

Mark E. Wildermuth's recent *Feminism and the Western in Film and Television* provides an interesting overview of women in western films from the 1930s, throughout the Cold War era and beyond, and also includes a chapter dedicated to women in television Westerns between 1954 and 2001. By tracing the development of feminist and proto-feminist thinking in films that traditionally have been governed by masculinity, the author examines some pro-feminist Westerns, films in which women function as agents of their destiny both in the public and the private sphere and who, most interestingly, show "reluctance to adopt violence as a way to establish justice."[3]

3. Heroines in Western Films?

With regards to female characters in Western films, other critics like Heba and Murphy claim that "their representations have not had the same iconic immediacy and value. As a result, women's identities in Western movies remain to be constructed, not only through the narrative of the film, but through the minds of the viewers as well."[4] In their illuminating article on "Hegel's dialectic and women's identities in Western films," Heba and Murphy affirm that the Westerns between the 1930s and 1960s, "have an ideological tendency toward representing women's identities in ways that reinforce traditional social roles in the cultural master narrative. Movies from the '70s on demonstrate an increasing number of heteroglossic and x-glossic representation of women's identities that challenges those traditional identities."[5] While some of the terminology employed by these critics is useful, I will instead refer to Bakhtin's theoretical opus in order to frame a different approach to the subject matter at hand.

As Dale Bauer writes, "For Bakhtin language bequeaths us many social voices, and these voices construct both selves and character-selves. The explicit and implicit interplay of these voices reveals the way a specific historical and cultural context fashions the self."[6] In *Problems of Dostoevsky's Poetics* Bakhtin affirms: "I am conscious of myself and become myself only while revealing myself for another, through another, and with the help of another. The most important acts constituting self-consciousness are determined by a relationship toward another consciousness ... the very being of man ... is the *deepest communication. To be* means *to communicate....* I cannot become myself without another ...."[7] According to Bakhtin, one is not able to know oneself, without the interacting presence of the other. As Danow points out, "Bakhtin approaches the problem of the self and the other in terms of one's own speech and the alien word of the other ... one's otherness derives from the particular use of language by the self. But the word of the self also expresses a world view; each message bears that view as an encapsulated ideology."[8]

Within the cultural context expressed through the language of the self, gender differences also play a part. In this sense we are going to look at discourse as a bearer of gendered identification. Bakhtin speaks about monoglossic discourse that has "the forces that serve to unify and centralize the verbal-ideological world."[9] The monoglossic utterance is the language of authority, and, "its function is to re-inscribe cultural myths of power and their representations."[10] Heteroglossia discourse

3. Heroines in Western Films?

conversely exists to challenge the dominant ideology. It opposes what is given as absolute. According to Bahktin it "permits a multiplicity of voices."[11] X-glossia, the term borrowed from the above two critics, Heba and Murphy, is the moment of transformation in which a new identity is created that transcends the binary opposition of heteroglossia (self versus the authoritative voice) or the impositions of the language of power (monoglossia). It is the creation of something new, of new identities.[12] In x-glossia the word and intention of the self and the other are transcended. The linked utterances of the self and the other interpenetrate on the interlacing of the dialogic word of the self and the other.[13]

In the classic Western, the woman is normally portrayed as a center of civilization: She is the one who changes the hero's destiny; in the end he will be absorbed into the community and, as a family man, he will contribute to progress. In this way the feminine values of the civilized East will be implanted in the West, and the "masculine West" will change forever. As Pam Cook writes:

> If the good mother represents the feminine ideal of the Western, what then of the "bad girls," the law-breakers against which the ideal is measured? These shady ladies threaten the applecart by challenging men on their own ground; adventurers all, they demand equal status and refuse to take second place, at first, anyway; they wear pants and brandish guns, own land, property and business, demand sexual independence. It's true that this is usually only temporary—if the tomboy has not abandoned her transvestite garb for the arms of the hero by the end of the movie, then she comes to a sticky end.[14]

Pam Cook is right; many heroines start out wearing pants and carrying a gun, but by the end of the movie they transition to dresses with ruffles and prepare themselves to marry the hero, leaving adventures to the men.[15] A case in point is Jessica Drummond (Barbara Stanwyck) in the celebrated *Forty Guns* (Samuel Fuller, 1957). Jacqueline Levitin in a polemic, but interesting article, states that the classic Western theoretical works by Will Wright (*Six Guns and Society*, 1976), John G. Cawelti (*The Six-Gun Mystique*, 1984) and Jim Kitses (*Horizon West*, 1970) all display a general dismissal of any problem related to female spectatorship and she, instead, poses the following questions:

> How might one account for the Western's effect specifically on women?
> How might one explain the Western's appeal for the female spectator?
> Is there no place for woman on that ritual frontier in any function greater than a prop in the male game of revolt and choice?
> Could she ever play the role of the hero?
> Would she want to be a hero in terms of power and violence? And can the

3. Heroines in Western Films?

convention of the Western permit women to be westerners without at the same time destroying the genre?[16]

For Levitin the traditional heroine is seen as supporting cast, as a passive character; schoolmarm or prostitute, the women in the Western are always waiting around for the hero to make his choice because it is always the male who propels the narrative with his action.[17] Jane Tompkins, following Levitin's path, identifies, in one of the rare feminist studies dedicated to the Western genre, the major roles of women in the genre as victims, damsels in distress who need to be rescued by the hero, or as motives for the man's action because they need to be rescued or vindicated. Women are usually controllers of the power of language, but doomed to be dismissed by the male counterpart.[18] Blake Lucas, on the other hand, in an article titled "Saloon Girls and Ranchers' Daughters: The Woman in the Western," contests the notion that women are unimportant in the Western, that they are marginal or have only a symbolic role. He claims, instead, that the insistence on the marginalization of women in the Western has undermined a genre that has been without equal "in its 1946–1964 golden age."[19] He writes: "It's time to see the Western in a different light—not as a masculine genre, but as one supremely balanced in its male/female aspect and one of the finest places for women in all of cinema."[20]

Lucas makes an interesting argument and defends the importance of women in the classic Westerns, mostly in the films of the 1940s and 1950s, but he discards the revisionist Westerns, and he seems to be unaware that even if it is true that formidable roles for women do exist in many famous films—*Stagecoach*, *My Darling Clementine*, *Two Rode Together*, *The Lawless Breed*, to cite a few—these women are important inside the structure of the films for their role either as ranchers' daughters or saloon girls, creating tension and richness in the relationship between the sexes on screen, but they are rarely in command of their own fate. Nobody denies that the women in Ford's films and in many other classic Westerns fulfill complicated and unforgettable roles as spiritually complex creatures, full of emotions and tormented by love and sorrows. However, it is undeniable that these women are essential only insofar as they are part of a love triangle—sometimes a woman and two men, sometimes a man and two women. They constitute the romantic interest of the hero, and as such they embody more decent impulses than their male counterpart and usually have a cathartic influence on

3. Heroines in Western Films?

the male protagonist otherwise bent on revenge, and often at risk of losing his humanity, as, for example, in Anthony Mann's films.

According to Lucas, "while men have commonly driven the action of a film in an external way, women have often driven it within themselves."[21] The critic is therefore attributing to women the domain of feelings, spirituality, and love. Lucas thinks that believing, like many (feminist) critics do, that "women are respected in relation to how much they are imitative of men as figures of action" has undermined their roles in cinema, and has contributed to the undoing of the Western genre on the whole.[22] Surely there are some unforgettable women in the Western genre as Lucas affirms, like for example Kathleen (Maureen O'Hara) in *Rio Grande* (1950), Hallie (Vera Miles) in *The Man Who Shot Liberty Valance* (1962), Dallas (Claire Trevor) in *Stagecoach* (1939) and so forth, but these roles, in the majority of the cases, reproduce relationships that celebrate the importance of women inside the patriarchal system. These women are rarely in command of their own fate. They are important, but not equal to men; their destiny is forged by the men around them. They are reacting to instead of acting in their lives.[23]

Our general objection to Lucas' analysis is that he forgets to mention, for example, films like *Johnny Guitar* (Nicholas Ray, 1954), *Rancho Notorious* (Frits Lang, 1939) and *Duel in the Sun* (King Vidor, 1946), important movies in which the woman role is subversive if not rebellious; furthermore, he is not considering other female roles like the "Indian princess" or the "half-breed," ignoring problems of miscegenation and racism altogether, and limiting his study to the role of the white woman. Finally, denying that in order to be an interesting character a woman does not need "to literally shoot her way into the center of action" is a very ideologically loaded affirmation. The women who know how to shoot, ride and fight like a man are not the ones who need help or protection, and they are very different from those pallid and often passive figures who, no matter how deep and profound the emotional weight they exercise on the men, are appendixes of the hero.

Trying to resolve the apparent dichotomy between the feminist critics who view the roles of women in the Western as restrictive and other critics who are content with the fundamentally charming, but marginal function of women as propellers for the narrative of the hero, we now recur to Bakhtin's dialectic system of monoglossia, heteroglossia and x-glossia to analyze how identities for women are constructed in Western films.

Monoglossia: The Submissive Woman and Shane (1953)

In many Westerns the pioneer woman has a monoglossic identity because she represents the most traditional roles available to women, usually inside the family, as mother and wife. As a monoglossic construction she is valued as the one who can procreate, nurture the family, raise the children and take care of her husband; she is the depository of the most traditional cultural values of family, community and faith.[24] Because the authoritative word, according to Bakhtin, demands unconditional allegiance, the voice of the pioneer women is minimal, and the male counterpart often ignores her.

Shane (1953, dir. George Stevens) is one of the best example for the construction of the monoglossic identity for women.[25] In *Shane*, Marian (Jean Arthur), wife of Joe Starrett, the farmer, is the co-protagonist of a story that deals with the conflict between homesteaders and ranchers in the Grand Tetons valley.[26] Shane (Alan Ladd) is the gunfighter who one day arrives at the farm of Joe Starrett (Van Heflin) and decides to stay and help the settler for a while. After much happening in both camps, the gunslinger saves the day, liberating the community from the evil rancher and then, riding into the sunset, disappears as most Western heroes do.

The film is a fascinating example of monoglossia for different reasons. Marian, at the very beginning of the film, is singing while cooking in the kitchen, and she observes what happens outside mostly through the window. The camera captures her peeping through, looking into the yard where Shane and her husband are talking. From the initial sequences, it is evident that her realm is the house and the kitchen: She takes care of her son, little Joey, and she is a good cook. She is fulfilling well her role of mother and wife. She continually suggests the proper behavior to her son and cooks an elaborate dinner for her husband and the guest. But she hardly ever speaks; the many medium shots of her show that she understands, feels, stares, and internalizes what happens, but keeps silent.

It soon becomes apparent that Marian does not advance the film narrative through her action; like the other pioneer women of the film—the wives of the other settlers—she utters few lines, agreeing with her husband or corroborating what he says. When the rancher's men appear, she remains silent like the other women, standing beside her man who

3. Heroines in Western Films?

Shane (Paramount, 1953). Directed by George Stevens. At right: Alan Ladd as gunslinger Shane. Also shown are Val Heflin as farmer Joe Starrett, Jean Arthur as Joe's wife Marian, and Brandon De Wilde as little Joey Starrett. The peaceful farmer talks with the rancher's thugs, while Shane observes the scene in silence (Photofest).

does the talking. In the few occasions in which she voices her opinion and she disagrees with the gunslinger or her husband, the two men listen to her, but they ignore what she says. At a certain point she tells Shane that she does not want Joey to learn how to shoot, exclaiming, "We'd all be much better off if there wasn't a single gun left in this valley, including yours!" clearly wishing for a more civilized way of living, for a more peaceful society in which conflicts could be solved without resorting to violence, something that unfortunately cannot happen because there is no "law" in the valley yet. When Marian desperately tries to convince her husband not to go face evil rancher Ryker (Emile Meyer) because most likely he will be killed, he replies: "It's a chance I got to take," clearly ignoring her pleading. The silencing of Marian becomes even more apparent in the most dramatic moments of the film. When Shane tries to stop Joe from going to town to confront Ryker, they get in

Monoglossia: The Submissive Woman and Shane *(1953)*

a fight, but all Marian can do is to follow their fight through the kitchen window, screaming, "Stop! Stop!" to no avail.

Like all the other pioneer women, Marian is also absent from certain spaces. When the farmers have a gathering to decide what to do against the abuses perpetrated by the rancher, no women are present. The meeting takes place at the house of Joe Starrett, but Marian is relegated with her son to another room where she keeps admonishing the youngster to be quiet because "the men are taking." The women are also absent from the town—comprised only of a saloon, a general store and a blacksmith shop—where Ryker and his minions seem to dwell all the time. The villains of the film are a group of men without wives and children who idle in the saloon, where no women can enter. Marian and the other farmers' wives are relegated mostly to their homes and yards. The division of the filmic space delineates visually the monoglossic construction of the gendered identities: The farmers are pictured mostly outside, the ranchers are seen riding around or idling in the saloon, the women are working in the homes. This division outlines the fixed borders of two worlds as prescribed by the patriarchal system in which female identities are circumscribed to the private area, while male identities are constructed in the public sphere, in action. Women clearly have a passive role while men have an active one.

The action is carried by the farmers and the rancher's gang through their violent interaction. In this perspective, it becomes clear that the women in the film exist only to further the male characters' purposes. They motivate the farmers indirectly. The homesteaders are fighting the rancher because they want to live in peace in the valley, have a school, keep their land, see their families grow and multiply and develop into a community.[27] This proves that the existence of the women and the children in the film functions only as the ideological motivation that propels the male protagonists of the story, the farmers, to act the way they do.

From an iconic point of view Marian is dressed in practical clothes because she does hard work. All the settler women wear working attire. They do not look glamorous, with the exception of Marian, who, during the Fourth of July celebration, wears a nice dress. However, we soon discover that she is sporting her wedding dress because she does not own any decent-looking clothing. What keeps Marian and the other women in this life of toil and marginality? All along, Joe Starrett praises his "little woman who surely can cook" as the best thing that ever happened to him, the best cook, the most loyal companion ("You are the most honest

3. Heroines in Western Films?

and the finest girl that ever lived!" he says), complimenting her for carrying on her duty of wife and mother flawlessly. Marian embodies the ideal mother/wife, the one idealized by patriarchy, the devoted spouse, the nurturing mother, and the submissive wife.[28] Her identity, like the identities of all the other female settlers (most of the time pictured while carrying small infants, surrounded by three, four children of different ages) is grounded in the patriarchal archetype of the perfect family, the one in which each member has a definite role and abides by it.

Luckily for the viewer the movie acquires a more complex meaning if we look into the inner emotional life of the four protagonists of the film (Marian, Shane, Joe Starrett and little Joey), escaping from the strictures imposed on each identity by the authoritative voice. It being understood that the inner life of the characters, made of glances, silences (mostly filmed in long shots) remains constrained inside the characters' selves so as to preserve the rules of patriarchal behavior. The attraction between Marian and Shane is obvious, even her husband and her son recognize it, but Marian, shaking Shane's hand before his final departure, can only mutter a polite "Take care of yourself!" Even in the moment of farewell to a man to whom she is clearly attracted she cannot step out of her traditional role of faithful wife and dedicated mother. Shane, torn between his loyalty to Joe whom he likes, the farmers whom he respects, and his affection for little Joey, kills Ryker and his men, gets wounded and, before leaving, tells Joey to say to Marian that now, as she had wished, "There aren't any more guns in the valley." It would seem that Marian has finally been *listened to*, but we would be wrong. Shane, the gunslinger, cannot change himself ("A man has to be what he is, Joey ... can't break the mold"). Killing is what he is good at, and he cannot avoid confronting the evil gunslinger Jack Wilson (Jack Palance), hired by Ryker. He needs to measure himself against Wilson first and foremost, before protecting the farmers, fulfilling the desire of a woman he is attracted to or proving to a kid he loves that he is the fastest gun. Hence, even at the end of the film, Marian's wish comes true only because it coincided with other, more pressing motives.

Shane, therefore, is a filmic narrative that engages with, negotiates and reworks the cultural fiction of femininity, constructing for the viewer a female identity that fits the ideal of the American society of the 1950s, in which many women were as disempowered as the ones who inhabit the symbolic world of the Western Frontier. Fortunately, the western myth is not as monolithic as it appears in *Shane*. Other filmic texts of the period became the arena of the struggle of the changing relationship between men and women, as Jacinda Read states, "...Stories of the West could become stories of feminism and femininity. Indeed, the western myth's ability to transcend its roots in history perhaps makes it the ultimate narrative of transformation."[29]

Heteroglossia: The Transgressive Woman and High Noon (1952)

Heteroglossic discourse exists to challenge the dominant ideology of monoglossic tradition, because, according to Bakhtin, "it permits a multiplicity of voices."[30] Heteroglossia challenges, negates, deviates from and opposes the authoritative voice. Town women, unlike pioneer women, often dress as sexualized objects.[31] As wives, widows, whores, servants, schoolmarms and fiancées, they wear fine, elegant, sometimes daring clothing; their attire and their behavior often position them outside the traditional terms of patriarchy. The filmic visual codes (low necklines, fine fabric, ribbons, hats, accessories, chest and waist emphasis, undergarments), the decision they take and the space they inhabit act as signs that denote transgressive identities. The town women's identities often go against the grain of what is considered the traditional female role.

High Noon (1952, dir. Fred Zinnemann) is one of the best examples for the construction of heteroglossic identity for women.[32] A superficial viewing of *High Noon* would reveal that it is, being based on the quest of a male hero, a traditional Western, even if, in this case, we have an unlucky hero who is abandoned by his countrymen and left alone to fend for himself. Digging a bit deeper into the layers of the filmic text, we discover that there are more subversive counter-narratives, both inside the main narrative—the one that belongs to Marshal Will Kane, the hero—and inside the one that pertains to the two women co-protagonists, Amy Fowler Kane, the white Quaker newlywed, and Helen Ramirez, the Mexican ex-lover of Kane. We are faced with a classic love triangle, one man and two women, but in this case the triangle is reassembled in unusual ways. The two women are not competing for the same man; they are ganging up against him. When we first encounter the two females, we are certain that Amy, as the blonde, white skinned and bonneted young woman, is the pure flower, the submissive wife—in a word

3. Heroines in Western Films?

the "good girl"—while Helen's first medium shot reveals a dark-skinned, dark-eyed, raven-haired woman in a dress with a low neckline—simply a "bad girl." The dichotomy of so many Westerns—bad girl versus good girl, with the bad girl who dies at the end sacrificing herself in repentance for her carnal sins while the good girl survives—is not something that applies here.[33] From the start we are constantly reminded that these women are different; everything that we would expect does not happen. The film is indeed, as Gwendolyn Foster says, "a metanarrative of difference."[34] The non-white woman is not a victim of her passion, and if she is a "fallen woman," she is also a very affluent one, being a successful businesswoman. The white woman is not a submissive wife; in fact, she rebels against her husband's decision to stay and fight the outlaws the minute her wedding ceremony is over. The two females clearly operate outside societal restrictions and are capable of independent decisions. On top of this, even though they both love the same man, they bond together and help each other. See the lingering shots of them riding together in a wagon toward the station and conversing and understanding each other in Helen's hotel room.

The film opens with Sheriff Will Kane (Gary Cooper) getting married to Amy Fowler (Grace Kelly). It is his last day as town marshal of Hadleyville because his wife is a Quaker and she opposes gun violence; hence, they will leave town to start a new life as owners of a store somewhere else in the West. Sudden news announces that the assassin Frank Miller (Ian MacDonald) will be on the noon train and, with his gang, is seeking revenge on Kane who sent him to jail years ago. A few minutes into the film the tension arises: Kane debates whether to leave or stay, while everybody else urges him to leave. He leaves, but then decides to come back to face the outlaws. It is at this point that Amy's personality comes to the fore. In the opening scenes she appears as a young, innocent bride, dressed in white with a hat, ribbons and frills and full of smiles and the viewer would expect her to abide by her husband's decision. However, when confronted with her husband's willingness to stay and face the Miller gang, Amy tells him that if he does not leave town with her, she will leave him ("No, I won't be here if you don't go with me now. I will be on the train when it leaves!"). It is evident that Amy has no intention to submissively wait and see if, in an hour and a half, she will be a widow or not. Kane, on the other hand, ignores his wife ultimatum. Like most Western heroes, he abides by a typical code of honor ("I've never run from anybody before.... I have got to stay!"). For most of the

Heteroglossia: *The Transgressive Woman* and High Noon *(1952)*

film Amy sits in the lobby of the hotel waiting for the noon train, until, realizing that Helen Ramirez (Katy Jurado) is her husband's ex-lover, she gets the courage to go and talk to her, assuming that her husband wants to stay and fight because of his past love interest, and hoping that the old flame can convince him to leave town.

Mrs. Ramirez constitutes the mirror image of Amy. She is as beautiful as Amy, but has dark skin, dark hair, dresses in dark colors, sports a very revealing neckline and is Mexican. She is a woman with a past: She was the lover of the outlaw Frank Miller, of Will Kane and now of Harvey, the marshal's young deputy. Helen is an outsider in this community, racially and morally, but she is also the successful owner of a profitable general store and a saloon, and therefore economically independent. She clearly lives outside the norm, having no husband. When she decides to leave in order to avoid Frank Miller, she refuses to be ordered around by her lover, Harvey, who wants her to stay; when he tries to force himself on her, she makes a point of showing him that she is the one who chooses the man that can touch her, slapping him on the face, and then kicking him out of her hotel room and her life.[35]

Emotionally she is a bit more fragile than she appears and it is evident that she admires Kane and she still loves him. However, in the face of the coming trouble she does not let her feelings interfere with her self-preserving decision to sell the store and move on, because she is convinced that nobody will help the marshal, and he will probably be killed.[36] Like Kane, she has a moral code. Knowing the town people and their hypocrisy, having lost Kane to another woman, she must forge ahead and can neither interfere with Kane's decision nor help him. Helen, is an outsider, the "Other," ostracized because of her gender, race and morality, and has to fight for herself to preserve her independence as well as her survival as an unmarried, racially different woman.

High Noon as a film text breaks many Western conventions even before we start looking at the heteroglossic identities of the two female protagonists. The story pivots around a male hero who becomes afraid and contemplates fleeing, and a community that abandons a man who deserves to be helped. Ideologically, it can be read as a parable of the anti–Communist witch-hunt of the House Un-American Activities Committee (HUAC) in Hollywood in the 1940s and 1950s, or as a morality play about a failing society.[37] Visually it is in black and white and, unlike most Westerns, feature no landscape views, no mountains, and no prairies. It is a rather claustrophobic film, constructed like a perfect

3. Heroines in Western Films?

mechanism whose movement is propelled by the ticking of a clock, signaling the approaching noon and the moment of the showdown.[38]

The spaces inhabited by the characters are all public: the railway depot, the saloon, the hotel lobby, the town marshal's office, the barber shop, the church, and the town streets. It could be argued that Helen is the only woman who inhabits a sort of private space, but considering that many characters have access to her hotel room, even that space could be considered semi-public.[39] Both Helen and Amy interact with men in the same public spaces, the station, the hotel, and the marshal's office, with the exception of the saloon populated only by males.

From an iconic point of view Amy and Helen are shown to be objects of the male gaze: sexualized, beautiful and elegant.[40] The other town women, mostly seen in the church because it is Sunday morning, are well dressed and not afraid of speaking; at least one church goer voices her disgust at the fact that nobody wants to help Kane who has done so much for the community. The conventional patriarchal voice is shown only in one instance, when Kane goes to the house of a friend to ask for help and this man forces his wife to lie to the marshal, admonishing her with a sharp, "Do as you are told! Do you want me to get killed? Do you want to be a widow?" However, although most of the town's women in the film speak their minds, they all seem to be ignored by the men.

High Noon (United Artists, 1952). Directed by Fred Zinnemann. Newlyweds Grace Kelly as Amy Fowler Kane, and Gary Cooper as Marshal Will Kane. In the background the clock shows it is high noon and time to confront the outlaws (Photofest).

Let's ask ourselves then what or who

Heteroglossia: The Transgressive Woman and High Noon *(1952)*

propels the action of the film. Most of the male characters hide in the saloon, the church or the barber shop waiting for the showdown. What advances the narrative is the interaction between Kane, the Miller gang and, surprisingly, Amy. Upon hearing the first gunshot, she jumps off the train and runs to see if Kane is alive; then, realizing that her husband is in danger—being pinned down between the fire of two outlaws—she shoots one of them in the back and makes it possible for the marshal to kill Frank Miller. Shooting an outlaw not only goes against Amy's own beliefs, but shooting the man in the back breaks any kind of moral code.[41] Amy transgresses the rules of the community and the rules of patriarchy, and becomes an independent agent of her life, deciding her future and taking her destiny into her own hands.

At this point the viewer has to ponder what motivated Amy's change of mind. We must assume that the challenging discourse of Helen Ramirez—"What kind of woman are you? I don't understand you? Why don't you fight with your man?"—was convincing and persuaded Amy to act. Helen's discourse is of decisive significance in the evolution of Amy's consciousness, because as Bakhtin claims, "consciousness awakens to independent ideological life precisely in a word of alien discourses ... from which it cannot initially separate itself. ... When thought begins to work in an independent, experimenting and discriminating way, what first occurs is a separation between internally persuasive discourse and authoritarian enforced discourse."[42] Through the alien discourse of the "other," Amy starts seeing the world with different eyes and becomes more like Helen: Each takes charge of her own life outside the strictures of what society considers proper female behavior. Amy's identity, like Helen's, becomes transgressive because it is no longer inscribed in family-centric terms. The two women clearly refuse to be passive victims of events, of men, and of other people's decisions.

Through the two female protagonists the film also attempts to make sense of the dichotomy between public and private. The theme of the single individual abandoned by society in the moment of need—Kane versus the town community—is recast in the case of the two strong female protagonists as private sphere against public sphere, between what is important for them against what is important for society. Helen, instead of staying and being protected by Harvey, decides to forge ahead. Amy, instead of sitting and waiting for the outcome of the duel, decides to participate in it. With their deeds, they both step outside the feminine identities sanctioned by society. *High Noon* challenges the cultural

3. Heroines in Western Films?

fiction of femininity, constructing for the viewer two female identities that show, in the American society of the 1950s, women were changing, starting to transcend the prescribed models and oppressiveness of patriarchy, and transforming their lives.[43]

The heteroglossic discourse of the two female characters matches the counter-narrative of the main hero. If we apply Bakhtin dialogic screen to this filmic text we discover that *High Noon* is not only a text that makes room for the voices of the "Other," but it also deconstructs the image of the mythical heroism of the male hero in subtle ways. Both Forman, the scriptwriter, and Zinnemann, the director, cooperated to "humanize" the male hero.[44] The courage of the marshal is paired with images of him desperate for help and wandering from the judge's office to the saloon and from the barber shop to the church in sequences that are stark and realistic because they are filmed without soft focus filters to better highlight his pain—images that are "paced to the strolling-minstrel measures of a fine Dmitri Tiomkin score" as Bosley Crowther reminds us.[45] The sequences of the aging Cooper sweating and wincing in pain as he walks in sun-drenched streets are memorable.[46] Kane suffers moments of despair and doubt during which he contemplates leaving town. However, his crisis of conscience and his interior drama never make him abandon his decision to stay and fight.

Visually the use of short cuts, shot-reverse-shots, and closeups make *High Noon* look different from other Westerns. Consider that when the prairie and the wilderness—already conspicuously absent from the screen—get mentioned, they are no longer a place of freedom, but a dangerous area in which Amy and Kane will be defenseless. As the marshal points out, "They'll just come after us. Four of them and we'd be all alone on the prairie." Long shots with sweeping ranges, mountains, cattle and horses, typical of the classic Westerns, have also disappeared from the film. Zinnemann uses only a few long shots to bring attention to the empty railway tracks, tracks that seem to stretch toward a distant horizon from which evil will descend in the person of Frank Miller, so that these few long shots leave an ominous and desolate impression with the viewer.

Furthermore, Zinnemann inserted the story inside a precise time frame; in fact there are twelve inserts of a clock ticking, reminding us (and Kane) that the moment of the showdown is approaching, and creating suspense more typical of a thriller than a Western. Evans considers

Heteroglossia: The Transgressive Woman and High Noon *(1952)*

Marshal Kane motivated by the categorical imperative of a true Kantian hero because he is determined to achieve justice regardless of the consequences to his person, his friends, and his family, and he always speaks the truth regardless of the consequences of his actions, pursuing only what is morally necessary.[47] After his wedding, Kane resigns as marshal (because his Quaker wife opposes violence), so no professional obligations would stop him from leaving. Even the townsfolk encourage him to depart. Why does he stay? Certainly, as Evans claims, his sense of honor and the wellbeing of the community are one and the same for Kane, but he goes against the desire of an entire community, his friends and his wife. Why?

In spite of his heroic role Kane is, in fact, an outsider. Like Helen and Amy, he does not belong in this community where greed, envy, cowardice, and hate dominate. We agree with Smyth who affirms that *High Noon* is a film that violates the rules of the genre, because it is one of "Hollywood's most high profile renegade, a true genre hybrid that unsettled critics Robert Evans and André Bazin and offended conservative filmmakers Howard Hawks and John Wayne."[48] Let's ask ourselves how the movie offended so many people and how it strayed from the genre. To do so we need to go back to Bakhtin. Certainly, the iconography, the introductions of gender and racial issues (with two independent women) challenged the Western code, but ideology is the key word here. The movie was found ideologically offensive because the community portrayed in the film is foul. Hadleyville proves to be, as the judge defines it, "a dirty little village in the middle of nowhere" not worth saving. The corruption that winds through the town inhabitants is the negation of Manifest Destiny. It is the destruction of the western myth.[49] This West is no longer a mythical place given to mankind (at least to the white part of it) for a second chance to build a better world. This West is a sorry place, so disgusting that, after killing the outlaws, the hero flings his marshal's star into the dirt before getting on the wagon with his wife (the only one who helped him), and disappearing.

Zinnemann not only changed the look of the Western, but he also introduced independent heteroglossic protagonists and turned the West into a claustrophobic place. First and foremost, however, he dared to deconstruct the western myth, long before the new historians did. *High Noon*, under the semblance of being a classic Western, is a film about rebels—about three characters who refuse to follow the norms, who refuse to conform and choose to be outsiders, preferring to follow

3. Heroines in Western Films?

what matters to them rather than what matters to society in general and to patriarchal society in particular.[50]

X-glossia: Transformational Women and Westward the Women *(1951)*

As we have demonstrated above, monoglossic women are prevented from constructing their own identity because their self is defined by the authoritative voice of patriarchy. Heteroglossic women go against what is considered the proper role of women in society and are therefore transgressive. X-glossic women are neither silenced nor rebelling; their identity transcends this binary opposition. They undergo a transformation and they cannot be coded as extensions of the male characters, victims of patriarchy, or spectacles of the male gaze; they become something unexpected, something new.[51] While monoglossia is centripetal, reductivist and brings closure, heteroglossia and x-glossia are centrifugal and bring openness. They contrast the authoritative utterance that seeks to foreclose on possible further dialogue. Heteroglossia and x-glossia allow polyphony, that is they offer a persuasive voice that opens new perspectives. As Bakhtin points out: "The semantic structure of an internally persuasive discourse is not finite, it is open; in each of the new contexts that dialogize it, the discourse is able to reveal even newer ways to mean."[52] In x-glossia the word and intentions of the self and the other are transcended. The linked utterance of the self and the other "interpenetrate ... on the interlacing of the dialogic word of the self and the other."[53]

Westward the Women (1951) is one of the best examples of the construction of the x-glossic identity for women.[54] The movie is, in many ways, a revolutionary Western because it problematizes concepts of masculinity and femininity. Underneath an apparently conservative master narrative, one of mail-order brides, the film debunks the concept of traditional female roles, constructing a new identity for women that reconciles femininity, motherhood and solidarity with independence, self-assertion and bravery. At first it seems that the domineering wagon-master Buck (Robert Taylor) will succeed in turning these women into men, but, in the course of the story Buck himself gets more "feminized" and the women more "masculinized" without losing sight of

X-glossia: Transformational Women and Westward the Women

their capacity for love, compassion, and nurturing. They change without sacrificing their femininity. The film does not shy away from dealing with violence against women (slapping, bull whipping, rape) and with an execution-style shooting, obviously departing from many of the established codes of the classic Western.

The story uncharacteristically focuses on a large group of women who, in their diversity, constitute a group of alien voices (Irish, French, and Italian; some of them do not even speak English) and heterogeneous people (virgins, matrons, schoolmarms, ex-prostitutes, a pregnant girl, widows, tomboys, immigrants). Linguistically, the insertion of foreign languages into the discourse of the film creates a polyphony that has a dual function. In the specific case of the French ex-prostitute Danon (Denise Darcel), the foreign utterance is used to oppose the machismo of Buck.[55] In general, the use of the foreign idioms forces Buck to confront the "Other," presenting him with different views of the world that challenge his prejudiced and gendered vision of existence. Other idioms also populate the discourse of the film. Patience for example, the virago

Westward the Women (MGM, 1951). Directed by William A. Wellman. Robert Taylor (at right) as tough trailblazer Buck Wyatt and Denise Darcel as French ex-prostitute Fifi Danon are surrounded by some of the women of the expedition. Buck teaches Fifi and the other women how to use a rifle (Photofest).

of the group, speaks English but uses a nautical language that comes from seafaring and is clearly an appropriation of the male language of sailors. This lingo gives Patience a distinct individuality, but also challenges patriarchal constructs. As Helene Shugart writes: "I am defining feminist rhetorical appropriation as a process by which ... stories, songs, myths, rituals, legends, fables [I would add speech] ... that advance ... an oppressive ideology of gender are referenced clearly in such a way that the messages apparent in the new text [in our case new discourse] challenges those traditional conceptions of gender."[56] Patience, using words like starboard, portside, running aground, and mackerel face, sails through the wilderness with self-assurance and, in spite of the comic relief of a speech pattern that is out of place, is not afraid of silencing Buck or of telling the men, "You can look us over, but don't think you're going to do the choosing." The virago operates an invasion of a master language but, by appropriating the meaning of the "alien" language, she can use it in liberating and different ways.[57] This polyphony of voices opens the text to multiple point of views that interact, correct and interfere with the hegemonic discourse of Buck, forcing him to concede, give in, become more human, and revisit his idea that physical prowess is the only arbiter of identity.[58]

Visually, when we first meet the one hundred thirty-eight women at the gathering in Chicago—before starting the trip to marry the love-starved pioneers awaiting them in a beautiful California valley—they are dressed like proper town ladies with hats and long dresses; they seem to embody the perfect idea of domesticity. They are knitting and embroidering while waiting their turn to sign up, busying themselves in endeavors that will be useful in their future family life. The viewer assumes that they are looking forward to a conventional life: marriage, husband and kids. Buck tells them straight away to jettison their fluffy dresses and to wear more sturdy, working clothing because the trail will be brutal. When we see them on the trail, they are wearing less appealing attire but, despite the hardship, they still take care of their bodies and appearances whenever they have a chance to do so. On their difficult journey through flash floods, Indian attacks, and a desert their clothing becomes ragged, torn, and dirty, and the women look more disheveled, beaten. When they finally get to their destination they ask Buck to find material to make dresses because they want to appear like "ladies" and not "tramps." When they show up at the settlement, they wear clothing made out of tablecloths and curtains. They put

X-glossia: Transformational Women and Westward the Women

flowers in their hair and clearly try to look their best. The first impression would be that, at the end of their journey, these women are operating, as at the beginning, inside the master narrative of patriarchy, animated by vanity and their dream of domesticity.[59]

The visual filmic codes are not the only conveyers of meaning though. The viewer needs to combine them with the other signifying elements of the filmic discourse, especially with space. According to Deleuze, the genre film is a kind of movie that rests upon an action presented primarily as a reaction to an environment.[60] Hence, the staging of space in the Western is crucial. In Westerns, in fact, the title often refers explicitly to a place or a cardinal point. *Westward the Women* clearly contains in itself the indication of the priority that should be given to a place, the West, and to a movement, to the west. Through the title, the viewer understands that the film deals mostly with open ranges, wilderness and prairies, and that there is no division between private and public space. The women and the fifty men who at the beginning are hired to protect them share the same public, open space. As a critic claims, in the conquest of the West, "it was surely the space that gave man the opportunity of an adventure, but it is the man who eventually transformed the space through its mobility, who tamed it, who changed a desert into a garden—even though at the end of the story, the hero's mobility turns into an endless wandering through a space where he does not belong anymore."[61] If what stated above describes perfectly the male hero of *Shane*, in the case of *Westward the Women* we need to re-examine how space transforms women.

Agacinski claims that in the Western genre "bodies interact with space, get transformed by it, or try to transform it."[62] It is certainly evident that the women of the film manage to tame the wilderness and open a trail, but it is a bit more complicated to show how the wilderness changes them.[63] However, in establishing how this is done we discover how x-glossia operates in the filmic text. The colonizing of the space does not give the women the same opportunity it affords to male heroes. The wilderness offers these women the opportunity to show that they can do a man's job, that they are equal to men if not better, because the inhospitable environment forces them to acquire endurance, strength and courage in order to survive.[64] But colonizing the space for the women means much more than getting sterling qualities. It allows them to develop traits that ultimately will change them from "good women" into "great women."[65]

3. Heroines in Western Films?

Along the arduous voyage, the women are pushed constantly by Buck to work more, to do better, under the implied challenge that they are inferior to men. The women live up to the challenge. After the Indian attack and many deaths, when Buck is ready to turn back and abort the crossing, the women, disagreeing with Buck, challenge his authority and decide to continue with or without him. Up to this point the female travelers have endured fatigue, insults and threats by Buck, and they have obeyed; after the Indian attack, however, they refuse to turn back, expressing a united solidarity that overwhelms the wagonmaster who, for once, caves in.

From this instance on, the women develop a sense of sisterhood that helps them to overcome serious obstacles while at the same time retaining nurturing, understanding and compassionate feelings: sadness at the killing of an injured horse, emotion at the sight of a colt and mare running happily together in the corral of the settlement, sense of cooperation when holding up the broken wagon when a child is born, and sadness for the many deaths after the Indian attack.

Once these women reach the edge of the desert, they get rid of all the pretty things that belonged to their eastern life, such as nice vases, paitnings, furniture and fancy garments, in order to travel lighter. Objects that clearly mattered to them in their previous domestic life are discarded because they are no longer important. It is clear

Westward the Women (MGM, 1951). Directed by William A. Wellman. Robert Taylor is Buck at the beginning of the trail. The medium shot emphasizes the fact that he is arrogant and bossy (Photofest).

X-glossia: Transformational Women and Westward the Women

that before reaching California they rid themselves of the vestiges of traditional domesticity, so that by the time they enter the desert they have gone through a sort of cleansing. They have left behind their old selves and are ready for a new identity. In spite of the harsh environment of the desert, they derive great joy from the birth of a child. When they reach the valley of the settlers they demand material to redress themselves and be presentable, making again a unified front so that Buck is forced to follow their decision. When they reach the settlers and dismount the wagons, the viewer sees that they are wearing pants with holsters and six-shooters underneath the more feminine attire, and, following Patience's lead, *they* choose their grooms. What has happened to these women? At the end of their journey they do get married and look forward to having a family life; in apparent abidance to patriarchy they even accept to be the objects of the male gaze. However, they are no longer the same women who left Chicago. They have built new selves; they have become the agents of their destiny. They are the ones pushing the narrative forward according to their desires; in a word they are redefining the rules of gender, going against hegemonic stereotypes of what female identity should be.

How can we reconcile domesticity and a transformative new identity in these women? The viewer is able to bridge this dichotomy because the discourse of the film also addresses female desire and sexuality. The male gaze-centered cinematic code is subverted by the female gaze-centered one. Buck tries to establish clear rules of separation between males and females before the start of the journey with very poor results. Uncharacteristically for a Western, the viewer is shown the "female gaze," as well as the "male gaze." Not only do the hired cowboys stare at the women as objects of desire, the women also gaze at the cowboys. There is attraction that is consensual, and also a non-consensual violent interaction that happens off screen. In the first case the man gets punished by Buck with expulsion from the caravan. In the second case, he executes the man, and Maggie, defending Buck, kills a cowboy who is about to shoot the master in the back. With one man gone and two men dead the rest of the hired hands abandon the expedition and go back east.

On one hand, Buck's extreme punishment stems mostly from the fact that the rapist has disobeyed his orders and not so much from a desire to punish the outrage. The cowboys, on the other hand, flee because they think Buck's punishment exceeds the crime, apparently

3. Heroines in Western Films?

agreeing with the rapist's statement that "nothing happened to her [Laurie] that hadn't happened to her before," following the old stereotype that an ex-prostitute cannot be raped.[66] The erotic desires of the women are voiced by Patience talking to the photograph of the man she has chosen (usually addressed *in absentia* as "mackerel face"), in the tender interaction between the pregnant Rose and the young cowboy Cid (the only one who does not go east because he is in love with the girl), in the happiness of the women when they reach the valley that is equal to the excitement shown by the settlers when they know that the women have finally arrived (extreme close up of one of the pioneer running towards the camera, shouting "Women! Women!") and, for the most part, in the verbal exchanges and body language of Danon, the French ex-prostitute, with the stern wagonmaster, her love interest.

Danon, attracted to Buck from the beginning, shows no inhibitions in teasing him verbally, at first making comments on his unshaved face then boldly invading his physical space and openly challenging him with a directness that shocks his tyrannical and patriarchal attitude towards women. Buck perceives Danon as a threat to his virility, his machismo and his view of sexuality and becomes more and more aggressive and sadistic toward the beautiful woman, picking on her and getting irritated by her incomprehensible language and her sexualized behavior. Buck with his "look of tortured eyebrows expressing the resolve and anger of the supremacist male"[67] seems to suffer from repression (especially toward "good women") and manifests a hate towards females in general and Danon in particular that, provoked by the circumstances, gets channeled into a sadistic streak. When Danon makes a mistake, he bullwhips her, and when she rides away, he catches her and slaps her twice, exclaiming:

> BUCK: Did I knock some sense into you?
> DANON: Yes, I'll be all right now.

Then the two embrace and kiss each other passionately. Obviously, every time Buck's authority is challenged by the opposite sex, he feels undermined and, to exercise his dominance, he resorts to violence.[68] His violence is a sign of patriarchal authority. He needs to discipline everybody who steps out of line; not only his men, but also the women need to remember that they must obey. Because Danon is defiant, in Buck's logic, she needs to be punished. However, the fact that he chases after her, deserting his post at the camp (let's not forget that while he

X-glossia: Transformational Women and Westward the Women

is pursuing Danon the Indians attack the wagons with daring results), makes the viewer a bit suspicious of his motivations. The kiss and the sudden submissiveness of Danon complicate the issue even further. Why will Danon be all right now? Her answer denotes submission on one level, but on the other, we need to examine the sequence in which they ride on the same horse back to camp.

Forgetting the lesson, Danon starts to address Buck in a way that should enrage the man, telling him that he is her object of desire: "... from the first time I saw your beautiful face.... It is a nice rugged face. Beard and all. I loved it. Did you like to hear that? Well, I like to hear it too." At this point the alpha male, confronted with an open declaration of attraction, does not react violently as one would expect, but admits that he is happy to get so much admiration. It is clear that in the war of the sexes, Danon is the victor: She has stormed the fortress of his masculinity and made a breach, even if, in the course of the battle, she has had to endure a few slaps. Some critics see in Danon a trace of masochism or, according to Freudian theory, a reactivation of pre-oedipal desires, but the psychoanalytical explanations, as interesting as they might be, seem to dismiss that Buck's behavior, as disturbing as it might seem at first, can also be read as his last reaction before capitulating to the "Other."[69] From the Indian attack on, his apparently monolithic identity changes. Through the polyphony of voices, the women manage to turn him into a more decent human being. Buck shifts from machismo to respect, while the women follow an equally x-glossic trajectory from traditional identities to empowerment without sacrificing the best qualities of femininity.

The young Japanese cook is another strong influence on Buck. With his small stature and his compassionate view of the world, Ito is a male who shows a sort of "feminized" masculinity, far from the domineering machismo of his boss. Expressing his disagreement and his criticism in Japanese to Buck, he compels the wagon-master to repeat with aggravation, "What did you say?" but, in this process, he also forces him to review, to defend, or to modify his decisions. Ito is the only character who exhibits a positive personality that remains constant all through the story. He is the only character whose identity does not undergo transformation. He is Buck's sidekick, his conscience and his more "feminine" side. The other older, paternalistic but decent male, Roy Whitman (Roy McIntire), owner of the California valley and the one who organizes the mail-order-brides enterprise, gets killed during the Indian attack, and

3. Heroines in Western Films?

therefore disappears from screen, passing his legacy to the wagon master. By the end of the film, Buck, chosen by Danon, offers her his arm so they can happily join the line of the soon to be married.

Westward the Women, thus, is a filmic narrative that challenges most of the established cinematic codes: the women of the film propel the narrative with their actions, acquiring the status of heroines; they redefine common gender assumptions with their sexuality; they defeat patriarchy with their polyphony; with their identities they transcend traditional models of monoglossic and heteroglossic constructions, becoming something new. The transformation of the women is articulated not around masculinity versus femininity, but around femininity itself. These women no longer operate following the standards of femininity set by patriarchy; they have gone beyond. They resemble some postwar American females who were setting for battles that had just begun in those years, battles that were going to come to the forefront a while later with feminism.

4

Hybridity and (De)Construction of Femininity and Masculinity in *Rancho Notorious, Johnny Guitar* and *Duel in the Sun*

Mary Ann Doane considers "Hollywood classic cinema as the locus of an especially powerful and influential filmic organization of sexual difference," claiming that "one need only register the compulsive heterosexual coupling which constitutes the closure of innumerable Hollywood films" to see how heterosexuality is magnified, performed and insisted on.[1] The girl marrying the cowboy hero is certainly the happy ending of many classic Westerns from *Stagecoach* (1939) on. However, in this very populous filmic genre, there are exceptions even within the conspicuous output of the classic era Hollywood production. Three films made in the postwar era succeed, in different ways, in constructing an unusual image both of femininity and masculinity, altering the rules of the filmic genre to which they belong. They are *Duel in the Sun*, 1946, directed by King Vidor, screenplay by David O. Selznick based on a novel by Niven Busch[2]; *Rancho Notorious*, 1952, directed by Fritz Lang, screenplay by Daniel Taradash based on an original story by Silvia Richards[3]; and *Johnny Guitar*, 1954, directed by Nicholas Ray, screenplay by Philip Yordan, based on a novel by Roy Chanslor.[4]

All three films break with the conventions of the Western genre: They are melodramas that focus on female protagonists with an emphasis on issues that are supposed to be relevant to women or that could appeal to a female audience. If films portray on screen "the collective drives, conscious and unconscious, of the American women," these

4. Hybridity and (De)Construction of Femininity and Masculinity

works can be considered woman's films.[5] Furthermore, the conscious adherence to the patriarchal order is absent in these movies, and the foundation of these stories is nothing less than a rebellion against the patriarchal order articulated differently in each work.

Melodrama, according to David Lusted, is "a fictional mode equivalent to romance or mystery which can operate in any genre ... [it] dramatizes contemporary political and social issues through a set of morally charged Manichean relationships. ... A central trope of melodrama is the dramatic connection between social and psychic repression, leading to an excess of misery in the central protagonist and matched by emotional tension in the audience. ... In cinema, particularly, this is evident in forms of spectacle and in the visual excess of a stylized fictional world."[6] For Lusted, melodrama in the Western genre does not imply just gender, but also problems related to masculine identity, including social relations inside a hierarchy of social classes.[7] According to the critic, melodrama incorporates socially marginalized groups, including fragments of the working classes, ethnic minorities, sub-cultures, i.e., "groups whose experiences of social [and emotional] oppression and desire for change are the subjects imagined through melodrama."[8]

If in the classic Western violence seems to obsess the male heroes—usually virile, adventurous and unbeatable—in the Western melodrama trauma gets added to violence. The moral order is hardly ever restored. Violence brings punishment, but never positive resolution. The happy ending is non-existent. The villain can be vanquished, but no moral order is restored because in order to achieve their goal, the male protagonists cause general destruction. The male heroes, like the female ones, are usually tortured individuals, caught between harrowing desires, often unacceptable to society. These protagonists are either prisoners of models of masculinity coded in contradictory ways, or victims of passions they cannot restrain. There is a pervasive excess in these characters. They suffer a crisis or a change of identity that often cannot be reconciled.

While most melodramas such as Douglas Sirk's show a romantic triangle, some form of betrayal and, usually, a resolution offering examples of redemption and moral rectitude, these films do not. Here the excessive emotions externalized through action express anger at different manifestations of injustice. The films of this chapter address different notions of class, gender, racial issues, and social injustice, and therefore they address femininity and masculinity along very different lines from the ones of the traditional Westerns (i.e., *Shane*, *The Searchers*). The male and female protagonists of these films do not conform to the canon. In the best scenario they remain marginalized from society (*Johnny Guitar*); in the worst (*Rancho Notorious*, *Duel in the Sun*) they plunge into lawlessness through violence.

Rancho Notorious: *The Filmic Text (1952)*

Rancho Notorious, by famous director Fritz Lang, subverts the Western genre on multiple levels.[9] First of all, the romantic couple of the story is not the one seen in the opening scene, a close-up in which the camera lingers on the passionate kiss between a young cowboy and a pretty girl. The romantic couple at the center of the story consists of a more mature male (Mel Ferrer as outlaw Frenchy Fairmont) and a more mature woman (Marlene Dietrich as Altar Keane), who is tough as nails and successful, but with a past. Lang is clearly diverting from the norm, setting the viewer up for a standard romance that gets denied a few minutes into the start.

At the plot level, the role of the male hero (Arthur Kennedy as Vern)—the young cowboy who is supposed to get married in eight days and contribute to the progress of the small town where he lives in early 1870s Wyoming—is shattered a few moments into the film by the murder of his fiancée Beth. There will be no wedding, no family, no life in the community for Vern because of Beth's brutal rape and murder. Beth, the only woman in the film who has the potential to be a "proper wife" and a nurturing member of society as the formula requires, is eliminated in the opening sequence. The schoolmarm/fiancée of the hero, the one who fits the Hollywood heterosexual ideal, disappears at the beginning of the story, making it impossible for the film to end traditionally. Marriage as narrative closure is negated in the film. The young girl's murder opens a trajectory that brings Vern to follow a path of vengeance, straying from the law and, in the end, getting killed. As a consequence, the movie develops along lines that prevent any happy ending: The unconventional romantic couple, on which the movie focuses half way through, Frenchy and Altar, and the male hero Vern, become the protagonists of a story in which everybody dies violently in the end. Thus, we have a closure that resembles more the *noir* genre than the typical Western.

Another absent component of the Western formula is the

4. Hybridity and (De)Construction of Femininity and Masculinity

community. The town in which Vern and Beth live at the beginning of the film seems to be inhabited by decent people, but once these folks face the danger of entering Sioux country to pursue Beth's assassins they turn their back on Vern. The townspeople are not supportive of the grieving hero as they should be. In fact, the posse abandons the search because its members abide by the law only as long as it does not interfere with their economic interest. Vern's fellow countrymen have more important things to do (like branding cows and taking care of business) than "pursuing justice." As a result, the hero continues alone in his quest for revenge.

The 1950s was the time of the House Un-American Activities Committee and it is no surprise that, here, we find a community that does not help the hero. Will Kane (Gary Cooper) as marshal of Hadleyville had suffered the same fate in *High Noon* (Fred Zinnemann, 1952). The critique of society does not stop with Vern's town, Whitmore, Wyoming, where the citizens are cowards. The other two filmic communities, Gunsight (where Frenchy is kept in jail) and Chuck-a-Luck (Altar's ranch), offer a pretty unsavory image of civilization. The latter is made up of a lawless gang of murderous and despicable individuals, with the exceptions of Frenchy and Altar, both forced on the wrong side of the tracks by different reasons—male exploitation for her and social injustice for him. The former is instead a more interesting case because it shows how corrupt politicians are worse than outlaws.

Vern arrives to Gunsight during election day; the "law and order" party is winning, but its members seem to be leaning toward an idea of justice that implies lynching. In the jail, where Vern is taken after he shoots up the saloon, executed on purpose in order to meet up with Frenchy, he encounters a bunch of crooked politicians ousted from power by the new party, but who are still in cahoots with the corrupt ex-sheriff. Vern opts for staying with Frenchy affirming, "...give me an outlaw over these thieves any time, at least he takes his chances in the open!" The reasons for his choice are determined by the fact that he wants to find Altar and her establishment, but he clearly despises the politicians who have stolen the town's money and want to bribe the two cowboys into freeing them. Another fundamental rule of the Western genre is deconstructed by Lang who creates societies that are not at all fitting into the myth of the Frontier, i.e., "land, liberty and the pursuit of happiness." As Fuller claims, the postwar Westerns present a different kind of heroes, "obsessive, violent and often masochistic: these

Rancho Notorious: *The Filmic Text (1952)*

angry, alienated protagonists lent the films psychological depth and moral complexity, helping to reinvigorate the genre and better enable it to grapple with the socio-political concerns of the Cold War era."[10]

For the first fifteen minutes of the film the viewer believes that the protagonist is indeed a male character—the usual good cowboy on the path of vengeance—but there is a twist. On one hand, the hero is so blinded by his desire for revenge that he is willing to become an outlaw to achieve his goal, and, by the end of the film, he is almost as violent and manipulative as the man he has set out to kill. On the other hand, Vern's wanderings in search of the ranch-hideout called Chuck-a-Luck, puts him in contact with various male characters whose flashback memories allow him to finally piece together the location of the assassin, as in a detective story. Through the flashbacks, we discover that the owner of the mysterious ranch is a charming dance hall singer (Altar Keane) who one day rebelled against male exploitation, won a fortune at the roulette, and skipped town.

The memories of the men and woman who knew Altar—recreated on screen in long flashbacks—combine the male and female points of view, revealing that both male and female characters admire her. Dora, the saloon singer and former friend of Altar, sees her as a free-spirited, elegant, rich woman courted by lots of men, capable of refusing a cattle baron if she fancied a cowpuncher; the men see her as a rebellious, beautiful, wild (see the "bar-race" with the saloon girls as jockeys on the shoulders of the customers), and a fun sexual object. In both cases Altar appears as a woman animated by a desire for independence, willing to take charge of her destiny outside the norms of any patriarchal authority. From the first flashback, Altar gets center stage because these recollections create a mythic aura around her, and because all the events revolve around searching for her and her hidden ranch.

The moment Vern meets Altar, we discover that she is the only woman ruling over an establishment made up of male bandits. She has established her own law in Chuck-a-Luck, creating a community in which everybody follows her rules. Even if she has chosen a companion, the highwayman Frenchy, she is the only boss. The fact that Altar is played by Marlene Dietrich serves to complicate the story; the viewer is compelled to add to the image of the ex-saloon girl Dietrich's own star persona, her past roles as fallen angel, and the diva of so many previous films.

Jeanine Basinger says, "'Persona' is the word used to define the

4. Hybridity and (De)Construction of Femininity and Masculinity

quality that a great star projects to an audience and that the audience accepts as being true to the star's nature."[11] Marlene Drietrich was a star whose screen persona challenged the inevitability of women's oppression with roles in which she had the right to satisfy her desires like men do.[12] In Josef von Sternberg's films of the 1930s, Dietrich appeared as a cabaret singer, dressed in man's white tie or top hat and tails, in men's military uniforms, or wrapped in elegant dresses as a diva, in roles that were not traditional for women.[13] In Sternberg's films a stunning visual use of light and shadow photography, accurate costumes and set designs contributed to create a *femme fatale* image, enhanced by Dietrich's ironic detachment and sophistication, so the "off-screen persona added layers to the screen image."[14] In *Rancho Notorious*, the expectation of the female character as appendix of the male hero, either as schoolmarm/wife or saloon girl/prostitute, is negated by the star persona of Dietrich,

Rancho Notorious (RKO Radio Pictures, Inc., 1952). Directed by Fritz Lang. Marlene Dietrich as Altar Keane, owner of the infamous ranch and dressed in a sexy gown, charms the sheriff and his posse, sending them after a red herring (Photofest).

Rancho Notorious: *The Filmic Text* (1952)

even though Dietrich was 50 years old when the film was made. Altar comes across as beautiful and fascinating as ever, and the film turned out to be an ideal vehicle for re-launching the star's career and reiterated the image that Sternberg had created for her in the 1930s.[15]

Basinger, looking at the role of female stars in terms of the woman's place in society, comes up with three different categories. Applying Basinger's theory to *Rancho Notorious* I conclude that Marlene Dietrich as Altar Keane falls into the category of "unreal women," meaning, "stars whose beauty, elegance, and sexual appeal are somehow beyond the ordinary. ... They are not supposed to be role models for anyone, because no one could imagine these women to be duplicated in real life; they are too out of the ordinary."[16] For Basinger, these stars provide all kinds of escape and yearning for both men and women, but they are the ones who appeal mostly to men because they are objects of desire on which the male gaze lingers.

The building of Altar into a *femme fatale* is made iconographically via many low-angle medium shots and close-ups of her singing act at the ranch, in front of the outlaws who lust for her and admire her beauty and elegance (i.e., the various close-up shots of their faces smiling, entranced in admiration).[17] Lang cleverly magnifies the impact of the vamp lingering on the intradiegetical gaze of the male characters that seems to be an extension of the extradiegetical gaze of the male audience. In this way Altar becomes a goddess for the cowboys as well as for us viewers. Altar's attire—a high fashion, princess-like dark ruffled dress with a low-cut and huge skirt—makes her appear like a dream, an almost unreal apparition. Altar's singing act is also dramatically enhanced by her attitude; she is teasing the public, alluring the men, flirting with them, passing herself out as a sex object, and somehow making the audience forget that she governs the ranch with an iron fist.[18]

Altar can also transition easily from pants, holster and six-gun to her princess-like dress. For most of the film she wears male clothing; only in a couple of instances does she cross-dress as a woman, clearly covering her position of authority with a masquerade of "traditional" femininity.[19] Altar as a vamp is clearly a woman in control who offers contradictory images of femininity. She can be at the same time both the phallic woman and the fetishized woman. Altar is sexy, but she is also in command; with her singing act and her masquerade she can manipulate the male audience and cease to be threatening. While singing, in fact, she returns the gaze, staring at the men, alluring them, but always

4. Hybridity and (De)Construction of Femininity and Masculinity

remaining unreachable.[20] As Vern says to Altar many times in the course of the film, she is a "pipe dream."

Altar embodies the "unreal woman," the creature who populates male fantasies, and is the opposite image of Beth, the fiancée/wife traditional woman. In this sense Altar is Chuck-a-Luck, and the ranch is her Shangri-La: A private utopia, isolated from the rest of civilization, a paradise for the outsiders/outlaws where the only law is *her* law. In order to escape a male-dominated world, Altar/Dietrich has created her own private universe, where she has rights normally denied to women (sexual life outside marriage and power over men). The relationship between Altar and Frenchy, as a critic claims, "undermines the idea of romance, the rigidity of gender roles and the picture of the homesteading community presented in the film's opening."[21]

The gaze is central in the film's discourse on masculinity and femininity, and it is visually enhanced by the filmic text through lingering shots that either follow the trajectory of the eyes of the characters or put the viewers in the position of the receiver of the look. Kinch the villain catches glimpses of Beth outside her shop while riding into town; he keeps looking at her until he decides to rob the shop, attracted by what he sees. When he enters the shop, he keeps staring at the girl in a long closeup filmed from a low angle so that we see his stare transitioning from greed (the open safe has money) to lust (the pretty girl, her face, her neckline). Aware of what is happening, Beth stares back at him in a closeup from top down that emphasizes her position as victim and returns the male gaze with one full of fear. When Vern meets Altar for the first time, he let his eyes go up and down on the woman, in such an insolent way that she exclaims, "…he uses his eyes too, doesn't he? … He is a little fresh!" and later she says to him, "You are always using your eyes!" There is a web of gazes in the story that intensify the gender discourse.

Lang was the first one to use a theme song in a Western.[22] The ballad sung over the opening credits tells us about a story of "hate, murder and revenge," setting the mood for tragedy, but the opening scene, showing a long tender kiss, seems to contradict the song lyrics. The words of the ballad comment on the story, in fact, and the song happens at certain crucial points, dividing the story into three parts. The prologue spans from the opening kiss to the moment in which Vern finds one of the dying robbers (who, in his last breath, mentions "Chuck-a-Luck") and explains why Vern is a man bent on revenge. The quest deals with

Rancho Notorious: *The Filmic Text (1952)*

Rancho Notorious (RKO Radio Pictures, Inc., 1952). Directed by Fritz Lang. Outlaws Mort Geary (Jack Elam; left) and Jeff Factor (John Kellogg) complain about Altar Keane's (Marlene Dietrich; center) exorbitant loot percentage, but she does not budge. Dressed like a man, Altar makes sure that everyone understands that she is the boss (Photofest).

Vern's desperate search for information on Chuck-a-Luck, the mysterious place where Beth's assassin is supposedly hiding. In his peregrinations the young man questions authorities, saloon owners and sheriffs, until he discovers the name of Altar Keane and connects her to the outlaw Frenchy, finding out that he is in a jail at Gunsight. The denouement, or main part of the story, starts with the ballad reinforcing the theme of murder and revenge, and focuses on the interaction of Frenchy, Altar and Vern at the ranch. From this point on, the song ceases until the very end.

The ballad returns in the last sequence of the film. After Altar's death, we observe through a long shot Frenchy and Vern riding away while the vocalized voice-over informs us that that very day they will die fighting, falling with empty guns. Lang clearly uses the ballad to give structure to the filmic text that, thanks to this melodic scansion, acquires thematic cohesion. However, the ultimate outcome of Lang's

4. Hybridity and (De)Construction of Femininity and Masculinity

construction is building expectation in the viewer via delayed action. Every time Vern is on the verge of acquiring a new piece of information that will help him to reach the truth, another action/event always interferes. He spots the brooch on Altar's dress, but before he can react, a warning is sounded and everybody has to flee; he is talking to Wilson, one of the outlaws, about the filly he just rode in a double/sexual entendre, and he is expecting a reaction, when two other outlaws arrive interrupting the conversation; he is about to kill Kinch, Beth's murderer, when a sheriff interrupts the duel, arresting the murderous cowboy. In this endless deferring of the truth and of the resolution, the spectator ends up sharing Vern's desperation.[23]

Lang's also creates a romantic triangle between Frenchy, Altar and Vern, using it to destabilize the canonical use of the archetype. Frenchy and Altar's affair is disturbed by the arrival of Vern who pretends to seduce Altar in order to discover who has given her the brooch that belonged to his fiancée. The love triangle, the jealousy and the tension among the three are created intentionally and unscrupulously by Vern. The love triangle is an act: A man (Frenchy) is in love with a woman (Altar) who is charmed by a younger man who pretends to be fascinated by her. For Vern, Altar is a means to obtain information, not a true love interest because he cannot love anybody, being too traumatized by Beth's murder, too angry, and too eaten up inside by hate and revenge.

Fate ruined Vern's life the moment he became a victim of unfortunate circumstances, the same as Frenchy has been a victim of social circumstances (trying to rectify a wrong, he killed a man and started on a path of violence that could never be stopped). The romantic, elegant gentleman-like Frenchy is a decent person who became a gunslinger because a corrupted rancher stole his homestead, and he could not recur to civil justice.[24] The fundamental trope of the Western, the moral rightness of the heroes, acquires a lot of new nuances here. The two male protagonists are nothing like Shane. For them exacting justice has unleashed a violence that has brought destruction. The use of violence to restore justice/peace/progress so celebrated in many traditional Westerns is totally negated in *Rancho Notorious*.

In this way, Lang manages to subvert completely the Western formula; he constructs a microcosm in which the community is made up of outlaws, the protagonist is an anti-heroine, and the hero is a cowboy so blinded by revenge he becomes an outlaw himself (he even robs a bank). Altar subverts the saloon girl character of so many Western films,

Rancho Notorious: *The Filmic Text (1952)*

creating a female who is self-sufficient and practical—she's nobody's property. Even if it is true that she sacrifices herself in the end, taking a bullet in order to save Frenchy's life, her death should not be interpreted as the final sacrifice that redeems the "fallen woman" of her sins. Altar's death is an act of volition, a decision to save the man who loved her, in the realization that her "empire" has crumbled.

At this point we should ask ourselves what Lang's film is about? What is the theme? Like many other Westerns, Lang's film centers on a revenge story. But, this is a story in which all the protagonists die in the end. Both the lyrics of the ballad and the interaction between the three protagonists have, as sub-text, the trope of time. From the first flashback until the moment we meet Altar at the ranch, a good span of years has passed. Therefore, the various recollections show a younger and more rambunctious saloon gal than the mature female boss of Chuck-a-Luck. When Vern meets Altar, she has been living for years with Frenchy and she is still beautiful, but she fears aging. On her birthday, she says to her companion: "Don't ask me how old I will be tomorrow. Every year is a threat to a woman!" Altar addresses Frenchy as "you old mustang" implying a sexual liaison, but also the fact that he too has aged. When Vern rides a wild bronco and tames it, Frenchy is envious of his strength and comments, "I might have done that kind of riding twelve years ago." In a fit of jealousy, the gunslinger says to Altar, "Once in a lifetime a woman means something to a man. ... Time holds us together, and time is stronger than a rope."

After a few kisses between Altar and Vern, before telling him to leave the ranch for good, she exclaims, "I wish you would go away and come back ten years ago!" The former barroom belle is falling for the young and handsome cowboy, but time is what keeps them apart; it is too late for Altar as she has too much history and too many years with Frenchy. The passing of time as a threat to Altar's beauty superimposes itself on the *star persona* of Dietrich, who, at the time of filming *Rancho Notorious*, was already fifty and certainly concerned about losing her fame and beauty.[25]

On the thematic level, Lang manages to construct a melodrama in which the real enemy of the anti-heroine is not Vern, the rebelling outlaws tired of paying too much to her in exchange for shelter, or the posse looking for the outlaws, but age. Parallel to the theme of the revenge of the male protagonist is the tragedy of a beautiful woman who can still keep men under control with her beauty, but she wonders

4. Hybridity and (De)Construction of Femininity and Masculinity

for how much longer, and for how long she can still redirect the male gaze to her advantage. In her mature years, Altar becomes vulnerable and she falls for a younger man's attention, breaking her own rules and setting in motion a series of tragic events that ultimately kill her. The ex-saloon girl, in her pride and vulnerability, is mirroring Dietrich herself, an aging star who felt that her *persona* was bound to wane with time. Even though Dietrich, in Lang's film, succeeded in keeping up the image of the *femme fatale*, certainly aging must have been a prime concern.[26]

If revenge and time are two of the themes on which the story is based, we also need to look at a deeper level: The female protagonist, who until the end of the film has maintained her power, gets destroyed, not by the bullet or by her failing charm (over men), but rather by the moral accusations of Vern. The moment Vern learns who gave her the brooch, and therefore gets to the end of his long quest, he drops the act and attacks Altar verbally, rebuking her for her free sexuality ("What do you see? A bedroom or a morgue?") and for breaking her own gender rules claiming that the men come to Chuck-a-Luck to hide behind her skirts, and accusing her of ruling over a "cemetery," an empire built upon killing and violence. Vern is verbally punishing Altar for acting according to her desires.

Once Vern tells Altar that her past "dirty life" as a dance hall gal is nothing in comparison to the filth of her present life—revealing at the same time that her empire is built on killing, he is impermeable to her attraction, and showing that her charm has failed—she is psychologically destroyed. The end of her control over men is complete: The outlaws are rebelling against her as a boss and the young cowboy has used her only for his revenge scheme. Even before losing her life, her whole existence has ceased to mean anything because Vern has taken away any power she had. Altar has again become a vulnerable female. When she decides to save the life of the man who loves her in the final showdown against the rebelling criminals, she steps in front of a bullet not because she wants to make amends for her past life as in many classic Westerns, but because she chooses to die rather than revert to her old life of bondage as a saloon-girl. Like Altar, the male protagonists, consciously or unconsciously, opt for death in the end: Vern because he cannot go back to what he was, and Frenchy because his life is ruined by the loss of Altar just as Vern's existence had been destroyed by Beth's death. Frenchy, accepting his fate as he leaves the ranch in the last sequence of the film, replies to Vern who warns him that the lawmen might be waiting to ambush them, "We all get taken soon or later."

Finally, we cannot conclude our analysis of *Rancho Notorious* without pondering on the title. The movie was originally titled *The Legend of Chuck-a-Luck*, but Howard Hughes, who financed the movie, changed it because he believed that very few people would be familiar with the name of the vertical roulette wheel of gambling barrooms called chuck-a-luck.[27] Hughes was right. The choice of the adjective "notorious" has, like Lang's filmic text, a complex meaning denoting something that can be both famous and infamous. The final title of the film is indeed more appropriate than the insipid and descriptive original one.

The ranch called Chuck-a-Luck is indeed famous and the ballad that accompanies the story proves it, but within the filmic diegesis it is a despicable place for Vern, who sees it as an emblem of moral decadence and crime. The hideout is infamous for the young cowboy because here a female has created a world by following her desires of independence, freedom and power in open defiance to male authority. This is the interpretation filtered through Vern's male subjectivity (probably shared by the male audience of the time) who remains, from beginning to end, a pretty conservative character and a traumatized subject incapable of curing himself of his obsession.[28] On the other hand, for the women watching the film Altar is a "pipe dream," one of those fanciful, impossible creatures who somehow can defy the system and construct a parallel world according to different rules.[29] Altar is the woman who obtains, for a time, complete freedom and independence, a model probably totally far-fetched for the Cold War American women of the 1950s, but a powerful paradigm of the female desires that were starting to brew under the surface of the male dominated society of the era.

Johnny Guitar: *Paratext*[30]

The film was scripted by Philip Yordan from a novel by Roy Chanslor, published in 1953 and dedicated to Joan Crawford.[31] Chanslor and his wife were old friends of Crawford. The famous actress was so fascinated by the story of Vienna, the female protagonist, that she bought the rights to the novel, liking the idea of two gun-toting women in the West, and then resold the rights to Republic Pictures with the stipulation that she would star in the movie.[32] The 1954 edition of the novel

4. Hybridity and (De)Construction of Femininity and Masculinity

by Pocket Books shows on the back cover an enthusiastic, autographed statement from the actress with a drawing of her face.[33] Chanslor and Nicholas Ray adapted the novel and transformed it into a script, but the film credits only Philip Yordan as the screenwriter; the latter was called in to revise it after Crawford complained to the studio, protesting that she did not have enough screen time or interesting dialogues ("I have no part. I just stand around with boots on and have a few stupid scenes. I want to play the man. I want to shoot it out in the end with Mercedes McCambridge instead of playing with myself in a corner. Let Sterling play with himself in the corner...").[34] The saga of the feuds between Crawford, the cast and the director spilled out of the set into local and national newspapers and magazines, but, in the end, as McGillian notes, "It was good for the picture" because the spillage created great publicity. The film did well at the box office, even if most American critics at the time demolished it; Bosley Crowther of *The New York Times* even called it a "fiasco."[35]

Overseas, however, French critics affiliated with *Cahiers du Cinéma* praised the movie, calling it a "Freudian, political, personal" Western and the work of an *auteur*, in short, an extraordinary film.[36] As Pamela Robertson claims, the *auteurists* (Truffaut, Rivette) liked the film, but asserted the primacy of the masculine plot over the feminine one, placing the film in the context of Ray's male *Rebel Without a Cause* filmography, and preferring the character of Johnny Guitar over the female characters. The genre theorists, on the other hand, considered the film a "hybridization," a Western that had too much in it, being psychoanalytic, erotic, and perverse at the same time.[37] Some later critics read into it a critique of McCarthyism/Cold War: They saw the protagonist, Vienna, as a sort of Will Kane (*High Noon*), an individual left alone to face a lynching mob dominated by hysteria. More recently, Leo Charney defined *Johnny Guitar* as "a film in which everything conspires against restraint: territory expands, time recurs, genre bends, sex roles fluctuate, and, above all, socio-political realities mix allegorically into the fictional tapestry."[38] For Pamela Robertson, instead, the "excess" at which Charney points is camp; she writes: "*Johnny Guitar* is camp because it is a fundamentally incoherent text, both a failed Western and an awkward star vehicle, which reflects a set of early-1950s ambivalences about female sexuality." For the critic, the excessive masculinization and the obsessive hate that links the two feuding female protagonists together opens a space for reading into it a "butch-femme role-play."[39]

Johnny Guitar: *Peritext and the Novel (1953)*

To make the situation even more complicated, the film got inscribed into the social context of its time in direct ways. Ward Bond was chosen to play McIvers, who, with Emma, is one of the leaders of the lynching mob; being a founding member of the virulent Motion Picture Alliance for the Preservation of American Ideals, both Ray and Yordan thought it was appropriate to turn him into a "caricature of an anti–Communist vigilante."[40] For the male leading part the director chose Sterling Hayden, who had admitted his ties to the Communist Party and had given "names" to the HUAC in 1951 but, since then, had been deeply regretting his choice; both Ray and Hayden "shared HUAC scars."[41]

The web of circumstances that went into the making of *Johnny Guitar*, its ties to the socio-political era, the writing and the modifications of the screenplay, and the disparity of the critics—even today divided between the disparaging and the celebratory—convinced us that one way to penetrate the filmic surplus of meaning would be to start from its origin—the novel by Roy Chanslor.

Johnny Guitar: *Peritext and the Novel (1953)*[42]

A glance at the original cover of *Johnny Guitar* is enough to help us realize that we are not far from the realm of pulp fiction. Under the title, we read: "A novel of gamblers, outlaws and lynching mobs in the American West," and, below, a female and a young man in a stagecoach look with concern toward a gunman on a horse about to rob them. The image is rendered in vivid colors—yellow and maroon predominate—and, like many covers of pulp fiction magazines, is meant to attract the reader by picturing a crucial moment of the story.

From the 1800s to 1950s "pulp" described an affordable, low-brow fiction, depending on formulas and genre, aimed at exciting, astonishing, and scaring the readership. In this category we had romance, science fiction, crime, horror, and Wild West adventures.[43] Chanslor's novel clearly belongs to this last category. If pulp fiction, "has often reflected the society at hand, its hopes and dreams, ideals and prejudices, taboos and sexual fantasies," analyzing Chanslor's novel will give us a fertile ground of comparison with the homonymous film.[44]

The story is recounted by an omniscient narrator in the third person from the characters' different points of view and is set in the vicinity of Powderville, Wyoming, in Elysian Fields, a small town in which

4. Hybridity and (De)Construction of Femininity and Masculinity

Front cover of Roy Chanslor's novel, *Johnny Guitar*, published by Simon & Schuster in 1953.

Johnny Guitar: *Peritext and the Novel (1953)*

the sheriff and Mr. and Mrs. Small reside. The outlaws live in a cabin, Lonergan's lair, hidden in the mountains. The Bills, a saloon populated by its owner Vienna and her croupiers, sits by itself in the middle of nowhere. Vienna, the protagonist, is presented as a "fine bold woman in black pants and red silk shirt," with a penchant for shocking townsfolk.[45] She rides a stud instead of a mare because the norm demands that a woman ride a mare; she wears a gun belt with a Smith & Wesson .38 caliber pistol, and she is a successful business woman. From the moment we encounter her, we realize that she is an outsider. Town women pretend to ignore her and "respectable citizens," like the general store owner, Mr. Small, call her "a Jezebel."[46] Nobody knows where she comes from or what her last name is. She is known only as Vienna, the owner of The Bills. As soon as Johnny Guitar, a handsome gambler newcomer in town, meets Vienna, he is attracted to her. From this point on, romance is in the making and, as the plot thickens, more adventures come into play.

As in the movie, the action is created by the interaction of three communities: the outlaws (Turkey, the Dancing Kid, Corey and Bart Lonergan, the gang leader), Vienna and her saloon helpers, and the town people (Emma, Mr. Small and the posse). The novel starts with a stage coach robbery that triggers a series of repercussions. Turkey, one of the robbers, kills the man riding shotgun during the hold-up. He is recognized by Mr. Small and he, his wife Emma and the sheriff look for the bandit at Vienna's saloon. Vienna hides Turkey to avoid mayhem, but the criminal ambushes and kills Mr. Small and the sheriff and wounds Emma while getting himself fatally injured. From this moment on, the chase starts. Emma, enraged by the killing of her husband—whom she has always detested and despised when alive—becomes obsessed by exacting "a tooth for a tooth" revenge; assuming that Vienna is the Dancing Kid's girlfriend and, therefore, an accomplice to her husband's murder, she assembles a lynching party that hangs the crew of The Bills.

Vienna is miraculously saved by Johnny Guitar while Emma burns the saloon down. Vienna, Johnny, and Sam, a Bills dealer and old friend/sidekick of Vienna, take refuge in Lonergan's lair where Johnny passes himself off as an outlaw in order to win money at cards. When Johnny's true identity as a professional gambler is discovered, Bart Lonergan decides to kill him. Vienna warns the gambler of the danger. Johnny guns down Bart, and the three take off. The rest of the outlaws chase them, but get intercepted by Emma's posse. The Dancing Kid, his girlfriend Elsa,

4. Hybridity and (De)Construction of Femininity and Masculinity

and Emma die in the shootout, while Sam, Vienna and Johnny Guitar ride free toward a rosy future.

In the novel, outlaws and posse are props used to make the romantic story more interesting; the characters are moved by very simple passions: revenge and hate in Emma's case, and greed in the case of the outlaws who kill for money. The archetypal story of good versus evil is acted out on a canvas at the center of which lies the romance between two pure souls, Johnny and Vienna, the good people (with Sam). To consolidate the position of Vienna and Johnny as hero and heroine, Chanslor also weaves in the story of their past lives. We discover that Johnny comes from a rich, aristocratic family in New Orleans, took the fall for love of a woman who turned out to be unworthy of it, and went to jail in a highly chivalric gesture to spare her the shame of the crime. Vienna is the daughter of a well-to-do family destroyed by an epidemic, who, as an orphan, was cared for by a prostitute and grew up innocently in a contaminated environment where she learned to distrust love. With the inclusions of these life narratives we are venturing into the realm of 19th century *feuilleton* fiction, which used to narrate the ups and downs of heroic figures who usually managed to preserve their innocence through terrible trials.

Chanslor's novel is a sort of big puzzle, many elements of which transmigrate into the film, but ended up being rearranged. At the plot level, all the elements of the original story reappear in the film but are re-contextualized in a more sophisticated way. The novel is essentially a vehicle for narrating a romance between Vienna and Johnny, and to make their story more alluring, their love reveals itself thanks to the various adventures the two go through. From the moment Johnny meets Vienna, he is attracted to her. After rescuing her from hanging, he falls in love; while avoiding the posse he decides to marry her; and in Lonergan's lair he convinces her that love is the most important thing in life. The 1950s "feminine mystique" that dictated that "the object of female desire and the basis for female satisfaction should be maternal and domestic," is at the core of the novel.[47] The book that seemed so original to Crawford in its depiction of an anti-conformist female protagonist is, in reality. promoting an old stereotype while dressing it up under a layer of modernity that is just cosmetic. Vienna dresses like a man, carries a gun and is the boss and a tough business woman fond of money, but, in the end, she recognizes that Johnny is right, that love is the most important thing in life, and becomes, we assume, a perfect wife. The book is peppered with a lot of corny statements that are borderline ridiculous:

Vienna: "I can't give you love, Johnny," "I don't want to be a woman," "Love! It's a cheat, a trap for women! I don't want love! I'll take money," "I don't want to love you. I don't want to lose my freedom, my independence, myself."[48]

Johnny: "Women are made for love," "I'm going to take care of you the rest of my life," "I am a man who plays for keeps," "You are so wrong, Vienna. [Love] is not sickness, it's health, it's not weakness, it's strength. Its's being alive...."

The title of the novel is appropriate, as Johnny Guitar is indeed the principal agent of the story; it is he who changes Vienna from a "rebel without a cause" into a more docile female specimen.[49] Without denigrating the importance of love in human relationships, we must admit that the book clearly functions as an ideological weapon aimed at showing that the most important things in life for a woman are not independence and freedom, but love and submission to a man, i.e., the book is a call to re-enter the ranks of patriarchal authority launched to those women out there who tried to "masculinize" themselves and strayed from the proper roles. We need to be thankful to Ray and Yordan for having created a movie that adds different sub-texts and complicates the love story between Vienna and Johnny Guitar.

Johnny Guitar: *The Filmic Text (1954)*

If *Rancho Notorious* portrays a *noir*-ish frontier, *Johnny Guitar* showcases a *dark*-frontier.[50] Darkness, in fact, predominates in the most astonishing sequences of the film, such as the ones in which the lynching party rides furiously around the massive burning flames of Vienna's saloon. Such scenes inspired Truffaut to label Ray "the poet of nightfall."[51] The film was shot in Trucolor stock, an unusual choice for a Western, because it oversaturates reds and greens, creating a striking palette.[52] Ray did many of the set designs for the film (Vienna's saloon, the cabin, the waterfall), creating distinct places for the three warring communities of the story.[53] On one side, the happy-go-lucky Dancing Kid (Scott Brady) and his friends (young Turkey, evil Bart, sick Corey), hard-working men who, accused unjustly of crimes, decide to rob a bank in order to punish the town's moral majority. On the other side, are the

4. Hybridity and (De)Construction of Femininity and Masculinity

evil townsfolk: Emma Small (Mercedes McCambridge), McIvers (Ward Bond) and the posse, who own the town and the bank. In between the two camps are Vienna (Joan Crawford) and her saloon croupiers with newly arrived Johnny Guitar (Sterling Hayden), sitting on a piece of land on which the railroad will soon pass, making it worth a fortune.

Through an ideological lens we could easily read in the above juxtaposition a distant reference to the Johnson County War in Wyoming in the late 1880s when cattle barons declared war on small settlers. We are aware that it would be equally possible, and probably more in tune with the contemporary climate of the era, to see the movie as a critique of McCarthyism, i.e., the moral majority on a hysterical crusade against some individuals (Vienna and company) and some marginal groups (the Dancing Kid gang). However, we would like to point out that class plays an important role in the story.[54] The Dancing Kid gang are peons squashed between two equally powerful factions, the land owners and the emerging class of railroad tycoons.[55] The railroad will bring progress, but also changes, and with them, capital and wealth will change hands. Vienna, in this sense is emblematic, because as the owner of a profitable establishment and of a piece of land on which a depot will be built, she commands power. She is not greedy. She very democratically divides her gains into equal shares among her workers, protecting them, using fairness (i.e., Tom: "I would have never known I would like to work for a woman") and opposing violence and killing as much as possible. She represents an illuminated form of ruling, one that promotes willing cooperation among the workers in opposition to the use of brute force and coercion promoted by the McIvers' bunch. In this sense, the landowners represent the past and Vienna the future.

If we agree with the filmic metaphorical depiction of a moment in history in which two opposed factions are conflating, the subversive and revolutionary force of the film comes to the fore.[56] Who are the real victims here? The working bunch turned criminals, the Dancing Kid and company, is a marginal community persecuted by the establishment and, therefore, the victims, together with Vienna, who as a relative newcomer who established herself in the area only five years earlier, is considered an outsider to the community (also morally). The miners turned bank robbers are the small people who, living off their hard work and not possessing much, get squashed between two overpowering forces: the railroad and the cattle barons (Emma, McIvers and the posse). Ray's and Yordan's invention is at its best in the moment in which the peons of

Johnny Guitar: *The Filmic Text (1954)*

the story refuse to fade easily into the night, and instead decide to rebel and strike back (robbing the bank). By the end of the film, the marginal group, one way or another, gets dispatched, but the McIvers' bunch is also pretty much a spent force. In fact, the posse retreats, letting Vienna and Johnny Guitar get on with their life and probably their (future) wealth (the depot).

Many critics have pointed out the lack of cohesiveness, the excess and the strangeness of Ray's Western, but we disagree. In our opinion, the film is beautifully constructed, like a pyramid of many co-existing layers of different subtexts. First of all, the film is a melodrama full of passions, highlighted emotions and dramatic events, or as Martin Scorsese says, "operatic."[57] If one subtext illustrates the revolutionary impulse of a marginal group, and the forming of a new "ruling class," in a reading of the film as a political Western we need to consider that there is another subtext equally important: gender.

Vienna, the heroine, appears in the opening sequences dressed like a cowboy, sporting fitted black pants, shirt and boots, towering over the croupiers of the barroom from a balcony (shot from bottom-up), dispensing orders to everybody ("Sam, light a lamp! Hang a lamp outside!," "Spin the wheel, Eddie!," "Keep the wheel spinning, Eddie!"). Tom the cook emphasizes her powerful position saying to Johnny Guitar, "Never seen a woman who was more a man. She thinks like one, acts like one, and sometimes make me feel like I'm not."[58] When Johnny comes back, after having abandoned her years before, and has the courage to confront her and demand proof of faithfulness, Vienna does not fall into the apologizing mode typical of the fallen women of traditional Westerns. When Johnny asks, "How many men have you forgotten?" she retorts with, "As many women as you have remembered," breaking the stereotype of the repenting attitude, and demanding an equal treatment from the male counterpart. Vienna is an autonomous, tough woman who has acquired wealth (land and saloon) selling her body after she was abandoned by Johnny. She is not hiding how she became rich; instead, she defends her choice, saying to Johnny that there is an inherent injustice in the moral double standards by which men judge women ("A man can lie, steal, and even kill. All a woman has to do is slip—once—and she's a tramp.")[59]

Their sparring is the result of a turbulent love story rendered through interesting repartees that are imaginative and full of nostalgia and regrets for what life could have been, but was not. We are very

4. Hybridity and (De)Construction of Femininity and Masculinity

distant from the corresponding infantile dialogues of the novel. Vienna and Johnny are clearly a good match, and it is amusing to watch their verbal interaction on screen, especially in front of the Dancing Kid who, having been Vienna's latest romantic interest and being unaware of the love story between the two, feels displaced and troubled for most of the film.[60]

Jeanine Basinger suggests that Joan Crawford as Vienna falls into a category she calls "exaggerated women."[61] These are actresses who had a long career, and "their accumulated film history of women portrayed began to weigh on their performance. By virtue of their longevity [all in middle age] and star power they took on a presence that moved them beyond reality and the stance of role model [...] into something high-powered, dangerous, exaggerated. And extraordinary." These women embodied an intimidating femininity. Their status as established movie stars combined with their age gave them powerful roles impersonating powerful women. As Basinger reminds us, they were women who, "in their offscreen lives had climbed to the top in a difficult profession and who fought to stay there." As a consequence, especially in the case of Crawford, there is a combination of ambition and anger that together with her unconventional beauty—bony structure, large mouth—in time made her face become masklike, and her persona look like the embodiment of a suppressed rage. Vienna comes indeed very close to the personification of Crawford's *star persona*, being a woman who fought hard to get where she is ("I am not ashamed of how I got what I have"), who had to toughen up along the way, and who clings to what she has with all her might in a world made by men and for men, where she needs to *be* like a man, *act* like a man and *appear* like a man in order to survive.[62]

Pamela Robertson sees Crawford's *star persona* at the time of *Johnny Guitar* as the butch variation of the castrating woman, "a domineering shrew, jealous of women and competitive with men."[63] Some critics underline also the "blurring of gender boundaries and sexual identities ... character nuances and neuroses."[64] There is certainly a gender fluctuation in Vienna that is visually rendered by her transitions between male attires, regular female clothing (skirt, going to the bank) and an extremely feminine dress, pure white fluffy princess-like with ample skirt (before the lynching). The changes of costume, however, are not cosmetic. At times they corroborate her toughness (dressed like a man, threatening the lynching mob with a gun), and at others show her

Johnny Guitar: *The Filmic Text (1954)*

Johnny Guitar (Republic Pictures, 1954). Directed by Nicholas Ray. From left: Ernest Borgnine as Bart Lonergan, Ben Cooper as Turkey Ralston, Frank Marlowe (obscured) as Frank the bartender, Royal Dano as Corey, Joan Crawford as Vienna, and Scott Brady as the Dancin' Kid. Vienna, in cowboy attire and gun, confronts the posse and defends the Dancin' Kid and his gang (Photofest).

hidden vulnerability that comes out only in certain instances such as when injured Turkey pleads for his life, when she hugs in a *pietà*-like embrace the dying Tom, and when she realizes that Johnny hasn't changed, remaining gun-crazy. In these moments, her pride and strong will cannot cover up her feelings.

Vienna is of equal parts masculine and feminine, embodying a pretty evolved and balanced type of modern woman: transgressive, but capable of choosing; vulnerable, but courageous; aggressive, but tender; compassionate, but determined. The female/male dichotomy is re-created visually by Ray in Vienna's environment. The public space, the saloon, is stylish and elegant, all reddish wood, with gigantic chandeliers and spinning roulette wheels; it is the kingdom of business where Vienna makes money, while the upstairs is her private space. Her apartment is

4. Hybridity and (De)Construction of Femininity and Masculinity

elegant and refined—with white tablecloths, crystal glasses, bone china dishes and silver—and nobody is allowed up there unless invited. Vienna is clearly capable of keeping the public area, in which she is tough and masculine, separated from the private one, in which she is more vulnerable and feminine.

Vienna wears the frilly, virginal white gown when she confronts the lynching mob. In that moment she is masquerading herself as a respectful lady who plays the piano in her home ("I'm sitting here in my own house, minding my own business, playing my own piano") in order to convince McIvers and Emma that she is innocent (as she is).[65] She is offering herself as a spectacle of perfect femininity, making herself intelligible to them by playing a role they can identify with (and not as a challenging/castrating masculine figure). In this way she hopes to diffuse the situation, but, unfortunately, the discovery of the wounded Turkey in

Johnny Guitar (Republic Pictures, 1954). Directed by Nicholas Ray. Joan Crawford plays Vienna, dressed in a fluffy white dress; she fails to convince the posse/lynching mob that she is the picture of domesticity (Photofest).

Johnny Guitar: *The Filmic Text (1954)*

the saloon destroys Vienna's ploy. In the androgynous appearances of Vienna, we could be tempted to read signs of sexual ambiguity, in part corroborated by her visceral hate/relationship with Emma, but on the whole many factors of the filmic text work against reading too much into this interpretation.

Mercedes McCambridge as Emma, on the other end, in her sulfuric, above-the-lines acting as the antagonist of Vienna, opens the door to different gender readings including forms of lesbianism.[66] She appears most of the time in long dresses that envelope her like a nun, in black like an aging spinster, with nothing in her attire that denotes femininity. She definitely seems to be suffering from neurosis. We assume that she has been sexually repressed by the rules of "proper society." She is unmarried and not particularly sought after by men. She is rich and, therefore, her social position allows her to be able to be heard by the town men (McIvers and the hostile bunch) and, in her lynching frenzy, she finally acquires the power over men that she cannot have otherwise. She seems to be channeling her sexual frustrations into the obsessive persecution of her objects of desire. In this perspective, the Dancing Kid becomes a potential unattainable partner (both socially and morally), and Vienna becomes the female she would unconsciously like to be, sexually free and independent, something she would never be able to be. In a case of sour grapes, Emma hates and craves to destroy what she cannot have or be. As Vienna says, "She's in love with the Kid. He makes her feel like a woman and that frightens her." Vengeance becomes for Emma a way to unleash her frustrated sexual energy, placating it through acts of orgasmic violence—the screaming of commands while hanging Turkey, the hysteric laughing contemplating the flames devouring Vienna's saloon, the complacent grin when she wounds Vienna during the final duel. Emma exists in a sort of "gray zone" between masculinity and femininity, trapped in a no-man's land inhabited by only two passions, violence and xenophobia.[67]

If the "masculinization" of Vienna goes against the Western traditional formula, so does the "softening" of the male protagonist, Johnny, who arrives in town with a guitar and no guns, uses irony and words as weapons, speculates about love and dreams, disappears when the lynching mob arrives, and only toward the end of the movie plays the hero (saving Vienna). Sterling Hayden as Johnny turned out to be a good choice. Tall and handsome, he has an understated way of playing his character as a cowboy who knows how to deflate potentially explosive

4. Hybridity and (De)Construction of Femininity and Masculinity

situations. At Vienna's saloon when the hostile cattlemen, the sheriff and the Dancing Kid's bunch arrive, tension goes up. Everybody seems to be ready to start shooting, until Johnny, asking the Kid for a cigar and McIvers for a light, says, "Some men got the craving for gold and silver [looking at the Kid], others need lots of land with herds of cattle [staring at McIvers], and there are those who like whiskey and women" [glancing at Vienna and talking about himself], concluding, "When you boil it all down, what does a man really need? Just a good smoke and a cup of coffee."[68] Before starting to play his guitar, Johnny summarizes in a nutshell the drives and desires of every man in the saloon and somehow, through irony, shows them how a shooting would be unnecessary. Even without a gun, he beats Bart Lonergan in a fistfight before shooting the gun out of Turkey's hand, and, in the end, he kills evil Bart. He proves that he is a true Western hero (but with a less conservative understanding of the opposite sex).[69]

At the beginning of the movie, the opening credits start rolling while the harrowing musical score by Victor Young, containing the theme of Johnny Guitar's song, is heard over an establishing shot of reddish, rocky peaks and green trees.[70] In the first sequence, the camera (in long-shots) follows a rider on a white horse, carrying a guitar on his shoulders, who gets spooked by an explosion that blows the top of a nearby mountain apart. He keeps lazily riding on when he hears some shots and, from far away, watches a stagecoach robbery and a man killed down in the valley. He keeps on going, and finally arrives at a secluded saloon, Vienna's, in the middle of a terrible dust storm. If we consider this sequence as a sort of introduction to the story, it becomes evident that violence rules in this environment.

The opening sequence tells us exactly what to expect; this land is clearly a dangerous place full of surprises. All along a powerful orchestration of violent acts allures and excites the viewer. Chanslor's story is retained in a certain way, but its meaning and structure are re-orchestrated through Ray's filmic re-inscription of violence. The conflict between the groups follows a snow-balling progression from false accusation to ultimatum (McIvers' ultimatum to leave the town), from unjust lynching to hunting down, and ultimately to multiple shootouts. Violence as the result of deeply rooted economic/social conflicts ties Ray's story together, and can be considered more than a subtext, the canvas upon which the narration is weaved. Moving from subtext to subtext the discursive registers shift from economics (landowners

Johnny Guitar: *The Filmic Text (1954)*

versus railroad) to class (cattle barons versus emerging class) and from sexuality (interaction between Emma, The Dancing Kid, Johnny Guitar, and Vienna) to gender (male versus female). If Hollywood cinema, as J. David Slocum affirms, "through masculine protagonists, public conflicts and resolutions ... employs certain images of violence ... in the process of exploring and, for the most part, validating the prevailing ideology," it becomes clear that Ray did not follow this path with *Johnny Guitar*.[71]

Ray's film does not perpetuate given representations of gender, social relations/power structures, or subordination as we have demonstrated in our previous analysis of the filmic text. If the Western is about "men with guns," Ray has altered the cliché. At the end, two women, Emma and Vienna, confront each other in a duel; Emma wounds Vienna, but Vienna finishes Emma off. Rebellious individuals pitted against violent authority was not new in Hollywood cinema, but it was a novelty in a Western, especially because they negated Slotkin's idea of "regeneration through violence." The bad/good guys of Ray's film, the Dancing Kid gang, get eliminated, evil Emma gets killed, but the future of the community remains unknown. Will the landowners continue to hold their power through violence? Violence is used in the film to overcome competition and to affirm hierarchies, not to right wrongs, and not for the good of the society in general. The victims/marginal groups react and respond to violence, but only because they are forced to. The representation of violence in Ray's film runs counter the Western code because he has altered gender roles, turned the repressive authoritative patriarchal group into the bad guys, and, through the marginal rebellious groups, challenged the reactionary politics of the Cold War contemporary era.

Many critics complain about the title, claiming that the movie is more about Vienna than Johnny. We are inclined to think that Johnny is, with Vienna, the co-protagonist of the story, being the one who saves her from lynching; it is true that without him the story would not go on. It is also true, however, that throughout the film he keeps a distance and a sort of detachment from the action (to the Dancing Kid gang during the robbery: "I am a stranger here myself"), but he is the one who predicts what is going to happen and knows what to do. He tells Vienna that she needs to leave, or the posse will kill her. She does not listen to him, being determined to keep what is hers, and, as a result, she needs to be rescued by Johnny. Many critics would like Johnny to be more aggressive and overpowering, à la John Wayne, while Hayden's soft-spoken and

4. Hybridity and (De)Construction of Femininity and Masculinity

unassuming way of acting made him look too marginal.[72] As one critic rightly claims, it is obvious that Johnny is, "uninterested in any destiny, manifest or otherwise, except his own and Vienna's."[73]

Therefore, through Johnny, Ray has deconstructed the traditional masculinity of the Western hero, creating a gunslinger who prefers a guitar to a gun, is not concerned with the progress of society, and values his private life over everything else. He is certainly a man with unrealized dreams, bitter memories and a crave for love. On the other hand, we cannot forget that Johnny is, in reality, famous gunslinger Johnny Logan, even if for the majority of the film he is "masquerading" his masculinity and, like Vienna, shows a capacity for gender flexibility, adapting himself to different situations (irony and detachment in talking, strength and determination in fighting). He is a tough guy, but a more modern and complex one.[74] As Geoff Andrew affirms, "For Ray genre was merely a convenient tool, which could be ... distorted according to the demands of his subject: America was his canvas, upon which he painted subtle strokes of bold, angry, yet tender color, and movement to express his private feelings of isolation and despair. For him, the grasping insensitivity of his homeland, with its conformism and complacency, its capitalism and crime, was forever threatening to consume the confused outsider."[75]

Duel in the Sun *(1946): Paratext*

Duel in the Sun was released in 1946 and, if we had respected chronology, we would have considered it at the beginning of this chapter, but we did not.[76] The reason for having examined first *Rancho Notorious*, secondly *Johnny Guitar* and lastly *Duel in the Sun* is based on the "syndrome of progressive expansion" they exhibit. The few characters of *Rancho Notorious* become larger communities in *Johnny Guitar,* and finally embodiments of history and politics in *Duel in the Sun*. The love triangle of the first film, doubles up in the second, to enter, in the last one, many mirror-like reverberations. These universes keep enlarging themselves, englobing psychology, sexuality, taboos, race, gender, social classes, capitalism, patriarchy and politics in filmic texts that become so full that they bulge at the seams. Unlike many other reputable critics of the time, we are not implying here any negative critique, rather, we are underlining the increasing complexity of these productions.

Duel in the Sun *(1946): Paratext*

In 1947, Bosley Crowther wrote in *The New York Times* a scathing review of *Duel in the Sun*, affirming that "[Mr. Selznick's] multimillion-dollar Western is a spectacularly disappointing job.... Most of the picture is devoted to the romantic quirks of a tawny-skinned Scarlett O'Hara who wants the noble brother with her heart, but can't help loving the scoundrel with her notably feeble flesh."[77] The movie, in spite of the many negative reviews, was a huge box-office success, even if it had gone over budget and had cost Selznick more than $6 million dollars.[78]

David O. Selznick was a Hollywood mogul and famous producer. In 1923, he started working as an MGM script reader. In 1933, he married Irene Mayer, daughter of Louis B. Mayer, owner of MGM, and in 1936 set up his own production company: Selznick International. During his career, he fully immersed himself in the films he produced to the point of functioning as director (often uncredited) and scriptwriter. He managed to "father" extremely successful films that have become classics such as *Gone with the Wind* (1939, directed by Victor Fleming, eight Oscars) and *Rebecca* (1940, directed by Alfred Hitchcock, two Oscars); between 1923 and 1957 he produced a total of 87 films. The life, career, and passion for cinema of David O. Selznick is documented in two big volumes: *Showman* by David Thomson and *Memo from David O. Selznick*, edited by Rudy Behlmer.[79]

As in the case of *Johnny Guitar*, many factors, private and public, intertwined in the making of *Duel in the Sun*. In 1941, Selznick had met a young, gorgeous, aspiring actress in New York, whose name he would change to Jennifer Jones. In a few years he would turn her into a Hollywood star and eventually, after a long affair and a troublesome divorce, would marry her in 1949.[80] By 1944 Selznick wanted to make a "huge picture" that matched his reputation and would equate his previous successes. He wanted it in Technicolor with epic scenes and, above all, wanted "to display Jennifer's sexual splendor on the screen."[81]

Niven Busch, an old friend of Selznick's, had written a novel in 1944 titled *Duel in the Sun* that had not been a big hit when published, but he had sold the rights to RKO and was screenwriting it. Selznick got interested in a role for Jennifer and thought that she would be perfect in the part of the "mixed-blood" Pearl Chavez, the heroine of the story who disrupts the life of the McCanles brothers with her beauty and sex-appeal. Selznick did not like the end of the story, so, in 1945, he bought the rights and started to re-write the screenplay.[82] He hired King Vidor as

4. Hybridity and (De)Construction of Femininity and Masculinity

director and cast Gregory Peck and Joseph Cotton respectively as Lewt and Jesse McCanles.[83] The script, however, became an endless work in progress: It started at 170 pages and grew to 199. Selznick changed scene after scene, claiming that they were not capturing Jennifer's sexual glory, and interfered with the making of the movie so much that six months into the shooting, the director (King Vidor) walked off the picture, and Selznick had to hire another director, William Dieterle, to finish the movie.[84]

When the film was released in December 1946, it was dubbed "Lust in the dust." It was rebuked by moral guardians, had problems with censorship, appalled critics and was considered scandalous in general because of its treatment of sexuality. The movie credited King Vidor as director but was very much the creation of Selznick as shown by the many memos that he wrote to Vidor, to his successors (William Dieterle, and Otto Brower, Reeves Eason, second unit directors), and to all the filmmaking personnel including Dimitri Tiomkin who wrote the musical score.[85] These letters reveal the passion, the obsession and the controlling megalomania of Selznick, who pushed everybody to the limits, as the below excerpt shows:

> I financed my pictures myself, and make them myself, and I have been on the set constantly with only the finest directors in the business, and you are certainly not familiar with my operations if you think that anybody working for me could for one moment keep me away from my pictures in any of their stages. Furthermore, Mr. Vidor was thoroughly aware that ... there were strict orders on the set that not a single scene was to be photographed, and not even a single angle of a single scene, until I was telephoned to come down on the set to check the lighting, the setup, and the rehearsal. ... I would then not merely check the exact direction of the scene, and ninety-nine times out of one hundred change it, but I would stay until I personally approved a take.[86]

If we examine Selznick's communications together with a lecture he gave at Columbia University in 1937 titled "The Functions of the Producer and the Making of Feature Films," it becomes evident that *Duel in the Sun* is indeed a case in which the producer overpowered the director (and everybody else on the set), and became the principal creative force behind the film, from screenwriting to distribution.[87] *Duel in the Sun* is, therefore, an unusual case, a movie that stemmed from public and private influences, and an over-the-top epic Western that contains too much. It is imperative, at his point, to look at the original text, Niven Busch's novel, to grasp the many transformations that Selznick imposed on the filmic story.[88] This analysis will help us to make sense of the contrasting critical positions that still proliferate, and to understand why the movie is considered an uneven melodrama, worth watching, but overdone, daring for its time, but still sizzling with sexual undertones.[89]

Duel in the Sun: *The Novel (1944)*

The story is narrated in the third person by an omniscient narrator and starts *in medias res*, recounting a period of the life of the heroine, Pearl Chavez, when she was riding alone through the vast empire of Senator McCanles, an enormous ranch called the Spanish Bit. From the incipit, we learn that Pearl does not behave as girls are supposed to: "She came and went in that land without women with as little notice as a man, always on a good horse, neither loafing nor in a hurry. ... She'd stop and eat at any line riders' camp she ran across—a custom that her uncle's foremen never encouraged, but to which they gradually became accustomed."[90] After a few paragraphs, we discover that this unusual girl has inherited beauty and Indian blood from her mother's side, she is very poor, and she had been sent to live with her rich cousins after the untimely, violent death of her father.[91] Here, the story of what happened to Pearl begins to unfold. We go back to a moment in 1883 when, at twelve years old, she arrived in town on the Dodge-El Paso stagecoach, and we stop again in 1889 when, happily married to Jesse McCanles, she leaves the territory to start a new existence elsewhere.[92]

As in the case of Chanslor's novel, *Johnny Guitar*, all the plot components of the fictional text reappear in the filmic one, but they become more complex because psychology and politics enter the fray. Busch's plot is basically a romance complicated by social differences, set at the time of the conflict between the railroad empire and the large landowners of Texas. Pearl is seduced by Lewt, the wild, but charming son of the senator. She falls for him and wants to be "bespoken" because, since arriving at the ranch, she has felt like an outsider, being poor and of mixed heritage. When she realizes that young Lewt wants to keep the relationship secret, she decides to marry an older cowboy, foreman Sam Pierce. The day of the wedding, Lewt, out of jealousy, shoots Sam, thus becoming a wanted man. The young cowboy flees and starts robbing stagecoaches and trains, condemning himself to a life on the run. Pearl tracks him down to kill him out of revenge, but she falls for him again

4. Hybridity and (De)Construction of Femininity and Masculinity

and starts riding with him. They both get caught by a posse and end up in prison. Lewt escapes from jail, helped by his two other brothers and his father, but Pearl refuses to escape with him, claiming she is too sick. Jesse, the good son of the McCanles (a lawyer, ostracized by the senator because he sided with the railroad) defends her in court, even if she is, in part, guilty. Pearl is acquitted and falls in love with Jesse, but, just before her wedding, receives a letter from Lewt. Afraid of being chased by him and of succumbing to him again, she tracks him down and kills him. Finally, free from the clutches of the obsessive passion that chained her to Lewt, she marries Jesse.

The novel is a traditional romance set in a western environment, in which the differences among social classes come to the fore in the relationship between Pearl and the McCanles. The patriarch, Senator McCanles, detests Pearl because he considers her the ruin of his son, Lewt. His wife, a Southern belle from a rich plantation family, tries to show Pearl how to behave in society, convincing her that Lewt would not be a good match for her, and claiming that her husband would never allow someone of mixed-race to marry into his powerful family. The outcome of the story, however, contradicts Mrs. McCanles' prediction. In the end, Pearl does marry a McCanles, even though he is disinherited.

Lewt seems interested in having fun with Pearl and with gambling, riding, and shooting. He is divided between feelings for her that he cannot comprehend and dreams of freedom and adventure; he is oblivious to any class difference and even to his father's will. Jesse, on the other hand, even though he fought for the railroad in opposition to his family, throws away his career as a future statesman and railroad representative when he decides to defend Pearl. Class, politics, love and sex all play a part in the story, but the ideas and desires that move the main protagonists remain vague. What drives them is mentioned, but never developed. The novel has a happy ending both for the romantic couple (Jesse and Pearl) and for the McCanles family; they lose a son but continue to prosper under the guidance of a younger sibling, Gil McCanles.

In the story Pearl appears as a young woman who knows that she was born "on the wrong side of the tracks." She is of mixed race and poor, with no education or skills like most women of the time. She is conscious of attracting men; she knows that she wants to become a "respected" member of society, and that the only way she can do it is through marriage. She acts wildly and does respond to the violent advances of Lewt. She is passionate, but sex outside wedlock is not what she wants. Feeling

Duel in the Sun: *The Filmic Text (1946)*

the oppression of patriarchy and the weight of racism, she feels guilty about her sexuality. She wants to escape her lower social and racial condition through marriage. She is even willing to marry an honorable, but much older man, Sam Pierce, even if she does not love him, to reach her goal. So, despite the unusual construction of femininity (a woman who rides like a man and can use a gun), Busch creates a character who is trying to conform more than to rebel. In the end, all her issues get resolved by a happy marriage and a move to the frontier where nobody knows her and everybody is foreign, immigrated and eager to start anew. Busch uses the traditional happy ending as a sponge to erase any possible racial and class evils.

The male characters in the story all seem to be incapable of introspection. The patriarch is moved mostly by the desire to maintain his cattle empire. Lewt cannot figure out why he kills for Pearl. Jesse seems unaware of his attraction for the girl almost until the end of the novel. Both Lewt and Jesse recur to violence to solve threats to their macho sense of honor when dealing with the opposite sex—the first kills a man in cold blood, and the other plans to kill both Lewt and Pearl if she goes back to his brother. The brothers' masculinity exhibits all the characteristics of authorial patriarchy: For them to love is to own. The larger political issue, the battles between railroad and cattle barons, government and landowners, industrialists and agrarians, is left dangling in the story as a backdrop and is never explored or resolved one way or another.

Duel in the Sun: *The Filmic Text (1946)*[93]

Selznick changed the end of the novel and had Pearl and Lewt shoot each other in a big conflagration of love and hate, as it should be in any serious case of *amour fou*.[94] If *Johnny Guitar* exhibited a showdown between two women, here we face a duel to the death between two lovers. The happy end of the traditional Western formula was not only subverted by Selznick—it was "perverted" through deadly eroticism. The film, like the novel, remains centered on the heroine, the "mixed-blood" Pearl Chavez (beautiful and sexy Jennifer Jones), and her relationship with the McCanles family. As in the novel, the interactions between all the characters revolve around desire, gender, race and class, but these items get explored more in depth in the filmic melodrama. The identities of the main characters are determined in the movie by their social

4. Hybridity and (De)Construction of Femininity and Masculinity

position, and the gender relationships, influenced by social hierarchies, reveal the hypocrisy of the patriarchal family.

Duel in the Sun is a film that narrates how patriarchy operates, how it oppresses both sexes and how only the ones who conform can live a happy and prosperous life. As David Lusted notes, "A central trope of melodrama is the dramatic connection between social and psychic repression, leading to an excess of misery in the central protagonist."[95] The "excess of misery" is exactly what troubles Pearl; in her desperation, or in her "hysteria," the spectator needs to read social oppression, psychic repression and desire for change.[96] Pearl is never happy in the film because all her attempts at inclusion are rebuked by the ruling class. She knows she is an outcast because of race, marginalized because of poverty, and uneducated, thus, she is totally dependent on the good heart of the McCanles family. Pearl's impossibility to enter the symbolic order triggers her hysteria, and prevents her from enjoying the outcome of her powerful sensuality because the moral dichotomy between *madonna* and whore weighs on her shoulders. Should she be a "good girl" and be chaste like her father advised and Mrs. McCanles hopes? Or should she commit sin following her desire like her mother did? Pearl is a woman trapped in a world where men make the rules, and even if she tries to rebel against this order, she never manages to escape it. The young woman drifts socially and morally between platonic love for Jesse and passionate love for Lewt, between the "good boy" and the "bad boy," because she has no guidance, no positive models to follow. In her misery, however, she is not alone. Every main character seems to be victimized by the symbolic order. Ultimately, the film is about how patriarchy as social paradigm breeds unhappiness in all areas of human life for male and female subjects alike.

The expressionistic use of the Technicolor surpasses the one of *Johnny Guitar*. Bright orange rocks, red sky, and bleaching sun permeate the landscape together with the many *chiaroscuro* of the interior shots filmed on set. The vivid colors of Pearl's attire scream her ethnicity. Her ample, colorful gipsy-skirts, her sleeveless shirts, her cleavage and her provocative way of walking broadcast sensuality. She is excessive, but she is like a magnet, irresistible, and as "wild as a bobcat," as Lewt asserts. In watching the film, the viewers forget the almost cartoonish vividness of the colors and the stage-like acting of the protagonists, because the drama of the two lovers caught and racked by passion, pride, and revenge overpowers all the other aspects of the film.

Patriarchy and Failed Masculinities

Duel in the Sun **(Selznick Releasing Organization, 1946). Directed by King Vidor (and Otto Brower). Jennifer Jones is Pearl Chavez and Gregory Peck is Lewton "Lewt" McCanles. The two lovers first shoot each other, and then die together in a final embrace (Photofest).**

The movie opens with a prologue (voice-over by Orson Welles) that frames the story and transforms it into a legend of two doomed lovers who died in a last embrace at Squaw's Head Rock after having shot each other. The same bright sky over the arid landscape that opens the film reappears in the end. The red sun is the visual equivalent of the burning and sizzling passion of Lewt and Pearl, consumed by the flames of Eros and Thanatos.

Patriarchy and Failed Masculinities

In spite of the central romance of *Duel in the Sun*, if we analyze the filmic text we realize that it is, in reality, a study of the effects of two types of patriarchal control: the ferocious, old-fashioned ruling of Senator McCanles, and the more democratic, but paternalistic

4. Hybridity and (De)Construction of Femininity and Masculinity

style of his son, Jesse McCanles. Both authoritative orders bring negative consequences to the subjects and to the rulers themselves. The brutal, tyrannical, and racist old Senator McCanles governs his family and his empire with an iron fist through force and coercion. Despising Pearl for her Indian heritage (he jokes about her name, the color of her skin, and the way she dresses), the senator prohibits Lewt from marrying Pearl because he does not want to have his empire transformed into an "In'jun reservation." It is this ideological set of beliefs that eventually destroys Lewt. Pearl, tired of being kept marginal, decides to marry Sam Pierce. Lewt kills him, becoming an outlaw without ever asking himself where the maddening jealousy that pushed him to kill a man in cold blood comes from. Trapped between the discriminating class system of the senator and the racial politics of his society, Lewt is doomed to take the path of violence once he realizes that lying to Pearl and promising to marry her does not work anymore. Lewt's mental makeup prevents him from comprehending fully what he feels for Pearl, so much so that he manages to express his true feelings only on the verge of death when any ideological construct gets peeled off by the finality of the moment and the truth comes out:

> LEWT (*bleeding to death, being shot twice*): Pearl, no use of lying no more, I am through, Pearl! Can you hear me? I am dying, I am going fast! Come up! I want to see you, I got to see you, where are you? Hurry! I got to hold you just one more before.... I love you, I LOVE YOU! Hurry, honey.... PEARL!
> PEARL (*crawling among the rocks toward Lewt, mortally wounded*): Lewt, hold on, Lewt, hold on, wait for me, I love you, I love you! I had to do it!
> LEWT: Of course you did, don't cry, don't cry, let me hold you, little bobcat. [He dies and she dies holding him].

Throughout the film, Lewt treats Pearl as a possession, an object to take and drop at his whim: "Pearl Chavez is my girl, and she will always be my girl, until I decide she is not." Prone to daring acts, Lewt uses violence to stop those who threaten to take Pearl away from him, without ever looking into the origins of his love/obsession/jealousy/lust and without ever considering Pearl's feelings or desires. He convinces himself (and the senator) that he "is just having a good time" with Pearl. However, in spite of his socially and economically privileged position, he is as much a victim of the white male order as Pearl is, an order that prohibits crossing racial lines in fear of miscegenation.[97]

Jesse, on the other hand, respects Pearl and is generous with her, even offering to send her to school. He is a lawyer who believes in the law, in progress (he is in favor of the railroad), and in peaceful resolutions of conflicts. He is a product of a "new order" or enlightened capitalism. He is the offspring of a new entrepreneurial class very distant from the senator's feudal idea of ruling by force. On the whole, Jesse is a more positive character than Lewt or the senator, but ineffectual just the same. Despite his good feelings, he fails Pearl. His desire to turn Pearl into a "lady" is a generic idea that involves learning "how to waltz, wear pretty dresses, make small talk" and, we suspect, above all, learning the "proper role" of a woman in respectable society. If Lewt treats Pearl as a possession, Jesse treats her as a pretty decoration, something beautiful to admire and keep around. Under close scrutiny, Jesse, is not very dissimilar from his brother Lewt when it comes to the other sex. Peeling away his mild manners and his kindness, we discover that he loves Pearl, but leaves her because he cannot forget or forgive her for having had sex with Lewt ("I don't think I will be able to forget," he says to Pearl). As a consequence, he decides to marry a "lady," the white, insipid, but well-bred rich daughter of the railroad magnate and totally domesticated Helen, a mirror image of his mother, Laura Belle.

Lewt and Jesse are both the byproducts of male hegemonic order, with Lewt embodying the more virulent side (more in line with the senator), and Jesse the gentler kind. If Lewt is a man caught between his sexual desires and the restrains imposed by his social class, Jesse has a more fluid identity. He migrates from one symbolic order to another, adapting to the new codes, transforming himself into a man who deems social position and political career more important than love (he will become governor) and giving priority to his public life over his private one (marrying Helen can be construed as a tactical move for his career).

The outcome of this duality is in both cases unsavory. The hegemonic code is so powerful that it prevents both these characters from exploring their true feelings. Everybody is victimized. Lewt does not go public with his love for Pearl and triggers a series of events that force him into a life on the run; Jesse does not have the courage to declare his love to Pearl and so he loses her. The message of the movie is indeed subversive. It is a denunciation of the dangers of patriarchal domination.[98]

Douglas Brode points out that the machismo of men like old Senator McCanles and his son Lewt, men who spend all their life attempting to live up to a code decided by an arch conservative society that prescribes fixed roles on men and women—repressing their inner sensitivity—triggers chaos and ends up tragically.[99] The senator in the film is crippled by

4. Hybridity and (De)Construction of Femininity and Masculinity

a horse-riding incident, but he is also emotionally crippled by his incapacity to show his true feelings toward his wife. Only when Laura Belle is about to die does the senator confess he always loved her, even if he has spent his entire life pretending to hate her and fearing she loved another man (Pearl's father, an educated, more sensitive fellow). The senator himself is a victim of the same passion—unbridled jealousy—that has turned Lewt into a murderer. Both the senator and Lewt want to own the women they love. They want to put their brand on them. The other male figures of importance in the film also represent failed masculinities. Pearl's father (Herbert Marshall as Scott Chavez) is an outcast who, having lost fortune and social status by marrying an Indian woman, is considered a "renegade squaw man" by his peers.[100] The Rev. Jubal Crabbe, the Sinkiller (Walter Huston), appears as a lecherous old man who administers faith with the butt of his revolver and is more moved by the looks of Pearl than by his duty of keeping her on the right path.

Patriarchy and Failed Femininities

Robin Wood says Selznick had an interest in women-centered melodramas, in women who struggle to survive in a world where men made the rules. According to the critic, there is a fascination in Selznick's films with transgressive women.[101] In *Duel in the Sun*, Selznick certainly continued this tradition. The young woman at the center of the film is no traditional role model, being pulled between primitive drives and the desire to suppress them. These two aspects of her personality are the reflections of her two role-model mothers: the wild biological Indian mother and the adopted mother, ladylike Laura Belle. Laura Belle has been playing the role of the proper and submissive wife, bringing only unhappiness to herself, while the Indian mother has been killed by her husband for her exuberant sexuality. Both women embody a failed form of femininity. As a result, Pearl, trapped between these two models, oscillates all along between being a good girl as Laura Belle wants and following her passionate instincts like her mother did, between "becoming a lady" or continuing on the path of her dead mother. These two identities are alternating constantly inside Pearl. When being lady like wins, she is pulled toward Jesse, when the wild side wins she is pushed toward Lewt.

Pearl's two mothers are both flawed role models. The biological one

Patriarchy and Failed Femininities

is like a destructive force of nature; she is the "Other," the wild native, alluring, but dangerous, the one that can be colonized by the white male, but if she cannot be controlled she needs to be suppressed, and, in fact, she gets killed by her husband because of her illicit behavior.[102] In spite of her high social status, Laura Belle's wealth and her "being a lady" is terribly ineffectual in her family and, even if she has been a nurturer, a proper wife, a perfect mother and everything else the dominant discourse required, she is victimized by her husband. She is the embodiment of the "proper lady," but she is frustrated, unhappy, repressed, and naïve. Facing these failed femininities, Pearl is doomed to become transgressive, and, despite the many promises she makes to Laura Belle to be a "good girl," she remains wild, being too passionate to endure the rules of patriarchy with patience and submission.

While romance between the cowboy and his sweetheart in Westerns usually reassures the viewers that, regardless of the changes in their society, the hegemonic order on which their life turns remains secure, interracial romance erodes that certainty. The sexualized maidens challenge notions of chastity and moderation, testing the boundaries of gender and social behavior.[103] These tainted blood women challenge class with their desire to exit marginality, marrying into white society, and threatening miscegenation. Pearl wants to marry Lewt, but such a union is considered a sin by the patriarchy because, besides disrupting racial laws, it also goes against class relations between dominant and dominated groups. In prohibiting Lewt from marrying Pearl, Senator McCanles is stopping an inferior subject (for race, gender and wealth) from entering into a white, rich, powerful class. On the other hand, the senator approves of the relationship as long as Lewt has "a good time" with the sexualized maiden outside of the official social circuits. In constructing these unjust dynamics Selznick ingeniously showed the ruinous results of deviant behaviors, punishing the lovers with death, while letting the virtuous conformist couple (Jesse and Helen) survive on one hand while, on the other, in turning the deviant behavior of Pearl and Lewt into a legend, he celebrated the mad lovers.

At the beginning of the film, the voice-over describes Pearl as "a wild flower sprung from the hard clay, quick to blossom and early to die." With this elegiac narration, the doomed love story enters the mythical, the everlasting, in which existing social codes and moral structures no longer have importance. In this way, Selznick tested the boundaries of hierarchy and gender, pushed the envelope of morality, sex and race,

4. Hybridity and (De)Construction of Femininity and Masculinity

celebrating a romance that, by the standard of his era, was inappropriate.[104]

Another woman important in the overall structure of the film, for delineating a generally accepted way of living that includes racism as the "norm," is Vashti (Butterfly McQueen), the negro maid of Mrs. McCanles. Vashti does not have enough screen time to influence Pearl as an example of femininity, but as the whiny, empty-headed Negro servant—a character-type resumed from *Gone with the Wind* (1939)—she does prove that in a subtle and almost kind manner, all the members of the McCanles family are racists. Everybody treats the maid as an underdeveloped human being who needs to be tolerated, but who needs to be sent on her way as soon as possible. Mrs. McCanles often shakes her head at Vashti and tells Pearl that she cannot even learn the basics. Vashti's function is comic relief. With her out of place comments, she makes the viewer smile and diffuses the tension on screen. However, because everybody, including Pearl, is intellectually and socially superior to Vashti in the household, the implied assumption is that all black people are, like the maid, deficient and inferior.[105] Furthermore, the facts that she cannot read or write and that she is continually reminded by Mrs. McCanles to "go about your business" without asking questions, shows us that Vashti is forced to remain underdeveloped and invisible and, as a consequence, is condemned to a serving condition and to submission

Duel in the Sun **(Selznick Releasing Organization, 1946). Directed by King Vidor (and Otto Brower). Gregory Peck is Lewt McCanles and Jennifer Jones is Pearl Chavez. The medium shot emphasizes the violent nature of their passion, made of lust, love, shame and revenge (Photofest).**

(when she talks everybody routinely interrupts her before she finishes speaking). The racial "Others" in the film, Pearl and Vashti are both tolerated, but contained in their social underclass niches.

According to Stanley Corkin, melodramas have "the potential to exact an emancipatory power through their capacity to trigger a level of response that accesses emotion, to allow the viewer an affective identification with those who have been subjugated."[106] It is clear that in the film the highly dramatic final showdown triggers a high level of response in the viewer who identifies with the vanquished ones. As the critic suggests, by casting the way in which patriarchy subjugates the ones who do not conform in terms that trigger pathos, "the text is instrumental in bringing about a feeling of outrage for the injustice that is being dramatized" on the screen.[107]

Capitalism and Patriotism

Selznick wanted to have many "epic scenes" in *Duel in the Sun*. Most of these scenes are part of the sequences in which the senator and his private army of cowboys converge at the east side of his ranch to block the passing of the railroad. Hundreds of riders are filmed in long shots, galloping over hills and converging in a valley; long tracking shots focus on the horses' legs moving at full speed. At the picket line we observe hundreds of coolies working for the railroad, watching Senator McCanles' approaching army with apprehension, but when the conflict seems to explode the cavalry enters the scene and hundreds of mounted soldiers gallop in, lining up along the fence to protect the railroad people. The movements of the various parties are filmed mostly in long shots that capture the impressive use of men and horses. These sequences, together with other long shots of large herds of cattle crossing the railroads going north to be sold and large groups of wild horses about to be corralled, please the eye of the spectator and reinforce the idea that the senator rules over immense wealth.

Even though Senator McCanles displays an impressive force, the railroad goes through. The conflict between the railroad magnate and McCanles is avoided because the latter is overwhelmed by patriotic feelings and declares that he cannot shoot at soldiers holding the flag of the United States under which he had previously fought. The senator's surge of emotion and sense of national identity is organized in a

4. Hybridity and (De)Construction of Femininity and Masculinity

shot-reverse shot sequence in which the camera for a few seconds captures in medium shot a soldier holding a huge Stars and Stripes banner with a flag waving in the wind. It is at this moment, that Jesse crosses the picket line and changes camp, siding with the politicians and railroad tycoon, ostracizing himself from his family, and opening up a new trajectory for his life and career. The conflict between railroad and landowners, between industrialists and cattle barons recalls many historical conflicts and fits well in the construction of the epic scenes; it is also in line with the Western classic formula that requires some form of clash on which to articulate the narrative.[108]

Senator McCanles represents a form of old-fashioned capitalist/patriarchal authority that has accumulated material wealth, securing through violence a vast portion of virgin land, and maintained his conquest through subordination. The senator has conquered and colonized the land, and he intends to hold on to his empire no matter what. Jesse, on the other hand, understands that technology is changing the dynamics of power, that the predatory patriarchal mode of his father is soon to be replaced by a new ideology, a new form of capitalism, a more democratic one, based on respect for the law, reforms and progress, a system not necessarily less predatory, but organized in different ways (Jesse to the senator: "I want one McCanles to give to the state instead of taking from it!"). Jesse embodies a form of benevolent paternalism. Slotkin defines paternalism as an ideology that "involves the projection onto social and political realms of the values and power relationships," characteristics of a traditional (read "idealized") family. "The ruler of the microcosm is a benign, but powerful father, whose moral authority and political legitimacy is authenticated by the natural sentiments of spousal and filial affection and respect. The father mitigates the rigor of his authorship by the essential affectionate and protective attitude toward his dependents; and the dependents, for their part, accept their place in his universe [willingly, without rebellion]."[109]

From the above, it becomes clear that both orders, the old and the new, demand submission. The only difference is that the latter is less violent than the former. In this panorama, the viewer concludes that even Jesse, as the more positive character of the story, is not so perfect after all. He still commands obedience. We are left wondering, who then are the real heroes/heroines of the filmic text? Pearl, tainted by the stigma of blood and unbridled passion, remains the purest soul of all, the only one capable of sacrifice. She kills Lewt to save Jesse. In her last act she destroys herself only to realize that Lewt is her true love and the wild mate she always wanted.[110]

To conclude, we want to highlight how *Rancho Notorious*, *Johnny Guitar* and *Duel in the Sun* "manipulate the sense of virtue and evil to render a form of suffering visible, shifting the composition of the community."[111] These films provide an interesting outlook on femininity, masculinity, sex, race, and class that dazzles our senses, and tickles our fancy with a spectacle of epic, erotic and violent scenes, with a discursive register that keeps shifting from class to sexuality to race, thanks to a clever orchestration between story, structure and moving image. These films are not failed Westerns as many critics affirm; they are hybrids that have exceeded the boundaries of the Western genre, smuggling into it romance and melodrama and altering the archetypal formula of good versus evil with incursions into psychology, class domination, and race.[112]

5

New Paths of the Western in the Third Millennium
The Lone Ranger, *Yesterday and Today*

The Western Genre Today

To start a discussion on contemporary Westerns, one should consider whether and how the films of the third millennium constitute a legacy of the past, or to what extent they mark a radical shift from it instead. Steve Neale affirms that "genres are inherently temporal: hence, their inherent mutability on the one hand and their inherent historicity on the other."[1] If "genres do not follow a schema of growth, flowering and decay," we must conclude that the diminishing number of Westerns made in the last decades, when compared with the big production of the 1950s, is not something connected to the permanent "exhaustion" of the genre, because the genre can rejuvenate itself constantly, being the result of "*processes* ... dominated by repetition, but ... also marked fundamentally by difference, variation, and change."[2] As Neale, quoting Jauss, writes, when genres lose their "effective power through continual reproduction, they are forced to the periphery by new genres often arising from a 'vulgar' stratum, if they cannot be reanimated through a restructuring (be it through the playing up of previously suppressed themes ... or through the taking up of materials or the taking over of functions from other genres)."[3] To this effect the function of hybridization in the formation of genres is of key importance and, as a consequence, "change" becomes a key factor in examining the general health of a given genre. After Neale, we can conclude that there is no danger of an imminent death of the Western genre because the genre has been renewing itself all along in spite of the decreasing output.

The Western Genre Today

It must be noted, though, that the use of the term "change" in this chapter does not imply "evolution,"[4] in the sense of birth, flourishing and death, but a process of constant development. In the beginning (that for most critics was 1939) the American cowboy embodied the values of puritan society, celebrating the "making" of a nation, and hiding the extermination of the natives under the "epic of the conquest." In the immediate post-war era, Westerns tried to renegotiate their "guilty conscience" in paternalistic films in which the Indians were allowed some more screen time and space. From the 1960s on, the myth of a "world in which justice always prevails and violence regenerates" was debunked by films like *The Professionals* (1966) and *The Wild Bunch* (1969). Unscrupulous capitalists embodied the idea of progress and criminals, who were morally superior to the lawmen who chased them, became the "heroes:" to believe in a just world was no longer possible, not even on screen. In the same years, the cynicism of Sergio Leone's anti-heroes shattered the archetype of the West. The frontier became a land of prevarication in which only the cleverest and fastest survived, where the process of acquiring personal wealth could lead to a few good deeds, and John Wayne was replaced by Clint Eastwood, a more up-to-date "anti-hero."[5] By the time the Vietnam war ended, counter-culture and battles for human and civil rights caused a re-visitation of "history" on screen, generating a long string of films that revaluated Native Americans [from *Soldier Blue* (1970) to *Dances with Wolves* (1990)]. The 1990s saw a string of very successful Westerns, ranging from an ambitious treatment of violence in *Unforgiven* (1992), women as gunfighters in *The Ballad of Little Jo* (1993), *Bad Girls* (1994), and *The Quick and the Dead* (1995), to more traditional features like *Tombstone* (1993), *Wyatt Earp* (1994), and *Wild Bill* (1995). Because these films were made by renowned directors, featured stars, and won awards, the decade has been celebrated as a "revival" period.[6] Since then, the number of Westerns made every year between 1990 and 2017 has been small, but not insignificant.[7]

Peter Falconer maintains that, in the past few decades, the Western genre seems to have entered an "afterlife" or a "more marginal, residual mode of generic existence in which older meanings and resonances face very different conditions of popular interest and understanding."[8] There seems to be, according to the critic, uncertainty about the commercial viability of Western productions, and about the contemporary audiences' capacity to appreciate these films.[9] As a result, contemporary

5. New Paths of the Western in the Third Millennium

incarnations of the genre tend to bridge such a historical gap through an accurate, almost obsessive, iconographic abundance of period details, and often through a retrospective narration (i.e., *True Grit*, 2010; *The Lone Ranger*, 2013) in which our access to the past is mediated by the memory of an older narrator who has had a more direct connection with it,[10] an interesting point of view that describes well the narrative pattern of the 2013 version of *The Lone Ranger*.

To sum up, most critics see the genre as a trajectory of films that started in the silent era as horse operas, evolved into classics between 1939 and the 1960s, then acquired more complexity and looked at the American past under a revisionist lens from the 1970s on (revisionist/post–Western), and eventually started to decrease in number and popularity.[11] As tempting as it might be for studying purposes to neatly divide the Western production in well-defined slots, we prefer to consider the Western as a fictional *space* in which at different times contemporary values/worries/ideals/attitudes/desires were inserted into stories set into the past (mostly the frontier between 1860 and 1890). These stories though were a way to talk about the present, especially if one assumes, with Jameson, that our reading of the past always depends on our experience of the present.[12] It is undeniable, however, that the mythology of the frontier (Manifest Destiny, national identity, nature of justice, regeneration through violence, white heroes) prevailed in most of the Westerns made during the studio system (1939–60), less so from the 1960s on, but even nowadays it is possible to make good Westerns imbued with traditional values such as *Open Range* (2003), *Appaloosa* (2008), and *The Salvation* (2014).[13]

Carter is dubious of the "extent to which the cinematic Western wholeheartedly endorsed either the triumphalist version of Anglo-American history *or* the dominant contemporary ideologies prevalent at any given period," and he discourages any view of the Western as "a servile accomplice to dominant ideologies."[14] Certainly, as Jameson notes, a cultural artifact as a symbolic act contains more than the dominant narrative promoted by the text, because a variety of subtexts often disclose contradictions, subversions, displacements, incongruences, and marginalized voices reduced to silence that resist the hegemonic message.[15] However, any filmic text is bound to convey some form of message or worldview to the viewer.

If establishing the survival of the genre is a positive step, this affirmation does not solve another problem that has to do with our contemporary commodified society that caters to specific sectors of consumers, and tends to repeat only commercially successful filmic formulas to maximize financial gain. In our post-industrial society, filmic production seems to be intended for consumer consumption, and to be channeled towards blockbuster productions.[16] According to many, the Western with all its correlations of myth-making has migrated into other Hollywood genres like action movies or science-fiction (e.g., *Star Wars* and similar) and that is why its production is dwindling.[17] As Miller and Van Riper note: "The numerous dramatic elements that the science-fiction and the Western genres hold in common—loner heroes exploring the unknown, encounters with exotic 'Others,' and expansive settings that begin where civilization ends—make it easy to export traditional Western plots and characters into outer space."[18] Especially because in outer space the conflict between good versus evil can be stripped to the bare bone, and the archetypal can be de-politicized and reduced to a basic fairy tale kernel.

Enter The Lone Ranger: *Prologue*

One of the most successful franchises of all time, "The Lone Ranger" started in 1933 on the radio, transitioned to television in 1949, to feature films in 1956–1958, and in 1981 migrated, always very successfully through the decades, into pulp novels, comic books, various merchandise (outfits, board games, buttons, pocket knives, etc.), fan clubs, and cartoons.[19] Its characters, the Lone Ranger and Tonto, are icons that contributed to creating and popularizing the Western genre through generations of viewers.[20] For having created a fantasy West—an adventurous and mythical image of how the West was conquered—it is important to compare the 1949–57 television series of the Lone Ranger with the 2013 remake made by Verbinski that turned out to be critically and commercially disappointing.[21] Using adaptation theory, we are going to show how the critics misread the film, and how Verbinski reformulated the story of the Lone Ranger to create a West that, paradoxically, ended up being less "fictional" than the original one of the 1950s television.

Verbinski's *The Lone Ranger* is a *sui generis* adaptation of a classic televisual text and famous icon of popular culture. It is not a classic case of novel to film, but a non-canonical adaptation from a televisual serial text to a feature film, a process in which the hypotext (the 1950s *Lone Ranger* TV episodes) was remade and condensed into a 149-minute film. In so doing, the director faced the problem of adding, compressing or subtracting from the original narrative, but at the same time he enjoyed more freedom and a wider possibility of choices than if the hypotext were a novel.[22] If Verbinski escaped from the restrictions caused by the "devotion of the author's words," he still had to worry about the creation of a new filmic text that would appeal to a mass contemporary audience as the original *Long Ranger* did.[23] As Julie Sanders affirms: "An adaptation signals a relationship with an informing source text or original. ... Appropriation frequently effects a more decisive journey away from the informing text into a wholly new cultural product and domain."[24] To determine if the 2013 version of *The Lone Ranger* is a reinterpretation or an appropriation, requires an analysis of the hypotext and of the new hypertext vis-à-vis adaptation discourse. Once we answer this question, we will be able to delineate the transformation of the Western genre through two exemplary texts, one that epitomized the high point of the Western's popularity in the 1950s, and another that will show us what happens when such a Western icon gets transferred into the second decade of the third millennium.[25]

The Lone Ranger *Yesterday or How the West Was Conquered*

"The Lone Ranger" was broadcast for the first time in January 1933 from WXYZ radio in Detroit.[26] The program became immensely popular and, as Parker underlines, "by the program's twentieth anniversary, the fictional 'masked rider' was known to virtually every man, woman, and child in the United States," becoming "an American institution."[27] "The Lone Ranger" was created originally by WXYZ's owner George Trendle to solve the station's financial problems. Trendle reasoned that the Westerns had done so well on screen that he could replicate that success on the air via a program conceived as patriotic, respectful of the American heritage, and an example of "good living and clean speech."[28] Fran Striker was the prolific writer of the 156 radio episodes that ran for more than twenty years. Later on, he also collaborated on the TV series. He based his narratives on a formula centered on the battle between good and evil with stereotypical characters, suspense, and lots of action,

The Lone Ranger *Yesterday or How the West Was Conquered*

with a Lone Ranger who usually outwits the outlaws with the help of the native Tonto, solves the situation, and captures the evildoers.[29] The hero of the show embodied "all desirable virtues" and his character was a "composite of all men who uphold the laws of God and Man."[30]

The radio show became a TV series in 1949 and ran until 1957, with Clayton Moore in the role of the "masked white savior," and Native American Jay Silverheels as Tonto, the "apprentice white man."[31] Fitzgerald emphasizes how, during the Cold War, the Lone Ranger partook of the ideological fighting against the Communist world, promoting God, country and justice. The almost perfect ranger (clean, white hat, on a white horse, speaking perfect English) motivated only by the love of justice, and not by personal gain, is an ideal authoritative figure[32]; his conduct is a model for any adult or child.[33] He rides around in anonymity (only a few people know him as John Reid) and his identity, obfuscated by a black mask, becomes a symbol of the invisible American white power that exercises its might in the frontier. His many disguises contribute to make him mysterious and, therefore, more legendary.[34]

The masked cowboy gallops on his clever horse Silver around the wilderness, punishing villains that prevent the development of white civilization and progress in a land that is always associated with the pioneers and only sporadically appears to be populated by Native Americans. The implication is that the white pilgrims are God's chosen people, and Manifest Destiny their deserved gift. The only ubiquitous specimen of Native American is Tonto, the sidekick and helper of the ranger. But this Native speaks in broken English and, therefore, the language establishes an implicit racial hierarchy; his white companion speaks perfect English, therefore he must be more educated than the native and, as a consequence, superior to him. Furthermore, Tonto is a "vanishing native" that has accepted the values of the colonizer. With his poor English and his eagerness to follow the commands of the Lone Ranger, he is "a guardian of the laws that gave rise to plunder," and to the genocide of his peoples.[35]

The Lone Ranger's mildly respectful attitudes towards other races (see for example the episodes entitled "War Horse" and "The Renegades"), together with his regard for the law (in the end, the villains are always handed over to the sheriff) and his reluctance to kill (he usually incapacitates the criminals), transformed the TV show into an ideal vehicle for the promotion of values that were supportive

5. New Paths of the Western in the Third Millennium

of "authoritarianism ... and vigilantism." The Lone Ranger became a "metonym for benevolent white supremacy."[36] It is obvious that the archconservative views of the creator, Trendle, a staunch Republican, had filtered from the radio shows into the TV series.[37] In spite of the proposed respect for other races that, according to its creators, pervaded the show, Tonto, is incapable of free thinking. He does not see himself as a man robbed of his identity and his land. He can only obey orders, and, as a result, the viewer assumes that natives can coexist with the white man if they not only absorb the hegemonic values of the master, but also promote those same values eagerly, becoming themselves enforcers of the dominant group's norms.[38] From the Depression to the Cold War era, the inevitability of American imperialism and its influence over the "underdeveloped world," in need of being rescued by the white man, remained a constant in the show. The submission of the "savages" became a moral duty, and their cooperation a given.[39]

Tonto was played by Jay Silverheels, a Native American of the Grand River Six Nations of Canada who became famous "playing a role that he knew to be a clumsy portrayal of his own people."[40] Fame, however, allowed him to spearhead the casting of Native Americans in films, against the practice of using white actors with "painted faces"; denounce the racist discrimination and typecasting suffered by Native Americans; and create the Hollywood Indian Actors Workshop "in an effort ... to change the negative film image of Indians," facilitating in this way the career of other native stars like Chief Dan George, Graham Greene, Wes Studi, Tantoo Cardinal, Tina Keeper, Gary Farmer, Russell Means and many more.[41]

Every TV episode of *The Lone Ranger* begins with the masked rider galloping on a splendid white horse called Silver, filmed in medium tracking shots from a vehicle running alongside, while, on the soundtrack, the William Tell Overture blares on, complementing the fast-paced sequence. While the man is galloping he shoots at a target, supposedly an outlaw that remains out of frame. Then, the masked man is shown in a full shot from bottom up, while he emphatically says to his animal "Hi-Yo, Silver!" and a voice over describes him as a "fabulous individual" known as the Lone Ranger who, in "the early days" brought "law and order" to the wild West.[42] The horse shares the same heroic qualities of his owner, in fact Silver seems to "understand" what is happening around him. He senses danger, often rescues his master and, at times, even knocks the bad guys unconscious. As soon as the story sets

The Lone Ranger *Yesterday or How the West Was Conquered*

out, Tonto shows up, calling his master "kemosabe," that supposedly, in some native American language, means "trusty scout."[43] At the end of each episode, a character always asks, "Who is that masked man?" Invariably, somebody else answers, "He is the Lone Ranger!" Every time a sheriff has doubts about the identity of the Lone Ranger, he unfailingly

The Lone Ranger TV show (ABC–TV, 1949–57). Clayton Moore is the Lone Ranger, Jay Silverheels is Tonto, and in the background is Silver, the Ranger's faithful horse. The composition of the picture with the Ranger towering over Tonto emphasizes the superiority of the cowboy over the native, who is, in fact, kneeling at his feet (Photofest).

produces a silver bullet (his symbol of justice) and every suspicion vanishes.[44]

Each episode is pegged to a conflict or a dangerous situation that is solved by the Lone Ranger with the help of Tonto. For every episode Striker worked out an interesting plot device based on the withdrawal of some crucial information. Every time the ranger faces a problem he says, "I think I have a plan," but immediately the screen goes black and we transition directly to the actualization of his plan via the actions on screen. In this way the audience gets glued to the screen, awaiting in suspense for the denouement of the events. Often the plan involves a masquerade, the Lone Ranger sheds his mask for a fake beard and disguises himself as an "old timer," an ex-soldier and so forth. Because each episode is constructed in this fashion—conflict-plan-implementation-setback-victory—our interest is enhanced, especially because, at first, both the Lone Ranger and Tonto seem to succumb to the villains, but then, in the end, they manage to defeat them, proving that justice always triumphs (at least on screen).[45]

Allen Chadwick maintains "'The Lone Ranger and Tonto' has been and continues to be a pervasive and powerful representation of the American frontier hero, serviceable to the changing requirements of dominant white fantasies about American frontiers."[46] And "fantasies" is certainly a key word in interpreting this TV show, considering that the filmic West created on screen is populated almost exclusively by white pioneers whose progress toward civilization is menaced by white criminals. This tall tale is corroborated by the scarce appearance of Native Americans and by the fact that Tonto is the last surviving member of his tribe, a vanishing noble savage. The idea, as in *Broken Arrow* (Delmer Daves, 1950) is to create a world in which either the genocide of the natives has been erased because it was silenced or omitted, and the good Indians are friends with the good whites, or one in which the two parties coexist peacefully because the "red men" have accepted willingly a reservation life regulated by government treaties.[47]

Even if the last episode of *The Lone Ranger* was broadcast long ago, we can still revisit the deeds of Tonto and the masked man on DVD, however, we cannot escape the unavoidable uneasiness caused by the fake rhetoric and the bombastic didacticism. The West remains, notwithstanding, as it has always been, a vast fictional space in which to rework many of the contradictions, myths and guilt that contributed to the creation of the American national identity.

The Lone Ranger *(2013): Paratext*

Produced by the same creative team behind the successful *Pirates of the Caribbean* franchise (Jerry Bruckheimer Film and Walt Disney Pictures as producers, Johnny Depp as star, Ted Elliott, Terry Rossio and Justin Haythe as screenwriters, and Gore Verbinski as director), *The Lone Ranger* (2013) is estimated to have cost $215 million, with some critics figuring the cost around $250. When the film opened in the U.S. and Canada over the July 4 weekend, it made just $29.9 million at the box office as opposed to *Man of Steel*, which cashed in $125 million over the same period. Disney was afraid that the movie might be a financial flop. However, by November 2013, five months after its theatrical release, *The Lone Ranger* had reached $260 million worldwide thus, more or less, breaking even.[48]

The fear of a financial disaster was fueled by bad reviews. Reviewers destroyed the film: "*The Lone Ranger* is a movie with no constituency to speak of. It is a gigantic picture with a klutzy, deeply un-cool hero ... based on a property that most young viewers don't know or care about";[49] "Taking a pop cultural icon well past its expiration date (*The Lone Ranger* first debuted on the airways in 1933) and meshing it with ludicrously overzealous budgeting proved a faux pas for Disney";[50] "*The Lone Ranger* wants to be a lighthearted action-adventure and a sober-minded reflection upon the atrocities committed against Native Americans. But it doesn't have the artistry—or the juggling skills—to accomplish both at the same time, and so it ends up being neither."[51]

As it would be impossible to cite all the negative responses, it is useful to summarize the main points of such vehement criticism. First of all, Verbinski's film seems to copy-cat a long series of Westerns in having the narrative framed by an aged Tonto (Johnny Depp) relating his fanciful tale to a kid (wearing a Lone Ranger mask) in a Wild West Exhibition housed in a San Francisco fairground. One obvious comparison is Arthur Penn's *Little Big Man* (1970). Just like Penn's mummified, 121-year-old Jack Crabb narrates his adventures to another character, so does Verbinski's Tonto. However, unlike Jack Crabb, Tonto uses irony and subverts the innocence that made the original Tonto character a favorite of the public, having lost any trace of past idealism and being unable to take himself seriously. As a consequence, some critics claim that Hollywood remakes of classics should stop because they usually fail miserably. Verbinski's film should be called "Pirates of the Wild

5. New Paths of the Western in the Third Millennium

West" for its cartoonish violence, plentiful carnage, cannibalism, too many baddies, and convoluted and predictable plotlines. On top of all this, critics do not seem to know what to do with the director's modes, because they seem to fluctuate from the funny to the serious, and then back again, so we are not sure if the story told by Tonto could be taken as a tall tale or as a politically correct recounting of the conquest of the West. Two competing storylines seem to belong to two different kinds of films. One, more realistic, follows the vicissitudes of the Lone Ranger/John Reid (Armie Hammer). The other, more surreal and wacky, is driven by Tonto's weird appearance (he sports a dead-crow tiara and white face-painting) and actions, and extends to his own life story. The lighthearted action adventures mix and superimpose themselves with the sober-minded reflections upon the atrocities committed against Native Americans, in a constant alternation of two conflicting narratives that go from horror to wisecrack, from slapstick to black comedy banter, leaving the viewer confused and uncertain.

The fact that a good film is often initially misjudged and then, through the years, becomes a cult film or well-renowned has happened many times over in the history of cinema, and we believe this could be the case of Verbinski's movie. The critics got disoriented by a story narrated in an unusual way (discordant registers, contradictory points of views) in a Hollywood blockbuster that weaves irony, unreliable narrators, *vampiresque* bunnies, improbable stunts (such as the ladder stunt reminiscent of Buster Keaton's *The General*) and extreme violence on the canvas of a well-known classic narration (the 1950s template of the Lone Ranger and Tonto).

The few good elements praised by the reviewers focus on the characterization of Tonto who is no longer a servile "noble savage" dominated by the Lone Ranger: Tonto no longer speaks in pidgin English, and he understands reality with more acumen than his white male counterpart. Moreover, Rossini's William Tell Overture Finale, the same music that accompanied the opening and closing of all *The Lone Ranger* TV episodes, is used at least three times at crucial moments: during the initial bank robbery, in sequences filmed in Monument Valley with deserts and canyons (amazing camera work by Bojan Bazelli),[52] and in the finale, during the spectacular denouement of the film, peppered with breathtaking action scenes: trains running parallel, intersecting each other, crashing locomotives, and exploding bridges.[53]

Verbinski clearly acknowledged his indebtedness to the original

The Lone Ranger *(2013): Paratext*

text because, by using the same title, he underlined an obvious bond with the antecedent text. Furthermore, he followed the original story of the televisual *Lone Ranger* that comprises episodes 1–3, narrating the coming to existence of the Lone Ranger as a vigilante-hero, and used it as the plot line for his narration. The premise revolves around the massacre of a group of Texas Rangers at the hand of the Cavendish gang. A wandering Indian, Tonto, comes upon the scene and, realizing that one Ranger is still alive, nurses him back to health. When the Ranger gets well, he decides to hide his identity (wearing a mask), so Cavendish and the whole world will assume that he is dead, and, in this fashion, he wages war against Cavendish and other criminals in the West. If the skeleton of the hypotext can be recognized, the director also added new "pulp," delaying for two hours and a half the killing of Cavendish, during which time the search for the villain is interrupted by diversions, flashbacks and flash forwards.[54]

If seriousness was the pervasive tone of the original Ranger and of Tonto, in the hypertext seriousness and playfulness alternate themselves all along. Verbinski not only modified the original story by adding to it, but he also adapted it to a new physical environment. From the beautiful, but indefinite western landscape of the hypotext, he set his film in Monument Valley (Ford's country), Canyon de Chelly National Monument and other locations that have been mythologized by many classic Westerns. Verbinski's operation, therefore, signals the presence of a new hypertext that is at the same time faithful to the original (the old plot remains, and the audience will have no problem in recognizing the story) and adds new life to it, decoding and recoding the hypotext.

In *The Lone Ranger* (2013) we face a *ghost*, the distant presence of the old version of the masked man and his Native American friend, who coexist with a more up-to-date and ironic version of the duo. Furthermore, Johnny Depp's *persona* draws attention away from the story because the audience gets captured by his performative virtuosity that works as an echo of his personifications of Captain Sparrow in the *Pirates of the Caribbean* filmic cycle, a fact that, on one hand, distances the hypotext but, on the other, infuses new blood into the old story. Captain Sparrow and Tonto are both characterized by excessive iconography, the use of self-irony and by being benevolent tricksters, but, while the *Pirates* franchise was successful critically and financially and the public loved Captain Sparrow, the same audience was not so enchanted by the new Tonto. Verbinski and his entourage proved

5. New Paths of the Western in the Third Millennium

capable of handling outsized projects with *The Pirates* cycle (2003, 2006, 2007, May 2017) and *Rango* (2011); the director proved to be a good *metteur-en-scène* who knew how to make a movie with thematic consistency, and to work in a popular adventurous genre ("the pirates" as an action/adventure sub-genre is not so dissimilar from the Western). Why, then, did the 2013 film fall short of everybody's expectations?

As Martin Zeller-Jacques claims, "For a film's producers, the appeal of a comic-book adaptation has its potential as a pre-sold franchise with a ready-made audience. Such an audience's response to the text will be heavily dependent upon its engagement with its source(s), and the adaptation risks ignoring this at its peril. However, as we shall see, conceptualizing a source in a narrative as complex and long-running as an established super-hero comic-book [a TV series in this case] is even more fraught than in literary adaptation studies. Every fan will have a different conception of what constitutes fidelity and will be able to point to ample textual evidence supporting his or her claim."[55] As the critic points out, the failure of the recent *Lone Ranger* is due to the lack of appeal for the old fans as well as not providing an exciting experience to new viewers. We can say that, when examining a hypotext that comes from a 50-year-old serialized narrative that appeared in many forms, "… we are examining a text marked by contradictory forces: by the pressure to reimagine an old narrative for an established audience, and the pressure to repackage old properties for a new audience."[56] This discrepancy is precisely what, in our opinion, created problems for the film.

The hypertext discarded many elements of the mythos that were dated and substituted them with contemporary ones, creating new subtexts that run parallel and intertwine with the main text, i.e., the story derived from the hypotext.[57] An additional problem was the fact that the film is a long flashback in which an unreliable narrator recounts his life-story going back and forth in time; the chronological disruption contributed in part, in our opinion, to the unpopularity of a film that was advertised as a linear action-adventure film.

The Lone Ranger *Today or How the West Was Lost*

Verbinski and his collaborators have created a very ambitious filmic text whose analysis requires bearing in mind the hypotext and

The Lone Ranger *Today or How the West Was Lost*

the principles of adaptation, but also necessitates Deleuze's cinematic theory to isolate certain features of its narrative. The overall structure embraces two points in time, 1933 and 1869, and two places, a Wild West Exhibition in a San Francisco Fairground, and different parts of Texas (Colby, Comanche Border, Indian Territory).[58] These points in time and space are connected by the reappearance of special objects, sounds or words that via a sophisticated system of "interferences" weave the narration together, eliminating the risk of having the filmic story perceived as a sequence of independent recollections of the past.[59]

The film opens with an establishing long shot that shows the ongoing construction of the Golden Gate bridge over San Francisco Bay[60]; the camera pans down and follows a masked kid dressed in a Lone Ranger costume entering a fairground and heading to a Wild West Exhibition. Once inside, he observes the bison and the grizzly bear and then is attracted to the statue of a Native American. In a series of reverse shots in which the kid approaches the statue and the camera zooms in on the Native face, we see the Indian moving his eyes, coming to life. This scares the little guy who drops his bag of peanuts and, with his fake gun, shoots repeatedly at the Indian. The old, wrinkled-up Native (Johnny Depp with prosthetic make-up effects) seems to recognize the boy (asking him, "kemosabe, you bring horses?"), trades a dead mouse for a bag of peanuts, feeds crumbled nuts to the dead bird sitting on his tiara and, finally, when the kid, taking off his mask, asks, "Who did you think I was, anyway?" He does not answer but exclaims, "Never take off mask!"

At this point, a cut takes us to the edge of a cliff overlooking a gorgeous view of Monument Valley, where two men on horses are deciding what course of action to take, and one of them wonders if he should wear a mask. By their attire we assume they are the Lone Ranger, alias John Reid (Armie Hammer with black mask, white hat, white horse), and Tonto, the younger version of the old Native of the Exhibition (Johnny Depp with the same tiara with a dead raven, but with white war paint and black streaks on his face).[61] A few shots later, the pair gallop into a village while the William Tell Overture blares on the soundtrack, enter a bank and warn the customers that it is a robbery. But, while they advance, the frame freezes and they remain suspended in midair. After a couple of seconds we hear the voice over of the kid saying, "Wait a minute.... You are saying you are Tonto...;" at the same time the young Tonto inside the freeze frame turns towards the camera, while everything else

5. New Paths of the Western in the Third Millennium

remains still, as if he is listening to the boy's voice (an impossibility), then we are back again inside the Exhibition in San Francisco.

On another occasion, Tonto and the Lone Ranger are lost in the desert, and a cut brings us back to the boy in the Exhibition, asking old Tonto, "You are lost, aren't you? Train tracks? I thought you were in Indian territory!" The Indian does not reply. He is holding an arrow and his eyes seem to follow the trajectory of an imaginary arrow when, all of a sudden, the sound of a flying arrow is heard in the sound track and the noise becomes intra-diegetic when we see the arrow arriving and piercing John Reid's shoulder in the desert.

As we have observed in the above examples, the events that happen to Tonto's younger self in the flashbacks are stitched together via some form of overlapping in which the voice of the boy carries over into a frame which he cannot be part of, an object in the hands of old Tonto in the diorama reappears in the following flashback (i.e., the arrow, the stone), or a word (i.e., mistake, mask, plan, bad trade) becomes the key that connects what Tonto says to the kid in the present with what happened before.[62] We are obviously facing a self-reflexive text, a text that playfully draws attention to its own fictionality and artifice and enjoys its ability to break the laws of time and space. In the film, the wall dividing past and present seems to have become porous, with objects, sentences, and sounds transitioning between the two realms.[63]

Old Tonto's story, however, is kept in check by the presence of the young interlocutor, who is a careful listener and an obvious fan of the Lone Ranger radio show—in fact, he is sporting Lone Ranger attire—and is not gullible. When the kid discovers that the native is indeed Tonto, the companion of the Lone Ranger, he cannot accept that the two robbed a bank ("But the Lone Ranger and Tonto were the good guys; they did not rob banks!"). To the inquisitive mind of the child, who is obviously very knowledgeable of the source-story, Tonto answers with a mysterious sentence that acquires meaning only at the end of the story: "Come a time, kemosabe, when good men must wear mask!" At this point a cut takes us to "Colby, Texas, 1869" where Tonto's story begins with a railroad executive, Latham Cole (Tom Wilkinson), looking at his pocket watch. It is the year in which the Transcontinental Railroad construction that united the country coast to coast was completed. We are 7:09 minutes into the film, the main story starts and the overlapping pattern we observed will repeat itself all along the narration.

Tonto, skipping back and forward in time while recounting his story

The Lone Ranger *Today or How the West Was Lost*

in a long flashback, appears as an unreliable narrator, while, in reality, it is the non-linearity of his recounting that makes him appear as such. His story starts in the beginning with a bank robbery that is interrupted by a freeze frame and concludes itself at the end of the film. Inside the main flashback—the events narrated by Tonto through which we can piece together what happened to him and how John Reid became the Lone Ranger—there is another flashback that is the story of "Tonto as a boy" recounted by the Comanche Chief, a story that took place many years before 1869 and helps us to understand much of what Tonto says in the present. On top of this, each time we transition to the past we move to a different location and observe different events that are happening in different places, sometimes simultaneously. Furthermore, even if Tonto's storytelling is kept in check by the very poignant questions of his young listener, the Indian often ignores him. Sometimes Tonto's answers make no sense, and we must wait until we advance forward in the narration before we comprehend the meaning of what he has said previously.

When Tonto speaks about rigging a bridge with nitroglycerine, the boy reminds him that he has missed something:

> BOY: Where did you get the explosives?
> TONTO: I told you.
> BOY: No, you did not!

The youngster is right; Tonto did forget to mention that piece of the puzzle. Sometimes an event repeats itself, like the bridge explosion or the bank robbery, but only because the second time we finally learn the outcome. The first time we watch the bank robbery, the happening is stopped *in medias res*, and we do not know what comes afterwards. In the case of the bridge, we see the failing of the fuse, and we keep wondering if the bridge ever blew up. Only at the end of the film do we learn how the duo acquired the explosives and blew the bridge. The bank robbery sequence shown at the beginning is replayed, but this time the two manage to enter the vault and find the nitroglycerine. Therefore, inside old Tonto's flashback story most of the incongruences (but not all) eventually get corrected, even if for a while the viewer (and the boy) remain perplexed. It is obvious that the audience's and the boy's point of view coincide; in fact, we believe that Verbinski created the boy-character in order to have an attentive listener who asks the narrator for clarifications, and, above all, somebody who has a precise knowledge of the hypotext.

5. New Paths of the Western in the Third Millennium

We must conclude that Tonto is indeed a special kind of narrator who often enjoys being mysterious not only with his interlocutor (the boy), but also with his companion, John Reid. When the Indian manufactures a silver bullet to kill Butch Cavendish (William Fichtner), he says to the masked man, "Silver made him what he is and so will return him to earth!" Only later on, we (and the Lone Ranger) find out the connection between Cavendish and the metal. As a boy, Tonto, in exchange for a pocket watch, showed young Cavendish and the future railroad magnate, Cole, the site of a huge silver lode; the discovery triggered the extermination of Tonto's village, and created his tribeless situation. The Lone Ranger (like the viewers and the boy) learns about young Tonto's story only toward the end of the film while talking to the Comanche chief.[64] Tonto not only withholds information, but also manipulates the Lone Ranger, convincing him that he is immortal ("spirit-walker"),[65] having come back to life after an apparent death, and feeding him an awful lot of fake Indian lore as truth, as in the sequence inside Red's (Helena Bonham Carter) brothel:

> LONE RANGER: Are all these women professionals?
> TONTO: Yes!
> LR: How do you know all this?
> TONTO: A vision said it would be so.

But then a prostitute addresses Tonto by name, so we know that he is a customer and had no vision. A bit later, in Red's office, Tonto grabs the Lone Ranger's drink, and gulps it down, claiming it is a sign of respect among the Comanche people, but, when the Lone Ranger repeats the gesture in front of the Indian chief, he almost gets killed, so we realize that Tonto had lied.

It follows that in the Tonto-character there is more at work than a desire to complicate the narration. His purpose is to create semantic gaps. Sentences like "Never take off mask!" (said by old Tonto to the boy who just took off his mask inside the Diorama), or "Silver made what he is and so will return him to earth!" (told by Tonto while giving a silver bullet to John Reid), or "Dan spends a lot of time in Indian territory..." (mentioned by Rebecca to John), or "It is not Cavendish he is worried about..." (told by one of the Texas Rangers to the others, referring to Dan Reid), or "Wendigo getting away!" (told by Tonto to John Reid on the roof of the train, and again in the brothel to Red) are utterances planted in a narration in which they remain obscure. Both the

The Lone Ranger *Today or How the West Was Lost*

intra-diegetic listeners and the extra-diegetic ones, the viewers, cannot understand what they mean. The reasons for such a complex way of narrating are many. Withholding information is certainly a way to keep the audience glued to the screen, getting them involved in the narration, but, in our opinion, this unusual narrative pattern aims at subverting the original hypotext.

The film can be read as a story in which a Native American helps a naïve white man to see how the world works. As in any education, the process goes by degrees. Every step of the way the "innocent" John Reid—who has noble ideals, no experience of real life, and a bookish culture—makes blunders, and it is up to Tonto to rescue him. It takes two hours before the young lawyer changes into the legendary Lone Ranger, embraces the mask, and starts pursuing the evildoers. Education certainly does not happen instantaneously. Changing a mindset is a slow process that takes time, and it is in the recounting of this process that the irony of the film dwells. The irony stems from the fact that the civilized white man, the lawyer John Reid, continuously blunders about and needs to be rescued by an astute and wise Noble Savage.[66] This Tonto, entrepreneurial and cunning, has very little in common with the naïve and obedient Indian of the hypotext. The new Tonto is a "savage" who educates a young, cultured white lawyer to the ways of the world, teaching him to see what hides behind the word "progress," what lies beneath big speeches, and how history can be manufactured to the advantage of a few.[67] Hence, we are facing a Tonto that is enterprising enough to direct (and sometimes manipulate) his "pupil" toward the right path.

The education of the white man occupies the majority of the film because the young John Reid is a slow learner. Being fixated on the idea of "pursuing justice in a court of law," wanting to arrest the criminals alive in an environment in which everybody shoots first, and refusing to carry a gun himself, John becomes the main source of humor. The anachronistic behavior of the lawyer does not fit the frontier, the same way as his suit and his enormous white cowboy hat are out of place. John is a source of humor also for the intra-diegetic characters.[68] Tonto shakes his head repeatedly at him and often raises his eyes in disapproval because John makes mistake after mistake. The new attorney shares the same strong faith in the law that animated the original Lone Ranger, without realizing that he operates in a world in which such belief is anachronistic. The viewers, therefore, are forced to sympathize with the Indian in many occasions, especially when he tries to convince

5. New Paths of the Western in the Third Millennium

the "spirit-horse" to resuscitate "great warrior" Dan Reid instead of his "half-wit, wet-brain" younger brother (John Reid); or when John asks what "kemosabe" means and the native, wittingly, responds, "Wrong, brother!" The "kemosabe" that in the hypotext meant "trusty scout" is transformed in the hypertext into something totally different. Verbinski did not eliminate anything of the source story; all the "items" are kept, but they have been subverted. The story of the mask, the white horse, the silver bullet, are recoded in ways in which the meaning is altered, because much else is added to the basic story of the coming into existence of the Lone Ranger.

In order to see what transformations Verbinski operated on the hypotext we must look at the most important object that the two texts share: the mask.[69] In the hypertext, the black leather mask, cut from the vest of the assassinated Dan Reid, is not worn by John Reid at first; in Verbinki's film Dan's younger brother and only survivor of the Texas Ranger massacre seems to think that wearing a mask is a ridiculous idea because it is not needed in a civilized society in which the laws of men, and not the laws of nature, prevail.[70] John, as the new county prosecutor fresh from law school back East, is totally adamant. In spite of Tonto's attempts to show him that his behavior is ineffective, he is so slow in understanding how the world functions that it takes two thirds of the film before he finally sees the light, and decides to become the masked man who fights evil.

In the televisual show, John Reid embraces the mask as soon as he is rescued by Tonto, actively promoting "law and order," always respecting the authorities—cavalry, sheriffs, judges etc.—because he operates in a system that punishes the criminals. The newer Lone Ranger is seeking justice like his older version, but his fight is ineffectual because he is sporting the same ideals of his predecessor in a world in which justice cannot prevail because the system is corrupted.[71] The moment in which John figures out that the myth of progress is just rhetoric fed to the masses (i.e., the many public speeches of the railroad magnate during which the content changes according to the political climate and the interests of the moments), that Cole is a predatory capitalist who, underneath the idea of progress, hides an imperialistic dream (Cole: "The one who governs the railroad, will govern the country!"), that the railroad man commands to the Cavalry, and that the army protects the interest of the great capital, he finally decides to wear the mask, exclaiming: "There is no justice! Cole controls everything… I'd rather be an outlaw!"

The Lone Ranger *Today or How the West Was Lost*

The Lone Ranger (Walt Disney Pictures, 2013). Directed by Gore Verbinski. Johnny Depp is Tonto, and Armie Hammer is John Reid (Lone Ranger). The long shot draws attention to the fact that Reid, having completed his "education," embraces the mask and becomes the Lone Ranger, finally "catching up" with Tonto in every sense (Photofest).

It is with this epiphany that John Reid decides to fight for justice as an outlaw, like Zorro or Robin Hood, and, therefore, as an anti-hero that rebels against the system, something that would have never occurred to the televisual Lone Ranger. It is at this point that old Tonto's warning ("Never take off mask!") uttered to the boy at the beginning of the film becomes clear—the boy should wear the mask and pursue justice in a world where otherwise there is none. The belief in a just system is negated by the hypertext and proved impossible in a world where greed and corruption prevail. The faith in the institutions, in "God and country" and in "progress," that were the pillars of the hegemonic message of the TV show are completely subverted. Ironically enough, in this world only fighting as an outlaw can bring a measure of (limited) justice.

This is a topsy-turvy world in which Texas Rangers and settlers are assassinated, Indian villages are destroyed, and an entire Comanche tribe gets mowed down by a Gatlin gun to protect the interest of a man and his march of "progress."[72] Verbinski rewrites the history of the West, depicting it as a space whose colonization and exploitation of

5. New Paths of the Western in the Third Millennium

resources commanded the genocide of the Native Americans.[73] The fictional West of Verbinski is violent and cruel and at times funny, but he never stops showing how Manifest Destiny—the greatest chance given to (white) mankind to build a more just society—gave rise to an imperialistic country dominated by dreams of power. During the Depression and the Cold War, Trendle and Striker made the original Lone Ranger a believer of Turner's myth of the Frontier, a myth that, at that time, was still unshaken by history. In the third millennium, the director had to be wiser and more revisionist. As a consequence, if the original text (both radio and televisual show) created on screen a perfect fable of how the West was conquered (or should have been), Verbinski created instead a grim fable in which he showed, with humor and pathos, how the West was lost to "progress," making the viewers aware that in the fictional *space* of the West we can indeed insert many different fables, some closer to reality than others.

As Rizzo writes, Verbinski's film "deviates from the rules of everyday human-centered vision and experiments with new forms of perceptions."[74] The director does not create a unifying narrative, but, through framing, camera movements, and the order in which shots are edited together—basically via his ordering of the narration—he generates "new modes of thinking that challenge conventional patterns of thought."[75] Avoiding linear storytelling in portraying the events, the viewer can go beyond conventional ways of thinking and escape from the strictures of a unifying conclusion or a stable point of view with which to identify. The two sequences of apparently disconnected images that occur when John Reid grabs a "cursed" silver piece of ore (inside Red's brothel), and the one during his temporary death-like state (on top a very tall Indian burial structure, situated over a huge butte) are hallucinatory, and surreal. They seem to be loosely connected images that, defying chronology, show bits and pieces of what has happened in the past and what will happen in the future. If we analyze them more carefully, however, we discover that in the end the two sequences can be reintegrated into the logic of the filmic narrative, albeit keeping in mind that the surreal quality of these sequences disorients the eye and operates through sensation rather than representation.[76] These two sequences and the insistence on certain recurrent images (pocket watch, Indian pendant, white hat, black mask, Texas Ranger star, azure scarf, bird seeds) are time-images, indicating that the filmmaker privileges temporality over spatiality.[77]

The montage that in the movement-image film operates through

The Lone Ranger *Today or How the West Was Lost*

a cause and effect logic, so that the action progresses in a linear fashion, in the 2013 version of the Lone Ranger is disrupted. The jumps between time zones, places, events, and strange realities (a horse who eats scorpions, drinks beer, wears a hat, climbs on roofs and trees; carnivorous-cannibalistic-*vampiresque* bunnies that fight and hiss like wild beasts; a dead raven that flaps his wings)[78] create a time-image film, in which time is no longer subordinated to movements. Let's see now if, at the end of the film, all these disruptions are reterritorialized so that all the pieces of the story fall into place, and to which extent they do, if they do at all.[79]

We would like to focus on the end of Verbinski's film to see how he recodes the hypotext and how successful his construction of a time-image film is. Tonto and the Lone Ranger—who has finally proved himself to be a "great warrior" like his brother—dispatch (in a very clever action sequence with two trains running in parallel)[80] the bad guys: Cole, Cavendish and the Cavalry Captain Jay Fuller (Barry Pepper, with blond long hair, made up to look like General George Custer). The Hollywood style happy ending would not, however, do justice to a text as complex as this. Once the baddies die, the masked man goes back to Colby where the Chairman of the Transcontinental Railroad thanks him for his deed and, offering him a gold pocket watch, says, "It is always nice to have a lawman on the side of progress!" It is the very word, progress, that makes the masked man walk away from the podium, bid farewell to his love interest, Rebecca, and take off on his white horse. The hero that, in the end rides off towards the horizon, choosing his quest over his love interest, is something that John shares with his old counterpart, the TV Lone Ranger. Nevertheless, the viewer cannot forget that the Chairman and his main share-holders are still advocating "progress" in the same sense that Cole did, and he might be inclined to conclude that this kind of progress cannot be stopped, only opposed, and that the struggle must go on. It is evident that the director recodes the end of the televisual episodes with totally different results.

The filmic test does not finish here because our masked hero reconnects with Tonto in the wilderness. While the two men are riding together, the camera focuses on the ground in a close-up that makes the two riders vanish out of focus, while a *vampiresque* bunny devours a scorpion, and then turns toward the camera as if looking at the viewer, proving that nature is still out of balance. The reappearance of the carnivorous bunny seems to confirm that there is still evil in the world, that

5. New Paths of the Western in the Third Millennium

things are not in order, and that we have not reached a happy conclusion even if the baddies are dead. To enhance our confusion, a cut takes us back to the Exhibition in San Francisco, where the lights are dim because it is evening and time to close; Tonto, dressed in an old fashion suit and a bowler hat with a suitcase nearby, seems ready to leave when the boy says to him, "So the wendigo, nature out of balance, the mask man, is just a story, right? I know it is not real ... or is it?" Tonto replies that it is up to him to decide and throws something at him that turns out to be a silver bullet. While the kid is observing the bullet, Tonto vanishes and in his place a raven appears. The bird flies out of the Exhibition into the night sky of San Francisco Bay; the kid is now convinced that Tonto's story is real, because he repeats the native's command ("Never take off the mask!") and, smiling, puts on his mask.

A cut brings us back to the wilderness where the Lone Ranger imitates the typical proud riding posture and the boisterous battle cry of the original masked man, "Hi-Yo, Silver. Away!," but in this hypertext Tonto disapproves of his gesture, admonishing him to never do it again. The salute that ends every episode of the hypotext is transferred verbatim into the hypertext with opposite results. The Lone Ranger here apologizes to Tonto for his excessive pride and prima donna gesture before they both start galloping away to the notes of the William Tell Overture, the same music used in the opening and closing of every televisual episode in the source-text. The screen becomes black and the main credits start rolling down, but, after a while, we are surprised by a sudden close-up of the unstable feet of an old man that a fix camera captures while he walks away. When he has covered enough distance from the camera, we recognize him thanks to his suit, his bowler hat and his suitcase. It is old Tonto that, while the credits of the visual effects, the special effects, etc. continue to roll over him, is going, we assume, home. The old man becomes smaller and smaller, advancing further and further in the middle of Monument Valley. He has abandoned the painted backdrop scenario of the San Francisco Exhibition and now is back in the wilderness, in his natural habitat.

Such a delayed and unusual ending, interrupted twice by the credits, definitely prevents the attentive viewer from coming to a unifying conclusion. Verbinski offers us multiple possibilities instead of a stable point of view with which to identify.

The filmic text is a rhizomatic system of lines that cannot be ordered easily in a hierarchical order, even if a certain measure of order

The Lone Ranger *Today or How the West Was Lost*

is achieved. As Deleuze explains, the molecular plane and the molar plane interact together constantly in this filmic text.[81] We could agree with the kid who, holding a silver bullet in his hand and having concrete proof of what Tonto told him, believes his story. But, even if we might agree in part with the boy, we cannot stop asking ourselves how Tonto could vanish and a raven appear in his place. Has the spirit of the raven sitting on his tiara finally come back to reclaim its dead body? How could old Tonto get to Monument Valley? Was Tonto capable of becoming a raven and escaping from jail at one point? Is the raven part of the other many strange realities that populate the film? Is Tonto part of these strange realities too? After all, in 1869 he traded an empty bag of peanuts that was the exact copy of the one the boy gave him in 1933.

We are facing a time-image film that does not reconcile all it presents into a unifying story or into a stable point of view, but challenges conventional patterns of thoughts, re-writing the Western *trope* in a completely new way, and transforming the usually realistic narration of the hypotext into an hypertext in which all the elements of the original survive, but are recoded through irony, humor, surprise, action, and ideological critique. Verbinski is clearly pushing the boundaries of the genre to create a new type of Western, an intense rather than representational film. The interferences, the "overlapping," the superimpositions of images, the surreal sequences, the disruption of the hierarchical order (repeated sequences, delayed end, no respect of chronology, impossibilities) disorient the average viewer (and also the critics) who were expecting a more traditional text that would not require so much attention on the part of the audience.[82]

The music and the arrangements suit perfectly what is happening on screen, and the matching of the two achieves amazing perfection in the action scenes. The sound track contains big, orchestral, operatic music and small ensemble music and is sometimes intra-diegetic as in the case of the religious group ensemble and Colby's marching band. The location, Monument Valley, and many of the events remind us of a long list of allusions to other famous Westerns. Rangers wearing dusters riding into a station and waiting for a train recall another group of men waiting for Harmonica in *Once Upon a Time in the West* (1968; by Sergio Leone); the music of this sequence also evokes Ennio Morricone's famous sound track. The images of John and Tonto approaching Rebecca's burning farm, supposedly raided by Indians, brings to mind the same sequence in *The Searchers* (1956; by John Ford) in which Ethan

5. New Paths of the Western in the Third Millennium

Edwards finds his family massacred. The Presbyterians and the League of Temperance revive another religious group that appears at the beginning of *The Wild Bunch* (1969; by Peckinpah) and gets caught in cross fire.[83] The blowing up of the wooden bridge reproduces the scene of *The Good, the Bad, and the Ugly* (1966; by Leone) in which Blondie and Tuco put charges under a bridge to help the Union army win a battle.[84]

To conclude, the 2013 version of the Lone Ranger is a special case of adaptation, an adaptation that happens inside the same culture, and not across different ones. We believe that the word "remake" would not properly fit in this case and that the word "adaptation" would be more correct because we face a hypertext in which "a unit of culture ... spreads and replicates, transforming itself to fit with whatever new habitat it finds itself in," and the third millennium is certainly a new habitat in which to situate the old story, being populated by a new audience and by new ideologies or lack of them.[85] The new version contains a comic exuberance that the older version lacked, presenting a rhythmic orchestration of actions, violence and strange realities and making it difficult to decide if the narration commands the events or if the action rules the narration. The ending of the film resists narrative closure and opens up many possibilities. At the outset we meet old Tonto in a sort of museum of the Wild West. The frontier is obviously over and can only be remembered in a diorama. Like the bison and the grizzly bear, the Native American is a specimen of a species so endangered that he gets exhibited in a sort of museum. Starting from this premise—that the Indians are a vanishing breed—it is comforting to see that, in the end, the narration has empowered Tonto, liberating him from the strictures of the stereotypical characterization of the original, so much so that he has stopped being someone who succumbs to servitude and submission, managing to go back where he belongs. Re-imagining the Lone Ranger story along different lines than the source has allowed the film to offer the viewers alternative forms of consciousness in addressing Native Americans.

Chapter Notes

Introduction

1. There are, of course, exceptions to the rule. Heroes/heroines, for example, die in the following films: the splendid *Colorado Territory* (1949, Raoul Walsh), the sad *The Great Silence* (1968, Sergio Corbucci) and the cruel *The Hateful Eight* (2015, Quentin Tarantino).

2. For the moment, I am leaving aside all the political implications and repercussions that stem from the colonization of the *real* West, because I deal with these issues and the way they reverberated on screen in Chapter 2, where I focus on the relations between Native Americans, their genocide and the image of the celluloid Indians. In the rest of the volume, I am dealing with the West as an imaginary space.

3. By "golden age" I mean the period in which a multitude of Westerns were released every year: the 1940s and '50s.

4. This is not an exhaustive list, but indicative of an output that is still vibrant.

5. John Ford employed Navajos in his films, the Sioux were hired for *A Man Called Horse*, the Crows for *Little Big Man*. See *The Only Good Indian: The Hollywood Gospel*, by Ralph E. Friar and Natasha A. Friar (New York: Drama Book Specialists, 1972), p. 257. The extras were found on reservations, and often employed for far less than union scale. See Ward Churchill, *Fantasies of the Master Race: Literature, Cinema, and the Colonization of the American Indians* (San Francisco: City Lights Books, 1998), and, by the same author, *Struggle for the Land: Native North American Resistance to Genocide, Ecoside, and Colonization* (San Francisco: City Lights Books, 2002); Ella Shohat, "Gender and the Culture of Empire," in Hamid Naficy and Teshone Gabriel, eds. *Otherness and the Media: An Ethnography of the Imagined and the Imaged* (Langhorne, PA: Harwood Academic Publishers, 1993); and Roxanne Dumbar-Ortiz, *An Indigenous Peoples' History of the United States* (Boston: Beacon Press, 2014). Kilpatrick criticizes the revisionist Westerns in which the white hero indianizes himself, as in *A Man Called Horse* (1970), affirming that in this film the natural superiority of the white man prevails; the indianized hero is the one who learns everything the Indians do, but he learns it so well and so quickly that he becomes their leader. The critic also points out the many inaccuracies of the Sioux rites and customs portrayed in the film. See *Celluloid Indians* (Lincoln: University of Nebraska Press, 1999), pp. 79–84. We agree in principle with the critic, and we think there is a need for more Native American actors and directors who can express their point of view in Western films (Paryz and Leo, p. 5). Paryz and Leo in *The Post–2000 Film Western*, however, also affirm that there have been some significant films produced after Costner's and Eastwood's films like *True Grit* (Joel and Ethan Cohen, 2010) and *Django Unchained* (Quentin Tarantino, 2012) among others, almost contradicting themselves.

6. Paryz and Leo, *The Post–2000 Film Western*, p. 5.

Notes—Introduction

7. For an assessment of the Western after 1990 see also Andre Patrick Nelson, ed., *Contemporary Westerns: Film and Television Since 1990* (Lanham, MD: The Scarecrow Press, 2013), pp. xiii–xxi.

8. There is a strong topsy-turvy mirror effect between *The Hateful Eight* and *The Great Silence*, Corbucci's 1968 Western. Both use a snowy, wintery setting and share a grim and tense story. In Tarantino's film all the bad guys die. In Corbucci's all the good guys perish, leaving only hateful bounty hunters to prosper. Tarantino's fascination with Corbucci's *Django* (1966) for music and theme is also testified to by his *Django Unchained* (2012).

9. Pioneer critical studies of the western include: Robert Warshow, "Movie Chronicle: The Westerner," in *The Immediate Experience* (New York: Doubleday, 1962); Leslie Fiedler, *The Return of the Vanishing American* (New York: Stein and Day, 1968); Jim Kitses, *Horizons West* (London: Thames and Hudson, 1969), often quoted for its set of binary oppositions: individual/community, nature/culture, West/East and so forth; John G. Cawelti, *Six Gun Mystique* (Bowling Green, OH: Bowling Green UPP, 1971); André Bazin, *What Is Cinema?* (Berkeley: University of California Press, 1971); Philip French, *Westerns* (London: Secker and Warburg, 1973); Will Wright, *Six Guns and Society: A Structural Study of the Western* (Berkeley: University of California Press, 1975), which put forth a taxonomy of plot structures in Western films; Edward Buscombe, *The BFI Companion to the Western* (New York: Atheneum, 1988), a seminal overview of the genre's iconography; Douglas Pye and Ian Cameron, eds., *The Book of Westerns* (New York: Continuum, 1996), highlighting narrative closure in the Western; Edward Buscombe and Roberta Pearson, eds., *Back in the Saddle Again: New Essays on the Western* (London: BFI, 1998); John G. Cawelti, *The Six-Gun Mystique Sequel* (Bowling Green, OH: Bowling Green UPP, 1999), in which Cawelty expands his study of formula narrative patterns: e.g., the journey, the empire, the outlaw, the revenge and so on. A paradigmatic study that frames Western cinema within American history are Richard Slotkin's three volumes: *Regeneration Through Violence: The Mythology of the American Frontier* (Middletown: Wesleyan UP, 1973), *The Fatal Environment: The Myth of the Frontier in the Age of Industrialization* (Middletown: Wesleyan UP, 1985) and *Gunfighter Nation: The Myth of the Frontier in Twentieth Century America* (New York: Atheneum, 1992). For the Italian Western see Christopher Frayling's *Spaghetti Westerns: Cowboys and Europeans from Karl May to Sergio Leone* (London: Routledge, 1981) and *Sergio Leone: Something to Do with Death* (London: Faber and Faber, 2000).

10. David Lusted, *The Western* (London: Longman, 2003). For a solid overview of the "revisionist" Western between 1969 and 1980 (that is, from Sam Peckinpah's *The Wild Bunch* and Michael Cimino's *Heaven's Gate*) see *Still in the Saddle: The Hollywood Western, 1969–1980* by Andrew Patrick Nelson (Norman: Oklahoma UP, 2015), pp. 15–41.

11. See also three books by McFarland & Company (Jefferson, North Carolina): Bob Herzberg, *Hang Them High: Law and Disorder in Western Films and Literature* (2013); David Meuel, *The Noir Western: Darkness on the Range, 1943–1962* (2015); Joseph Maddrey, *The Quick, the Dead and the Revived: The Many Lives of Western Film* (2016).

12. Neil Campbell (citing Stuart Hall), *Rhizomatic West: Representing the American West in a Transnational, Global, Media Age* (Lincoln: Nebraska UP, 2008), p. 25.

13. Campbell citing Paul Giles, *Rhizomatic West*, p. 3.

14. Campbell, *Rhizomatic West*, pp. 8–12. According to Campbell, who follows Deleuze and Guattari in their study of painting, the "deframing power (...) opens ... up [the existing frame] onto ... an infinite field of forces ... all of which give the picture the power to leave the canvas. The painter's action never stays within the frame and does not begin with it" (*Post Westerns* (Lincoln: Nebraska UP, 2013), p. 4.

15. Campbell, *Rhizomatic West*, pp. 24–25.

Notes—Introduction

16. Campbell, *Rhizomatic West*, p. 25. See also, from the same author, *Post-Westerns* (Lincoln: Nebraska UP, 2013), p. 8–9.

17. A fold is a form of connection according to Deleuze (as opposed to Althusser's articulation) between multiple levels of meaning that is open-ended, unexhaustive, unlimited and non-exclusive.

18. Campbell citing Paul Gilroy, *Rhizomatic West*, p. 28.

19. "Meme" is an idea, behavior or style that spreads from person to person within a culture, a unit of culture or imitation. It was originally coined by Richard Dawkins, an evolutionist biologist, in *The Selfish Gene* (Oxford, UK: Oxford UP, 1999), p. 191–197. See also for a direct application of the "meme" in the field of cinema studies Iain Robert Smith, *The Hollywood Meme: Transnational Adaptations in World Cinema* (Edinburgh: Edinburgh UP, 2017), pp. 31–33.

20. See the chapter on the culture industry in Theodor Adorno and Max Horkheimer, *Dialectic of Enlightenment* (New York: Herder and Herder, 1969).

21. See Ivo Ritzer's article "Spaghetti Westerns and Asian Cinema: Perspectives on Global Cultural Flows," in *Spaghetti Westerns at the Crossroads*, Austin Fisher, ed. (Edinburgh: Edinburgh UP, 2016), p. 166.

22. Campbell, *Rhizomatic West*, p. 40.

23. Molly Haskell, *From Revenge to Rape: The Treatment of Women in the Movies* (Chicago: University of Chicago Press, 1987), p. 168.

24. Jonna Eagle. *Imperial Affects* (New Brunswick: Rutgers UP, 2017).

25. Steve Neale, *Film Genre Reader III*, Barry Keith Grant ed. (Austin: University of Texas, 2003), p. 169.

26. The story narrated by the radio show was "translated" almost verbatim into the TV series as David Wilson Parker demonstrates in his dissertation "A Descriptive Analysis of the Lone Ranger as a Form of Popular Art," Northwestern University, 1956, pp. 210–327.

27. Ian R. Smith, *The Hollywood Meme: Transnational Adaptations in World Cinema* (Edinburgh: Edinburgh UP, 2017), p. 31.

28. Neil Campbell, *Post-Westerns* (Lincoln: Nebraska UP, 2013), p. 357.

29. See William Mcclain, "Western, Go Home! Sergio Leone and the 'Death of the Western' in American Film Criticism," *Journal of Film and Video* 62, no. 1–2 (Spring–Summer 2010): pp. 52–66.

30. See Brian Hosmer and Larry Nesper, eds. (New York: SUNY Press, 2013) (e-book).

31. In this volume, every time I use the term "classic Westerns" I am referring to the filmic production of the Hollywood studios at the time of their maximum splendor. The movies of this period do exhibit certain common features and often hegemonic narratives; however, a classic Western could be made today using the same "print," proving that this type of film is not necessarily circumscribed to a certain time frame. It goes without saying that there are films in this period that do contain different traits and exhibit subversive narratives as we demonstrate in the present study, because Westerns, like all cultural artefacts, are not monolithic. What I want to point out is that when I use the term "classic Westerns" I am not hinting at any evolutionary genre pattern (i.e., glory then and decline now), rather, I am simply singling out films with a cluster of predominant characteristics as the ones contained, for example, in *Shane*: male hero, marginal female characters, Manifest Destiny, conflict whose solution will facilitate progress and civilization, positive resolution, etc. However, the genre formula can exhibit different and, I hope, infinite combinations.

32. Jane Tompkins, *West of Everything* (Oxford: Oxford University Press, 1992), pp. 8–67. See also Susan Suleiman, *The Female Body in Western Culture: Contemporary Perspectives* (Cambridge, MA: Harvard University Press, 1986).

33. Shelley Armitage, "Who Was That Masked Man? Conception and Reception in *The Lone Ranger*," in *The Post–2000 Film Western*, Marek Paryz and John R.

Notes—Chapter 1

Leo, eds. (New York: Palgrave Macmillan, 2015), p. 64.

34. "Variation" has to be interpreted as in Neale's quote.

35. Campbell, *Post-Westerns—Cinema, Region, West* (Lincoln: Nebraska UP, 2013), p. 24. Campbell talks about post-Westerns, but his definitions would also apply to my selection of Westerns.

36. Neil Campbell, *Post-Westerns—Cinema, Region, West* (Lincoln: Nebraska UP, 2013), p. 24.

Chapter 1

1. See Ella Shohat and Robert Stam, *Unthinking Eurocentrism* (New York: Routledge, 1994), p. 340.

2. According to Antonio Gramsci's theory of cultural hegemony, popular culture is the site of struggle between the forces of resistance of subordinate groups and the forces of incorporation associated with dominant groups in society. As a result, texts and practices of popular culture swing between two poles, resistance and incorporation, and also between the discourse of the text and the discourse of the reader, who brings his/her own cultural formation and his/her historical moment to the reading. Cf. *Antonio Gramsci: Prison Notebooks* (New York, Columbia UP, 1996).

3. See Ella Shohat and Robert Stam, *Unthinking Eurocentrism*, p. 340.

4. Ian Tyrrell's article is available online at http://iantyrrell.wordpress.com/what-is-transnational-history/. For the new directions of historic research, see the splendid volume *Beyond the Nation: Pushing the Boundaries of U.S. History from a Transatlantic Perspective*, edited by F. Fasce, M. Vaudagna, and R. Baritono (Torino: Otto-Nova Americana in English, 2013).

5. See *Transnational Cinema: The Film Reader*, Elizabeth Ezra and Terry Rowden, eds. (London: Routledge, 2006), pp. 1–70.

6. See *Transnational Cinema: The Film Reader*, Elizabeth Ezra and Terry Rowden, eds., pp. 4–5.

7. See *Transnational Cinema: The Film Reader*, Elizabeth Ezra and Terry Rowden, eds., pp. 4–5.

8. See Anne Jackel, "Dual Nationality Film Productions in Europe after 1945," *Historical Journal of Films, Radio and Television* 23, no. 3 (2003). In particular, see the successful coproduction treaty signed between Italy and France in 1949, regularly revised and renewed through the years, so that by 1957 over 230 French-Italian films had been made (p. 232).

9. See Andrew Higson, "The Limiting Imagination of National Cinema," in *Transnational Cinema* (Ezra and Rowden, 2006).

10. See Tim Bergfelder, "National, Transnational or Supranational Cinema? Rethinking European Film Studies," *Media Culture & Society* 27, no. 3 (May 2005). Leone's films were at the time considered "oddball" and were dismissed by the critics. The revaluation of the spaghetti Westerns started with Christopher Frayling's *Spaghetti Westerns: Cowboys and Europeans from Karl May to Sergio Leone*, a pioneer work that opened the floodgates to more accurate studies and to more balanced assessments of the Italian Western.

11. In the course of this chapter, I will demonstrate that Sergio Leone's *A Fistful of Dollars* is not a remake of Akira Kurosawa's *Yojimbo*, but, for working purposes, at the beginning of my argument, I will use the term "remake" as an umbrella term.

12. In "The Limiting Imagination of National Cinema," (in *Cinema and Nation*, Mette Hjort and Scott MacKenzie, eds. London: Routledge, 2000) Andrew Higson claims that "the meanings that an audience reads into a film are heavily dependent on the cultural context in which they watch it." A movie distributed abroad, according to Higson, will have three possible outcomes: "cultural imperialism" with liberating effects on the indigenous culture; negative effects corrupting the local culture, or, ultimately, the film will be interpreted according to an "indigenous frame of reference," in the sense that it will be translated into the local idiom (p.19).

Notes—Chapter 1

13. Linda Hutcheon, *A Theory of Adaptation* (New York: Routledge, 2006), p. 170–77.

14. For the fortune of the spaghetti Westerns see Christopher Wagstaff "A Forkful of Westerns: Industry, Audiences and the Italian Western," in *Popular European Cinema*, Richard Dyer and Ginette Vincendau, eds. (London: Routledge, 1992).

15. Elizabeth Ezra and Terry Rowden, eds., *Transnational Cinema* (New York: Routledge, 2006), p. 19.

16. Leone's film was not the first Italian Western. Giulio Ferroni's *Il fanciullo del West* dates back to 1942; Mario Amendola's *Il terrore dell'Oklahoma* was released in 1959; Riccardo Blasco and Mario Caiano's *Duello nel Texas* in 1963. Even in 1964, the year *A Fistful of Dollars* was distributed, a number of Westerns were produced. A chapter entirely dedicated to pre-Leone Western films can be found in Matteo Mancini, *Spaghetti Western*, Vol. 1 (Edizioni Il Foglio, 2012). Leone, however, established new conventions and popularized the Italian Western; his films launched the "spaghetti phenomenon" and started a *filone* that lasted about a decade and produced 493 films. Pre-Leone Westerns were tired reworkings of the American formula. For the spaghetti phenomenon see Flavia Brizio-Skov's article, "Dollars, Bullets and Success: The Spaghetti Western Phenomenon" in *Popular Italian Cinema— Culture and Politics in a Postwar Society* (London: I.B.Tauris, 2011), pp. 83–106; Christopher Frayling, *Sergio Leone: Something to Do with Death* (London: Faber and Faber, 2000) and Christian Uva, *Sergio Leone—Il cinema come favola politica* (Roma: Ente dello Spettacolo, 2013).

17. Leone's Western trilogy is *A Fistful of Dollars* (1964), *For a Few Dollars More* (1966), and *The Good, the Bad, and the Ugly* (1966). *A Fistful of Dollars* was distributed in the USA only in 1967 because of the legal battle with Toho Films, Kurosawa's studio producers. See Christopher Wagstaff's "Italian Genre Films in the World Market," in *Hollywood and Europe: Economics, Culture, National Identity 1945–95*, Geoffrey Nowell-Smith and Stephen Ricci, eds. (London: BFI, 1998).

18. For a detailed history of the cinematic laws and politics in the postwar era see Lorenzo Quaglietti, *Storia economico-politica del cinema italiano 1945–1980* (Roma: Editori Riuniti, 1980).

19. See "Il cinema italiano batte ogni record" in *Il cinema italiano dal dopoguerra a oggi*, Mino Argentieri, (Roma: Editori Riuniti, 1998), pp. 65–67.

20. Paul Ginsborg, *A History of Contemporary Italy. Society and Politics 1943–1988* (London: Palgrave Macmillan, 1990).

21. The image of the *Italiano Medio* (lower middle-class Italian) was created thanks to the male stars of the time: Vittorio Gassman, Alberto Sordi, Ugo Tognazzi among others, the so called *mattatori* of Comedy Italian Style.

22. On the golden age of Italian national cinema see "Il cinema italiano batte ogni record" in *Il cinemai italiano dal dopoguerra a oggi*, Mino Argentieri (Roma: Editori Riuniti, 1998), pp. 59–79.

23. Alan Williams, ed., *Film and Nationalism* (London: Rutgers UP, 2002), p. 5. Many *auteurs* "re-wrote" Italian recent history—the Resistance, World War II, Fascism—or registered the consequences of the economic miracle and the persistence of many taboos in Italian society in films like *Divorce Italian Style* (Pietro Germi, 1962) and *Seduced and Abandoned* (Pietro Germi, 1964). See also Andrea Bini's article, "The Birth of the Comedy Italian Style" in *Popular Italian Cinema*, Flavia Brizio-Skov, ed. (London: I.B. Tauris, 2011), and Andrea Bini's *Male Anxiety and Psychopathology in Film— Comedy Italian Style* (New York: Palgrave and Macmillan, 2015).

24. Even if it would be worth examining the transnational/national nature of other popular genres of the time like horror, the *mondo* documentaries, the *poliziottesco* or the James Bond-style spy films, I am not going to deal with them here for obvious reasons of space. I am limiting my discourse to the Italian Western, using the *peplum* only as a counter example of the *spaghetti*. For the fortune of Italian cinema in the 1960s see Adelio

Notes—Chapter 1

Ferrero, Giovanna Grignaffini, Leonardo Quaresima, eds., *Il cinema italiano degli anni '60* (Firenze: Guaraldi, 1977), pp. 9–39.

25. The Alfieri Law, promulgated in 1938 and enforced in 1939, was not a ban on foreign imports though. Rather, imports of foreign films became a state monopoly. As a reaction, the four major studios (Paramount, MG, Warner and Fox) withdrew their films—which made up almost all of the U.S. imports—from the Italian market until the end of World War II.

26. See Lorenzo Quaglietti, *Storia economico-politica del cinema italiano 1945–1980* (Roma: Editori Riuniti, 1980) and Mino Argentieri, *Il cinema Italiano dal dopoguerra a oggi* (Roma: Editori Riuniti, 1998), pp. 65–67.

27. Runaway production is a phrase commonly used by Hollywood's film producers to describe the outsourcing of production work to foreign countries/locations. In the 1950s–60s, Hollywood Studios were attracted by low filming costs and migrated to Cinecittà Studios (Rome). Overseas, they could reinvest the revenues from the American films shown in the Italian distribution circuit, according to measures signed in the late 1940s by Giulio Andreotti, then Secretary to the Council of Ministers, under which the recouped funds could be spent in Italy, but not exported. See Christopher Frayling, 2000, p. 64; Camille Johnson-Yale's "Frozen in Hollywood: Postwar Film Policy and the New Power-Geometry of Globalizing Production Labor." *Critical Studies in Media Communication* 32, no. 1 (March 2015), pp. 33–47 and, by the same author, also *Runaway Production: A Critical History of Hollywood's Outsourcing Discourse* (Dissertation, University of Illinois, Urbana-Champagne, 2010), pp. 1–133.

28. Peter Bondanella and Peter Pacchioni, *A History of Italian Cinema* (New York: Bloomsbury Academic, 2017), pp. 163-165.

29. See the illuminating article of Elena D'Amelio, "The Hybrid Star: Steve Reeves, Hercules and the Politics of Transnational Whiteness," *Journal of Italian Cinema & Media Studies* 2, no. 2 (2014): pp. 259–277.

30. See Frank Burke, "The Italian Sword-and-Sandal Film from *Fabiola* (1949) to *Hercules and the Captive Women* (1961): Texts and Contexts," in *Popular Italian Cinema* (London: I.B. Tauris, 2011), pp. 17–51.

31. See A. Brogi, *Confronting America. The Cold War Between the United States and the Communists in France and Italy* (Chapel Hill, NC: North Carolina UP, 2011), and D. Ellwood and G. P. Brunetta, eds., *Hollywood in Europa: industra, politica, pubblico del cinema 1945–60* (Firenze: Casa Usher, 1991).

32. See Christopher Frayling, *Sergio Leone: Something to Do About Death* (London: Faber and Faber, 2000), p. 119.

33. See Frayling, 2000, pp. 46–79. Leone's father, Vincenzo Leone, aka Leone Roberti, was born in 1879. He became a renowned filmmaker during the silent era until the 1920s, directing Francesca Bertini in many films. He eventually fell out of Mussolini's grace, got ostracized by the regime, and stopped directing after the war, even if he made a few more films up to 1941. See Frayling, 2000, pp. 25–48.

34. See Frayling, 2000, pp. 77.

35. Between 1958 and 1963, 170 *pepla* were made in Italy. See Frayling, 2000, pp. 82.

36. See Frayling, 2000, pp. 91–96.

37. See Frayling, 2000, pp. 110–117.

38. See Frayling, 2000, p. 119.

39. See Frayling, 2000, p. 125.

40. See the chapter "Fistful of Dollars" in Frayling, 2000, pp. 118–165; and Christian Uva in *Sergio Leone—Il cinema come favola politica* (Roma: Edizioni Fondazione Ente dello Spettacolo, 2013), pp. 112–144.

41. See Frayling 2000, p. 77.

42. Dasheill Hammett [Maryland, 1894–1961], *Red Harvest* (New York: Avenel Books, 1980). For a critical analysis of Hammett's novels see Peter Wolfe, *Beams Falling: The Art of Dashiell Hammett* (Bowling Green: Bowling Green UP, 1980); and LeRoy Lad Panek, *Reading Early Hammett* (Jefferson, NC: McFarland, 2004); Richard Layman and Julie M.

Notes—Chapter 1

Rivett, eds., *Selected Letters of Dashiell Hammett 1921–1960* (Washington, D.C.: Counterpoint, 2001); Julian Symons, *Dashiell Hammett* (New York: Harcourt Brace Jovanovich, 1985).

43. Northrop Frye, *Anatomy of Criticism*. Princeton, Princeton UP, 1957, p.46.

44. For Frye, the ironic mode is typical of detective stories, but as we move away from the Sherlock Holmes period, the stories become more and more brutal and begin "to merge with the thriller as one of the forms of melodrama." In melodrama the core themes are "the triumph of moral virtue over villainy, and the consequent idealizing of the moral views assumed to be held by the audience (*Anatomy*, p. 47).

45. *Anatomy*, pp. 48–49.

46. Critics have wondered why Hammett at the *incipit* of the novel has the Op meet Bill Quint, a character who never surfaces again in the story. Bill Quint is a union organizer who gives the Op the "low down" on what happened to Personville. The story recounted by Quint tells how the miners, who in the 1920s demanded better working conditions, obtained them from the owners of the mines. But when the copper business got bad, the agreements were eventually revoked, and strikes and bitter struggles ensued. The bosses called in thugs and gunmen as strike-breakers. The owners succeeded in breaking the organized labor union. By the end, the workers' organization was a spent force, but the thugs did not leave town and started to gain power infiltrating the channels of command, corrupting the institutions. The critics seem to agree that introducing Quint as a speaker in favor of the labor struggle in the beginning of the novel, and then making him vanish from the story, is a loose end the author did not tie up. The brief encounter does not seem to justify, according to them, the inclusion of this episode as a defense of organized labor against brutal capitalism. Many believe that the episode is a reverberation of Dashiell Hammett's personal experience when he was sent to Anaconda, Montana, in 1917, as a Pinkerton operative to work for the copper mine owners against the striking miners. We, on the other hand, are convinced that Hammett knew very well what he was doing, and he knew that he needed to anchor the central theme of the story, the corruption of a community, on something that could justify the extreme situation in which the Op finds himself in Personville. See Julian Symons, *Dashiell Hammett* (New York: Harcourt Brace Jovanovich, 1985), pp. 39–57; Leroy Lad Panek, *Reading Early Hammett* (Jefferson, NC, and London: McFarland, 2004), pp. 121–148.

47. The characters that Goldoni used in *The Servant of Two Masters*—Pantalone the Venetian merchant, Brighella the innkeeper, Smeraldina the maid, Truffaldino the servant, the doctor and so forth—are all stock characters of the *commedia dell'arte*. The actors used to wear a particular mask and attire while performing, and each of them was characterized by specific qualities that were well known to the public of the time. Pantalone is the father who is bent in marrying his daughter to a man she does not love; the maid is usually cunning and witty; the innkeeper is smart etc. See Filippo Zampieri, ed., *Carlo Goldoni—Opere* (Milano: Ricciardi Editore, 1954).

48. See Carlo Goldoni, *The Servants of Two Masters* (London: Nick Hern Books, 2012). pp. xvii—xxviii.

49. See Frayling, 2000, pp. 125.

50. *Miles Gloriosus* is a comedic play written by Plautus (c. 254–184 B.C.). The title can be translated as "The Swaggering Soldier" or "Vainglorious Soldier."

51. In his long career as a film-maker Kurosawa wrote the majority of his scripts, and he also controlled every aspect of his films, including editing. However, Hammett's *Red Harvest* was not credited in the film. See Mitsuhiro Yoshimoto, *Kurosawa* (Durham: Duke University Press, 2000), pp. 53–68.

52. See Hutcheon, *A Theory of Adaptation*, 2006, p. 111.

53. See Hutcheon, 2006, p. 145.

54. The *jidaigeki* or samurai films were set in the Tokugawa or Edo period between the 1600s and 1867. They were fictitious historical narratives usually set in an idealized feudal Japan of the 17th

Notes—Chapter 1

century. The samurai of feudal times followed a code of honor called *bushido*, under which they protected their lords and committed *hara-kiri* (self-inflicted disembowelment with a blade) if disgraced or defeated. In the 1950s, *jidaigeki* produced by Toei Studio changed the genre; the hero is a superior swordman who ultimately triumphs and kills the villain, the thematic core being the battle between good and evil. However, its fighting scenes are rendered in a ritualistic rather than realistic way. Japanese cinema is often defined in terms of *jidaigeki*, or period films, and *gendaigeki*, or modern films. Kurosawa made eleven samurai films, three of which were based on original scripts—*Seven Samurai*, *The Hidden Fortress*, and *Kagemusha*; *Yojimbo* is based on a script that is a transcoding of an American novel; *Rashomon*, *Sanjuro*, and *Red Beard* are adaptations of modern Japanese literary works; *The Men Who Tread on the Tiger's Tail* is the adaptation of a Kabuki play; *Throne of Blood*, *The Lower Depths* and *Ran* are adaptations of foreign works. The success of Kurosawa's iconoclastic *Yojimbo* sealed the decline of Toei's samurai production. In the 1960s, following the extreme popularity of Kurosawa's *Yojimbo* and *Sanjuro* (1962), a new type of samurai film emerged. This short-lived (roughly a decade) cycle of films portrayed extreme graphic violence, fast-paced sword fighting, and were thus called *zanzoku eiga* (cruel film). See Mitsuhiro Yoshimoto, *Kurosawa* (Durham: Duke University Press, 2000), pp. 54–142; Eric Cazdin, *The Flash of Capital—Film and Geopolitics in Japan* (Durham: Duke University Press, 2002); Donald Richie, *The Films of Akira Kurosawa* (Berkeley: University of California Press, 1996), especially pp. 147–162.

55. The farmer's son says to his father: "Who wants a long life eating porridge? I want to eat good food, wear nice things. A short, exciting life for me!" At the end, Sanjuro, sparing his life, tells him: "Go home. A long life eating porridge is best!" This dialogue together with the farmer's exclamation, "Everybody's after easy money!" reinforces the fact that youth seems to have fallen prey of consumerism, money has become the key to happiness, and happiness seems to be found in goods and not in family relationships.

56. Irony is not only achieved through the dialogue, but also at the iconic level: The samurai has ticks, makes funny faces, walks strangely, and some of the characters look cartoonish. At the acoustic level some sounds like the swooping of a sword cutting through flesh are amplified.

57. See Hutcheon, *A Theory of Adaptation*, 2006, pp. 145–159.

58. See Yoshimoto, 2000, p. 289.

59. See Yoshimoto, 2000, p. 245

60. See Dimitris Eleftheriotis, "Genre Criticism and the Spaghetti Western" in *Popular Cinemas of Europe* (London: Continuum, 2001), pp. 92–133.

61. See Eleftheriotis, 2001, pp. 104–105 and Brunetta, 2003.

62. See Hutcheon, 2006, pp. 176–177.

63. See Yoshimoto, 2000, p. 245.

64. See Yoshimoto, 2000, p. 231.

65. In an interesting article titled "Japanese Swordfighters and American Gunfighters," J. L. Anderson writes that the *jidaigeki* was influenced especially by the silent Westerns starring William S. Hart that arrived in Japan around 1920. The critic does not provide any evidence for his claim, but he states that Hart's ruthless skill with a weapon and his fits of violence are similar to the behavior of traditional samurai heroes (*Cinema Journal* 12, no. 2 (Spring 1973): pp. 1, 2).

66. See Anderson, 1973, p. 2. The myth for America would be the conquering of the West and for Japan the Tokugawa and Meiji periods during which the *shogunate* system of military rulers and feudal lords started unraveling.

67. Nature is still portrayed sometimes in the samurai films—ponds, cherry blossoms, flowers—but, according to Anderson, these are symbolic of the emotional states of the characters, or create the "mood" of the scene (Anderson, 1973, pp. 9–10).

68. See Frayling, 2000, pp. 118–125.

69. Leone quoted in Frayling, 2000, p. 125.

70. The film is a gangster story set in the days of Prohibition in the corrupt

Notes—Chapter 1

border town of Jericho, Texas, where two crime syndicates (Italian and Irish) fight one another until, one day, John Smith (Bruce Willis), an "amoral" gunslinger, arrives in town and offers his services to both sides, pitting them against each other. Hill's film copycats Leone's *A Fistful of Dollars*.

71. The coffin maker in *Yojimbo* is a sympathetic character; he helps Gonji, the *sake* vendor, and the samurai, but he is a bit more ambivalent. When he gets scared, he flees and abandons Gonji, who is left alone to carry the canister in which the wounded samurai is hidden. Piripero, on the other hand, is more courageous and sides with the gringo from the very beginning of the film.

72. In *Yojimbo*, the rescue of the woman causes the wild beating of the samurai. Even if she appears only in a short sequence, the woman is fundamental for the development of the plot, however, she is not a full-blown character. In *A Fistful of Dollars*, Marisol has the same propelling function, but she has more screen time and is more developed as a character. In short, the *sake* vendor as innkeeper Silvanito, the coffin maker as Piripero, and Marisol as the kept woman become more prominent characters in Leone's film.

73. As I mentioned before, Sanjuro meets the farmer's son again before the end, while fighting Ushitora's clan. Sanjuro spares his life, sending him home to the farm, claiming that an honest long life eating porridge is better than a rich, but short life of crime.

74. See Tadao Sato, *Currents in Japanese Cinema*, translated by Gregory Barrett (New York: Kodansha International, 1982), pp. 116–123 and pp. 15–115.

75. In *Shane* (George Stevens, 1953), or in *High Noon* (Fred Zinnemann, 1952) as in many other classic Westerns, the showdown usually occurs at the end. The American classic Westerns continued to be produced into the '60s, until films like *The Professionals* (Richard Brooks, 1966) and *The Wild Bunch* (Sam Packinpah, 1969) were released. By then Leone's Westerns had also been distributed in the U.S. (1967). The influence of the Italian Western, together with the 1960s counter culture contributed to the alteration of the mold of the classic Western. See Austin Fisher, *Radical Frontiers in the Spaghetti Western* (London: I. B. Tauris, 2011), p. 226.

76. The Stranger does not hesitate to transport the corpses of two dead soldiers from the river bank to a cemetery to provoke a shooting between the Rojos and the Baxters.

77. See Christopher Frayling. *C'era una volta in Italia—Il cinema di Sergio Leone* (Bologna: Cineteca Bologna, 2014), p. 7.

78. *A Fistful of Dollars* was filmed in Almeria, a region of Southern Spain, in the Tabernas Desert, a zone that supposedly resembles the U.S. Southwest for its windswept plains, aridity, rocky ravines and dried out riverbeds. Some sequences were also shot near Madrid, in La Pedrizia of Colmenar Viejo.

79. The "Man with no name" shares many qualities with the Japanese bodyguard; he has a wicked sense of humor, is ironic, looks scruffy and measures his words. If the gringo is unshaven, rides a mule, and keeps a cigarillo stump permanently hanging from his lips, Sanjuro twitches his shoulders, chews on a toothpick, and sports an unusual way of walking that is enhanced, as we mentioned before, by the rhythm of the music.

80. Frayling, 2000, p. 163.

81. Hammett's novel got to Leone only via Kurosawa's film, as we read in Frayling's *Sergio Leone: Something to Do about Death*. Therefore, I compared *Yojimbo* with *Red Harvest*, but *A Fistful of Dollars* with *Yojimbo*.

82. See Dimitris Eleftheriotis, "Genre Criticism and the Spaghetti Western" in *Popular Cinemas of Europe* (London: Continuum, 2001), pp. 92–133.

83. Eleftheriotis, 2001, pp. 92–133.

84. See Stefano Rosso, ed., *Le Frontiere del West* edited (Milano: ShaKe Edizioni, 2008) in which various Italian historians re-read critically the myth of the American Frontier, deconstructing Turner's thesis.

85. D.P. Martinez, *Remaking Kurosawa—Translations and Permutations in*

Notes—Chapter 2

Global Cinema (New York: Palgrave Macmillan, 2009), p. xix.

86. *A Fistful of Dollars* is one of the most successful films ever made moneywise; see charts in Austin Fisher's *Radical Frontier in the Spaghetti Westerns* (London: I.B. Tauris, 2011), Appendix A, pp. 219–222. Part of this chapter has appeared on the journal of *Cultural and Religious Studies*, Vol. 4, Number 3 (March 2016).

Chapter 2

1. Today we would be too politically conscious to formulate a statement like the one of Bazin without acknowledging the fact that cinema has celebrated and repeated over and over a narrative that absconded history. The epic conquest of the West was, in reality, paved by genocide and expropriation. Cinema did manage to create the myth of the Frontier, a myth (albeit a white myth) for which today we can only apologize, but it exists and, like most things that have populated the imagination of generations, will be difficult to deconstruct. There is no doubt that Hollywood cinema did promote an incorrect image of the indigenous people, repeating it ad infinitum, at least in many classic Westerns, and it is true that Bazin did celebrate *Stagecoach* (1939, John Ford) without much thought about the fact that the Indians appear as "hollering savages" in the film (i.e., the stagecoach attack). Bazin, however, looked at the film only aesthetically; in fact, he was the first to consider *Stagecoach* "the ideal example of the maturity of a style brought to classic perfection. John Ford struck the ideal balance between social myth, historical reconstruction, psychological truth, and the traditional theme of the Western *mise en scène* ... *Stagecoach* is like a wheel, so perfectly made that it remains in equilibrium in its axis in any position." "The Evolution of the Western," in André Bazin's *What is Cinema?* Translated by Hugh Gray (Berkeley: University of California Press, 1967), vol. 2, p. 149.

2. Bazin, 1967, p. 151.

3. Bazin mentions the '50s cycle, but dwells in particular on Anthony Mann's Westerns: *Devil's Doorway* (1950), *Bend of the River* (1952), *The Naked Spur* (1953), and *The Far Country* (1954).

4. Richard Slotkin, "Foreword," in *Action Speaks Louder*, Eric Lichtenfeld (Westport, CT: Praeger, 2004), pp. ix–x.

5. Steve Neale, "Vanishing Americans: Racial and Ethnic Issues in the Interpretation and Context of Post-War 'Pro-Indian' Westerns," in *Back in the Saddle Again*, Edward Buscombe, ed. (London: BFI Publishing, 1998), pp. 8–28.

6. For very enthusiastic reviews of *Broken Arrow* see: Tinee Mae, "*Broken Arrow* Is a Picturesque, First Rate Film," *Chicago Daily Tribune*, August 29, 1950; "Movies Are Growing Up!—Here's Proof," *New York Amsterdam News*, August 5, 1950; Phillip K. Scheuer, "*Arrow* Unites Blood Brothers," *Los Angeles Times*, August 19, 1950; Lillian Scott, "Indians and Intermarriage Get New Treatment in *Broken Arrow* Film," *The Chicago Defender*, July 8, 1950. *Broken Arrow* was distributed nationwide by 20th Century Fox in August 1950. MGM waited to release *Devil's Doorway* until September, afraid that the movie content would be too daring for the contemporary public and, as a consequence, the film would flop at the box office. When *Broken Arrow* was well received critically and at the box office, MGM released *Devil's Doorway* banking on the national change of heart toward the Indians. *Devil's Doorway* was not so fortunate. It had lukewarm reviews, and some negative ones like "Films, *Devil's Doorway* Is Just Too Bad," (*Chicago Daily Tribune*, September 30, 1950, by Tinee Mae). Mann's film was obviously too ideologically advanced for its time.

7. Angela Aleiss, *Making the White Man's Indian* (Westport, CT: Praeger, 2005), pp. 73–76. The Hollywood branch of the agency scrutinized film scripts and made recommendations that were generally followed by the studios. Any idea that could be harmful to the projection of a democratic and egalitarian image of the country, and, as a result, could impede the victory of the war, had to be avoided.

Notes—Chapter 2

For this reason, white and dark-skinned Americans had to appear united in racial brotherhood.

8. Blacklisted people lost their jobs and for years could not work in the industry. Many, as a result, committed suicide, others emigrated abroad and some worked under pseudonyms or were fronted by friends and colleagues. See Dalton Trumbo, *The Time of the Toad* (New York: Harper, 1972) and Robert Rossen, Frank Krutnik et al., eds., *Un-American Hollywood: Politics and Film in the Blacklist Era* (New Brunswick, N.J.: Rutgers University Press, 2007), especially the chapter on "Red Hollywood."

9. The Roosevelt administration during the war enlisted Hollywood executives and producers to push the idea of America as a melting pot. National unity became a priority, especially in recruiting minorities into military service. The image of the Indians as homicidal maniacs became an embarrassment for the Department of State. The government stationed personnel in Hollywood to monitor and moderate such images. Twentieth Century Fox vice president Darryl F. Zanuck was in regular contact with the Eisenhower administration and met with White House staff to insert propaganda messages into films. See Michael Ray Fitzgerald, "Television Westerns, Termination, and Public Relations: An Analysis of the ABC Series *Broken Arrow*, 1956–1958," in *Film & History: An Interdisciplinary Journal of Film and Television Studies* 41, no. 1 (Spring 2011): pp. 50–72; and also Tricia Jenkins, *The CIA and Hollywood: How the Agency Shapes Film and Television* (Austin: Texas UP, 2012), pp. 38–40.

10. See Steve Neale, "Vanishing Americans: Racial and Ethnic Issues in the Interpretation and Context of Post-war 'Pro-Indian' Westerns," in *Back in the Saddle Again*, Edward Buscombe and Roberta E. Pearson, eds. (London: BFI Publishing, 1998), pp. 8–28.

11. Steve Neale, in "Vanishing Americans: Racial and Ethnic Issues in the Interpretation and Context of Post-war 'Pro-Indian' Westerns," writes that the liberal attitudes and the "Cult of the Indian" found a place in films of the '50s as well as in the television Westerns of the same period, in series like *Brave Eagle* (presenting the Indian point of view, CBS, September 1955–June 1956); *Broken Arrow*, inspired by the feature film with the same title and centered on Cochise (ABC, September 1956–September 58); *Laws of the Plainsman*, featuring an Apache marshal (NBC), etc. See Steve Neale in *Back in the Saddle Again*, Edward Buscombe and Roberta E. Pearson, eds. (London: BFI Publishing, 1998), p. 13.

12. See Steve Neale's article in Buscombe, 1998, pp. 8–28.

13. See the heated comments by Neale about this matter in his article (pp. 8–11), against John H. Lenihan (*Showdown*, Urbana: UP of Illinois, 1980), Richard Slotkin (*Gunfighter Nation*, New York: Atheneum, 1992) and other critics who tend to see the Indians as "empty signifiers" or "stand-ins" for other minority groups.

14. I am going to use the term "Indians" for the fictional characters represented in films, and the term "Native Americans" when I am referring to the human beings living at the time in the United States.

15. In her article, "Hollywood Addresses Postwar Assimilation: Indian/White Attitudes in Broken Arrow," Angela Aleiss affirms that a significant number of pro-Indian movies were produced in the silent era. These films were, in their simplicity, sympathetic to Indians, for example *Ramona* (D.W. Griffith, 1910), *The Squaw Man* (Cecil DeMille, 1914), *The Vanishing American* (George B. Seitz, 1925), and *Redskin* (Victor Schertzinger, 1929). Negative stereotypes of the Indians, however, were also present in many silent movies from the beginning (*American Indian Culture and Research Journal* 11, no. 1 (1987), pp. 67–68). See also by the same author, *Making the White Man's Indian: Native Americans and Hollywood Movies* (New York: Praeger, 2005), pp. 60–70.

16. Other minority groups such as African-Americans found themselves in

Notes—Chapter 2

similar unfortunate predicaments coming home after the war.

17. See Kenneth William Townsend, *World War II and the American Indian* (Albuquerque: UP of New Mexico, 2000), pp. 115–228.

18. However, conservative political authorities cut federal social assistance and programs in a country whose mobilization had created unemployment problems. The fear of a national economic crisis that could spiral the country into another Great Depression was felt deeply. Moreover, corporations had a vested interest in making reservation lands available for commercial exploitation, especially for mining. See Alison R. Bernstein *American Indians and World War II* (Norman: UP of Oklahoma, 1991).

19. See M. Elise Marubbio, *Killing the Indian Maiden* (Lexington: UP of Kentucky, 2006), pp. 61–65. For a comprehensive study on the Native Americans' situation see Clayton R. Koppes, "From New Deal to Termination: Liberalism and Indian Policy 1933–53," in *Pacific Historical Review* 46, no. 4 (November 1977), pp. 543–566.

20. See Alison R. Bernstein, *American Indians and World War II* (Norman: UP of Oklahoma, 1991).

21. For a comprehensive look at the Native Americans' situation after the war see Kenneth R. Philip, "Termination: A Legacy of the Indian New Deal," *Western Historical Quarterly* 14, no. 2 (April 1983), pp. 165–180. See also "Hollywood-ized History" in *Native Americans on Network TV—Stereotypes, Myths, and the "Good Indian,"* Michael Ray Fitzgerald (Lanham, MD: Rowman & Littlefield, 2014), pp. 53–75.

22. See Michael Ray Fitzgerald, *Native Americans on Network TV—Stereotypes, Myths, and the "Good Indian,"* (Lanham, MD: Rowman & Littlefield, 2014), pp. 69–70. Between 1949 and 1956 production of Westerns increased. Twenty-five Westerns were made in 1949, thirty-eight in 1950, forty-six in 1956, then, between 1957 and 1962, there was a slight decline due to the television competition and the collapse of the studio system. However, the genre appeal remained strong as the increase in the television Western productions demonstrates. See M. Elise Marubbio, *Killing the Indian Maiden* (Lexington: UP of Kentucky, 2006), p. 251.

23. According to Theodore Roosevelt, frontier life fostered the emergence of a new type of man who shared some of the same qualities of the Indian—a skillful hunter/fighter who could survive in the Darwinian arena of the Wilderness. The new man is a sort of hero who believes in democracy and the construction of a better world. See Thomas C. Dyer, *Theodore Roosevelt and the Idea of Race* (Baton Rouge: Louisiana UP, 1980), chapters 1 and 2.

24. It goes without saying that, when the pro-Indian films were made, many anti-Indian films were also produced. Inside this group we should distinguish between the mainstream Westerns and vitriolic Westerns. The mainstream Westerns follow the classic model of *Stagecoach*, in which the Indians are just a menacing presence and are not developed as full characters. Thus the viewer, knowing nothing about them, remains neutral toward them. In the others, such as *Arrowhead* (Charles Marquis Warren, 1953) or *The Stalking Moon* (Robert Mulligan, 1968) the Indian was denied not only civil rights, but even basic human rights. What is appalling in the case of *The Stalking Moon* is the fact that such a racist Western was made in the era of counter-culture.

25. See J. P. Telotte, "A Fate Worse Than Death," *Journal of Popular Film and Television* 26, no. 3 (1998): p. 127.

26. See, as an example, the case of *Broken Arrow* in which Sonseeahray (Debra Paget), the Indian wife of Tom Jeffords (James Stewart), the white cowboy/hero, dies in a (bad) white man ambush, but her death helps to seal the peace-treaty. After her death, Tom roams the wilderness alone, and any problem related to the integration of the Indian maiden into white society is avoided.

27. See Angela Aleiss, 1987, p.75.

28. To give an idea of what film critics saw in *Broken Arrow*, I quote an excerpt: "In the new picture, the Indians are no

Notes—Chapter 2

longer cliché or mutely accepted stock creations, but characters drawn with the blinds pulled back from history, and with an obviously fresh and unbiased attempt to tell the real story and the impelling reasons for the things that happened in Arizona territory in the sixth and seventh decades of the past century. The Apache Indian, thus becomes a living ... understandable human being ... and not implacably hostile." It is clear that the above critic considered Delmer Daves' film a historically accurate description of the events that took place in 1870s Arizona Territory. A redeeming quality of the article is the fact that the author welcomes *Broken Arrow* as a powerful weapon against racial prejudice and discrimination against the Indians. The critic also mentions *Home of the Brave, Lost Boundaries* and *Pinky* as great dramas in favor of Black-Americans' civil rights and breaks a lance for *Gentleman's Agreement,* claiming that a movie that dealt honestly with the Jewish question deserved the Oscar. *Broken Arrow* took a major step towards breaking conventional stereotypes of the Indians, at least superficially. Delmer Daves was a screenwriter and a director and in his long career he made eleven Westerns: *Broken Arrow* (1950), *Return of the Texan* (1952), *Drum Beat* (1954), *White Feather* (1955), *The Last Wagon* (1956), *Jubal* (1956), *3:10 to Yuma* (1956), *Cowboy* (1958), *The Badlanders* (1958), and *The Hanging Tree* (1959). For an overview of Daves' vast filmic output see: Michael Walker, "The Westerns of Delmer Daves," in *The Book of Westerns,* Ian Cameron and Douglas Pye, eds. (New York: Continuum, 1996), pp. 123–166.

29. The screen story shows that massacres have been committed by military forces and by settlers, but they were caused by a minority of fanatics and racists, distinct from the government and the majority of the white people who were decent human beings. In a nutshell, the film claims that a few rotten apples always spoil the bunch. In fact, for the love of balance, the whites also get ambushed by the evil warriors of Geronimo. In the end, after the killing of Sonseeahray, the white townsfolk say to Jeffords that the white perpetrators of the ambush have been apprehended and will be severely punished. Justice finally triumphs, and the viewer can go home happy; after all, the system works even in the face of daring challenges. As Fitzgerald claims, the federal government and the army appear in *Broken Arrow,* both the 1950 film and the TV series with the same title (aired by ABC between 1956 and 1958 for a total of 72 episodes), as protectors of the Indians, because the natives are childlike and need protection from their white fathers. Only a few bad apples among white society want to exterminate the Indians, but the rest of society does not. Putting the blame on some ignorant, white supremacist groups of individuals, the filmic narrative reassures the public that the system is sound and working; injustice and inequality are contained, and the viewer is reassured that, even if terrible things had happened in the past, society has made racial progress (*Native Americans on Network TV* (Lanham, MD: Rowman & Littlefield, 2014), pp. 68–69.

30. For a more detailed discussion of the Indian goddess-princess, see M. Elise Marubbio, 2006, pp. 66–71. Marubbio sees the love relationship between Sonseeahray and Jeffords as the mythical union between Adam and Eve in the American Eden. The idea is reinforced by Jeffords' statement during their honeymoon where he expresses his state of bliss by recalling Adam and Eve.

31. See the Navajo crisis in 1947: In spite of their wartime contributions, the Navajos were on the verge of starvation; national relief organizations had to intervene, sending food and aid. The embarrassing situation showed to mainstream America that most Native Americans were excluded from the postwar affluence the rest of the country was enjoying. The Navajo-Hopi Aid Relief was passed in 1950. In 1948, John Ford, a friend of the Navajo Indians of Monument Valley because of their participation in many of his movies, used his military connections to organize an airborne relief effort to deliver supplies to the Navajo. See *Monument Valley: John Ford Country,* Turner Entertainment DVD documentary, 2006,

included in the Warner Brothers DVD edition of *Fort Apache*.

32. The script of *Broken Arrow* is supposed to have historical roots because it is based on a famous novel, *Blood Brothers*, that recounts the historical events of the Southwest that led to the signing of a peace treaty between Cochise and General Howard—a treaty made possible by a cowboy named Jeffords who became friends with the Apache chief. The novel covers a period of nineteen years between 1855 and 1874, the year Cochise died. The film concentrates on the friendship between the cowboy and Cochise, giving the impression that the signing of the peace treaty is a consequence of their friendship. The extensive screen time devoted to Jeffords' friendship with the chief and his love interest allows the viewer to become familiar with the differences between the two cultures and to accept the foreign culture as "other but equal." Historicity in the film is bent because, in reality, General Howard was not a paragon of religiosity. After signing the treaty, he continued to wage war against many Indian tribes. The treaty was followed by many others and, in the end, the Apaches lost their native land. Cochise was a good friend of Jeffords, but he probably signed the treaty because he realized that the future of his people was threatened by the relentless advance of white civilization. The movie ultimately projects a respectful image of the Indians, but it covers up the expropriation of their territory. See "Hollywood-ized History" in *Native Americans on Network TV* by Michael Ray Fitzgerald (Lanham, MD: Rowman & Littlefield, 2014, pp. 55–57) on the insistence of historical accuracy in the *Broken Arrow* TV Series (1956–58) and the 1950 film of the same title.

33. See "Hollywood Addresses Postwar Assimilation: Indian/White Attitudes in *Broken Arrow*," *American Indian Culture and Research Journal* 11, no. 1 (1987): pp. 73–74.

34. Angela Aleiss claims that "*Broken Arrow* did more than simply 'echo' government attitudes: It indicates the film industry's response to the Indian's evolving role in society." (Angela Aleiss, 1987, p. 75).

35. Cochise had fought against American encroachment since 1861. In 1872, he signed the peace treaty and in 1874, after having honored the peace, died. Cochise had managed, by signing the treaty with General Oliver O. Howard, to hold on to his stronghold, the Dragon Mountains. After his death the government breached the agreement and consolidated the Cochise tribe with other Apache groups in New Mexico. Lodes of copper and uranium had been found on Cochise land and the government, according to Fitzgerald, worked to further the interests of mining companies. In 1872, President Grant created the San Carlos Apache Reservation. Geronimo respected the peace treaty until Cochise died, then he waged war until 1886, the year in which he was captured and never allowed to go back to his homeland. The Apache Wars lasted from 1849 to 1886. See Michael Ray Fitzgerald, "Television Westerns, Termination, and Public Relations: An Analysis of the ABC Series *Broken Arrow*, 1956–1958," *Film & History: An Interdisciplinary Journal of Film and Television Studies* 41, no. 1 (Spring 2011): pp. 65–72.

36. In January 1863 Cochise's father in law, Mangas Colorada, was captured by General Joseph Rodman West. The Americans duped Colorada into a conference under a flag of truce and, during what was to be a peaceful parley session, they took the unsuspecting Mangas Colorada prisoner, tortured him and later murdered him. See E. Buscombe, ed., *The BFI Companion to the Western* (New York: Atheneum, 1988), pp. 91, 180; Edwin R. Sweeney, *Cochise-Chiricahua Apache Chief*, (Norman: University of Oklahoma Press, 1991), pp. 204–205; David Roberts, *Once They Moved Like the Wind—Cochise, Geronimo, and the Apache Wars* (New York: Simon and Schuster, 1993), pp. 19–122.

37. *Devil's Doorway* is the only Anthony Mann Western with an Indian in the leading role and is an exception to the rule. In the '50s cycle, there are other Westerns that are centered on an Indian

Notes—Chapter 2

protagonist, for example *Sitting Bull* (dir. Sidney Salkow, 1954), *Chief Crazy Horse* (dir. George Sherman, 1955, with Victor Mature as Crazy Horse), *Taza, Son of Cochise* (dir. Douglas Sirk, 1954, with Rock Hudson as Taza), *White Feather* (dir. Robert D. Webb, 1955), *Comanche* (dir. George Sherman, 1956), *Walk the Proud Land* (dir. Jesse Hibbs, 1956), and *Apache* (dir. Robert Aldrich, 1954, with Burt Lancaster as Geronimo). All leading roles are played by white actors with painted faces. These films tend to follow the *Broken Arrow* model, sugar-coating history. *Devil's Doorway*, like *The Last Hunt* and *The Last Wagon*, goes against the grain.

38. The sheep herders are not necessarily evil; they have been misguided by Coolan into believing that there is free land in the valley. Because of a drought in the North, they have come down to Wyoming hoping to find pastures for the sheep that otherwise would starve. So, the sheep herders, like the Shoshone Indians, have no choice; they have no place where to go, and they are forced to fight for their survival. The situation mirrors the one between pioneers and Native Americans in the 19th century, as both had no choice but to fight for the possession of the land that meant their survival.

39. For the Dark Frontier see David Meuel, *The Noir Western—Darkness on the Range, 1943–1962* (Jefferson, NC: McFarland, 2015), pp. 122–128.

40. In the valley, protected by Devil's Doorway pass, the Shoshone Indians who have fled the reservation can get a home.

41. His American identity has been erased by a society that refuses Poole any rights.

42. At the end of the movie, Orrie, in her misguided attempt to save Poole's life, calls in the cavalry of the United States, thinking of protecting Poole and his Indians from the town posse that is attacking them. To speed the army deployment, she telegraphs the nearest military post saying that Shoshone Indians, escaped from a reservation, are hiding in Poole's valley. The cavalry arrives with orders to take the Indians back to where they came from. But Poole and the last surviving Shoshone Indians do not want to leave the valley and prefer to die fighting; as a result they get mowed down by the soldiers. Poole and his Indians, if let alone, could have probably won the fight against the townsfolk, but instead, thanks to Orrie's meddling, they all get killed. In the end, only Indian women and children go back to the reservation. The lawyer, revealing the presence of the escaped Shoshone Indians, also breaks the promise made previously to Poole.

43. See Jacquelyn Kilpatrick, *Celluloid Indians* (Lincoln: University of Nebraska Press, 1999), pp. 42–47. Lately, economic historians have proved that property rights existed among some indigenous people of North America. See Terry L. Anderson et al., eds., *Self-Determination: The Other Path for Native Americans* (Stanford: Stanford UP, 2006).

44. See the chapter entitled "The Cowboy Talkies" in *Celluloid Indians* by Jacquelyn Kilpatrick (Lincoln: University of Nebraska Press, 1999, pp. 36–64).

45. A sentence attributed to General Philip Sheridan, commander of the military forces in the West at the time of the Indian Wars in the Great Plains (1866). See Peter C. Rollins and E. O'Connor, "Hollywood's Indian: The Portrayal of the Native American in Film," *The Journal of American History* 86, no. 1 (June 1999): p. 95.

46. For the importance of the land as Mother Earth for the Native Americans see also Jacquelyn Kilpatrick, *Celluloid Indians* (Lincoln: University of Nebraska Press, 1999), pp. 65–67.

47. The title of the film refers to the pass, Devil's Doorway, that leads into Poole's valley, Sweet Meadows. But the suggestive title hints, in our opinion, to the two opposite points of view that are at the foundation of the story. For the white community the pass is indeed the "door to the devils," as beyond it Poole and the Shoshone Indians will not let the land go without a fight. For the Shoshone Indians, on the other hand, the pass is what separates them from the "white devils" who claim their land, their freedom, and ultimately their existence.

48. See the "Cult of the Indian," in

Notes—Chapter 2

Gunfighter Nation, Richard Slotkin, pp. 366–378.

49. The original short story by Guy Trosper titled "The Drifter" was rewritten three times before becoming a screenplay. In the previous version there are no Indians; the story got changed to be centered on Indians and racial injustice with the purpose, we believe, to make sure that the past (1865) could speak to the present (1946).

50. See Steve Neale's article (in *Back in the Saddle Again*, page 25), Alison R. Bernstein (*American Indians and World War II: Toward a New Era in Indian Affairs*, 1991), Kenneth William Townsend (*World War II and the American Indian*, 2000) and Richard Slotkin (*Gunfighter Nation*, 1992).

51. For the great contributions of the Native American Code Talkers during the world conflict see Bishop Franco, *Crossing the Pond: The Native American Effort in World War II* (Denton: Texas: North Texas UP, 1999), pp. 62–67. See especially p. 196 for the story of Native American Ira H. Hayes, the decorated Marine war hero and Pima Native American, who became famous when he was immortalized in the iconic photograph of the flag raising on Mount Suribachi on Iwo Jima, in 1945.

52. MGM waited to release *Devil's Doorway* after the enormous success of *Broken Arrow*, fearing the public would not be ready to accept a Hollywood production in which the main hero dies in the end.

53. Richard Brooks was a screenwriter who turned director and often worked on both the script and the movie. He made many successful films in his long career (*Blackboard Jungle, Cat on a Hot Tin Roof, In Cold Blood, Looking for Mr. Goodbar*), but only three Westerns: *The Last Hunt* (1956), *The Professionals* (1966), and *Bite the Bullet* (1975). The first Western was not so successful. It cost $1.7 million and made $1.7 million in its initial run. The second was a hit, it made $8.8 million in its initial release. The third movie, made $5 million in its initial run, cost $4 million, and it placed at No. 46, barely making the list of the top fifty films of the year. See Douglass K. Daniel, *Tough as Nails—The Life and Films of Richard Brooks* (Madison: University of Wisconsin Press, 2011), chapters 5, 8 and 10.

54. In the case of Charlie, the hunt is his last because he dies. In the case of Sandy, we presume that he will never hunt buffalo again because his aversion to killing becomes more and more apparent over the course of the film. At a certain point, after having spotted the peaceful grazing buffaloes basking in the sun, he puts away his rifle and, like many of the animals, takes a nap. Later on, Charlie gets mad at him for not having killed any buffaloes for days.

55. It is interesting to note that Jimmy gets beaten up because he gives some water to an Indian prisoner. As a consequence, he is punished for his humanitarian efforts by a community that treats Indians like slaves.

56. Charlie chases Sandy and wants to kill him because he is convinced that Sandy stole the white buffalo skin and "his woman." He is delusional, because neither is true; the Indian woman secretly gave the white skin to Jimmy for the burial of his dead Indian friend (killed by Charlie), and the Indian girl is not Charlie's woman because she detests him. He has forced himself on her since he captured her.

57. See Peter C. Rollins, *Hollywood's Indian: The Portrayal of the Native American in Film* (Lexington: University of Kentucky Press, 1998), pp. 12–38.

58. See "Savage Nations" in *The Philosophy of the Western*, Jennifer McMahon (Lexington: Kentucky UP, 2010), p. 264 et al.

59. The bar fight between Poole and Coolan's henchman in *Devil's Doorway*, for example, was edited. The censors eliminated some frames of the bar fight sequence because they deemed some of the kicks unacceptable. See Joanna Hearne, "The 'Ache for Home' in Anthony's Mann's *Devil's Doorway*," *Film and History* 33, no. 1 (2003): p. 29. In the Western genre, the use of the past to speak to the present was a good way to avoid the attention of the Un-American Committee.

Notes—Chapter 2

60. See John H. Lenihan, *Showdown—Confronting Modern America in the Western Film* (Urbana: University of Illinois Press, 1980), p. 58.

61. Lenihan, 1980, p. 57.

62. See Philip French, "The Indian in the Western Movie," in *The Pretend Indians: Images of Native Americans in the Movies*, Gretchen Bataille, eds (Ames: Iowa State UP, 1980), pp. 104–110.

63. *The Last Wagon* cost $1,670,000 and the box office return exceeded $1.5 million, according to *Variety Weekly*, 1956. *The Last Hunt* was budgeted at $2,121,000 and in December 1956 the box office return was only $1,604,000, but worldwide it made $3 million. On the whole they were not very successful movies, public or criticwise. Bosley Crowther, a famous reviewer of the era, wrote, in *The New York Times* (March 1, 1956, p. 37), a lukewarm review of *The Last Hunt*, praising the chilly and disturbing sequences of the slaying of the buffaloes for their unfortunate realism, but added: "But, unfortunately, what follows the scenes of slaughter has little more to do with the buffaloes and is mainly an account of bitter conflict between two hard-bitten buffalo-hunting men. ... The equating of Indian-hating with a lust for slaughter is morally good. But it does seem to take to Mr. Granger an awfully long time to get around to freezing out Mr. Taylor. That's the way sermons sometimes go." On the whole, the critic does not find the movie novelistic at all. Crowther also published a review of *The Last Wagon* (*The New York Times*, September 22, 1956, p. 14) in which he slashed mercilessly at the film: "A Familiar and unexciting journey across a plateau of western clichés is made by XX Century Fox ... dragging a lot of Arizona scenery in color and Cinemascope. The only thing novel about it is a courtroom scene at the end. ... Richard Widmark plays the hero with an air of weary truculence, and Felicia Farr is monotonously respectful as the survivor who falls in love with him. The only character in the picture worth attention is the brutal sheriff ... he keeps things humming..."

64. See as an example, *Dances with Wolves*, directed by Kevin Costner in 1990. The film uses many Native American actors cast as Indian characters: Graham Greene (Kicking Bird), Oneida Indian; Rodney A. Grant (Wind in His Hair), Omaha Tribe; Floyd "Red Crow" Westerman (Ten Bears), Dakota Sioux; Tantoo Cardinal (Black Shawl), Cree and French; Nathan Lee Chasing His Horse (Smiles a Lot), Lakota Sioux; Michael Spears (Otter), Lakota Sioux; Wes Studi (Toughest Pawnee), Cherokee; Steve Reevis (Sioux /Warrior), Blackfoot Nation. The film was shot on location in South Dakota and in Wyoming, in Sioux territory. The Indian characters do speak Lakota (one of the three languages of the Great Plains Sioux tribes) and subtitles are provided.

65. See Vine Deloria, *Custer Died for Your Sins: An Indian Manifesto* (Norman: Oklahoma UP, 1988, p. 202). I would also add that the Western is essentially an "action" film. The filmic story needs a conflict with an antagonist—usually played by Indians or outlaws—which in the end can be resolved through a violent confrontation and many exciting sequences. The Indians, unfortunately, ended up being the designated enemies. I would like to point out that the Indian attack is what has made the genre so everlasting and so popular with the audience. Often, the most memorable part of a Western is the Indian attack; the galloping horses, the screeching war hoops, the tumbling of riders and horses, and the arrows create fast action sequences that prepare the viewer for the last-minute arrival of the cavalry (with blaring bugle and unsheathed sabers), and the resolution of the situation. The abilities and agility of so many Native American stunt-actors greatly contributed to making the genre into an exciting spectacle.

66. Gretchen Bataille, ed., *The Pretend Indians* (Ames: Iowa State UP, 1980), p. 50.

67. Bataille, 1980, p. 56.

68. Valdez Moses writes an interesting analysis of the Indian in *Fort Apache* (John Ford, 1948), *Little Big Man* (Arthur Penn, 1970), *A Man Called Horse* (Elliot

Notes—Chapter 2

Silverstein, 1970), *The Return of a Man Called Horse* (Irvin Kershner, 1976), *Dances with Wolves* (Kevin Costner, 1990) and *Dead Man* (Jim Jarmush, 1995). Starting from Tzvetan Todorovs's *The Conquest of America: The Question of the Other*, and the Spanish conquest of the continent, the critic traces the persistent binary view of the Amerindian—a view that has remained fixed ideologically through centuries and has ended up permeating many Hollywood Westerns—as the noble savage (De Las Casas) or the inferior/demonic savage (Sepulveda). He argues that because Hollywood production was not aimed at a Native American public, the portrayal of the Indian had little to do with any modern attempt to discover or understand the "Other," but was motivated mostly by the desire to criticize the defects of contemporary American society ("Savage Nations: Native American and The Western," in *The Philosophy of the Western*, Jennifer McMahon ed. (Lexington: Kentucky UP, 2010), pp. 261–290.).

69. On the inferiority of the cinematic Indians see also Jacquelyn Kilpatrick, *Celluloid Indians* (Lincoln: University of Nebraska Press, 1999), pp. xv–35.

70. See Peter C. Rollins, *Hollywood's Indian: The Portrayal of the Native American in Film* (Lexington: University of Kentucky Press, 1998), p. 33.

71. "The Plains Indians include such tribes as the Sioux, the Cheyenne, and the Crows, who lived in tipis, hunted buffalo, danced the Sun Dance, and lived—and often died—on horseback. The Plains Indian was the most dashing figure among the American Indians because the Plains made him a horseman. Moreover, he was a fighter and is bound up with the conquest of the country, to say nothing of his connection with the Custer Massacre." Grechen Bataille, *The Pretend Indians* (Ames: Iowa State UP, 1980), pp. 64–65. The horse was introduced into the New World by the Spaniards, and it then diffused to North America, initially from the settlements around Santa Fe in 1600s. This spreading process went on through the 1700s, gradually providing the Indians of the Southwest and the Great Plains with the economic and military advantage of the use of horses. See Bataille, 1980, pp. 85–90.

72. See Ralph E. Friar and Natasha A. Friar, *The Only Good Indian; The Hollywood Gospel* (New York: Drama Book Specialists, 1972), p. 205.

73. Some of the most popular Native American actors were: Charles Stevens, grandson of Geronimo who was in more than 100 films between 1915 and 1961; Chief Thundercloud played Geronimo in *Geronimo* (1939) and Tonto in *The Lone Ranger* (1938); Jay Silverheels played Geronimo in *Broken Arrow* and *The Battle of Apache Pass*, Lakohna in *The Cowboy and the Indians*, Tonto in the *The Lone Ranger* TV series, etc.; Iron Eyes Cody had a career as an "Indian" in motion pictures that spanned 50 years, but he was in reality an Italian-American who faked his origins; Chief Dan George (Old Lodge Skins in *Little Big Man*, Lone Watie in *The Outlaw Josey Wales*); Wes Studi (a Pawnee in *Dances with Wolves* 1990, Magua in *The Last of the Mohicans*, 1992, Geronimo in *Geronimo: an American Legend*, 1993, and Eytukan in *Avatar* 2009). Jay Silverheels was very active in promoting Native Americans in motion pictures. He was behind the Indian Actors Guild, founded in 1966, to promote the use of native people in native roles, the training of Native Americans in horseman skills, and the teaching of dramatic skills. He helped to form an Indian Actors' Workshop at the Los Angeles Indian Center with the help of other Indian actors. For more on Native American actors see Bob Herzber, *Savages and Saints* (Jefferson, NC: McFarland, 2008), p. 115.

74. See Gretchen Bataille, *The Pretend Indians* (Ames: Iowa State UP, 1980), p. 57. The Native Americans and the few critics who spoke out against the misrepresentation of Indians in films during the first half of the century were isolated voices (p. 58). The misrepresentation of Indians also includes the use of other races and nationalities (Latinos, Middle-Eastern and Asian people) in the role of the Indians.

75. See John Price, "The Stereotyping of North American Indians in

Notes—Chapter 2

Motion Pictures" in *The Pretend Indians*, Gretchen Bataille, ed. (Ames: Iowa State UP, 1980), p. 73. Price also notes that most of the Indians did not regularly ride horses, hunt large game, wear tailored hide clothing or wear feathers in their hair. The use of feather headdresses is correct for about two dozen Great Plains tribes of the late 1800s, but they are false for more than 500 other Native societies in North America (p. 75).

76. Bataille, 1980, p. 87.

77. About the representation of Indians in the movies see Edward Buscombe, *'Injuns!': Native Americans in the Movies* (London: Reaktion, 2006). Buscombe affirms that Indianness is an artificial construction imposed by whites and produced for white consumption; whites even imposed names like Navajo, Sioux on the tribes (pp. 10–19).

78. For an amusing, but truthful description of the filmic stereotypes see J. Kilpatrick who writes: "The typical Hollywood Indian of the '40s and '50s wore long, flowing, feathered headdress, a breechclout (with swimming trunks underneath, of course), and moccasins, and he wielded a fierce-looking tomahawk. His sister, the Indian Princess wore a long, beaded and fringed buckskin dress and a beaded headband with one feather sticking straight up in the back. They lived in tipi, and he hunted buffalo—or settlers—and carved totem poles while she picked berries, slaved away at the buffalo hides, or fashioned pottery. A man described as Sioux might have been found wearing a Navajo blanket over his chest, carrying weapons from a northeastern tribe, wearing an Apache bandanna, and standing in front of a northwestern tribe's totem pole. These individual details of the celluloid Indians were obviously not all figments of a Hollywood imagination. Most of them could be found somewhere in the five hundred separate cultures, but Hollywood was the only place where the whole simulacrum came together." *Celluloid Indians* (Lincoln: University of Nebraska Press, 1999), p. 51.

79. It goes without saying that the filmic scenes of the "Indian attack" in which the braves attack the whites and get mercilessly mowed down by the whites' repeater guns, even if cinematographically attractive, are indeed offensive. The fact that the Indians keep coming, frame after frame, to get killed in great numbers without stopping or changing tactic, makes them look like senseless beings, incapable of judgment. Historically, the "Indians Wars" proved that the "redskins" were indeed skillful fighters, even when facing enemies with superior weaponry. See Ralph E. Friar and Natasha A. Friar, *The Only Good Indian: The Hollywood Gospel* (New York: Drama Book Specialists, 1972), p. 205.

80. John Ford employed Navajos in his films, the Sioux were hired for *A Man Called Horse* and the Crows for *Little Big Man*. See Friar and Friar, 1972, p. 257. The extras were found on reservations and often employed for far less than union scale.

81. See Ward Churchill, *Fantasies of the Master Race: Literature, Cinema, and the Colonization of the American Indians* (San Francisco: City Lights Books, 1998), and, by the same author, *Struggle for the Land: Native North American Resistance to Genocide, Ecoside, and Colonization* (San Francisco: City Lights Books, 2002); Ella Shohat, "Gender and the Culture of Empire," in *Otherness and the Media: An Ethnography of the Imagined and the Imaged*, Hamid Naficy and Teshone Gabriel, eds. (Langhorne, PA: Harwood Academic Publishers, 1993); and Roxanne Dumbar-Ortiz, *An Indigenous Peoples' History of the Unites States* (Boston: Beacon Press, 2014).

82. Kilpatrick criticizes the revisionist Westerns in which the white hero indianizes himself as in *A Man Called Horse* (1970), affirming that in this film the natural superiority of the white man prevails; the indianized hero is the one who learns everything the Indians do, but he learns it so well and so quickly that he becomes their leader. The critic also points out the many inaccuracies of the Sioux rites and customs portrayed in the film. See *Celluloid Indians* (Lincoln: University of Nebraska Press, 1999), pp. 79–84. We agree in principle

Notes—Chapter 3

with the critic, and we think there is a need for more Native American actors and directors who can express their point of view in Western films, because the Native voice, so far, has been mediated through the indianized white hero and has, mostly, reverberated the way the progressive, non-racist whites see the natives and their culture. However, we also believe that the "indianization" of the white hero works well in highlighting the shortcomings of white civilization in films like *Little Big Man*, *The Last Wagon*, and *Dances with Wolves*. In the pro-Indian cycle, the cowboy/hero in the end integrates into his society and accepts the fact that his allegiance is to the whites as in *Run of the Arrow*, *The Savage*, *The Last Frontier*, etc., but, in the novelistic and revisionist Westerns this does not happen. Often the indianized hero chooses the indigenous way of life and the wilderness over civilization. An additional problem, as Marubbio and Buffalohead point out, is "Native Americans and First Nations people make up roughly 1 per cent of the population in the United States and 3.8 per cent in Canada. For a market-driven industry like Hollywood, such a small viewing demographic is invisible. While advocates in Hollywood supporting Indigenous filmmakers exist, it remains more profitable for Hollywood to continue reproducing the stereotypical images of Native people found in blockbuster period films set in the colonial period or the mid- to late nineteenth century. ... Such productions tend to valorize the actions of the Unites States against Native Nations during this nation-building eras." (M. Elise Marubbio and Eric L. Buffalohead, eds., *Native Americans on Film: Conversations, Teaching, and Theory* (Lexington: Kentucky UP, 2012), pp. 3–4). Furthermore, for these latter authors, the majority of the revisionist Westerns use the Indians "as a backdrop for the telling of a white person's story" (p. 5), depriving the natives of their voice because "... the continual consumption of these reified images of Indians validates a colonialist historic memory and denies critical acknowledgement of the lived reality of native nations" (p. 5). The idea is that the Western genre creates images of Indians from the point of view of non-natives, reinforcing stereotypes and national myths of conquest, perpetuating images of native peoples as exotic objects of interest ethnographically speaking (p.10), once the "noble" and the "hollering savage" have been dismissed. For the West as a center of imperial fantasies see also Lee Clark Mitchel, "Whose West Is It Anyway? Or, What's Myth Got to Do with It? The Role of America in the Creation of the Myth of the West," *American Review of Canadian Studies* 33, issue 4 (December 2003). Mitchel claims that Buffalo Bill's Wild West Show convinced millions of people in America and abroad that the reality of the West "exactly matched their own romantic imaginings, with dare-devil, bareback cowboy riding, actual Indian figures like Sitting Bull and Geronimo, trick marksmen like Annie Oakley, and authentic historical pageants" (p. 504).

Chapter 3

1. The list of the 1990s Westerns includes also *Tombstone* (1993), *Dead Man* (1995), *Wyatt Earp* (1994), *Wild Bill* (1995), *Posse* (1993), *Geronimo: An American Legend* (1993), to cite just the most famous.

2. See Martin Flanagan "Fighting to Be Seen: Looking for Women in the West: From *The Searchers* to *The Missing*," in *Myth and Violence in the Contemporary Female Text: New Cassandras*, Sanja Bahun-Radunović and V.G. Julie Rajan, eds. (Burlington, VT: Ashgate, 2011), pp. 112–15.

3. Mark E. Wildermuth, *Feminism and the Western in Film and Television* (New York: Palgrave-Macmillan, 2018), p. 4.

4. Gary Heba and Robin Murphy, "Go West, young woman! Hegel's Dialectic and Women's Identities in Western Films" in *The Philosophy of the Western*, L. McNahon and B. Steve Csaki, eds. (Lexington: Kentucky University Press, 2010), p. 309.

Notes—Chapter 3

5. Gary Heba and Robin Murphy, 2010, pp. 325–26.

6. Dale Baues, "Gender in Bakhtin's Carnival," in *Feminism: An Anthology of Literary Theory and Criticism*, Robyn R. Warhol, ed. (New Brunswick, NJ: Rutgers UP, 1991), p. 671.

7. Mikhail M. Bakhtin, *Problems of Dostoevsky's Poetics*. Caryl Emerson, ed. (Minneapolis: Minnesota UP, 1963), p. 287.

8. David K. Danow, *The Thought of Mikhail Bakhtin: From Word to Culture* (New York: St. Martin's Press, 1991), p. 60

9. Mikhail M. Bakhtin, *The Dialogic Imagination: Four Essays*, Michael Holquist, ed. (Austin: University of Texas Press, 1988), p. 270.

10. Gary Heba and Robin Murphy, 2010, pp. 310–311.

11. Bakhtin, 1988, p. 263.

12. Gary Heba and Robin Murphy, 2010, p. 312.

13. David K. Danow, 1991, p. 65.

14. Pam Cook "Women in the Western," in *The Western Reader*, Jim Kitses and Gregg Rickman, eds. (New York: Limelight Editions, 1998), pp. 295–296.

15. Pam Cook, 1998, p. 294.

16. Jacqueline Levitin, "The Western: Any Good Roles for Feminists?" in *Film Reader*, no. 5 (1982): pp. 95–108.

17. Lindsey Collins reminds us that the woman in the Western is often equated to the land; she is, like Nature, a "virgin space" to be conquered. The critic writes: "Many feminist philosophers, such as Luce Irigaray, Susan Bordo, Elizabeth Grosz, and Donna Haraway, have pointed out the ways that masculinist philosophical traditions have participated in this panoramic epistemology by coding the mind as immaterial, disembodied, and male, and conversely, the body as natural, material, and female. In this formulation ... natural landscapes are the passive feminine proving ground for masculine projects of technology and progress." "Landscapes of Gendered Violence," in *The Philosophy of the Western*, Jennifer L. McMahon and B. Steve Csaki, eds. (Lexington: Kentucky UP, 2010), p. 92). We agree with Collins; in *Shane* the women, like the land, need to be protected and "cultivated." See Lizzie Francke's "Perspectives: Western Women," in which she affirms that the frontier was no place for women, but the revival of the Western in the 1990s brought gender into the genre. She refers specifically to *The Ballad of Little Jo* (dir. Maggie Greenwald, 1993); in her article she offers an excursus of the Hollywood Westerns that focused on a female protagonist (*The Guardian Weekend Page*, December 4, 1993, p. 22). There is an interesting interview with Maggie Greenwald recorded by Tania Modleski in 1995, in which the director talks about female heroines in Westerns ("Our Heroes Have Sometimes Been Cowgirls: An Interview with Maggie Greenwald," *Film Quarterly* 49, no. 2 (Winter, 1995–1996): pp. 2–11.) In 2016 Tauris published *Euro-Western: Reframing Gender, Race and the "Other" in Film*, by Lee Broughton (London: Tauris), who claims, after a brief overview of some American Westerns with female protagonists at the center, that "British Westerns produced during the early 1970s introduced female characters who were able to act completely independently and physically strike against patriarchal order without suffering the gender-based punishment [usually death] or prescription [returning to a proper female role] still found in contemporary American Westerns" (p.188). Broughten does not seem to find any heteroglossic or ex-glossic female protagonists in the American Westerns, an argument that the present chapter proves incorrect.

18. Jane Tompkins, *West of Everything* (Oxford: Oxford University Press, 1992), pp. 8–67. See also Susan Suleiman, *The Female Body in Western Culture: Contemporary Perspectives* (Cambridge, MA: Harvard University Press, 1986).

19. Blake Lucas, "Saloon Girls and Ranchers' Daughters: The Woman in the Western," in *The Western Reader*, Jim Kitses and Gregg Rickman, eds. (New York: Limelight Editions, 1999), p. 301.

20. Blake Lucas, 1999, p. 301.

21. Blake Lucas, 1999, p. 310.

22. Blake Lucas, 1999, p. 310.

23. Claire Johnston, on this regard, affirms that "Iconography as a specific

Notes—Chapter 3

kind of signs based on certain conventions within the Hollywood genres has been partly responsible for the stereotyping of women within commercial cinema in general, but the fact that there is a far greater differentiation of men's roles than women's roles in the history of cinema relates to sexist ideology itself, and the basic opposition which places man inside history, and women as ahistorical and eternal." (in Richard Dryer, *Stars* (Durham: Duke UP, 1998), p. 92). It seems to us that Lucas is referring to this kind of "eternal femininity."

24. See Gary Heba and Robin Murphy, 2010, pp. 312–317.

25. *Shane* was directed by George Stevens in 1953, with the screenplay by A.B. Guthrie Jr., and was based on the novel by Jack Schaefer titled *Shane*. It starred Alan Ladd as the gunfighter Shane, Jean Arthur as the wife of the homesteader, and Joe Starrett (Van Heflin). In 1954, the film won the Oscar for Best Cinematography (Loyal Griggs), Best Picture (George Stevens) and Best Actor in a Supportive Role (Brandon De Wilde as the young son of Joe Starrett). Patrick McGee in his *From Shane to Kill Bill: Rethinking the Western* (Malden, MA: Blackwell, 2007) does an interesting close reading of *Shane* through the lens of masculinity, focusing on the role of the individual in relation to class struggle. In our analysis, we are mostly focusing on femininity instead.

26. For a general overview of *Shane* see Wyn Wachhorst, "Come Back, Shane! The National Nostalgia," *Southwest Review* 98, no. 1 (2013): pp. 12–25; Matthew J. Costello "'I Didn't Expect to Find Any Fences Around Here': Cultural Ambiguity and Containment in *Shane*," *Journal of American Culture* 27, no. 3 (September 2004): pp. 261–270; and Joseph Maddrey who affirms that "Shane reinforces the themes of the classic Western ... showing that 'right can have violence on its side,' but, at the same time, acknowledging that 'heavy responsibility' comes with violence, as Shane himself says to little Joey: 'There's no living with a killing, Joey!'" (*The Quick, the Dead, and the Revived* (Jefferson, NC: McFarland, 2016), p. 51).

27. On individual freedom and the importance of land rights see Stephen J. Mexal, "Two Ways to Yuma—Locke, Liberalism, and Western Masculinity in *3:10 to Yuma*" in *The Philosophy of the Western*, Jennifer McMahon and B. Steve Csaki, eds. (Lexington: Kentucky UP, 2010), pp. 69–87.

28. For an analysis of the family in *Shane* that mirrors the most archetypical of families, the holy family of Christian belief, see Jeff Malpas, "A Western Sense of Place: The Case of George Stevens' *Shane*," *GeoHumanities* 1, issue 1 (August 2015): pp. 35–50.

29. Jacinda Read, *The New Avengers: Feminism, Femininity and the Rape-Revenge Cycle* (Manchester, UK: Manchester UP, 2000), p. 125.

30. Bakhtin, *Dialogic Imagination*, p. 263.

31. For a discussion on the "gaze" and scopophilia see the ultra-popular article by Laura Mulvey titled "Visual Pleasure and Narrative Cinema." *Screen*, Autumn, 1975, Vol. XVI (3): 6–18.

32. *High Noon* was produced by Stanley Kramer, directed by Fred Zinnemann and written by Carl Forman. They all collaborated to the script and worked as a team. The movie, made with a fairly modest budget, was enormously successful at the box office. It won four Oscars: Best Actor (Gary Cooper), Best Film Editing (Elmo Williams and Harry W. Gerstad), Best Original Song (Dmitri Tiomkin and Ned Washington), Best Music Score (Dmitri Tiomkin) and went on to gather many other awards. For a detailed story of the making, the success, and the attacks against the film see Jeremy Byman's *Showdown at High Noon—Witch Hunts, Critics, and the End of the Western* (Lanham, Maryland: Scarecrow Press, 2004); and Joseph Maddrey, *The Quick, the Dead and the Revived* (Jefferson, NC: McFarland & Company, 2016), pp. 48–49.

33. In our case the "good girl" has already married the hero before the story starts.

34. Foster, G. "The Women in *High Noon* (1952): A Metanarrative

Notes—Chapter 3

of Difference," in *The Films of Fred Zinnemann: Critical Perspectives*. Albany, NY: University of New York Press, 1999. pp. 93–102.

35. Helen tells Harvey: "I don't like anyone to put his hands on me unless I want him to. And I don't like you to ... anymore."

36. Helen Ramirez is motivated by different factors: she wants to avoid being in town when Frank Miller arrives because, as Kane says, some townsfolk might have written to him about their affair, and, as a consequence, the outlaw may want to exact revenge; she still loves Kane and, therefore, she neither wants to see him dead, nor to be around to see him happily married to somebody else, in case he survives the showdown. She is also upset that Harvey tells the marshal that he is her lover. On top of all this, she does not like the townsfolk because they treat her as an outcast due to her "immoral" behavior. See the episode in which her co-partner in business comes to see her, entering by the hotel backdoor, so he won't be seen by the "moral majority"—community. It is clear that it is OK to do business with her in order to get money, but it is better to keep it under wraps. Hence, the evident hypocrisy of the townspeople.

37. Because of the unfortunate involvement of Carl Forman with the HUAC, the fact that he was blacklisted and had to flee (immediately after *High Noon* was completed) to the UK where he was in exile for many years, it is easy to interpret the film as an allegory of McCarthyism: the good individual (Forman), abandoned by the community (Hollywood cinematic community and American society at large), has to fend for himself while he is persecuted by an evil bunch (Miller gang/HUAC). See Matthew J. Costello who writes: "*High Noon* is thus a strong voice criticizing the cold war consensus for its lack of public virtue and its failure to support the noble, virtuous individual who risks all to defend a community unworthy of that defense." ("Rewriting *High Noon*—Transformations in American Popular Political Culture During the Cold War, 1952–1968,"

in *Hollywood's West* by John E. O'Connor. Lexington: Kentucky UP, 2005, pp. 175–180). According to J. Jeffrey Tillman's "*High Noon* and the Problem of American Political Obligation," the film can be interpreted as a depiction of the problems of political obligation centered on Kane who pursues an Aristotelian ideal of community based on virtue, while the rest of his fellow countrymen follow a Lockean idea of society, based on economic gain, because to help the marshal will certainly put at risk the future growth of the town: violence and instability will scare investors (in *Perspectives on Political Science*, Winter 2007, Vol. 36, No. 1, pp. 30–45). For a general treatment of the historical period of the Cold War see Stephen J. Whitfield, *The Culture of the Cold War*, especially the chapter entitled "Reeling: The Politics of Film," Baltimore: Johns Hopkins UP, 1996, pp. 127–151, and Tom Engelhardt, *The End of Victory Culture*. Amherst: Massachusetts UP, 1995. Other critics like John Francis Kreidl affirms that "the marshal [America] has wanted peace after cleaning up the town five years before, [i.e., World War II] and [now] reluctantly must buckle on his gun belt again in the face of new aggression [the Korean War], and eventually his pacifist wife [American isolationists] must see where her true duty lies and support him" [in *Nicholas Ray* (Boston: Twayne Publishers, 1977, p. 46)]. In spite of all the possible correlations existing between the socio-political climate and the content of films, especially inside popular culture and genre cinema, we tend to be cautious with these direct parallels between fiction and reality because fiction reverberates, alludes to, echoes reality, but a filmic text is a fictional representation with a surplus of signification.

38. Byman writes "Visually, *High Noon* is above all about the framing of specific shots and matching them to other carefully framed shots—such as the jump cut from the track to the church aisle—to increase the sheer oppressiveness..." ("The Making of *High Noon*," in Byman's *Showdown at High Noon*, p. 222).

39. For an in-depth analysis of

Notes—Chapter 3

Helen's space see Monica Montelongo Flores'"Helen's Hotel Room: The West, the Hotel and the Mexican Female Body as Decolonial Sites in *High Noon*." *Quarterly Review of Film and Video*," 32 (20015): 301–313.

40. See the attraction of one of the Miller's gang for Amy. After watching her buying a ticket in the station, she becomes the object of the young outlaw's desire. Later on, he is killed because, following his desire, he steals a woman's hat in a millinery shop, making a noise that alerts Kane of the approaching gang. The viewer assumes that the fashionable hat would have been a present for Amy. When he is shot by Kane, the man has the fashionable hat hanging from his gun belt.

41. David Lusted writes, "In Westerns, back-shooting—shooting an adversary from behind—transgresses the ritual of the gunfight, which demands that an opponent is faced. Back-shooters thereby offend not just the code of justice, but against the social codes ... by rejecting the public display of fair play." ("Social Classes and the Western as Male Melodrama," in *The Book of Westerns*, Ian Cameron and Douglas Pye, eds. (New York: Continuum, 1996), p. 72). In this sense Amy breaks both moral and social codes with her transgressive behavior.

42. Bakhtin, 1988, p. 345

43. One could argue that *Shane* is trying to impose on the audience a pre-war feminine role model, the one typical of patriarchy. *High Noon* instead proposes a more modern feminine role model that seems to reflect the changes that the war effort promoted among the female population at large, bringing about a more independent female individual in charge of her own life.

44. For an in-depth description of the motivations of Zinnemann and Forman, respectively director and scriptwriter of *High Noon*, see Stephen Prince's article "The Women of *High Noon* (1952)," and Leonard Quart's article "Historical Perspectives and the Realist Aesthetic in High Noon (1952)," in *The Films of Fred Zinnemann: Critical Perspectives*, A. Nolletti, ed. (Albany: State University of New York Press, 1999). Forman was blacklisted during McCarthyism and had to flee to the UK in order to work; Zinnemann, being an Austrian Jew who emigrated to the U.S. at the onset of Nazism (1929), knew what it meant to be persecuted, having lost both his parents in the Holocaust. *High Noon* could easily be read as a text in which one man (Kane), facing a danger (Fascism) that threatens his community, against all odds, alone and only guided by his moral compass, decides to fight back. We could read into it a reverberation either of what went on in Europe during Nazi-Fascism or in the USA during McCarthyism. In both cases we face a civilization on the brink of collapse.

45. Crowther is quoted in J. E. Smyth's article, entitled "The Western That Got Its Content 'From Elsewhere': *High Noon*, Fred Zinnemann and Genre Cleansing," in *Quarterly Review of Film and Video* 31 (2014): p. 50.

46. For a study of the filmic strategies of *High Noon* see Leonard Quart's article, "Historical Perspectives and the Realist Aesthetic in High Noon (1952)," in *The Films of Fred Zinnemann: Critical Perspectives*, A. Nolletti, ed. (Albany: State University of New York Press, 1999), pp. 79–92; and Jeremy Byman's "The Making of *High Noon*," in *Showdown at High Noon* (Lanham, MD: Scarecrow Press, 2004), pp. 207–243.

47. For an analysis of Kane as a Kantian hero see Daw-Nay Evans, "The Duty of Reason—Kantian Ethics in *High Noon*," in *The Philosophy of the Western*, Jennifer McMahon, ed. (Lexington: University of Kentucky Press, 2010), pp. 180–187. For Kant's influence on Westerns see also "The Cost of the Code—Ethical Consequences in *High Noon* and *The Ox-Bow Incident*," pp. 187–189 of the same source.

48. J.E. Smyth, "The Western That Got Its Content 'From Elsewhere': *High Noon*, Fred Zinnemann and Genre Cleansing," *Quarterly Review of Film and Video* 31 (2014): p. 42.

49. For a detailed discussion on the various motivations of Hadleyville inhabitants see Stephen Prince's "Historical Perspective and the Realist Aesthetic in *High Noon*," pp. 86–89. It is worth noticing that the only two people willing to

Notes—Chapter 3

help the marshal are an old drunkard and a fourteen-year-old boy, and, for obvious reasons, Kane has to decline their offer.

50. Pat Kirkham and Janet Thumin in "Me Jane" in *Me Jane—Masculinity, Movies and Women* argue that "transgression is in itself 'feminine' since to transgress patriarchal law—social, moral, ethical, political—is to put oneself outside of it, and, outside the symbolic boundaries of the masculine is, precisely, the realm of the feminine." (London: Lawrence & Wishart, 1995, p. 31) According to this perspective Marshal Kane could be considered an *ante litteram* feminist hero; no wonder that John Wayne and Howard Hawk reacted so ferociously to the film. For a complete view of what happened to *High Noon* when it was created and afterwards see Jeremy Byman, *Showdown at High Noon—Witch-Hunts, Critics, and the End of the Western* (Lanham, MD: Scarecrow Press, 2004). It is the depiction of Hadleyville's foul society and the fact that Kane in the end, completely disgusted, throws his marshal star into the dust that infuriated Wayne and Hawks, because Marshal Kane's final gesture is the negation of the Frontier myth.

51. The transformation of the women is not articulated around femininity versus masculinity, but around femininity itself. The women at the end of the story, as our filmic analysis demonstrates, no longer operate according to the standards of femininity established by patriarchy at the beginning of the story.

52. Bakhtin, 1988, p. 346.

53. Bakhtin, *Problems of Dostoevsky's Poetics* (Minneapolis: University of Minnesota Press, 1963), p. 81.

54. William Wellman directed nine films in the Western genre, most of them striking for the variety of tone and topics. Three of them are superb and unusual Westerns: *The Ox-Bow Incident* (1943), *Yellow Sky* (1948) and *Westward the Women* (1951). Wellman, who directed 83 films in his long career, was also the author of classic Hollywood hits like *Public Enemy* (1931), *A Star Is Born* (1937; Oscar for Best Director), and *Story of G. I. Joe* (1945), just to mention a few. *Westward the Women* is a neglected classic in which the director "interrogates the fragile stability of friendship, family, ethnicity, romance ... and (most radically of all) gender..." (Josh Anderson, "Westward Wellman," *Senses of Cinema*, issue 67 (July 2013): p. 2). In the same article Anderson goes on to define Wellman's film as a "a proto-feminist exploration of social norms," and a plain bizarre Western for 1951. The film deserves "a more central position in discussions of gender roles in classic Hollywood cinema" as Be Sachs points out in "*Westward the Women*: A Neglected Classic About Sexual Politics on the Frontier," in *Chicago Reader*, June 19, 2014. Frank Thompson in "The Wellman Westerns: An Appraisal," reveals, "The location work on *Westward the Women* turned out to be nearly as grueling for the cast and crew as for the fictional women in the film. The women were put through a three-week course where they were trained in the art of riding, roping, shooting and anything else that a pioneer woman might need to know.... This was to aid them immeasurably when the location work began at a place called Surprise Valley in the Mojave Desert. Apart from interiors, virtually no shooting was done at the studio. Wellman instructed cameraman William C. Mellor to use no filters (or as little as possible) to give the film a stark, glaring look" (in *American Classic Screen Features*, John C. Tibbetts and James Michael Welsh, eds. (Lanham, MD: Scarecrow Press, 2010), p. 106). Charles Schnee wrote the screenplay based on a story by Frank Capra. Critic Bosley Crowther, in *The New York Times* review that came out on January 1, 1952, defines Wellman's movie as an "uneven Western, part weeper and part burlesque. ... We cannot surrender entirely to the eloquent doctrine of the film," showing evidently an error of judgment not uncommon among the critics of the time; the negative or lukewarm reviews that the film received are probably the reasons why it has not been properly studied so far as a great proto-feminist Western.

55. This is true also in the case of Ito, the puny Japanese man and sidekick of

Notes—Chapter 3

Buck, who, disagreeing with the "big boss," mumbles in Japanese, aggravating the wagon-master and forcing him to repeat over and over, "What did you say?" Through the foreign utterance Ito influences Buck and manages to soften and redirect his behavior. Ito is a more "feminized male voice," capable of compassion and respect towards the "Other." The movie is an interesting case of Frontier polyphony.

56. See Helene Shugart "Counterhegemonic Acts: Appropriation as a Feminist Rhetorical Strategy," *Quarterly Journal of Speech* 83, no. 2 (1997): p. 211. For the languagescape of Frontier women see Annette Kolodny "Honing a Habitable Languagescape: Women's Images for the New World Frontiers," in *Women and Language in Literature and Society*, Sally McConnell-Ginet, Ruth Borker and Nelly Furman, eds. (New York: Praeger, 1980), pp. 188–202. In the same volume see also "Linguistics and the Feminine Challenge" by Sally McConnell-Ginet, pp. 3–25.

57. See Helene A. Shugart, "Counterhegemonic Acts: Appropriation as a Feminist Rhetorical Strategy," *Quarterly Journal of Speech* 83, no. 2 (1997) (1997): pp. 213–214.

58. For a discourse on Robert Taylor as Buck, the wagonmaster, see Peter William Evans, "Westward the Women: Feminizing the Wilderness," in *The Book of Westerns*, I.A. Cameron and D. Pye, eds. (New York: Continuum, 1996), pp. 207–211.

59. The character that supports a benevolent, but traditional idea of patriarchal domesticity is the owner of the California valley, Roy Whitman (John McIntire). He repeats often that there is nothing a woman won't overcome if facing the possibility of getting married. However, these women end up pursuing marriage on their own terms as we see when they reach their destination.

60. See Gilles Deleuze, *Cinema 1: The Movement Image* (Minneapolis: Minnesota UP, 1986), p. 25.

61. See Gilles Deleuze, *Cinema 1: The Movement Image* (Minneapolis: Minnesota UP, 1986), p. 26.

62. See Daniel Agacinski, "West and the City," *South Atlantic Review* 76, no. 2 (Spring 2011): p. 24.

63. The women are not going to follow the genre cliché and become adventurers that roam the prairies, i.e., they are not becoming a copycat of the classic male hero who chooses the wilderness over family life. They are not transforming themselves into men. In the end, they find their sweethearts and choose domesticity as in many traditional Westerns, but with a difference—they do it on their own terms, becoming the makers of their own destiny. In fact, they do the choosing, subverting gender rules. Let's not forget that underneath their nice attire they carry a gun.

64. The rhetoric used for talking about the conquest of the wilderness has traditionally used terms that equate the virgin land with the passive feminine in a discourse in which the landscape is talked about as a land to be conquered, subdued and possessed like a woman. As Slotkin (*Regeneration Through Violence*) reminds us, the frontier mythology has constructed the male hero as the one who can fight as savagely as the Indians and, at the same time, can tame the wilderness. On the verge of the desert, the protagonists of *Western the Women* are shot from bottom up, standing on dunes, beaten by the wind and the sun, in ragged clothing, but empowered by their fortitude; they are shot in small groups, in a phallic position, and in a way that gives them the same power that is usually reserved in Westerns for the male heroes. The spectacular cinematography tells us that the women do "belong" in the West because they have acquired the status of heroines.

65. See Susan Suleiman, *The Female Body in Western Culture: Contemporary Perspectives*, (Cambridge, MA: Harvard UP, 1986), pp. 463–474. Suleiman defines the story of *Westward the Women* as "an odyssey of pain toward equality."

66. On rape and revenge in the Western genre see "Frontier Femmes: Rape-Revenge and the Western" in Jacinta Read's *The New Avengers: Feminism, Femininity and the Rape-Revenge Cycle* (Manchester: Manchester UP, 2000), p. 143.

Notes—Chapter 4

67. See Peter William Evans, "Westward the Women: Feminizing the Wilderness," in *The Book of Westerns*, I.A. Cameron and D. Pye, eds. (New York: Continuum, 1996), p. 208.

68. For the interplay of domination, love and submission see Jessica Benjamin, *The Bonds of Love—Psychoanalysis, Feminism, and the Problem of Domination* (New York: Pantheon Books, 1988).

69. For a summary of psychoanalytic feminist thinking regarding masculinity see Jessica Benjamin, "Masculinity Complex: A Historical Take" *Studies in Gender and Sexuality* 16, no. 4 (October 2015): pp. 271–277.

Chapter 4

1. Mary Ann Doane, *Femmes Fatales: Feminism, Film Theory, Psychoanalysis* (New York: Routledge, 1991), p. 270.

2. Niven Busch was the author of three famous novels: *The Postman Always Rings Twice* (1946), *Duel in the Sun* (1946) and *Distant Drums* (1951); all three were made into successful films. He sold the screen rights to *Duel in the Sun* to David O. Selznick.

3. Daniel Taradash also wrote the script for *From Here to Eternity* (1953).

4. Philip Yordan was a prolific writer, and he served as a front for the writers who had been blacklisted during McCarthyism. Some of his films include *Broken Lance* (1954), *The Bravados* (1958), *The Man from Laramie* (1955), *The Last Frontier* (1955), *El Cid* (1961), and *The Fall of the Roman Empire* (1964); Roy Chanslor was the author of two renowned novels made into films, *Johnny Guitar* (1954) and *The Ballad of Cat Ballou* (1963).

5. Karen Hollinger, *Feminist Film Studies* (New York: Routledge, 2012), p. 39.

6. David Lusted, "Social Class and the Western as Male Melodrama," in *The Book of Westerns*, Ian Cameron and Douglas Pye, eds. (New York: Continuum, 1996), p. 65. See also Jonna Eagle who asserts that "melodrama pivots around identification with the position of the victim … this identification with suffering, victimization, and abuse alternates, in melodrama, with another set of appeals oriented around sensational action and violence." According to the critic, melodrama oscillates between pathos and action, introverted moments of identification and scenes of shocking violence. We could not agree more; in fact, in the films analyzed in this chapter, action/violence and pathos alternate constantly on screen, forcing the viewer to identify with the victims. (Jonna Eagle, *Imperial Affects* (New Brunswick: Rutgers, 2017), pp. 4–5.)

7. As Lee Clark Mitchell affirms, the Western genre "allows us to gaze at men, this gaze forms such an essential aspect … that it seems covertly about just that: looking at men." Undoubtably the critic is right, nevertheless, the Western films we are considering in this chapter are the exception to the rule because they focus mostly on women protagonists. *Westerns: Making the Man in Fiction and Film* (Chicago: University of Chicago Press, 1996), p. 159.

8. Lee Clark Mitchell, 1996, p. 65.

9. Fritz Lang was an Austrian-born director who, at the onset of Nazism in 1934, emigrated from Germany to the United States. He was part of the German Expressionist cinema movement of Weimar with works that are considered milestones in cinema history: *Dr. Mabuse* and *The Gambler* in 1922, *Metropolis* in 1927, *M* in 1931, and *The Testament of Dr. Mabuse* in 1933. In the United States, he made two Westerns besides *Rancho Notorious*—*The Return of Frank James* (1940) and *Western Union* (1941). Lang had a very limited budget for *Rancho Notorious* and decided to film it entirely in studio, shooting some of the exteriors in the Republic's Western Lot. Every time we watch a scene with a landscape—mountains or a desert overlooking Altar's ranch—it is noticeable that the actors are in front of a painted backdrop. The "fictionality" of the exterior *mise-en-scène* involving a landscape, however, does not detract from the movie, because, in a melodrama, the priority for the viewer remains the interaction between the characters, an

Notes—Chapter 4

interaction that happens mostly in beautifully recreated interiors (I also consider as "interiors" the sequences that involve outside shops, town streets, and the ranch courtyard, etc.—all the exteriors that are contained spaces). The film is based on a short story by Silvia Richards that was never published. At the time she had a relationship with Fritz Lang. The movie script, however, written by David Tarandash, is derived from Richard's short story. For behind the scenes of *Rancho Notorious* see Peter Bogdanovich, *Fritz Lang in America* (New York: Praeger, 1967), pp. 77–80 and Robert A. Armour, *Fritz Lang* (Boston: Twayne Publishers, 1978), pp. 125–127. Notice the lukewarm review of *Rancho Notorious* by Bosley Crowther in *The New York Times* of May 15, 1952.

10. Graham Fuller, "The Psychological Western," *Sight and Sound* 26, no. 5 (May 2016): p. 38. According to the critic, unlike the classic Westerns centered on the nation-building myth, many postwar Westerns reversed the traditional gender roles (see Altar who enjoys the same privileges as the male world), and the male hero image. Vern and Frenchy are outlaws who have no desire to reintegrate into society, and why should they? All the communities are pretty unsavory.

11. Jeanine Basinger, *A Woman's View—How Hollywood Spoke to Women 1930–1960* (New York: Knopf, 1993), p. 161–165. Nobody doubted that John Wayne's star persona was the all-American active male, and Greta Garbo's a mysterious and exotic woman. Even when they appeared in roles that would contradict their star image, the audiences identified "these actors and actresses by a particular type of role, the one they most believe them in." According to Basinger, an audience remembers what it wants to remember and discards what it doesn't like, so Wayne will always be the all-American hero who never dies and always wins in movies, and Garbo will remain a Mata Hari even if she plays the role of a loving mother or devoted wife.

12. See Florence Jacobowitz, "The Dietrich Westerns: *Destry Rides Again* and *Rancho Notorious*," in *The Book of Westerns*, Ian Cameron and Douglas Pye, eds. (New York: Continuum, 1996), p. 88.

13. The films that Josef von Sternberg directed with Dietrich in the leading role were *The Blue Angel* (1930), *Morocco* (1930), *Dishonored* (1931), *Shanghai Express* (1932), *Blonde Venus* (1932), *The Scarlet Empress* (1934), and *The Devil is a Woman* (1935).

14. Florence Jacobowitz, "The Dietrich Westerns: *Destry Rides Again* and *Rancho Notorious*," in *The Book of Westerns*, Ian Cameron and Douglas Pye, eds. (New York: Continuum, 1996), p. 88. Dietrich was married to Rudy Sieber, but they lived separately. She had an endless string of lovers and suitors of both genders. Her persona conveyed a transgressive edge that challenged the cultural notion of femininity at the time. See also Catherine Constable, *Thinking in Images* (London: BFI Publishing, 2005) for an analysis of the images of Dietrich as *femme fatale* in von Sternberg's films.

15. I am thinking of *Destry Rides Again*, 1939, directed by George Marshall, a comedic Western with a flamboyant, bubbling, gorgeous Dietrich and a young James Stewart—an enjoyable film peppered with incredibly energetic scenes of dancing and singing, that, unfortunately, falls into the genre cliché, when, in the end, we have the saloon girl sacrificing herself for the hero. The sequence of the "saloon race" in one of the flashbacks of *Rancho Notorious* is reminiscent of a similar sequence in *Destry Rides Again*, but the former is a much more atmospheric and *noir*-like film.

16. Jeanine Basinger, *A Woman's View—How Hollywood Spoke to Women 1930–1960* (New York: Knopf, 1993), p. 166.

17. The male admiration is also enhanced by the fact that she is the only woman in the ranch and in the film, if we exclude the unfortunate fiancée of Vern, Beth, who only enjoys a few minutes of screen time in the beginning before being killed.

18. The song has many *double entendre* and sexual innuendos on the difference between a handsome boy and a

Notes—Chapter 4

man, and concludes affirming that a boy should not be sent to do the job of a man. It alludes to Frenchy and Vern, the man and the boy, both attractive for different reasons; Altar clearly favors the "man" in the song, as she does at the end of the story, when she steps in front of a bullet to save Frenchy.

19. See Pam Cook, ed., *The Cinema Book* (London: BFI, 2007), p. 495. Cook claims that the female spectator of 1940s and 1950s Hollywood melodramas is involved in emotional processes like masochism, paranoia, narcissism and hysteria, because "the woman's film, in spite of its focus on a female main character, perpetuates these processes and thus confirms the stereotypes about the female psyche." The emotional investment of the viewer destroys the distance between spectator and object of desire on screen, turning the active desire of both the female character and the female spectator into "the passive desire to be the desired object." According to Cook, the female spectator seems to be consumed by the image on the screen, and not consuming it, undergoing processes that can bring over-identification with the object of desire, and as a consequence, "the masquerade is effective in that it manufactures a distance from the image. By wearing femininity as a mask, the female spectator can create the necessary difference between herself and the represented femininity on the screen."

20. From the singing sequences, it is evident that Altar uses her beauty to rule over the men. To stay at Chuck-a-Luck the outlaws must pay her 10 percent of the loot they acquire in their robberies; she is so inflexible that often the outlaws complain about her ruling. When they finally rebel against her, they say that she had it coming, having been "riding mighty high" for a long time. Obviously, Altar has been able to exact payment and impose her rules for a long time thanks to her charm, sexual appeal, and legendary past life. However, with the passing of time she is doomed to lose this prerogative. Altar is aware of this, and in fact she is afraid of aging. Vern's vengeance ploy only speeds up a process of destruction that was already in the making because Time would interfere with her beauty.

21. Florence Jacobovitz, "The Dietrich Westerns," in *The Book of the Westerns*, Ian Cameron and Douglas Pye, eds. (New York: Continuum, 1996), p. 93.

22. See Lotte H. Eisner, *Fritz Lang* (London: Secker &Warburg, 1998), p. 302.

23. When Altar introduces Vern to the outlaws upon his arrival at the ranch, Wilson, as soon as Altar leaves, says, "What a gorgeous filly!" "Filly" normally means a young female horse, but, in this case, an attractive woman. Vern, after taming a wild filly, addresses Wilson and Kinch saying, "She's a cocky filly, like a lot of women, takes a lot of breaking before she comes along nice and even." In this instance, the patriarchal and domineering point of view of Vern in regard to women comes to the fore. It is true that in this case he is provoking Wilson, whom he suspects was Beth's assassin, to get him to say something incriminating. However, we cannot forget that Vern's viewpoint has to be connected with the tirade he launches against Altar after she reveals who gave her the brooch.

24. Frenchy is also deeply in love with Altar (a desperate and possessive love); he risks being hanged for stealing a bottle of perfume for her birthday, and, in the end, when she plans to leave Chuck-a-Luck, he says to her, "You belong to me. ... There is not much I have been able to keep and if I lose you I might as well turn me into the nearest sheriff. ... I'll kill you before you leave."

25. Richard Dyer affirms that Dietrich's image, crystallized in Josef von Sternberg's films, remained the key note of the actress' career. Her appearance in Westerns (*Destry Rides Again*, 1939, *Rancho Notorious*, 1952) only reinforced the image of an "alluring, exotic female 'Other.'" He says, "Her aging, far from dimming this [image], contributed to it, partly by the degree to which her beauty remained, partly by her presentation, in films, concerts, records, and photographs, in this term: the 'Eternal Feminine' ... Glamour photographs from early and late in her career illustrate this continuity, in particular the way in which

Notes—Chapter 4

she 'emerges' out of a vague background that places her nowhere earthly, but rather in some 'Other' realm of existence and by her almost Oriental eyes that look straight into the camera" (in *Stars* (London: BFI Publishing, 1998), p. 64).

26. Lang talks about Dietrich's unhappiness; she became very disagreeable during the filming, constantly saying to him that "Sternberg would have done so and so," basically implying that Lang was not doing enough to make her appear as attractive as she was in the 1930s films. Peter Bogdanovich, 1967, pp. 77–78.

27. Lotte H. Eisner, *Fritz Lang* (London: Secker & Warburg, 1976), pp. 301–302.

28. Frenchy embodies a more benign image of patriarchy than Vern. The gunslinger can be with a woman with a past who is in charge. However, he still considers Altar his possession, being the only thing that matters in his life. As a consequence, he would rather kill her that let her leave the ranch, as he tells her before the showdown with the outlaws. Vern demands submission in a woman. He believes in the traditional female role. Frenchy demands ownership. He can neither part from Altar nor allow somebody else to have her. Obviously in Frenchy's opinion, to love somebody means to ignore the other party's volition, as in the typical *amour fou* stereotype that for centuries has justified the killing of women in the name of violent passion or offended honor.

29. It seems to me that the utopian construction of Chuck-a-Luck in *Rancho Notorious* falls perfectly into what Jameson calls "an ideological act ... with the function of inventing imaginary ... 'solutions' to unresolvable social contradictions." (Fredric Jameson, *The Political Unconscious* (Ithaca, NY: Cornell UP, 1981), p. 79.)

30. For the definition of paratext and, later in the chapter, of peritext see Gèrard Genette who distinguishes everything that is around a text in the following ways: "... the *peritext* and the *epitext* occupy exclusively and exhaustively the spatial field of the *paratext*; in other words ... *paratext* = *peritext* + *epitext*," in "Introduction to the Paratext" *New Literary History* 22, no. 2 (Spring 1991): p. 264. Genette clearly considers the peritext as comprising the title, the preface, the post-scriptum, the notes, etc., while all the messages outside the book (at a certain distance from the book)—media interviews, conversations, correspondences, private journals, etc.—constitute the epitext; the two together form the paratext.

31. Yordan describes the creation of the screen play of Johnny Guitar as such: "We chose Chanslor's novel without using a single word from it, only the title; and we went and wrote a story where the woman was the star, a rare thing in Westerns." (in John Francis Kreidl, *Nicholas Ray* (Boston: Twayne Publishers, 1977), p. 48.)

32. Patrick McGilligan in *Nicholas Ray* (New York: Harper and Collins, 2011, p. 244) writes: "The Hollywood press reported that the Western would have an unusually lavish budget for Republic. Besides a salary commensurate with her billing, the star would participate in the film's profits, because she owned the screen rights to *Johnny Guitar*, the novel on which the picture would be based." Johnny Guitar was delivered to Republic as a package deal by Lew Wasserman, the president of MCA, which was Hollywood's most powerful talent agency. Crawford became a "de facto producer," and therefore held a powerful decisional position in the making of the film (Joe McNeill, "*Johnny Guitar* in Sedona," *Sedona Monthly*, http://sedonamonthly.com/2003/10/Johnny-dearest; and Patrick McGilligan, *Nicholas Ray* (New York: Harper and Collins, 2011), pp. 244–261.)

33. On the back cover of the Roy Chanslor's novel *Johnny Guitar* (New York: Simon and Schuster, 1953), we read the following paragraph signed by Joan Crawford: "When I read Roy Chanslor's turbulent drama of the legendary woman known as Vienna and her Johnny Guitar, I wanted to do it on screen. For me there was a special excitement in the role of this fascinating woman and in the fast-paced drama of the story of the West. Republic

Notes—Chapter 4

has brought it to the screen in a Trucolor picture I think you'll enjoy."

34. Joe McNeill, "*Johnny Guitar* in Sedona," *Sedona Monthly*, pp. 245–255; the involvement of the director Nicholas Ray with Chanslor in the writing of the script remains a mystery. It seems that Chanslor wrote a first draft, consulting with Ray and Crawford, but then Yordan revised the script enhancing the actress's dialogue parts. Ray had had a fling with Crawford, but by the time they both arrived at the shooting location in Sedona, they were no longer on speaking terms. Yordan was called by the MCA agent, Lew Wasserman, to appease the situation because Crawford claimed that Ray was favoring the other actors, and that Hayden and McCambridge were conspiring against her (see "*Johnny Guitar* in Sedona," http://sedonamonthly.com/2003/10/Johnny-dearest and Joseph Maddrey, *The Quick, the Dead and the Revived—The Many Lives of the Western Film* (Jefferson, NC: McFarland & Company, 2016), p. 52).

35. See Joe McNeill, "*Johnny Guitar* in Sedona," *Sedona Monthly* pp. 259–261 for the negative reviews of the critics.

36. Joe McNeill, "*Johnny Guitar* in Sedona," *Sedona Monthly*, p. 260. André Bazin, reviewing the film on *Le parisien liberé* (February 18, 1955), considered *Johnny Guitar* a "super–Western," together with *Shane* (1953) and *High Noon* (1952); (in *Bazin on Global Cinema 1948–1958*, translated and edited by Bert Cardullo (Texas: University of Texas Press, 2014), p. 152).

37. Pamela Robertson, "Camping Under Western Stars," in *Guilty Pleasures: Feminist Camp from Mae West to Madonna* (Durham: Duke University Press, 1996), pp. 102–105.

38. Leo Charney, "Historical Excess: *Johnny Guitar*'s Containment," *Cinema Journal* 29, no. 4 (1990): p. 25.

39. See Pamela Roberts, 1996, pp. 112–124.

40. See Patrick McGilligan, 2011, p. 415. The Motion Picture Alliance for the Preservation of American Ideals was founded in 1944 by actors Ward Bond, John Wayne and director Cecil B. DeMille. From 1947 on, they supported the HUAC in its anti–Communist hunt in Hollywood (pp. 202–214). Nicholas Ray was summoned by the HUAC in 1950 (or 1951); he admitted that in his youth he had been a member of the Communist Party, but he met behind closed doors, so nobody knows what he revealed to the committee. The director, however, managed to elude the blacklist. Bond never realized what the real motivations were behind his being hired for McIvers' role—the irony apparently escaped him.

41. According to McGillian, the choice of Hayden in the leading male role was due to the fact that Ray and Hayden had the same business manager and both, going through stormy divorces, needed money (*Nicholas Ray*, p. 248).

42. See image of the front cover of the novel, *Johnny Guitar*, by Roy Chanslor (New York: Simon and Schuster, 1953).

43. For an overview of pulp fiction see Lee Server, *Encyclopedia of Pulp Fiction Writers* (New York: Checkmark Books, 2002), p. xi. Although the name pulp was "originally used to describe a mere physical characteristic of the periodicals of the 1880s to 1950s whose pages were made from the cheapest grade of pulpwood paper, the word came to have an expanded meaning ... pulp as a genus of imaginative reading matter ... primarily concerned with sensation ..." In the Wild West pulp, we have: Ned Buntline (who created the myth of Buffalo Bill in his works), Owen Wister, Zane Grey, and Louis L'Amour to mention the most famous. Some of these pulpsters moved on to work in the movies.

44. Lee Server, *Encyclopedia of Pulp Fiction Writers* (New York: Checkmark Books, 2002), p. xv.

45. Roy Chanslor, *Johnny Guitar* (New York: Simon and Schuster, 1953), p. 6.

46. Roy Chanslor, 1953, p. 15.

47. Pamela Robertson, 1996, p. 99. Women who entered the workforce during WWII were supposed to give their jobs back to men when the war ended.

Notes—Chapter 4

The "mystique" was part of this ideological campaign to turn working women back into housewives.

48. Roy Chanslor, 1953, pp. 124, 178, 177, 208.

49. Roy Chanslor, 1953, pp. 134, 178, 179, 207.

50. Michael Wilmington points out that Ray's *Johnny Guitar* shares with *Rancho Notorious* "bitter romance, simmering tension, and caustic social comment" (*Velvet Light Trap* 12 (Spring 1974): pp. 19–25).

51. Will Scheibel, *American Stranger—Modernism, Hollywood, and the Cinema of Nicholas Ray* (New York: SUNY, 2017), p. 37.

52. John Francis Kreidl, *Nicholas Ray* (Boston: Twayne Publishers, 1977), pp. 43–59. See also V.F. Perkins, "The Cinema of Nicholas Ray," *MOVIE A Journal of Film Criticism*, issue 7 (May 2017): pp. 75–83. Ray spoke of the importance of color saying: "The use of primary color in film is as significant as the use of a close-up. ... *Johnny Guitar* won awards for its use of color, and I'd insisted on keeping the posse in black-and-white all the way through" (in Nicholas Ray, *I Was Interrupted—Nicholas Ray on Making Movies* (Los Angeles, CA: University of California Press, 1993), pp. 57–58).

53. See Geoff Andrew, *The Films of Nicholas Ray* (London: BFI Publishing, 2004), pp. 70–77.

54. For a discussion on the importance of social class in the Western see Patrick McGee, *From Shane to Kill Bill: Rethinking the Western* (Malden, MA: Blackwell, 2007), pp. 59–68.

55. The Dancing Kid gang is made up of individuals who do not conform, as the sheriff points out: "You boys do not farm, do not ranch ... you spend plenty of money. Where do you get the money?" At the beginning of the film, the Kid's bunch is falsely accused of robbing and stealing because they are not doing what the majority of the community does. This is Ray, we think, jabbing at the anti-Communist witch-hunt at a time when anybody who did not conform (especially ideologically) would be persecuted as an enemy of the state.

56. As Lévi-Strauss suggests, "cultural artifacts are to be read as symbolic resolutions of real political and social contradictions" (in Jameson, *The Political Unconscious* (Ithaca, NY: Cornell UP), 1981), p. 80).

57. Introduction to the film in the DVD special features of Olive Films.

58. For a discussion on powerful women and "empire versus desire," see N. Megan Kelley, *Projections of Passing—Postwar Anxieties and Hollywood Films 1947–1960* (Jackson: University of Mississippi Press, 2016), pp. 172–177.

59. For a discussion on *Johnny Guitar* as a film that provides evidence of the changing attitudes toward sex and gender in the postwar era, see Richard Aquila, *The Sagebrush Trail—Western Movies and Twentieth-Century America* (Tucson: University of Arizona Press, 2015), pp. 178–179.

60. In the film, there are two love triangles, one between Vienna, the Dancing Kid and Johnny, that is revealed through the jealous interactions between the two men who both desire the same woman, Vienna, and the second one between Emma, Vienna and the Dancing Kid that is open to different interpretations. Emma seems to be attracted to the Kid, who clearly loves Vienna, therefore she hates Vienna (and the Kid) and wants to kill her (and him), being obsessive and neurotic; or Emma could be attracted to Vienna who instead loves the Kid, so she hates them both. We, instead, would be more inclined to see Emma as a sexually repressed person who dwells in an ambiguous gray zone between genders, in which violence and hate have suppressed any other natural passions, i.e., the realm of xenophobia.

61. Jeanine Basinger, *A Woman's View—How Hollywood Spoke to Women 1930–1960* (New York: Knopf, 1993), p. 166. "These are the ferocious women like Joan Crawford, Bette Davis, Barbara Stanwyck, and Katherine Hepburn, women who throw any film off balance by their frequently neurotic and exaggerated presence." (p.167)

62. For a discussion on Joan Crawford's Hollywood career see Pamela

Notes—Chapter 4

Robertson, "Camping Under Western Stars: Joan Crawford in *Johnny Guitar*," *Journal of Film and Video* 47, no. 1–3 (Spring–Fall 1995): pp. 33–49. In many previous movies Crawford had played the tough woman with a past, and, by 1954 when *Johnny Guitar* came along, she was at the top of her profession; by then, she had managed to be a big star for decades. The bossy-rebellious-tough *star persona* she had acquired served her well in the role of Vienna. (See Richard Dryer, *Stars* (London: BFI Publishing, 1998), p. 129.)

63. Pamela Robertson, 1996, p. 100. The critic is considering the publicity given to the off-screen animosity between McCambridge and Crawford, documented in their respective biographies, and in the testimonies by Ray and Hayden in various interviews. According to Robertson, in *Mildred Pierce* (1945), Crawford was impersonating a character "who usurps masculine power and must be punished or returned to femininity, thus reflecting a backlash against professional women coincident with the return of America GIs after the war and the need to reassert masculine authority in the workplace after the unprecedented wartime employment of women." (p. 89)

64. Pamela Robertson, 1996, p. 107.

65. For masquerade, see Mary Ann Doane, "Film and the Masquerade: Theorising the Female Spectator," https://academic.oup.com/screen/article-pdf/23/3-4/74.

66. See Judy Greenway, "Impossible Outlaws: Gender, Space and Utopia in *Johnny Guitar*," www.judygreenway.org.uk/wp/impossible-outlaws-gender-space-and-utopia-in-johnny-guitar.

67. For a study of Emma see also Jennifer Peterson, "The Competing Tunes of 'Johnny Guitar': Liberalism, Sexuality, Masquerade," *Cinema Journal* 35, no. 3 (Spring 1996): 3–18.

68. See Murray Pomerance's article, "A Teacup and a Kiss," about the importance of Johnny's teacup scene in the film (in *Lonely Places, Dangerous Grounds: Nicholas Ray in American Cinema*, Steven Rybin and Will Scheibel, eds. (New York: SUNY Press, 2014), pp. 123–137), and for the "wounded masculinity" that defines all Ray's heroes see pp. 148–149. I would agree with the "wounded masculinity" of Johnny only if interpreted in the sense of broken dreams, lost illusions, and dreamy detachment from reality.

69. For a debate about the gun as a phallic symbol see Fran Pheasant-Kelly, "The Sexual Signification of the Gun in Western Film," in *A Fistful of Icons*, Sue Matheson, ed. (Jefferson, NC: McFarland, 2017), pp. 124–141. Clearly Johnny is not the typical Western hero who chooses the schoolmarm in the end. He wants to marry Vienna who treats him as an equal.

70. The theme song is repeated many times during the most romantic moments of the story, but it is sung only once, by Peggy Lee, with lyrics at the very end of the film.

71. J. David Slocum, ed. *Violence and American Cinema* (New York: Routledge, 2001), pp. 4–5.

72. According to Dryer, the audience has preconceptions about the characters in certain genres: "We expect John Wayne to play a certain kind of character, and we expect anyone playing the male lead in a Western to fit broad parameters of cowboy characterization." Obviously, in the case of the character of Johnny (and in the film on the whole in its *mise en scène*) we face a polysemy of traits together with a multiplicity of coexistent discourses.

73. Michael Wilmington, "Nicholas Ray's *Johnny Guitar*," *Velvet Light Trap* 12 (Spring 1974), p. 22.

74. Let's not forget that Old Tom (John Carradine, a veteran of westerns), the saloon helper/cook, always shows admiration for Johnny; thus, when the young man arrives, he welcomes him saying, "That's a lot of man you're carrying in those boots, stranger. You know, there's something about a tall man that makes people sit up and take notice." Johnny Guitar is not as insignificant as some critics think.

75. Geoff Andrew, *The Films of Nicholas Ray* (London: BFI Publishing, 2004), p. 15.

76. *Duel in the Sun* was directed by King Vidor and based on a screenplay by David O. Selznick who produced the film.

Notes—Chapter 4

The screenplay was loosely based on the homonymous novel by Niven Busch published in 1944, but Selznick changed the ending, eliminated characters and substantially modified the story.

77. Bosley Crowther, "*Duel in the Sun*, Selznick's Lavish Western That Stars Jennifer Jones, Gregory Peck, Opens at Loew's Theatres," *The New York Times*, May 8, 1947.

78. Paul Monticone points out, "As the end of World War II approached, Hollywood studios reentered A-Western production, which had largely ceased at the beginning of the war. The box-office success of David O. Selznick's Technicolor super–Western, *Duel in the Sun* (1946), initiated a surge of A-Western production." ("The Noir Western: Genre Theory and the Problem of the Anomalous Hybrid," *Quarterly Review of Film and Video* 31, no. 4, (2014): p. 338). In March 1946, the estimated budget of *Duel* was $2.8 million; after all the rewriting, changing of scenes and continuous reshooting in Arizona, in April 1946 it had reached $6.28 million (David Thomson, *Showman* (New York: Knopf, 1992), p. 472). The film made $10 million at the box-office, and was extremely successful as Michael Coyne points out: "*Duel in the Sun* became the highest-grossing Western of the 1940s, ranking second only to *The Best Years of Our Lives* (1946) as the decade's box office champion; furthermore, after inflation-adjustment in 1981, *Duel* emerged as the greatest Western money-spinner of all time." The critic also colorfully describes the film: "*Duel* was a visual and narrative feast of opulent sensuality unequalled by anything else in the genre … the costliest, the most lushly Technicolored, the most lavishly cast, the loudest ballyhooed, and the sexiest horse opera ever made" (in *The Crowded Prairie: American National Identity in the Hollywood Western* (London: Tauris, 1997), p. 42). Mary Lea Bandy and Kevin Stoehr in *Ride, Boldly Ride—The Evolution of the American Western* define *Duel* as "grandiose, visually sumptuous, and often corny soap-opera-on-the-range … a lavish epic" (Berkeley: University of California Press, 2012, pp. 166–167).

79. David Thomson, *Showman* (New York: Knopf, 1992); Rudy Behlmer, ed., *Memo from David O. Selznick* (New York: Viking Press, 1972).

80. As Thomson writes "[Jennifer Jones] was twenty-two … whatever happened between David and the woman who would be Jennifer, this was also the meeting of an actress who wanted to be a star and of a man who measured his potency by what he could get the public to buy and believe" (*Showman*, p. 371). Selznick turned Jennifer into a star very fast; for her role in *The Song of Bernadette* (1943), directed by Henry King and produced by the mogul, she got an Oscar in 1944 (the film won three other Oscars). By then, Jennifer had initiated divorce proceedings against her husband, actor Robert Walker.

81. David Thomson, 1992, pp. 447–449.

82. In the filmic credits we read that the screenplay of *Duel in the Sun* was adapted by Oliver H.P. Garrett, and based on a novel by Niven Busch, but written by Selznick. Selznick kept writing and rewriting the script, continually adding and changing scenes as David Thomson explains in *Showman* (New York: Knopf, 1992) and it is confirmed by Rudy Behlmer, ed., *Memo from David O. Selznick* (New York: Viking Press, 1972).

83. The movie sports a great cast of legendary Hollywood players, besides Peck and Cotton: Lionel Barrymore as Senator McCanles, Lilian Gish as Laura Belle McCanles, and Walter Huston as Reverend Jubal Crabbe, the Sinkiller.

84. David Thomson, 1992, pp. 450–451.

85. David Thomson, 1992, pp. 448–449.

86. Rudy Behlmer, ed., *Memo from David O. Selznick* (New York: Viking Press, 1972), p. 355. The letter was sent to an attorney with a copy to King Vidor, and it was about who should be credited as director of the film. Selznick claims that the credit should go to Dieterle and Brower and not to Vidor, but the Movie Guild credited Vidor.

87. Rudy Behlmer, ed., *Memo from*

Notes—Chapter 4

David O. Selznick (New York: Viking Press, 1972), pp. 473–479.

88. Niven Busch was a novelist and renowned screenwriter who worked between 1932 and 1953 in the Hollywood Studios. Among his many successes for the screen there are notable Westerns: *The Westerner* (1940), *Belle Starr* (1941, based on his story), *The Postman Always Rings Twice* (1946), *Pursued* (1947), *Distant Drums* (1951, based on his story), *The Man from the Alamo* (1953), *The Moonlighter* (1953) and *The Treasure of Pancho Villa* (1955). He wrote 14 novels, the most famous of which are considered "psychological Westerns," and include *Duel in the Sun* (1944) and *The Furies* (1948), both turned into popular films.

89. Jeffrey M. Anderson, "Lust in the Dust," combustiblecelluloid.com, 1997; Jim Tudor, "*Duel in the Sun* (1946)—Blue-Ray Review" *Zekefilm*, August 23, 2017; Martin Scorsese in *A Personal Journey Through American Movies*. DVD. British Film Institute, Buena Vista Home Entertainment, 2000. Scorsese credits *Duel in the Sun* as the film that inspired him to become a filmmaker and considers it an extraordinary production.

90. Niven Busch, *Duel in the Sun* (New York: Pocket Books, 1977), p. 1.

91. Unlike the film, in the novel Pearl's father, Mr. Chavez, gets lynched for thieving, but does not kill his adulterous wife nor her lover.

92. Selznick, having Pearl and Lewt kill each other, changed the ending of the story. In the novel the heroine kills Lewt, but survives the ordeal and marries Jesse.

93. In the rolling credits we read "Screenplay by the producer David O. Selznick, suggested by a novel by Nivel Busch, adapted by Oliver H.P. Garrett." Selznick clearly wanted everyone to know that the screen play was his creation.

94. As Jim Hitt reminds us, "When David O. Selznick purchased the rights, he did so for purely monetary reasons. He disliked Westerns in general, but he said: 'Seeing how profitable Westerns always were, I decided that if I could create one that had more spectacle than had ever been seen in a Western, and combine it with a violent love story, then the two elements would give me a great success'" (in *The American West from Fiction (1823–1976) into Film (1909–1986)* (Jefferson, NC: McFarland, 1990), p. 255). Before *Duel*, there had been another Western loaded with eroticism; *The Outlaw* (1943), directed by Howard Hughes, starred Jane Russell in low-cut blouses and sexy poses, and two leading men (Jack Beutel and Walter Huston) divided between homoerotic and heterosexual love. The film was so daring for the time that the censors pulled it out of distribution in 1943 after only a week in theaters; Hughes eventually re-released it with cuts in 1946, and this unusual Western became a big box-office hit.

95. David Lusted, "Social Class and the Western as Male Melodrama," in *The Book of Westerns*, Ian Cameron and Douglas Pye, eds. (New York: Continuum, 1996), p. 65.

96. Robin Wood defines Pearl's hysteria as a "feeling of powerlessness ... a form of active, but impotent protest; if it lacks revolutionary effects, it has revolutionary meaning." For the critic, Pearl's hysteria "pervades every aspect of the film, determines its style, produces its storms, its lurid sunsets, the intolerable heat of its sun, and finally precludes any possibility of that satisfying and pacifying sense of resolution that is supposed to be a permanent and necessary feature of traditional narrative." ("*Duel in the Sun*—The Destruction of an Ideological System," in *The Book of Westerns*, Ian Cameron and Douglas Pye, eds. (New York: Continuum, 1996), p. 189). In the film, Pearl often, out of frustration, screams, "I am trash, trash, trash," a sentence that clearly elucidates her desperate state of mind, her "excess of misery."

97. Lewt has dreams of independence and adventure, and he does not want to take Pearl with him when he plans to flee to Mexico. However, considering the hypocrisy of the male order, according to which a white male can have sex with the "Other" as long as he does not commit himself publicly, we are inclined to think that Lewt is lying to

Notes—Chapter 4

himself, because the social order weighs on him so much that he is incapable of analyzing his feelings. Lewt's emotions, nevertheless, surface in bits and pieces in his conversation with Pearl, in "moments of truths" in which he seems to be deeply fond of Pearl: "You are my girl, honey. Anybody who was my girl is still my girl, that's the kind of guy I am. Nobody is taking my girl, nobody, never ..."; in another instance, talking about being on the run from the law, but needing to come to see her: "Just when I figure I am doing fine and dandy, I start thinking about you and nothing is any good." In the same conversation, referring to the killing of Pierce, he says to Pearl, who is holding a gun, ready to shoot him: "I go out and show you as much as I love you and you want to plug me?" It is evident that Lewt does not understand why Pearl is upset, neither is he capable of seeing that his abnormal reactions stem from a frustration born by the fact that he cannot marry Pearl (because of his social class), neither can he live without her (because of his passion/feelings). Miscegenation was considered a real threat by American society for the longest time. Jolie A. Sheffer reminds us that "as of 1949, twenty-nine states had laws prohibiting some form of interracial marriage" (in *The Romance of Race: Incest, Miscegenation, and Multiculturalism in the United States, 1880–1930* (New Brunswick, NJ: Rutgers University Press, 2012), p. 17).

98. We are aware that many critics believe that the movie has a happy and conservative ending because the "proper" couple, Jesse and Helen, will live happily ever after. We, rather, believe that the focus of attention in the film is the Lewt-Pearl couple, because the legend narrated by the voice-over (Orson Welles) at the beginning of the film celebrates their tragic death; on top of that, presenting the lovers' story in flashbacks, the film insists on the wild couple's fate. Selznick, in our opinion, gave the "moral majority" a traditional happy ending as in many classic Westerns (the future wedding of Jesse and his fiancée), while, at the same time, he kept the erotic lovers in the spotlight. It is obvious that Selznick made sure that the viewers' sympathy went to the unorthodox lovers.

99. Douglas Brode, *Dream West: Politics and Religion in Cowboy Movies* (Austin: University of Texas Press, 2013), pp. 65–73.

100. Mr. Chavez kills Pearl's mother and her lover in front of his daughter out of rage, jealousy and wounded honor. Condemned to hanging for the double murder, before the execution he quotes the verses of an ancient Persian poet that evoke the brevity of life. The sensitive Southern gentleman, having chosen love above class and race, has doomed himself, and, in the moment of death, he ponders about the futility of his and every action.

The poem by Omar Khayyam, a Persian poet of the 12th century, reads:

Oh, threats of Hell and hopes of Paradise!
One thing at least is certain—this life flies;
One thing is certain and the rest is lies;
The Flower that once has bloomed forever dies.

101. Robin Wood quotes three films that are concerned with the struggle of a woman to survive and establish herself inside the hegemonic discourse. According to the critic, *Gone With the Wind* (1939, directed by Victor Fleming), *Rebecca* (1940, directed by Alfred Hitchcock) and *Since You Went Away* (1944, directed by John Cromwell) show transgressive women who refuse to be contained by the rules of patriarchy ("*Duel in the Sun*—The Destruction of an Ideological System," in *The Book of Westerns*, Ian Cameron and Douglas Pye, eds. (New York: Continuum, 1996), p. 190).

102. M. Elise Marubbio talks about the sexualized maiden, a character who retains her "wildness" combining racial exoticism, sexual promiscuity and physical threat to the hero, defining her as "explicitly erotic, sexually active, not above a little infidelity." These maidens are tainted by miscegenation themselves and threaten white civilization with their otherness (*Killing the Indian Maiden:*

Notes—Chapter 5

Images of Native American Women in Film (Lexington: University of Kentucky Press, 2006), p. 75). In the film Pearl is exotic, sexualized, and definitely tainted by being a mixed-blood, but she seems to be moved by divergent drives, therefore Marubbio's definition of the sexualized maiden fits, in our view, more specifically Pearl's Indian mother. Pearl represents an unusual case of rebellion. Because she is a mixed-blood and poor, she is prevented from marrying into the white upper class; in order to enter the symbolic order, she wants to get married to defy the father's rules (Senator McCanles). Unlike other white women, marriage for her constitutes a rebellion, it is the only way she has to acquire social acceptance and escape marginality.

103. See Cynthia J. Miller's "'Wild' Women: Interracial Romance on the Western Frontier," in *Love in Western Film and Television*, Sue Matheson ed. (New York: Macmillan Palgrave, 2013), p. 85.

104. We are under the impression, after having read the biography of Selznick, that at the time of filming *Duel in the Sun*, he himself was feeling the same pulls that the filmic characters were experiencing: having to choose between divorcing his wife, Irene Mayer with whom he had two boys and strong economic ties, or continuing his affair with beautiful, and seventeen years younger, Jennifer Jones. According to his biography (*Showman*), he seemed to be unsure about what to do: remain married and drop the affair or get divorced and be free to continue his liaison. Selznick constantly seemed to oscillate between the wife and the lover, having feelings for both, one representing proper upper-class life, respectability, money and Hollywood royalty status, and the other embodying youth, beauty, sexuality, passion and "inappropriate love" for a married middle-aged man like him (David Thomson, *Showman* (New York: Knopf, 1992). Without being able to prove our supposition, we suspect that Selznick was caught between respectability and passion like Lewt and Jesse in *Duel in the Sun*.

105. See Walter Lippmann, *Public Opinion* (New Brunswick, NJ: Transaction Publishers, 1998), p. 96.

106. Stanley Corkin, *Cowboys as Cold Warriors* (Philadelphia: Temple University Press, 2004), p. 62.

107. Stanley Corkin, 2004, p. 62.

108. Because of the clash with his father, Jesse leaves Spanish Bit and goes to Austin where he works as a lawyer, leaving behind his beloved mother and Pearl. In this way, he starts his brilliant political career and gets engaged to the daughter of the railroad magnate.

109. Richard Slotkin, *The Fatal Environment—The Myth of the Frontier in the Age of Industrialization 1800–1890* (New York: Harper Perennial, 1994), p. 140.

110. Lewt falls for Pearl and, after courting her for a while (the swimming, the showing off with the horses, the Pinto given to her as present), he forces himself on her; it is a rape that turns into something else. The excessive nature of Lewt matches in many ways the volcanic personality of Pearl—the two would make a perfect match if arch-conservative ideology wouldn't derail everything. Lewt uses offensive sexist language calling Pearl "a pretty cute tamale" or a "bobcat," but Jesse also, at a certain point, tells Pearl "not to worry your pretty head." Both men are the products of a sexist society in which women are equated to food or to animals, and they are considered either sexually "edible," as in the case of Lewt, or decorative accessory as in the case of Jesse.

111. Agustin Zarzosa, *Refiguring Melodrama in Film and Television* (Lanham, MD: Lexington Books, 2013), p. 19.

112. For a discussion on genre see Steve Neale, "Questions of Genre," in *Film Genre Reader II* (Austin: University of Texas Press, 1995), p. 171.

Chapter 5

1. Steve Neale, "Questions of Genre" in *Film Genre Reader III*, Barry Keith Grant ed. (Austin: University of Texas, 2003), p. 169. According to Neale, the historicity of the genre that includes the memories of films the viewers have previously watched, and the corpus of the images created by the advertising campaigns—the articles, the reviews, the

Notes—Chapter 5

posters, etc.—also partakes of a process that includes variation and change. I interpret historicity (and I assume Neale does too) as in Jameson's theory: "... the historical origins of the things themselves and that more intangible historicity of the concepts and categories by which we attempt to understand those things ... (the historicity of its forms and of its content, the historical moment of emergence of its linguistic possibilities, the situation-specific function of its aesthetic) and something rather different which would instead foreground the interpretative categories or codes through which we read and receive the text in question." (*The Political Unconscious* (Ithaca, NY: Cornell UP, 1981), p. 9).

2. Neale, 2003, p. 171. Tag Gallagher in "Shoot-out at the Genre Corral: Problems in the 'Evolution' of the Western" maintains that in the Western genre there is "cyclicism rather than evolution," a critical stand closer to Neale than to Cawelti, French, Wright et al. (Barry Keith Grant ed. *Film Genre Reader II* (Austin: Texas UP, 1995), p 247).

3. Neale, 2003, p. 174.

4. Tag Gallagher in "Shoot-Out at the Genre Corral" offers a pretty forceful tirade in favor of evolution and against the "octet of genre critics:" Robert Warshow, John G. Cawelti, Philip French, Jack Nachbar, Will Wright, Frank D. McConnell, Leo Braudy, and Thomas Schatz. According to Gallagher, the evolutionists see the Western genre developing through stages similar to artistic styles: "the *experimental*, when the stylistic conventions become established; the *classical*, when they have been accepted by the public; *refinement*, when style becomes more elaborate; and *mannerist* when style becomes self-reflective [Schatz]." The above listed critics believe that "the later Western projects a less optimistic ... vision of the West's potential synthesis of nature and culture; the Western hero, once an agent of law and order, has become a renegade, a professional killer, an antihero, neurotic, psychotic ... the later Western is less simple, tidy, and naïve, more ambiguous, complex, and ironic, more self-critical and into the 'art of telling.'" (*Film Genre II*, p. 263) Gallagher admits that, like any other genres, the Western reflects its era, but denies that there is an evolutionary process, affirming instead that "a superficial glance at film history suggests *cyclicism*: "Despair and an appetite for realism were modish before World War I, escapism and genuinely happy endings became mandatory after the war. Films were moody and depressed during the early years of the Depression, when both surrealism and realism were in fashion; then with the censorship codes of 1934 films turned escapist and during the next ten years were awesomely repressed. A demonic period after World War II precedes a mingling of optimism and anguish in the 1950s, followed by extremism and schizophrenia in the 1960s, escapism mingling with serious concern in the late 1970s and 1980s" (*Film Genre II*, p. 268).

5. For a brief overview of the genre evolution in the 1990s see Chuck Berg, "Fade-out in the West: The Western's Last stand?" The critic claims that the genre, once severed from its ideological moorings in the 1960s, has produced in the 1990s an uneven crop of idiosyncratic films that have pushed the parameters of the classic Western to a breaking point; he argues that *Unforgiven* (1992) by Clint Eastwood is "the Western that killed off the genre," having created "a Westerner without the code" (in Wheeler Winston Dixon, ed., *Film Genre 2000—New Critical Essays* (New York: State University of New York Press, 2000), p. 219). Berg concludes, saying: "Given what we have seen of the 1990s, will the Western somehow find a way out of its current postmodern status as a body of free-floating signifiers usable only in parodic or mannerist or stay-vanity venture? Was *Unforgiven* the last deconstructive nail driven into the wooden coffin of the classic Western? While predicting the future is always risky, there is reason to think that, yes, the classical Western is dead. ...With the ideological gravity of the classical Western now demolished, what remains is a grab bag of exhausted and watered-down themes, high-fashion stylistics, and ... a

Notes—Chapter 5

nostalgia for an imagined past in which myth and fact are inextricably intertwined. ... The Western as a means of transmitting epic and unifying tales of American experience has passed" (p. 224). It is evident that pro-evolution critics like Berg seem to think that only classic Westerns are worth studying, and that everything that appeared before or after is not. The result is a view that considers the Western defunct or dying. For other analysis of the 1990s Westerns, see Stanley Corkin, *Cowboys as Cold Warriors: The Western and U.S. History* (Philadelphia: Temple University Press, 2004) and Tom Engelhard, *The End of Victory Culture: Cold War America and the Disillusioning of a Generation* (New York: Basic Books, 1995).

6. Jim Kitses and Greg Rickman, eds. *The Western Reader* (New York: Limelight Editions, 1998), pp. 85–92. On the Western revival of the 1990s see also Marek Paryz and John R. Leo, eds., *The Post-2000 Film Western: Contexts, Transnationality, Hybridity* (New York: McMillan Palgrave, 2015), pp. 3–4.

7. Consulting Filmsite.org and Magill's Cinema Annual Series, the number of Western films seems to be small, but constant.

8. See Pete Falconer, "Spaghetti Westerns and the 'Afterlife' of a Hollywood Genre," in *Spaghetti Westerns at the Crossroads—Studies in Relocation, Transition and Appropriation*, Austin Fisher, ed. (Edinburgh: Edinburgh UP, 2016), p. 262.

9. Pete Falconer, 2016, p. 263.

10. Pete Falconer, 2016, pp. 267–272.

11. For evolutionary views on the Western genre see Richard Slotkin, *Gunfighter Nation* (Norman: Oklahoma UP, 1992); Michael Coyne, *The Crowded Prairie* (London: I.B. Tauris, 1997); Carlton Smith, *Coyote Kills John Wayne* (Hanover, NH: New England UP, 2000); Steven McVeigh, *The American Western* (Edinburgh: Edinburgh UP, 2007); Patrick McGee, *From Shane to Kill Bill* (Oxford: Blackwell, 2007), John G. Cawelti, *The Six-Gun Mystique Sequel* (Bowling Green, OH: Bowling Green UPP, 1999); Thomas Schatz, *Hollywood Genres* (New York: Random House, 1981); Will Wright, *Six Guns and Society* (Berkeley: University of California Press, 1975).

12. Fredric Jameson, *The Political Unconscious* (Ithaca, NY: Cornell UP, 1981), p. 11.

13. We consider *Open Range* (Kevin Costner, 2003) a well-made, but very traditional Western, especially in the relationship between the male hero and the female main protagonist. *Appaloosa* (Ed Harris, 2008) and *The Salvation* (Kristian Levring, 2014) insert innovative motives into a traditional formula; the former, subverting *Unforgiven* (Clint Eastwood, 1992), is a story centered on forgiveness and the exploration of female sexuality/social climbing; Pete Falconer notices that the film is shot in a classical style that includes wide shots, long takes, and deep focus, together with great attention to historical details, especially in the case of weaponry, technology, and facial hair (Victorian style beards, moustaches) (Cf. Austin Fisher ed. *Spaghetti Westerns at the Crossroads* (Edinburgh: Edinburgh UP, 2016), p 268); *The Salvation* is a revenge story whose plot resembles in some way *High Noon* (Fred Zinnemann, 1952), showing a hero that, abandoned by the community in his moment of need, manages in the end to exterminate all the bad guys. The film has an interesting female character (Eva Green), a bad girl turned gunslinger who finally, rebelling against male hegemony, becomes an avenger; cinematographically the film sports an unusual palette with striking surreal colors (see Manohla Dargis, "In *The Salvation*, a Hero Lays Waste, Western Style," *New York Times Reviews*, February 27, 2015).

14. Matthew Carter, *Myth of the Western* (Edinburgh: Edinburgh UP, 2015), p. 117.

15. Fredric Jameson, 1981, pp. 28, 48–39. The *non dit* for Jameson is the political unconscious of the text.

16. See J. David Slocum, "Violence and American Cinema: Notes for an Investigation," in *Violence and American Cinema*, J. David Slocum, ed. (New York: Routledge, 2001), pp. 1–34.

17. See Matthew Carter, *Myth of the*

Notes—Chapter 5

Western (Edinburgh: Edinburgh UP, 2015), p. 1–4.

18. See Cynthia J. Miller and Bowdoin Van Riper, "The Fantastic Frontier" in *Critical Perspectives on the Western*, Lee Broughton, ed. (Lanham, MD: Rowman & Littlefield, 2016), p. 29.

19. For an in-depth exploration of the Lone Ranger franchise, its licensing history and its popularity among consumers from the 1930s to the post-war era, see Santo Avi, *Selling the Silver Bullet: The Lone Ranger and Transmedia Brand Licensing* (Austin: University of Texas Press, 2015).

20. *The Lone Ranger* TV series was aired on ABC at 7:30 pm, on Thursdays, and it was meant for family viewing, unlike other televisual Western series like *Gunsmoke* (CBS, 1955) and *Broken Arrow* (ABC, 1956) that were aimed at adults. *The Lone Ranger* depicted a West that was loosely based on history, and portrayed a society that needed a vigilante who would take the law into his own hands so that justice could prevail. See Michael Ray Fitzgerald, "Cold War Avengers: The Lone Ranger and Tonto in *The Lone Ranger* (1949–1957)," in *Native Americans on Network TV* (Lanham, MD: Rowman & Littlefield, 2014), pp. 29–52, and "The White Savior and His Junior Partner: The Lone Ranger and Tonto on Cold War Television (1949–1957)," *Journal of Popular Culture* 46, no. 1 (2013): pp. 79–108.

21. We are going to base our analysis on a certain number of episodes of the TV series for two reasons: first, the episodes are based on a very successful formula that keeps repeating itself *ad infinitum*; second, there are so many episodes it would be impossible to watch them all. For the formula, the construction of the episodes and of the characters that populate them, and for a detailed overview of the world of the Lone Ranger see David Wilson Parker, "A Descriptive Analysis of the Lone Ranger as a Form of Popular Art." (Dissertation, Northwestern University, 1956), pp. 210–327. Parker writes (p. 193): "*The Lone Ranger* was 'frozen' in form from the moment of its first success, and neither its hero nor its format have been materially altered since." Many TV episodes of *The Lone Ranger* can be watched on *Youtube* and on DVD.

22. I am borrowing the terms hypotext (original text) and hypertext (subsequent text) from Gèrard Genette who writes: "By hypertextuality I mean any relationship uniting a text B (which I shall call the hypotext) to an earlier text A (I shall, of course, call it hypertext), upon which it is grafted in a manner that is not a commentary" (*Palimpsests: Literature in the Second Degree* (Lincoln: Nebraska UP, 1997), p 5).

23. See Deborah Cartmell, ed., *A Companion to Literature, Film, and Adaptation* (Malden, MA: Wiley Blackwell, 2014), p. 8.

24. Julie Sanders, *Adaptation and Appropriation* (London: Routledge, 2005), p. 26.

25. The enormous popularity through the decades of *The Lone Ranger* makes it an exemplary text, an icon which generations of western fans identified with when it came to the genre.

26. As Michael Ray Fitzgerald points out, the fortune of the Lone Ranger was enormous: "The series came to television in 1949, during the early stages of the Cold War. The Ranger also appeared in various media, such as a series of paperback novels from 1936 to 1956 as well as two feature films released through Republic Pictures in 1938 and 1939. He also appeared in a weekly comic strip syndicated through King Features from 1938 to 1971, and in 145 comic books published by Dell Comics from 1948 to 1962." ("The White Savior and His Junior Partner: The Lone Ranger and Tonto on Cold War Television (1949–1957)," *Journal of Popular Culture* 46, no. 1 (2013): p. 79.

27. David Wilson Parker, "A Descriptive Analysis of the Lone Ranger as a Form of Popular Art" (Dissertation, Northwestern University, 1956), p. 188.

28. David Wilson Parker, 1956, pp. 188–190. Between 1935 and 1952 cowboy Hopalong Cassidy (William Boyd) became super famous first in films and then in the TV series with the same

Notes—Chapter 5

name; Roy Rogers and Dale Evans became very renowned with the extremely successful "The Roy Rogers Show," singing nine years on radio and then on TV between 1951 and 1957; Gene Autry was another singing cowboy who appeared in 93 B-Westerns between 1934 and 1953 and acquired great popularity with his show, the "Gene Autry's Melody Ranch." On the singing cowboys see Peter Stanfield, *Horse Opera* (Urbana: Illinois UP, 2002), and by the same author *Hollywood, Westerns, and the 1930s: The Lost Trail* (Exeter: Exeter UP, 2001). Most of these screen heroes sported very ethical, tolerant, patriotic values that were in line with the Lone Ranger Creed mentioned in Parker's dissertation.

29. David Wilson Parker, 1956, pp. 190–191. As Parker notes, "within a five-year period, the adventures of the Lone Ranger were released in novels, moving pictures, comic strips, and comic books. ... Within twelve years Lone Ranger merchandising grew to a million-dollar enterprise and showed signs of becoming even bigger." The television series was adapted from the radio episodes; in the credits we read: "Screenplay by Gibson Fox from the radio program by Fran Striker. ... A copyright feature of *The Lone Ranger* Inc. Created and produced by George W. Trendle." For a detailed explanation of the Western genre formula see the chapter entitled "Popular Cinema and Violence—The Western Genre," in *Popular Italian Cinema: Culture and Politics in a Postwar Society*, Flavia Brizio-Skov, ed. (London: I.B. Tauris, 2011), pp. 189–227.

30. David Wilson Parker, 1956, p. 192. Parker transcribes the Lone Ranger Creed (pp. 212–214):

The American Heritage

Our forefathers were men among whom uncommon valor was a common virtue. Those men have handed down a great heritage which you, and others like you, must protect and preserve. It is the heritage of every American. The right to live as free people in a land where there is true equality of opportunity.

It is your duty to be eternally vigilant—prepared at all times to fight those who dare to challenge our way of life. And you must build. It is your duty to make of this a greater nation—to build homes and farms and villages—mills, factories, and great cities.

Property is the fruit of labor. That some should be rich shows that others may become rich and hence is encouragement to industry and enterprise. Abraham Lincoln said: "Let not him who is houseless pull down the house of another. But let him labor diligently and build one for himself—this by example—assuring that his own shall be safe from violence when built."

You have for your own, a great nation—together with the will—the heart—the courage to make it even greater. This is your heritage. This is the heritage of every American.

Patriotism

The Lone Ranger is motivated by love of country—a desire to help those who are building the West. ... Patriotism means service to a community; voting ... the development of schools and churches. ... Patriotism means respect for law and order, and the selection of officials who merit such respect. Patriotism consists of the preservation of the things for which our ancestors fought and died. The preservation of the rights of freedom of speech and religion.

Fairness

The Lone Ranger never attacks from behind or takes unfair advantage of an adversary. The Lone Ranger registers disapproval of bullets—of men who take unfair advantage—of men who, even though within their legal rights, step beyond the bounds of fair play. ... The Lone Ranger advocates the American Tradition, which gave each man the right to choose his work and to profit in proportion to his effort; and to retain for himself fair proportion of his profits. The Lone Ranger also advocates the right to possess and hold worldly goods.

Notes—Chapter 5

Tolerance

The Lone Ranger's friend is an Indian. If the Lone Ranger accepts the Indian as his closest companion, it is obvious to the child listener that great men have no racial or religious prejudice. Nowhere in the stories is any minority group referred to in a derogatory manner. [It goes without saying that there is no mention of the fact that the Native Americans roamed this great country before the pilgrims!]

Sympathy

The Lone Ranger is a specific example of a man who can be strong, yet tender—a man who can fight hard, yet show mercy and compassion. ... The Lone Ranger chooses the side of the oppressed—the underdog—the little man in need of help ...

Religion

The Lone Ranger is not shown to be a member of any specific creed, but he is definitely a respecter of all creeds. He is generally visualized as a Protestant. ... He shows respect for preachers and worshippers of every denomination. ... The Lone Ranger believes that our sacred American Heritage provides that every individual has the right to worship God as he desires.

Pure Speech

The Lone Ranger by example, hopes to teach the strength and importance of pure speech. Easily the strongest character in every story, he is able to register in pure speech a greater impact than some of the characters whose limited understanding causes them at times to resort to slang and colloquialisms. The Lone Ranger is able to be forceful without swearing and emphatic without shouting.

Brutality, Gore and Sex

The relationship of the sexes in the stories is kept wholesome. The Lone Ranger has no love interest. Romance in other characters is clean. Triangle situations, faithlessness and sex in lurid form are never used. The sanctity of the home is emphasized. Blood and brutality are eliminated except where plots definitely demand them. In these cases they are held to a minimum. Drinking, gambling and smoking are not done by the Lone Ranger and are kept to a minimum with the other characters and avoided entirely unless needed for the plot.

According to this "sanitation," the program message should have been: "Home life is cemented. Parents are respected. Youth betterment is fostered. Democracy is taught. Community obligations are explained." On the whole the program was considered, ideologically speaking, a "force for good ... [that] combines all the finest attributes which make up our American concept of social justice and democracy ..." The didactical, political, hegemonic and, I would say, even propagandistic goals of the radio program (and of the TV series) are self-evident.

31. Michael Ray Fitzgerald, *Native Americans on Network TV—Stereotypes, Myths, and the "Good Indian"* (Lanham, MD: Rowman & Littlefield, 2014), p 29–30.

32. For Fitzgerald, the Lone Ranger, thanks to the many low-angle shots of him towering over the landscape atop a rock against the sky and the clouds, appears to the viewer as a godlike creature. The messianic trope also contains an implicit imperialistic message because, as Richard Dryer observes, "Men [framed] against the horizon are a cliché of aspirational propaganda" (in Fitzgerald, 2014, p. 32).

33. For Douglas Pye the Lone Ranger represents "the inheritance of romantic narrative in one of its simplest forms; it centers on the anonymous masked hero who possesses extraordinary powers that set him apart from ordinary men. He is virtually invulnerable—the nearest thing to a god without being immortal. He rides a horse of incredible beauty, which, like his master, has extraordinary gifts. And he is accompanied by a faithful Indian companion—a fact which draws attention to the direct line of descent from

Notes—Chapter 5

Fenimore Cooper. There is none of Cooper's complexity, of course, but instead a simple moral scale of polarized good and evil, with the basic terms and the hero's status never questioned" ("The Western Genre and Movies," in Grant, B. K. ed. *Film Genre Reader III*, B.K. Grant, ed. (Austin: Texas UP, 2003), p. 215). Tonto was supposed to be a companion who, according to Trendle, would not detract from the glory of the Lone Ranger, would talk little, but help a lot. Basically, a totally dominated subject. The Lone Ranger shares many of the qualities of the heroes of the *peplum filone* of Italian popular cinema (1950s): Ursus, Hercules, Maciste, etc., who fought evil usurpers and killed the tyrants of antiquity in order to put a good new ruler on the throne, reasserting the stability of the status quo, and making sure that no changes would destabilize hegemonic rule. The Lone Ranger, via his law enforcement actions, helps to consolidate the Anglo-American civilization, therefore promoting ideas of authoritarianism, vigilantism, and a benevolent form of white supremacy. See Fitzgerald, "Cold War Avengers" in *Native Americans on Network TV* (Lanham, MD: Rowman & Littlefield, 2014), pp. 40–41.

34. According to Dorfman, the mask "represents the anonymous nature of justice, the dedication to a cause that reaches the point of abnegation, and the renunciation of everyday aspirations." For Trendle and Striker, the masked man was motivated by a burning desire to help the settlers, by his love of country and never by his own personal gain (in *Empire's Old Clothes* (New York: Penguin Books, 1996), p. 101). We could say that the Lone Ranger certainly drained history of discontent, so the viewers could "consume" or enjoy the fable/myth. The Lone Ranger appeared in the middle of the greatest economic crisis of capitalism—the Great Depression—immediately after the Green Hornet, Batman, Flash Gordon, and Superman were created. Dorfman and other critics believe that it is not a coincidence that these protagonists were brought to light in a moment in which an entire economic system was collapsing. The new superheroes were a means to dream, a way out of the crisis. (p. 116).

35. Fitzgerald, 2014, p. 45. Vigilantism has to be intended as the subordination of the law to the actions of some special individuals like the Ranger, who pursue evil for the good of the majority and allow a measure of justice to happen. It goes without saying that without these individuals the authorities would not be able to keep justice afloat, hence we need the vigilantes, and we should also try to emulate them for the good of society.

36. Fitzgerald, 2014, pp. 41, 43.

37. See Mary E. Bickel, *George W. Trendle: Creator and Producer of the Lone Ranger, the Green Hornet, Sgt. Preston of the Yukon, the American Agent, and Other Successes* (New York: Exposition Press, 1971).

38. Fitzgerald, 2014, p. 43. The episodes that deal with Indians are few in number: "War Horse" (air date October 20, 1949); "Renegades" (November 3, 1949); "Rifles and Renegades" (May 4, 1950); and "White Man's Magic" (July 13, 1950). The Ranger is working like Jeffords in *Broken Arrow* (1950) to preserve peace between the two races, but his idea of preservation implies Indians' quiet acceptance of reservation life and/or assimilation, a step up from the eradication program of many classic Westerns, but still very far from considering the "Other" as equal. See Michael Ray Fitzgerald, *Native Americans on Network TV* (Lanham, MD: Rowman & Littlefield, 2014), p. 49.

39. See Stanley Corkin, *Cowboys as Cold War Warriors* (Philadelphia: Temple University Press, 2004). Fitzgerald labels natives like Tonto "the Regulators," i.e., minority characters presented as enforcers of the hegemonic group's values. For the treatment of the "Other" as Native Americans, Asians or other minorities see the interesting article by Tom Engelhardt, "Ambush at Kamikaze Pass" in which the critic argues that in most Hollywood films (war, western, science-fiction) the non-whites are depicted either as dependable/sidekick (like Tonto), sometimes helpless, or as evil and inhuman. However, the more they are independent

219

Notes—Chapter 5

and resist the white man's colonization the more they deserve extermination (*Bulletin of Concerned Asian Scholars* 3, no. 1, Winter-Spring 1971). According to Edward Said nothing could be better for the colonizer than a native subject who expresses assent to his superior knowledge and power, accepting his judgment on the backward nature of his own society; this is what happens to Tonto, when, deciding to be the sidekick of the white savior, he exclaims, "Me want law here too—for all." (Edward Said, *Culture and Imperialism* (New York: Vintage Books, 1993), p 149).

40. Zig Misiak, *Tonto: The Man in Front of The Mask* (Brantford, ON: Real People's History, 2013), p. 51.

41. Misiak, 2013, pp. 115–116.

42. Each TV episode starts with this voice-over narration: "This is the story of one of the most mysterious characters to appear in the early days of the West. He was a fabulous individual—a man whose presence brought fear to the lawless and hope to those who wanted to make this frontier land their home."

43. There are many theories on the origin of the words "kemo sabe," and there seems to be little agreement on the exact translation; supposedly it is a term that originated from a Native American language, but experts do not agree on which language, and therefore we chose the translation that best suits Striker's character.

44. For a detailed history of *The Lone Ranger* in books, comic strips, pulp and features films see Allen Chadwick, "Hero with Two Faces: The Lone Ranger as Treaty Discourse," *American Literature* 68, no. 3 (1996): pp. 614–616.

45. In the televisual episodes everything gets resolved in the happy ending. When the villains get reprimanded, everything goes back to normal; in this way the viewer is reassured that the status quo is re-established and justice prevails. The Lone Ranger never rebels against the law, he does not oppose society, and he acts on behalf of the system so that such a system can continue to prosper. See Ariel Dorfman, *Empire's Old Clothes—What the Lone Ranger, Babar, and Other Innocent Heroes Do to Our Mind* (New York: Penguin Books, 1996), pp. 96–97.

46. Allen Chadwick, "Hero with Two Faces: The Lone Ranger as Treaty Discourse," *American Literature* 68, no. 3 (1996): p. 610.

47. For a detailed analysis of *Broken Arrow* see Chapter 2. Chadwick, in "Hero with Two Faces," defines the creation of this kind of Wild West fantasy-history as "treaty discourse."

48. See Catherine Shoard, "*The Lone Ranger*: A Box Office Flop Rides into Town," *The Guardian*, August 7, 2013.

49. Matt Zoller Seitz, "The Lone Ranger," July 3, 2013, on rogerebert.com.

50. Daniel Kelly, "*The Lone Ranger*," August 8, 2013, on eFilmCritic.com.

51. "*The Lone Ranger* Tells Two Stories at the Same Time, Baffling Everyone," July 7, 2013, on dallasfilmnow.com. The reviews in the *Austin Chronicle*, the *Hollywood Reporter*, *The Independent Critic*, by Leonard Maltin on IndieWire, and Walter Chaw on filmfreakcentral.net as well as A.O. Scott, "Hero Rides Again, with Big Boots to Fill," *The New York Times*, were all negative. The only positive comments came from the many user reviews posted on IMDb; Peter Suderman in *The Washington Times*, July 3, 2013 was also (almost) sympathetic.

52. For a highly technical recount of the amazing results achieved in cinematography by Bojan Bazelli in the making of *The Lone Ranger* see Rachel K. Bosley, "Big Guns," *American Cinematographer* 94, no. 8 (August 2013): pp. 32–45. Bazelli recalls that "production decided to build a six-mile railroad that encircled our Colby town set in the desert outside Albuquerque, and we used that for the train action in the prairie. By making the track a circle, we could position the train wherever we needed to in order to maintain our backlight strategy at any time of the day."

53. See Catherine Shoard, "*The Lone Ranger*: A Box Office Flop Rides into Town," *The Guardian*, August 7, 2013; Peter Bradshaw, "*The Lone Ranger*—Review," *The Guardian*, August 8, 2013; Xan Brooks, "Johnny Depp and Jerry Bruckheimer Blame Critics for *Lone Ranger* Flop," *The Guardian*, August 6,

Notes—Chapter 5

2013; Peter Debruge, "Film-review: *The Lone Ranger*," *Variety*, June 30, 2013.

54. The televisual episodes are "Enter the Lone Ranger," "The Lone Ranger Fights On," and "The Lone Ranger Triumphs." Verbinski developed the original story of the silver mine that existed in the hypotext into a more substantial one, connecting it to the story of Tonto as a boy, and then linking Cavendish and Cole's silver-mine discovery to their railroad ploy. It seems that the director picked ideas about the criminal figures from various televisual episodes and then wove their development into a more complex narration than the one of the originals.

55. Martin Zeller-Jacques, "Adapting the X-Men Comic-Book Narratives in Film Franchises" in *A Companion to Literature, Film and, Adaptation*, Deborah Carmell, ed. (Oxford: Wiley Blackwell, 2014), p. 144.

56. Martin Zeller-Jacques, 2014, p. 147

57. Martin Zeller-Jacques, 2014, p. 147.

58. The film was shot in different locations in Monument Valley, Dead Horse State Park, and Moab in Utah; Canyon de Chelly, and Kayenta in Arizona; Alamosa and Creed in Colorado; Shiprock, Hurley, Angel Fire, Abiquiu, and Puerco Valley in New Mexico; and Long Pine and Sunland in California; however, for the viewer it is always Texas.

59. The story, reorganized chronologically, can be summarized as follows: An Indian boy (Tonto), in exchange for a cheap pocket watch, one day shows two white men a huge silver deposit. In order to keep the silver secret, the men, Cavendish and Cole, massacre the boy's tribe. Tonto, the only survivor, later decides to pursue the killers and exact revenge. Twenty years later, the two white men decide to harvest the ore using the approaching railroad. Cole uses Cavendish to kill the Texas Rangers because Dan Reid has discovered Cole's plan to simulate Indian raids in order to annul the peace treaty with the Comanches; then he uses the cavalry to kill the innocent Indians and get the ore valued sixty-five million dollars. It is at this point that John Reid, only survivor of the Texas Rangers, embraces the mask and, with Tonto, kills Cole, Cavendish and the cavalry captain.

60. It is 1933, the Lone Ranger radio show has just started to be broadcast, and the Golden Gate bridge is under construction; it will be finished in 1937.

61. Johnny Depp borrowed his iconic look from Kirby Sattler's painting entitled "I am Crow." Tonto sports the same dead crow headdress and the same white and black painting on the face. However, the costume is not accurate historically, but an invention of Sattler. See "Johnny Depp's Tonto Is Based on a White Man's Painting of an Imaginary Native American," https://gawker.com/5906868/johnny-depps-tonto-is-based-on-a-white-mans-painting-of-an-imaginary-native-american. There have been mixed feelings in the Native American community: some claim that the improvement in the Tonto character is a good sign, while others believe that a Native American, and not a white man with "painted face," should have been chosen for the role of Tonto. The way Tonto speaks in the 2013 screen version of the film is an improvement if compared with the pidgin English of the televisual Tonto, but it is still stilted, and choppy as "Redmen speak," proving that some stereotypes still persist (Chr. Alex Hider, "*Lone Ranger* Sparks Debate Over Native American Portrayal," *USA Today*, July 8, 2013).

62. When John Reid drags Cavendish in chains through the desert, a red meteor-like object crosses the screen and dissolves the image of the two men on a dune. As soon as we start wondering what this red "sun" is, we see the blotch dissolving in water, and realize that is a drop of opium that is poured into a glass of water by a Chinese woman that slowly comes into focus; the camera then pans over to where Rebecca lies recovering from her fall, after being "rescued" by Cole. This is another instance of "overlapping," a bit different from the others, but serving the same purpose.

63. The technique of "overlapping"

Notes—Chapter 5

the images is similar to what Rizzo talks about when she affirms that, disconnecting the linear logic of images and reconnecting them in different ways, generates new modes of thinking. Connecting images with artifice creates an "interstice" that increases our possibility of going beyond the limitation of conventional thought (see Teresa Rizzo, *Deleuze and Film* (New York: Continuum, 2012), p. 71).

64. The Comanche chief's story of "Tonto as a boy" is a "story within the story," and, in this case, a flashback inside a flashback.

65. A "spirit-walker" is, according to Tonto, "a man who has been to the other side and returned, a man who cannot be killed in battle," but, as we know, the Indian is a bit untrustworthy. Butch Cavendish, who eats the heart of Dan Reid, has a history of cannibalism, and seems to have consumed Red's leg also. According to Tonto, a "wendigo" is "an evil spirit born in the empty spaces of the desert with a hunger that cannot be satisfied, and the power to turn nature out of balance." I would interpret the cannibalistic hunger of Cavendish as a projection of his insatiable greed. He is a more brutal incarnation of the vice, while Cole, who is equally consumed by greed, is a more civilized version of the same desire, having been able to cover it with erudition, good manners, rhetoric, and hypocrisy. The costume and the disfigured-grimy look of Cavendish also classifies him as a brute, while Cole is always dressed in a spotless business suit, disguising well his predatory nature.

66. Northrop Frye talks about "an exquisite balance between comic heroism and comic irony," and we believe this describes well the predicament of John Reid for most of the film (*Anatomy of Criticism* (Princeton, NJ: Princeton UP, 1971), p. 44).

67. Tonto as portrayed in Verbinski's film would please Sherman Alexie, a Native American novelist who wrote a collection of short-stories in 1993 entitled *The Lone Ranger and Tonto Fistfight in Heaven* (New York: Harper Perennial, 1994). Alexie was advocating for a Tonto who rebels against the Ranger, acquiring his own identity and reclaiming his own land and his past. The new version of Tonto might achieve this goal, finally presenting a Native American who has rescued himself from the white men's stereotypes.

68. Dan makes fun of John's suit and of his big hat in two occasions; also, Cavendish comments on John's suit the first time he meets him. Pointing a gun at him, he exclaims, "Nice suit!"

69. The iconic objects that pertain to the two texts are the black leather mask, the white hat, the Ranger star, and the silver bullet, to which, I would also add the white horse, Silver. Verbinski, however, has inserted more iconic objects into his filmic narration: the bird seeds that Tonto feeds to the dead raven on his tiara every time he feels uncomfortable, in danger or uneasy; the pocket watch, and an azure scarf that belongs to Rebecca, but keeps reappearing on different characters. This scarf links the woman, Dan's widow, to John, symbolizing their romantic, but platonic relationship. The most powerful object of all is the pocket watch. Closeups of different pocket watches fill the screen at least fourteen times, thus becoming signifiers of different concepts of time. There is the Comanche time, the time of their extermination, a time to die, a time that the white man calls "progress" and will turn them into ghosts. There is Cole's obsession with time because for him time is money; it means profit, a way to connect the country rapidly together, a speedier road to success, to the stock exchange, and ultimately to power. There is the broken pocket watch of Tonto, broken like him because it reminds him of the massacre of his people, a broken time that will be "restored" only when the evildoers Cole and Cavendish die.

70. At the outset of the story, when we meet young lawyer John Reid on the train, he is reading *Two Treatises of Government* by John Locke and says to a passenger, "This is my bible!" Later, he recites Locke's words to Cole. John's quotation is referring to the treaty of political philosophy in which the philosopher argued that

Notes—Chapter 5

all men are created equal by God in the state of nature. But, while in the state of nature the individuals are under no obligations to obey one another, with the rise of civilization they need to obey laws to enter into civil and political society. The quoting of Locke reinforces the idealistic nature of the young attorney.

71. In a certain sense Verbinski's West is not too dissimilar from Leone's; see Chapter 1.

72. The Texas Rangers and the settlers are assassinated by the Cavendish gang; Tonto's village is destroyed by Cavendish and Cole; the Comanche tribes are mowed down by the cavalry because they are unjustly accused of killing the settlers (in reality Cavendish's men dressed like Indians perpetrate the crime). All these massacres are commissioned by Cole to protect his interests. Cole wants the railroads to go across the Indian territory in order to harvest the silver. To achieve his goal he has Cavendish's gang kill the Rangers, because Dan had discovered the truth, and was opposing his plan, and then he orders the raids of the settlements so to nullify the peace treaty with the Comanche Nation.

73. See Richard Slotkin, *Gunfighter Nation* (New York, Harper Perennial, 1993), pp. 347–353, 29–32.

74. Teresa Rizzo, *Deleuze and Film* (New York: Continuum, 2012), p. 70.

75. Rizzo, 2012, p. 71.

76. Rizzo, 2012, pp. 74–75.

77. Rizzo, 2012, pp. 59–76.

78. Verbinski's film is an artistic object that reflects on its own construction. Instead of minimizing the camera's presence and producing a narrative flow that approaches reality, the filmic text continuously plays against it. I want to mention a particular instance in which Tonto, making trade with a dead Ranger, gives him in return an empty peanut bag: How can Tonto, in the middle of the wilderness in 1869 have an empty peanut bag that looks exactly like the bag of peanuts that the boy gave him at the beginning of the film in 1933 inside the Wild West Exhibition? As we can see, the wall between past and present is porous.

79. We cannot forget, as Northrop Frye explains, that the filmic murderous (in our case also cannibalistic) violence is not only an attack on society by malicious individuals, but more a symptom of a society out of balance. In Tonto's repeated sentence, "Nature is out of balance," we need to include not only animals, but also humans. See Frye talking about ironic comedy in *Anatomy of Criticism*, p. 48.

80. The film was nominated in the "Best Achievement in Visual Effects" category at the 2014 Academy Awards, proving, as Rick Marshall writes, "...a film does not need to be successful at the box office—or well-liked by critics—to merit an invitation to the Oscar party" (p. 2). As Verbinski underlines in the same article, the train is a significant character in the film, symbolizing, even if negatively, "progress and the inevitability of change" (pp. 3–4). As Marshall points out: "John Reid and Tonto's adventures culminate in a third act that features two trains chasing each other on crisscrossing tracks, hurtling through a landscape of forests, deserts, cliffs, and tunnels. As the trains speed along in parallel with Tonto in one train and a host of villains in the other, John Reid pursues them while riding his trusty steed Silver, eventually overtaking them and—in one memorable sequence—galloping across the top of a train while it chugs along. Naturally, this all unfolds to the tune of the William Tell Overture, the iconic theme of the [televisual] Lone Ranger" (pp. 4–5). Verbinski's plan was to have the train sequence run through all the different environments shot in five different states and multiple sections of tracks, in order to keep at least half the action of the sequence happening in the frame as it was shot, and create the other half digitally "with footage of the actors on top of a train or shots of the train itself matched with digitally created environments that featured the other train chugging along in parallel" (pp. 5–6). The team also used a series of railroad cars that were mounted on tractor-trailer trucks. In the end, the visual team "had to push the limits of what they were capable of creating when it came to the rapidly moving surroundings. Between the ever-present

Notes—Chapter 5

smoke, the combination of digital and authentic elements, the natural transition between light and dark as the trains hurtled along, and the speed at which everything was moving—to name just of a few of the issues the visual effects designers faced—the initial plan to keep at least half of the action happening in front of the camera (instead of digitally added) had to be scrapped early in production" (pp. 7–8). The final action sequence is "all about timing and music" as the visual effect supervisor, Tim Alexander, points out (p. 5), and, we would add, it turned out to be spectacular. In Rick Marshall, "Oscar Effects: Going Locomotive in *The Lone Ranger*," February 27, 2014, www.digitaltrends.com/gaming/lone-ranger-fx/. See also "Gore Verbinski—The Lone Ranger: A Classic Western Shot On Film and Digital Formats," *Post*, August 2013, p.12, on http://www.postmagazine.com/Publications/Post-Magazine/2013/August1,2013/Directors-Chair-Gore-Verbinski-The-Lone-Ranger.aspx.

81. Rizzo, 2012, pp. 59–60.

82. Jackson Blair in "The Lone Ranger Rides Again! Sound Challenges of a Fun-filled Western," writes: "The Lone Range, starring Armie Hammer in the title role and Johnny Depp as Tonto, ... is a Western for a new generation of moviegoers, a deft blending of imaginative, cleverly staged action sequences, a compelling classic story and doses of humor, both silly and dark. This just might work." It looks like some critics recognized that the film is original and well done. The article also contains a detailed description of the use of sound effects and music, with interviews with the people who created them, explaining how the train noise, the Gatlin gun, the wind and the music by Hans Zimmer were blended together to follow a certain rhythm (in *Mix* 37, issue 7 (July 2013): pp. 32–35).

83. Scorpions also appear at the beginning of *The Wild Bunch*.

84. The structure of the bridge and the explosion recall a scene of *Two Mules for Sister Sara* (1970, Don Siegel) in which a nun (Shirley MacLaine) puts the charges on a structure made of wood very similar to the one in Verbinski's film, and then she and Hogan (Clint Eastwood) watch the explosion. John Reid dragging Cavendish in chains through the desert brings to mind a similar sequence of *The Good, the Bad, and the Ugly* in which Tuco drags Blondie through the desert, holding a cute pink parasol. In our hypertext, it is Tonto that carries the parasol crossing the Indian territory.

85. Ian R. Smith, *The Hollywood Meme: Transnational Adaptations in World Cinema* (Edinburgh: Edinburgh UP, 2017), p 31.

Bibliography

Adorno, Theodor, and Max Horkheimer. *Dialectic of Enlightenment*. New York: Herder and Herder, 1969.
Aleiss, Angela. *Making the White Man's Indian*. Westport, CT: Praeger, 2005.
Alexie, Sherman. *The Lone Ranger and Tonto Fistfight in Heaven*. New York: Harper Perennial, 1994.
Anderson, Terry L., et al. (eds.) *Self-Determination: The Other Path for Native Americans*. Stanford: Stanford UP, 2006.
Andrew, Geoff. *The Films of Nicholas Ray*. London: BFI Publishing, 2004.
Aquila, Richard. *The Sagebrush Trail-Western Movies and Twentieth-Century America*. Tucson: Arizona UP, 2015.
Argentieri, Mino. *Il cinema italiano dal dopoguerra a oggi*. Roma: Editori Riuniti, 1998.
Armour, Robert A. *Fritz Lang*. Boston: Twayne Publishers, 1978.
Avi, Santo. *Selling the Silver Bullet: The Lone Ranger and Transmedia Brand Licensing*. Austin: University of Texas Press, 2015.
Bahun-Radunović, Sanja, and V. G. Julie Rajan (eds.). *Myth and Violence in the Contemporary Female Text: New Cassandras*. Burlington, VT: Ashgate, 2011.
Bakhtin, Mikhail M. *The Dialogic Imagination: Four Essays*. Michael Holquist (ed.) Austin: University of Texas Press, 1988.
____. *Problems of Dostoevsky's Poetics*. Caryl Emerson (Ed.) Minneapolis: Minnesota UP, 1984.
Bandy, Mary Lea, and Kevin Stoehr (eds.). *Ride, Boldly Ride—The Evolution of the American Western*. Berkeley: California UP, 2012.
Basinger, Jeanine. *A Woman's View—How Hollywood Spoke to Women, 1930–1960*. New York: Knopf, 1993.
Bataille, Gretchen. *The Pretend Indians: Images of Native Americans in the Movies*. Ames: Iowa State UP, 1980.
Baues, Dale. "Gender in Bakhtin's Carnival." In *Feminism, an Anthology of Literary Theory and Criticism*. New Brunswick, NJ: Rutgers UP, 1991.
Bazin, Andrè. *What is Cinema?* Berkeley: University of California Press, 1971.
Behlmer, Rudy (ed.). *Memo from David O. Selznick*. New York: Viking Press, 1972.
Benjamin, Jessica. *The Bonds of Love—Psychoanalysis, Feminism, and the Problem of Domination*. New York: Pantheon Books, 1988.
Bernstein, Alison R. *American Indians and World War II*. Norman: UP of Oklahoma, 1991.
Bickel, Mary E. *George W. Trendle: Creator and Producer of the Lone Ranger, the Green Hornet, Sgt. Preston of the Yukon, the American Agent, and Other Successes*. New York: Exposition Press, 1971.
Bini, Andrea. *Male Anxiety and Psychopathology in Film—Comedy Italian Style*. New York: Palgrave and Macmillan, 2015.

Bibliography

Bishop, Franco. *Crossing the Pond: The Native American Effort in WWII.* Denton, TX: North Texas UP, 1999.
Bogdanovich, Peter. *Fritz Lang in America* New York: Praeger, 1967.
Bondanella, Peter and Peter Pacchioni, *A History of Italian Cinema.* New York: Bloomsbury Academic, 2017.
Brizio-Skov, Flavia. *Popular Italian Cinema: Culture and Politics in a Postwar Society.* London: I.B. Tauris, 2011.
Brode, Douglas. *Dream West: Politics and Religion in Cowboy Movies.* Austin: University of Texas Press, 2013.
Brogi, A. *Confronting America. The Cold War Between the United States and the Communists in France and Italy.* Chapel Hill, NC: North Carolina UP, 2011.
Broughton, Lee (ed.). *Critical Perspectives on the Western—From 'A Fistful of Dollars' to 'Django Unchained.'* Lanham, MD: Rowman & Littlefield, 2016.
_____. *The Euro-Western-Reframing Gender, Race and the 'Other' in Film.* London: I.B. Tauris, 2016.
Burgin, Victor, James Donald and Cora Kaplan (eds.). *Formations of Fantasy.* London: Metheun, 1986.
Busch, Niven. *Duel in the Sun.* New York: Pocket Books, 1977.
Buscombe, Edward. *The BFI Companion to the Western.* New York: Atheneum, 1988.
_____. *'Injuns!': Native Americans in the Movies.* London: Reaktion, 2006.
Buscombe, Edward, and Roberta E. Pearson (eds.). *Back in the Saddle Again-New Essays on the Western.* London: BFI Publishing, 1998.
Byman, Jeremy. *Showdown at High Noon—Witch-Hunts, Critics, and the End of the Western.* Lanham, MD: Scarecrow Press, 2004.
Cagle, Chris. *Sociology on Film. Postwar Hollywood's Prestige Commodity.* New Brunswick, NJ: Rutgers UP, 2016.
Calder, Jenni. *There Must Be a Lone Ranger.* London: Hamish Hamilton, 1974.
Cameron, Ian, and Douglas Pye (eds.). *The Book of Westerns.* New York: Continuum, 1996.
Campbell, Neil. *Post-Westerns: Cinema, Region, West.* Lincoln: Nebraska UP, 2013.
_____. *Rhizomatic West: Representing the American West in a Transnational, Global, Media Age.* Lincoln: Nebraska UP, 2008.
Cardullo, Bert. *Bazin on Global Cinema 1948–1958.* Texas: University of Texas Press, 2014.
Carter, Matthew. *Myth of the Western.* Edinburgh: Edinburgh UP, 2015.
Cartmell, Deborah (ed.). *A Companion to Literature, Film, and Adaptation.* Malden, MA: Wiley-Blackwell, 2014.
Cawelti, John G. *Six Gun Mystique.* Bowling Green, OH: Bowling Green UPP, 1971.
_____. *The Six-Gun Mystique Sequel.* Bowling Green, OH: Bowling Green UPP, 1999.
Cazdin, Eric. *The Flash of Capital- Film and Geopolitics in Japan.* Durham: Duke University Press, 2002.
Chanslor, Roy. *Johnny Guitar.* New York: Simon & Schuster, 1953.
Churchill, Ward. *Fantasies of the Master Race: Literature, Cinema, and the Colonization of the American Indians.* San Francisco: City Lights Books, 1998.
_____. *Struggle for the Land: Native North American Resistance to Genocide, Ecoside, and Colonization.* San Francisco: City Lights Books, 2002.
Codell, Julie F. (ed.). *Genre, Gender, Race, and World Cinema.* Malden, MA: Blackwell Publishing, 2007.
Cohen, Clélia. *Il Western: il vero volto del cinema americano.* Torino: Lindau, 2006.
Constable, Catherine. *Thinking in Images.* London: BFI Publishing, 2005.
Cook, Pam (ed.). *The Cinema Book.* London: BFI Publishing, 2007.
Corkin, Stanley. *Cowboys as Cold Warriors—The Western and U.S. History.* Philadelphia: Temple UP, 2004.
Coyne, Michael. *The Crowded Prairie: American National Identity in the Hollywood Western.* London: I. B. Tauris, 1997.

5. Bibliography

Danow, David K. *The Thought of Mikhail Bakhtin: From Word to Culture.* New York: St. Martin's Press, 1991.
Deleuze, Gilles. *Cinema 1: The Movement Image.* Minneapolis: Minnesota UP, 1986.
Dixon, Wheeler Winston (ed.). *Film Genre 2000. New Critical Essays.* New York: New York Press, 2000.
Doane, Mary Ann. *Femmes Fatales-Feminism, Film Theory, Psychoanalysis.* New York: Routledge, 1991.
Dorfman, Ariel. *The Empire Old Clothes. What the Lone Ranger, Babar, and Other Innocent Heroes Do to Our Mind.* New York: Penguin Books, 1996.
Douglass, K. Daniel. *Tough as Nails—The Life and Films of Richard Brooks.* Madison: University of Wisconsin Press, 2011.
Dumbar-Ortiz, Roxanne. *An Indigenous Peoples' History of the Unites States.* Boston: Beacon Press, 2014.
Dyer, Richard. *Stars.* London: BFI Publishing, 1998.
Dyer, Richard, and Ginette Vincendau (eds.). *Popular European Cinema.* London: Routledge, 1992.
Dyer, Thomas C. *Theodore Roosevelt and the Idea of Race.* Baton Rouge: Louisiana UP, 1980.
Eagle, Jonna. *Imperial Affects-Sensational Melodrama and the Attractions of American Cinema.* New Brunswick, NJ: Rutgers UP, 2017.
Eisner, Lotte H. *Fritz Lang.* London: Secker & Warburg, 1998.
Eleftheriotis, Dimitris. *Popular Cinemas of Europe.* London: Continuum, 2001.
Ellwood, D., and G.P. Brunetta, (eds.). *Hollywood in Europa: industra, politica, pubblico del cinema 1945–60.* Firenze: Casa Usher, 1991.
Emerson, Caryl (ed.). *Bakhtin, Mikhail M. : Problems of Dostoevsky's Poeticics.* Minneapolis: Minnesota UP, 1963
Engelhardt, Tom. *The End of Victory Culture. Cold War America and the Disillusioning of a Generation.* Amherst: Massachusetts UP, 1995.
Ezra, Elizabeth, and Terry Rowden (eds.). *Transnational Cinema: The Film Reader.* London: Routledge, 2006.
Fasce, Fernando, M. Vaudagna and R. Baritono (eds.). *Beyond the Nation: Pushing the Boundaries of U.S. History from a Transatlantic Perspective*s. Torino: Otto-Nova Americana in English, 2013.
Ferrero, Adelio, Giovanna Grignaffini, Leonardo Quaresima (eds.). *Il cinema italiano degli anni '60.* Firenze: Guaraldi, 1977.
Fiedler, Leslie. *The Return of the Vanishing American.* New York: Stein and Day, 1968.
Fisher, Austin. *Grindhouse.* New York: Bloomsbury Academic, 2016.
_____. *Radical Frontiers in the Spaghetti Western.* London: I.B. Tauris, 2011.
_____. *Spaghetti Westerns at the Crossroads.* Edinburgh: Edinburgh UP, 2016.
Fitzgerald, Michael Ray. *Native Americans on Network TV-Stereotypes, Myths, and the "Good Indian."* Lanham, MD: Rowman & Littlefield, 2014.
_____. "Television Westerns, Termination, and Public Relations: An Analysis of the ABC Series *Broken Arrow,* 1956–1958." *Film & History: An Interdisciplinary Journal* 41, no. 1 (Spring 2011): pp. 48–70.
Frayling, Christopher. *C'era una volta in Italia—Il cinema di Sergio Leone.* Bologna: Cineteca di Bologna, 2014.
_____. *Sergio Leone: Something to Do with Death.* London: Faber & Faber, 2000.
_____. *Spaghetti Westerns: Cowboys and Europeans from Karl May to Sergio Leone.* London: Tauris, 1998.
French, Philip. *Westerns.* London: Secker and Warburg, 1973.
Friar, Ralph E., and Natasha A. Friar. *The Only Good Indian; The Hollywood Gospel.* New York: Drama Book Specialists, 1972.
Frye, Northrop. *Anatomy of Criticism.* Princeton: Princeton UP, 1957.
Genette, Gérard. *Palimpsests: Literature in the Second Degree.* Lincoln: Nebraska UP, 1997.

Bibliography

_____. *Palinsesti—La letteratura al secondo grado*. Torino: Einaudi, 1997.
Ginsborg, Paul. *A History of Contemporary Italy. Society and Politics 1943–1988*. London: Palgrave MacMillan, 1990.
Goldoni, Carlo. *The Servants of Two Masters*. London: Nick Hern Books, 2012.
Goral, Pawel. *Cold War Rivalry and the Perception of the American West*. New York: Palgrave-Macmillan, 2014.
Gramsci, Antonio. *Antonio Gramsci: Prison Notebooks*. New York: Columbia UP, 1996.
Grant, Barry Keith (ed.). *Film Genre Reader II*. Austin: Texas UP, 1995.
_____. *Film Genre Reader III*. Austin: Texas UP, 2003.
Hall, Stuart (ed.). *Representation—Culture Representations and Signifying Practices*. London: Sage Publications—The Open University, 1997.
Hammett, Dashiell. *Red Harvest*. New York: Avenel Books, 1980.
Haskell, Molly. *From Revenge to Rape: The Treatment of Women in the Movies*. Chicago: University of Chicago Press, 1987.
Herzberg, Bob. *Hang 'Em High: Law and Disorder in Western Films and Literature*. Jefferson, NC: McFarland, 2013.
_____. *Savages and Saints*. Jefferson, NC: McFarland, 2008.
Hitt, Jim. *The American West from Fiction (1823–1976) into Film (1909–1986)*. Jefferson, NC: McFarland, 1990.
Hollinger, Karen. *Feminist Film Studies*. New York: Routledge, 2012.
Holmlund, Chris. *Impossible Bodies: Femininity and Masculinity at the Movies*. London: Routledge, 2002.
Hosmer, Brian, and Larry Nesper's (eds.) *Tribal Worlds: Critical Studies in American Indian Nation Building*. New York: SUNY Press, 2013.
Hutcheon, Linda. *A Theory of Adaptation*. New York: Routledge, 2006.
Indick, William. *The Psychology of the Western*. Jefferson, NC: McFarland, 2008.
Jameson, Frederic. *The Political Unconscious: Narrative as a Socially Symbolic Act*. Ithaca, NY: Cornell UP, 1981.
Jenkins, Tricia. *The CIA and Hollywood: How the Agency Shapes Film and Television*. Austin: Texas UP, 2012.
Kaplan, E. Ann (ed.). *Feminism and Film*. New York: Oxford UP, 2000.
Kelley, Megan N. *Projections of Passing—Postwar Anxieties and Hollywood Films 1947–1960*. Jackson: University of Mississippi Press, 2016.
Kendrick, James. *Film Violence: History, Ideology, Genre*. London: Wallflower, 2009.
Kilpatrick, Jacquelyn. *Celluloid Indians: Native Americans and Film*. Lincoln: University of Nebraska Press, 1999.
Kirkham, Pat, and Janet Thumin. *Me Jane—Masculinity, Movies and Women*. London: Lawrence & Wishart, 1995.
Kitses, Jim, and Gregg Rickman (eds.). *The Western Reader*. New York: Limelight Editions, 1998.
Kreidl, John Francis. *Nicholas Ray*. Boston: Twayne Publishers, 1977.
Layman, Richard, and Julie M. Rivett (eds.). *Selected Letters of Dashiell Hammett 1921–1960*. Washington, D.C.: Counterpoint, 2001.
Lenihan, John H. *Showdown: Confronting Modern America in the Western Film*. Urbana: Illinois UP, 1985.
Leutrat, Jean Louis, and Suzanne Liandrat-Guigues. *Le carte del Western: percorsi di un genere cinematografico*. Genova: Le Mani, 1993.
Lichtenfeld, Eric. *Action Speaks Louder*. Westport, CT: Praeger, 2004.
Lippmann, Walter. *Public Opinion*. New Brunswick. NJ: Transaction Publishers, 1998.
Loy, Philip R. *Westerns and American Culture*. Jefferson, NC: McFarland, 2001.
_____. *Westerns in a Changing America, 1955–2000*. Jefferson, NC: McFarland. 2004.
Lusted, David. *The Western*. London: Pearson-Longman, 2003.
Maddrey, Joseph. *The Quick, the Dead and the Revived—The Many Lives of Western Film*. Jefferson, NC: McFarland, 2016.

5. Bibliography

Martinez, D. P. *Remaking Kurosawa—Translations and Permutations in Global Cinema.* New York: Palgrave MacMillan, 2009.
Marubbio, M. Elise. *Killing the Indian Maiden. Images of Native American Women in Film.* Lexington: UP of Kentucky, 2006.
Marubbio, M. Elise, and Eric L. Buffalohead (eds.). *Native Americans on Film: Conversations, Teaching, and Theory.* Lexington: Kentucky UP, 2012.
Matheson, Sue. *Love in Western Film and Television.* New York: Palgrave-Macmillan, 2013.
_____. (ed.). *A Fistful of Icons—Essays on Frontier Fixtures of the American Western.* Jefferson, NC: McFarland, 2017.
McClain, William. "Western, Go Home! Sergio Leone and the 'Death of the Western' in American Film Criticism," *Journal of Film and Video* 62, no. 1–2 (Spring–Summer 2010): pp. 52–66.
McConnell-Ginet, Sally, Ruth Borker, and Nelly Furman (eds.). *Women and Language in Literature and Society.* New York: Praeger, 1980.
McGee, Patrick. *From Shane to Kill Bill—Rethinking the Western.* Malden, MA: Blackwell Publishing, 2007.
McGilligan, Patrick. *Nicholas Ray.* New York: Harper and Collins, 2011.
McMahon, Jennifer, and B. Steve Csaki (eds.). *The Philosophy of the Western.* Lexington: Kentucky UP, 2010.
McVeigh, Steven. *The American Western.* Edinburgh: Edinburgh UP, 2007.
Mellencamp, Patricia. *A Fine Romance: Five Ages of Film Feminism.* Philadelphia: Temple UP, 1995.
Meuel, David. *The Noir Western: Darkness on the Range, 1943–1962.* Jefferson, NC: McFarland, 2015.
Miller, Cynthia J., and A. Bowdoin Van Riper (eds.). *International Westerns: Re-Locating the Frontier.* Lanham, MD: Scarecrow Press, 2014.
Misiak, Zig. *Tonto: The Man in Front of the Mask.* Brantford, ON: Real People's History, 2013.
Mitchell, Lee Clark. *Westerns: Making the Man in Fiction and Film.* Chicago: University of Chicago Press, 1996.
Morsiani, Alberto. *L'America e il Western: storie e film della frontiera.* Roma: Gremese, 2007.
Nachman, Gerald. *Raised on Radio.* New York: Pantheon Books, 1998.
Naficy, Hamid, and Teshone Gabriel (eds.). *Otherness and the Media: An Ethnography of the Imagined and the Imaged.* Langhorne, PA: Harwood Academic Publishers, 1993.
Nelson, Andrew Patrick. *Still in the Saddle—The Hollywood Western, 1969–1980.* Norman: Oklahoma UP, 2015.
Nelson, Andrew Patrick, and Edward Buscombe (eds.). *Contemporary Westerns—Film and Television Since 1990.* Lanham, MD: Scarecrow Press, 2013.
Nolletti, Arthur. *The Films of Fred Zinnemann: Critical Perspectives.* Albany: State University of New York Press, 1999.
Nowell-Smith, Geoffrey, and Stephen Ricci (eds.). *Hollywood and Europe: Economics, Culture, National Identity 1945–95.* London: BFI, 1998.
O'Connor John E. *Hollywood's West: The American Frontier in Film, Television, and History.* Lexington: Kentucky UP, 2005.
Panek, LeRoy Lad. *Reading Early Hammett.* Jefferson, NC: McFarland, 2004.
Parker, David Wilson. "A Descriptive Analysis of the Lone Ranger as a Form of Popular Art." Dissertation, Northwestern University, 1956.
Paryz, Marek, and John R. Leo (eds.). *The Post–2000 Film Western.* London: Palgrave Macmillan, 2015.
Pettey, Homer B. (ed.). *The Western.* Vashon Island, WA: Paradoxa, 2004.
Pippin, Robert B. *Hollywood Westerns and American Myths: The Importance of Howard Hawks and John Ford for Political Philosophy.* New Haven: Yale University Press, 2010.

Bibliography

Quaglietti, Lorenzo. *Storia economico-politica del cinema italiano 1945–1980*. Roma: Editori Riuniti, 1980.
Ray, Nicholas. *I Was Interrupted—Nicholas Ray on Making Movies*. Los Angeles: University of California Press, 1993.
Read, Jacinta. *The New Avengers. Feminism, Femininity and the Rape-Revenge Cycle*. Manchester, UK: Manchester UP, 2000.
Richie, Donald. *The Films of Akira Kurosawa*. Berkeley: University of California Press, 1996.
Rizzo, Teresa. *Deleuze and Film*. New York: Continuum, 2012.
Roberts, David. *Once They Moved Like the Wind—Cochise, Geronimo, and the Apache Wars*. New York: Simon & Schuster, 1993.
Robertson, Pamela. *Guilty Pleasures: Feminist Camp from Mae West to Madonna*. Durham: Duke University Press, 1996.
Rollins, Peter C. *Hollywood's Indian: The Portrayal of the Native American in Film*. Lexington: University of Kentucky Press, 1998.
Rossen, Robert, Frank Krutnik, et al. (eds.). *Un-American Hollywood: Politics and Film in the Blacklist Era*. New Brunswick, N.J.: Rutgers University Press, 2007.
Rosso, Stefano. *Le frontiere del Far West. Forme di Rappresentazione del grande mito americano*. Milano: Shake Edizioni, 2008.
Rybin, Steven, and Will Scheibel (eds.). *Lonely Places, Dangerous Grounds: Nicholas Ray in American Cinema*. New York: SUNY Press, 2014.
Said, Edward. *Culture and Imperialism*. New York: Knopf, 1993.
Sanders, Julie. *Adaptation and Appropriation*. London: Routledge, 2005.
Sato, Tadao. *Currents in Japanese Cinema*. New York: Kodansha International, 1982.
Schatz, Thomas. *Hollywood Genres*. New York: Random House, 1981.
Scheibel, Will. *American Stranger—Modernism, Hollywood, and the Cinema of Nicholas Ray*. New York: SUNY, 2017.
Server, Lee. *Encyclopedia of Pulp Fiction Writers*. New York: Checkmark Books, 2002.
Sheffer, Jolie A. *The Romance of Race: Incest, Miscegenation, and Multiculturalism in the United Sates, 1880–1930*. News Brunswick, NJ: Rutgers University Press, 2012.
Shohat, Ella, and Robert Stam. *Unthinking Eurocentrism*. New York: Routledge, 1994.
Simmon, Scott. *The Invention of the Western Film: A Cultural History of the Genre's First Half-Century*. Cambridge, UK: Cambridge UP, 2003.
Slocum, David J. (ed.). *Violence and American Cinema*. New York: Routledge, 2001.
Slotkin, Richard. *The Fatal Environment: The Myth of the Frontier in the Age of Industrialization, 1800–1890*. New York: Harper Perennial, 1994.
_____. *Gunfighter Nation: The Myth of the Frontier in Twentieth-Century America*. New York: Harper Perennial, 1993.
_____. *Regeneration Through Violence: The Mythology of the American Frontier, 1600–1860*. Middletown, CT: Wesleyan UP, 1973.
Smith, Andrew Brodie. *Shooting Cowboys and Indians: Silent Western Films, American Culture, and the Birth of Hollywood*. Boulder: Colorado UP, 2003.
Smith, Carlton. *Coyote Kills John Wayne*. Hanover, NH: New England UP, 2000.
Smith, Ian Robert. *The Hollywood Meme: Transnational Adaptations in World Cinema*. Edinburgh: Edinburgh UP. 2017.
Smyth, J. E. *Reconstructing American Historical Cinema: From Cimarron to Citizen Kane*. Lexington: Kentucky UP, 2006.
Staiger, Janet. *Interpreting Films*. Princeton: Princeton UP, 1992.
Stanfield, Peter. *Hollywood, Westerns, and the 1930s: The Lost Trail*. Exeter: Exeter UP, 2001.
_____. *Horse Opera—The Strange History of the 1930s Singing Cowboy*. Urbana: Illinois UP, 2002.
Stoddard, F. Scott (ed.). *The New Western: Critical Essays on the Genre Since 9/11*. Jefferson, NC: McFarland, 2016.

5. Bibliography

Suleiman, Susan. *The Female Body in Western Culture: Contemporary Perspectives*. Cambridge, MA: Harvard University Press, 1986.
Sweeney, Edwin R. *Cochise: Chiricahua Apache Chief*. Norman: University of Oklahoma Press, 1991.
Symons, Julian. *Dashiell Hammett*. New York: Harcourt Brace Jovanovich, 1985.
Takacs, Stacy. *Interrogating Popular Culture*. New York: Routledge, 2015.
Tasker, Yvonne (ed.). *Action and Adventure Cinema*. New York: Routledge, 2004.
Thomson, David. *Showman*. New York: Knopf, 1992.
Tibbetts, John C., and James Michael Welsh (eds.). *American Classic Screen Features*. Lanham, MD: Scarecrow Press, 2010.
Tompkins, Jane. *West of Everything*. New York: Oxford UP, 1992.
Townsend, Kenneth William. *World War II and the American Indian*. Albuquerque: UP of New Mexico, 2000.
Trumbo, Dalton. *The Time of the Toad*. New York: Harper, 1972.
Uva, Christian. *Sergio Leone—Il cinema come favola politica*. Roma: Ente dello Spettacolo, 2013.
Varner, Paul (ed.). *Westerns: Paperbacks Novels and Movies from Hollywood*. Newcastle, UK: Cambridge Scholars Publishing, 2007.
Walle, Alf H. *The Cowboy Hero and Its Audience: Popular Culture as Market Derived Art*. Bowling Green, OH: Bowling Green UP, 2000.
Warhol, Robyn R. *Feminism: An Anthology of Literary Theory and Criticism*. New Brunswick, NJ: Rutgers UP, 1991.
Warshow, Robert. *The Immediate Experience: Movies, Comics, Theatre & Other Aspects of Popular Culture*. New York: Atheneum, 1971.
Whitfield, Stephen J. *The Culture of the Cold War*. Baltimore: Johns Hopkins UP, 1996.
Wildermuth, Mark E. *Feminism and the Western in Film and Television*. New York: Palgrave-Macmillan, 2018.
Williams, Alan (ed.). *Film and Nationalism*. London: Rutgers UP, 2002.
Wolfe, Peter. *Beams Falling: The Art of Dashiell Hammett*. Bowling Green: Bowling Green UP, 1980.
Wright, Will. *Six Guns and Society: A Structural Study of the Western*. Berkeley: University of California Press, 1975.
Yoshimoto, Mitsuhiro. *Kurosawa*. Durham: Duke University Press, 2000.
Zampieri, Filippo (ed.). *Carlo Goldoni—Opere*. Milano: Ricciardi Editore, 1954.
Zarzosa, Agustin. *Refiguring Melodrama in Film and Television*. Lanham, MD: Lexington Books, 2013.

Index

Numbers in **_bold italics_** indicate pages with illustrations

Across the Wide Missouri (1951, Wellman) 47
action movies 155
adaptations 2, 5, 9, 15, 20–1, 33; and *Yojimbo* 26, 27, 29; see also *The Lone Ranger*
African-Americans 48, 65, 148–9
Aldrich, Robert: *Apache* (1954) 47, 190*n*37; *Sodom and Gomorrah* (1961) 20
Almeria (Spain) 20, 21, 40, 185*n*78
Alton, John 62
American-ness 46–7, 59, 61–2
Antonioni, Michelangelo: *L'avventura* (1961) 17
Apache (1954, Aldrich) 47, 190*n*37
Apache Indians 52–5, 56, 58, 81; and *The Last Wagon* 68, 70, 71, 73
Apache Woman (1955, Corman) 47
Appaloosa (2008, Harris) 2, 154
Arizona 67
Arnold, Elliott: *Blood Brothers* 52
Arrowhead (1953, Warren) 188*n*24
art cinema 15
Arthur, Jean 89, **_90_**
The Assassination of Jesse James by the Coward Robert Ford (2007, Dominik) 1–2
assimilation 6, 49–50, 52, 65, 79
auteurists 122

Bad Girls (1994, Kaplan) 84, 153
Bagni, Gwen 67
Bakhtin, Mikhail 6–7, 10, 85–6; see also heteroglossia; monoglossia; x-glossia
The Ballad of Little Jo (1993, Greenwald) 84, 153
Bandidas (2006, Hill) 1, 2
Barboni, Enzo 20

Bascom, Lt George 58
Basinger, Jeanine 113–14, 115, 130
The Battle of Apache Pass (1952, Sherman) 6, 47, 58–9
Bazin, André 45–6, 99, 186*n*1
Ben-Hur (1959, Wyler) 18, 19, 20
Berk, Aaron: *Cowboys and Aliens* (2011) 2
Berk, Tyler: *Cowboys and Aliens* (2011) 2
The Big Sky (1952, Hawks) 47
Black Panthers 43
blacks *see* African-Americans
Blankfort, Michael 48, 52
Blaustein, Julian 52
blockbusters 155
Blood Brothers (Arnold) 52
Bond, Ward 123, 128
Bone Tomahawk (2015, Zahler) 2
Bonham Carter, Helena 168
Bonnard, Mario 19; *The Last Days of Pompeii* (1959) 20
Bosone, Reva Beck 50
Brady, Scott 127
Brode, Douglas 145
Broken Arrow (1950, Daves) 6, 47, 50–6, 160
Broken Lance (1954, Dmytryk) 47
Brooks, Richard 48, 192*n*53; *The Last Hunt* (1956) 6, 47, 74–9; *The Professionals* (1966) 153
Brower, Otto 138
buffalo 74, 75–6, 78–9
Busch, Niven 211*n*88; and *Duel in the Sun* 109, 137, 138–41

Cahn, Edward L.: *Oklahoma Territory* (1960) 47
Calhern, Louis 60
camera shots: and *Devil's Doorway* 62–3;

233

Index

and *Duel in the Sun* 149–50; and *High Noon* 94, 98; and *Johnny Guitar* 134; and *The Last Hunt* 74, 78; and *The Last Wagon* 68; and *The Lone Ranger* (film) 165–6, 172, 173, 174; and *The Lone Ranger* (TV series) 158; and Native Americans 53; and *Rancho Notorious* 115; and *Shane* 89; *see also* close-ups
Camerini, Mario 19
Campbell, Neil 4–5, 7
campness 122
Canyon de Chelly National Monument 163
capitalism 14, 27, 36, 38–9, 43, 136, 153; and *Duel in the Sun* 149–51
cattle barons 128, 149–50
cavalry 5, 52, 58–9, 68
Cawelti, John G.: *The Six-Gun Mystique* (1984) 86
censorship 16, 79, 138
Chadwick, Allen 160
Chandler, Jeff 52–3, 55
Chanslor, Roy: *Johnny Guitar* 109, 121–2, 123, *124*, 125–7
Charney, Leo 122
chase 67, 68, 125–6
Cheyenne Indians 57, 81, 82
chiaroscuro techniques 62, 142
Chief Crazy Horse (1955, Sherman) 190*n*37
Christianity 68, 70
Cinecittà 18, 182*n*27
cinematography 62, 67, 127; *see also* Technicolor
civil rights 6, 43, 50, 153
Civil War 59, 66, 70
civilization 55, 65, 83; and *Devil's Doorway* 66; and *The Last Wagon* 70, 72–3; and *The Lone Ranger* 157, 160; and Native Americans 56, 57, 58, 80; and *Rancho Notorious* 112, 116; and women 10, 86
class 8, 11, 110, 136; and *Duel in the Sun* 140, 141–2, 144, 145, 146, 147; and Italy 181*n*21; and *Johnny Guitar* 128
Cleopatra (1963, Mankiewicz) 18
Cline, Wilfred M. 67
close-ups 41–2, 75, 116
Cochise 52–3, 55, 58, 82, 190*n*35
Coen, Ethan: *True Grit* (2010) 2, 154
Coen, Joel: *True Grit* (2010) 2, 154
Cold War 14, 17, 18, 48, 50; and *Johnny Guitar* 122, 135; and *The Lone Ranger* 157, 172

colonization 40–1
Colorado Territory (1949, Walsh) 177*n*1
The Colossus of Rhodes (1959, Leone) 20
Comanche (1956, Sherman) 190*n*37
Comanche Indians 67, 70–1, 72, 81; and *The Lone Ranger* 167, 168, 171
comedy 16, 17, 24–5, 148, 169–70
Comencini, Luigi 19
commedia dell'arte 24–5, 183*n*47
Communism 17–18, 48, 157; *see also* House Un-American Activities Committee
community 10, 23, 32, 79–80, 86; and *Broken Arrow* 52, 53, 55; and *Devil's Doorway* 59–61, 63, 65, 66; and *High Noon* 95–7, 99; and *Johnny Guitar* 127–9, 135; and *The Last Hunt* 74–5; and *The Last Wagon* 67, 68, 70, 72–3; and *Rancho Notorious* 111–12, 113; and *Shane* 89, 91
consumers 155
Cook, Pam 86
Cooper, Gary 94, *96*, 98, 112
Cooper, James Fenimore 73
Cooper, Scott: *Hostiles* (2017) 2
Corbucci, Sergio 20; *Django* (1966) 178*n*8; *The Great Silence* (1968) 177*n*1, 178*n*8
Corkin, Stanley 149
Corman, Roger: *Apache Woman* (1955) 47
corruption 22, 27, 35, 39, 112, 170
Cosmatos, George P.: *Tombstone* (1993) 153
Costner, Kevin: *Dances with Wolves* (1990) 2, 49, 73, 80, 84, 153; *Open Range* (2003) 1, 154
costume 81; and *Duel in the Sun* 142; and *Johnny Guitar* 129, 130–1, 132–3; and women 86, 91, 93, 102–3, 105, 115; *see also* mask
Cotton, Joseph 138
counter-culture 43, 153
The Cowboy and the Indians (1949, English) 47
cowboys 39, 153, 216*n*28
Cowboys and Aliens (2011, Berk) 2
Crawford, Joan 121–2, 126, 128, 130–1, *132*, 208*n*62
Crazy Horse 81
critics 3–4, 161–2
Crowther, Bosley 98, 122, 137
culture 9, 15, 66; and Native Americans

Index

81–2, 83; and USA 18; and women 89; see also popular culture
Custer, Lt Col George Armstrong 81

Dakota Incident (1956, Foster) 47
Dances with Wolves (1990, Costner) 2, 49, 73, 80, 84, 153
Daniels, Harold: *Daughter of the West* (1949) 47
Darcel, Denise 101
Daughter of the West (1949, Daniels) 47
Daves, Delmer 57; *Broken Arrow* (1950) 6, 47, 50–6, 160; *Drum Beat* (1954) 47; *The Last Wagon* (1956) 6, 47, 67–73
Dawes Act (1887) 49
De Sicca, Vittorio: *La ciociara* (1960) 17
De Wilde, Brandon **90**
Deloria, Vine 80, 81
Depp, Johnny 161, 163, 165, **171**
desegregation 50, 65
Destry Rides Again (1939, Marshall) 204*n*15
detective fiction 22–4, 26, 27
Devil's Doorway (1950, Mann) 6, 49, 59–67, 73
Dieterle, William 138
Dietrich, Marlene 111, 113–15, **117**, 119, 120, 205*n*25
Disney 11, 161
distribution 15, 16, 21, 43
Django (1966, Corbucci) 178*n*8
Django Unchained (2012, Tarantino) 2, 178*n*8
Dmytryk, Edward 48
Doane, Mary Ann 109
Dominik, Andrew: *The Assassination of Jesse James by the Coward Robert Ford* (2007) 1–2
Douglas, Gordon: *Yellowstone Kelly* (1959) 47
Drum Beat (1954, Daves) 47
Duck, You Sucker! (1971, Leone) 40
Duel in the Sun (1946, Vidor) 7–8, 10–11, 47, 88, 109; and capitalism 149–51; and filmic text 141–3; and novel 139–41; and paratext 136–9; and patriarchy 143–9
duels 25, 141

Eason, Reeves 138
Eastwood, Clint 20, 35, 153; *High Plains Drifter* (1973) 43; *The Outlaw Josey Wales* (1976) 43; *Unforgiven* (1992) 2, 84, 153

English, John: *The Cowboy and the Indians* (1949) 47
epics 18–19, 20
Evans, Robert 99
Expressionism 15
extras 82–3

fables 39–40
Fabrizi, Aldo 19
Fairbanks, Douglas 33
Falconer, Peter 153
family 89, 91–2
Farrow, John: *Hondo* (1953) 47
Fellini, Federico: *La dolce vita* (1960) 17
female gaze 105–7
femininity 7, 8; and *Duel in the Sun* 146–9; and *High Noon* 97–8; and *Johnny Guitar* 131–3; and melodrama 109, 110–11; and *Rancho Notorious* 116; and *Westward the Women* 100–1
feminism 84, 88, 108
femme fatales 114, 115, 120
Ferrer, Mel 111
feuilleton fiction 126
Fichtner, William 168
film *noir* 62, 111
A Fistful of Dollars (1964, Leone) 5, 15, 20–2, 34–44
Flaming Star (1960, Siegel) 47
flashbacks 113, 119, 164, 166–7
Fleming, Victor: *Gone with the Wind* (1939) 137, 148
Ford, John 36, 46; *The Man Who Shot Liberty Valance* (1962) 46, 88; *My Darling Clementine* (1946) 87; and Native Americans 177*n*5, 195*n*80; *Rio Grande* (1950) 46, 88; *The Searchers* (1956) 8, 66, 175–6; *Stagecoach* (1939) 36, 46, 72, 87, 88, 109; *Two Rode Together* (1961) 87
Ford, Philip: *Ranger of the Cherokee Strip* (1949) 47
Forty Guns (1957, Fuller) 86
Foster, Gwendolyn 94
Foster, Lewis R.: *Dakota Incident* (1956) 47
Foster, Norman: *Navajo* (1952) 47
Fox *see* 20th-Century–Fox
France 122
Frayling, Sir Christopher: *Sergio Leone: Something to Do About Death* 19
frontier 1, 4, 9, 34, 64–5; and *Johnny Guitar* 127; and myth 73, 154, 186*n*1; and Native Americans 49

Index

Frye, Northrop 22, 23, 42
Fuller, Samuel 48; *Forty Guns* (1957) 86; *Run of the Arrow* (1950) 51
Fuqua, Antoine: *The Magnificent Seven* (2016) 2

Gallone, Carmine 19
gangster movies 26, 27
gender 7–8, 85–6, 136; *see also* masculinity; women
genocide 52, 79, 157, 160, 172
genres 2, 7, 8, 11, 152, 155
Geronimo 53, 56, 58, 82, 190*n*35
Gilmore, Stuart: *The Half-Breed* (1952) 47
Giraldi, Franco 20
Goldoni, Carlo: *The Servant of Two Masters* 5, 21, 22, 24–6, 183*n*47
Gone with the Wind (1939, Fleming) 137, 148
The Good, the Bad, and the Ugly (1966, Leone) 176
The Good, the Bad, and The Weird (2008, Jee-woon Kim) 2
good versus evil 8, 21, 22, 78, 151; and Leone 37; and *The Lone Ranger* 156–7; and women 93–4
Granger, Stewart 74, **76**, **77**
Grant, James Edward 67
Great Plains Indians 81
The Great Silence (1968, Corbucci) 177*n*1, 178*n*8
Greenwald, Maggie: *The Ballad of Little Jo* (1993) 84, 153

The Half-Breed (1952, Gilmore) 47
Hammer, Armie 162, 165, **171**
Hammett, Dashiell: Red Harvest 5, 15, 22–4, 26, 27–9, 32, 42, 183*n*46
happy endings 7, 40, 67, 71, 109; and *Duel in the Sun* 140, 141; and *Rancho Notorious* 110, 111
Harris, Ed: *Appaloosa* (2008) 2, 154
The Hateful Eight (2015, Tarantino) 2–3, 177*n*1, 178*n*8
Hawks, Howard 99
Hayden, Sterling 123, 128, 133–4, 135–6
Hayward, Jimmy: *Jonah Hex* (2010) 2
Heflin, Van 89, **90**
Helen of Troy (1956, Wise/Walsh) 19
heritage 6
heroines *see* women
heteroglossia 7, 93–100
Hiawatha (1952, Neumann) 47

Hibbs, Jesse: *Walk the Proud Land* (1956) 53, 190*n*37
High Noon (1952, Zinnemann) 7, 93–100, 112
High Plains Drifter (1973, Eastwood) 43
Hill, Walter: *Bandidas* (2006) 1, 2; *Last Man Standing* (1996) 34; *Wild Bill* (1995) 153
Hillcoat, John: *The Proposition* (2005) 1
historicity 55–6, 57, 58–9, 66, 190*n*32
Hitchcock, Alfred: *Rebecca* (1939) 137
Hollywood Indian Actors Workshop 158
The Homesman (2014, Jones) 2
Hondo (1953, Farrow) 47
Horizon West (1970, Kitses) 86
horror genre 2
horse operas 8, 49, 154
Hostiles (2017, Cooper) 2
House Un-American Activities Committee (HUAC) 48, 79, 95, 112; and blacklists 187*n*8; and *Johnny Guitar* 122, 123, 128
Howard, Gen Oliver O. 52, 55, 58, 70–1, 190*n*32, 190*n*35
Hughes, Howard 121
Hunter, Jeffrey 57
Huston, John 48; *The Unforgiven* (1960) 47
hybridity 7–8, 9; and *High Noon* 99; and Italian cinema 17–19; and *Johnny Guitar* 122; and spaghetti Westerns 32

iconography 40, 62
identity 65, 66, 157; and women 85–6, 93, 97–8, 105; *see also* national identity
ideology 47, 48, 56, 99, 154
imperialism 47, 158, 172; and *Broken Arrow* 52, 54–5, 56
Inarritu, Alejandro: *The Revenant* (2015) 2
Indian Claims Commission (1946) 65
Indian Wars 81
Indians *see* Native Americans
injustice 11, 39, 110
Italian cinema 16–19, 33, 181*n*16, 182*n*27
  see also Leone, Sergio
Italy 37–8, 43

Jane Got a Gun (2016, O'Connor) 2
Japan 27, 33–4, 37, 48–9
Japanese cinema *see* Kurosawa, Akira
Jee-woon Kim: *The Good, The Bad, and The Weird* (2008) 2
Jeffords, Tom 52–5, 58

Index

Jews 48, 49
jidaigeki (period/samurai) genre 27–32, 33–4, 183*n*54
Johnny Guitar (1954, Ray) 7–8, 10–11, 88, 109, 151
and filmic text 127–36
and paratext 121–3
and peritext 123, *124*, 125–7
Jolly Film 21
Jonah Hex (2010, Hayward) 2
Jones, Jennifer 137, 138, *143*, *148*
Jones, Tommy Lee: *The Homesman* (2014) 2; *The Missing* (2003) 1
Jurado, Katy 95
justice 154, 170–1; *see also* injustice

Kael, Pauline 45
Kane, Joseph: *The Vanishing American* (1955) 47
Kaplan, Jonathan: *Bad Girls* (1994) 84, 153
Kasdan, Lawrence: *Wyatt Earp* (1994) 153
Keller, Harry: *Rose of Cimarron* (1952) 47
Kelly, Grace 94, *96*
Kennedy, Arthur 111
Kitses, Jim: *Horizon West* (1970) 86
Kurosawa, Akira 183*n*51; *The Seven Samurai* (1954) 33; *Throne of Blood* (1957) 26; *see also* Yojimbo

Ladd, Alan 89, *90*
land 50, 56, 64–5; and *Devil's Doorway* 63–4, 65–6
Lang, Fritz 203*n*9; and *Rancho Notorious* (1952) 7–8, 10–11, 88, 109, 111–21
language 81, 87, 101–2, 157, 159
The Last Days of Pompeii (1959, Bonnard) 20
The Last Hunt (1956, Brooks) 6, 47, 74–9
Last Man Standing (1996, Hill) 34
Last Train from Gun Hill (1959, Sturges) 47
The Last Wagon (1956, Daves) 6, 47, 67–73
The Lawless Breed (1952, Walsh) 87
Lee, Sigmoo: *The Warrior's Way* (2010) 2
Lenihan, John H. 79–80
Leone, Sergio 16, 19–22, 25, 32–3, 153; *The Colossus of Rhodes* (1959) 20; *Duck, You Sucker!* (1971) 40; *A Fistful of Dollars* (1964) 5, 15, 20–2, 34–44; *The Good, the Bad, and the Ugly* (1966)

176; *Once Upon a Time in the West* (1968) 175
LeRoy, Mervyn: *Quo Vadis?* (1951) 18, 19
lesbianism 133
Levitin, Jacqueline 86–7
Levring, Kristian: *The Salvation* (2014) 2, 154
Little Big Man (1970, Penn) 49, 161
Little Bighorn, Battle of 81
Lone Ranger (character) 217*n*30, 218*n*33
The Lone Ranger (radio show) 8, 155, 156
The Lone Ranger (TV series) 8, 10, 155–60, 170
The Lone Ranger (2013, Verbinski) 2, 8–10, 11, 154, 155–6
and filmic text 164–76
and paratext 161–4
Lott, Milton: *The Last Hunt* 74
love stories 51–2, 53–4, 71–3, 111, 147–8; and *Johnny Guitar* 125, 126–7, 129–30; *see also* love triangles
love triangles 87–8, 93–4, 118, 139–40
Lucas, Blake 87–8
Lusted, David 110, 142

MacDonald, Ian 94
Maclean, John: *Slow West* (2015) 2
Maddow, Ben 48
The Magnificent Seven (1960, Sturges) 26, 33
The Magnificent Seven (2016, Fuqua) 2
male gaze 96, 100, 105–7
Maltz, Albert 48
A Man Called Horse (1970, Silverstein) 177*n*5, 195*n*82
The Man Who Shot Liberty Valance (1962, Ford) 46, 88
Manga Colorado 59
Mangold, James: *3:10 to Yuma* (2007) 1, 2
Manifest Destiny 4, 34, 43, 154; and *Broken Arrow* 54; and *High Noon* 99; and *The Lone Ranger* 157, 172
Mankiewicz, Joseph: *Cleopatra* (1963) 18
Mann, Anthony 46, 88; *Border Incident* (1949) 62; *Devil's Doorway* (1950) 6, 49, 59–67, 73; *Raw Deal* (1948) 62; *T-Men* (1947) 62
The Mark of Zorro (1920, Niblo) 33
Marshall, George: *Destry Rides Again* (1939) 204*n*15
Marshall Plan 18, 48
martial arts 2
Masaru, Sato 30

237

Index

masculinity 7–8, 109, 110–11, 143–6; and *Duel in the Sun* 141; and *Johnny Guitar* 131, 133–4, 135–6; and *Rancho Notorious* 116; and *Westward the Women* 100–1
mask 157, 160–1, 165–6, 168–71, 174, 219n34
mass culture 14
massacres 67, 68, 69–70, 189n29
Mathews, George 68
May, Karl 21
McCambridge, Mercedes 128, 133
McCarthyism *see* House Un-American Activities Committee
McQueen, Butterfly 148
Meek's Cutoff (2011, Reichardt) 2
melodrama 7–8, 10–11, 22–3, 109–10; and *Duel in the Sun* 141–2, 149; and *Johnny Guitar* 129; and *Rancho Notorious* 119–21
"melting pot" 5, 187n9
Mexicans 93, 94, 95
Mexico 21, 35, 40
Meyer, Emile 90
MGM 137
Miike, Takashi: *Sukiyaki Western Django* (2007) 2
minorities 48–9; *see also* African-Americans; Native Americans
miscegenation 51–2, 55, 88, 147; and *Devil's Doorway* 59, 61, 63
mise-en-scène 2, 35, 37, 40
The Missing (2003, Jones) 1
modernity 37, 46, 126
Mondo documentaries 16
monoglossia 6–7, 85–6, 88, 89–93, 100
Monument Valley 163, 165, 174, 175
Moore, Clayton 157, **159**
morality 28–9, 110; and *Duel in the Sun* 147–8; and *High Noon* 95, 99; and *Rancho Notorious* 118, 120
Morricone, Ennio 42, 175
Moses, Michael Valdez 81
Motion Picture Alliance for the Preservation of American Ideals 123
Motion Picture Bureau 48
Mulligan, Robert: *The Stalking Moon* (1968) 188n24
music 116–18, 119, 121; and *Duel in the Sun* 138; and *Johnny Guitar* 134; and Leone 42, 175; and *The Lone Ranger* (film) 162, 165, 174, 175; and *The Lone Ranger* (TV series) 158; and *Yojimbo* 30, 39

My Darling Clementine (1946, Ford) 87
myth-making 46–7, 49, 50–1, 56, 172; and frontier 73, 154, 186n1

national identity 4–5, 13–14, 26, 33, 154; and Italy 22; and *The Lone Ranger* 160; and USA 46–7; *see also* American-ness
Native Americans 6, 9, 10, 43; and actors 194n73, 195n82; and anti–Indian films 188n24; and assimilation 49–50; and film 79–83; and Ford 177n5, 195n80; and land 65; and myth-making 50–1; and Navajo crisis 189n31; and re-evaluation 153; and World War II 66; *see also* pro–Indian cycle; Tonto
Navajo (1952, Foster) 47
Navajo Indians 81, 189n31
Nazarro, Ray: *The White Squaw* (1956) 47
Neale, Steve 8, 47, 49, 152
Nelson, Ralph: *Soldier Blue* (1970) 153
Neorealism 15
Neumann, Kurt: *Hiawatha* (1952) 47
Niblo, Fred: *The Mark of Zorro* (1920) 33
Nichols, Dudley 48
noble savages 53, 73, 80–1, 82, 160, 162, 169
Nolan, Lloyd 74, **76**
Nott, Gerald: *The Quick and the Undead* (2006) 2
Nouvelle Vague 15

O'Connor, Gavin: *Jane Got a Gun* (2016) 2
Oklahoma Territory (1960, Cahn) 47
Once Upon a Time in Mexico (2003, Rodriguez) 1
Once Upon a Time in the West (1968, Leone) 175
Open Range (2003, Costner) 1, 154
the Other 5, 6, 47, 79, 83; and *Devil's Doorway* 59, 61; and *Duel in the Sun* 147, 149; and *High Noon* 95, 98; and *The Last Wagon* 71, 73; and Native Americans 51, 52; and *Westward the Women* 101
The Outlaw Josey Wales (1976, Eastwood) 43

Paget, Debra 53–4, 55, 57, 75, **77**
passion 11
patriarchy 2, 10, 88, 136; and *Duel in the Sun* 141, 142, 143–9, 150; and *High Noon* 96, 97; and *Johnny Guitar* 127;

Index

and *Shane* 91–2; and *Westward the Women* 102, 103
patriotism 149–51, 156
peace treaties 52, 54–5, 56, 57
Peck, Gregory 138, **143**, **148**
Peckinpah, Sam 46; *The Wild Bunch* (1969) 43, 153, 176
Penn, Arthur: *Little Big Man* (1970) 49, 161
peplum genre 18–19, 20, 21
photography *see* cinematography
pioneers *see* settlers
Pirates of the Caribbean franchise 11, 161, 163–4
politics 136, 139, 140
popular culture 14, 180*n*2
power dynamics 10
Price, John 82
private space 96, 131–2
pro–Indian cycle 6, 10, 47–9, 51–2; and changes 80, 82, 83; see also *The Battle of Apache Pass*; *Broken Arrow*; *Devil's Doorway*; *The Last Hunt*; *The Last Wagon*; *White Feather*
The Professionals (1966, Brooks) 153
progress 10, 37, 39, 47, 52, 80; and *Broken Arrow* 55; and *Devil's Doorway* 65, 66, 67; and *Duel in the Sun* 145, 150; and *Johnny Guitar* 128; and *The Last Hunt* 78–9; and *The Last Wagon* 72–3; and *The Lone Ranger* 170, 172–3
The Proposition (2005, Hillcoat) 1
prototexts 15, 22–6
psychology 8, 136, 139
public space 96, 103, 131–2
Puerto-Ricans 49
pulp fiction 1, 123

The Quick and the Dead (1995, Raimi) 84
The Quick and the Undead (2006, Nott) 2, 153
Quo Vadis? (1951, LeRoy) 18, 19

race 4, 8, 47, 48, 110, 136; and *Devil's Doorway* 59–62, 64; and *Duel in the Sun* 140, 141, 142, 144, 146, 147–9; and film 80–1; and *The Last Hunt* 74–9; and *The Last Wagon* 67, 69–71, 72–3; and *The Lone Ranger* (TV series) 157–8, 160; and white heroes 154; and women 88, 93–4, 95; *see also* Native Americans
radio 8, 155, 156

railroads 34, 128, 139, 140; and *Duel in the Sun* 149–50; and *The Lone Ranger* 166, 173
Raimi, Sam: *The Quick and the Dead* (1995) 84, 153
Rancho Notorious (1952, Lang) 7–8, 10–11, 88, 109, 111–21, 151
Ranger of the Cherokee Strip (1949, P. Ford) 47
Rango (2011, Verbinski) 2, 164
rape 105–6
Ray, Nicholas: *Rebel Without a Cause* (1955) 122; see also *Johnny Guitar*
Raymond, Paula 63
Rebecca (1939, Hitchcock) 137
Red Harvest (Hammett) 5, 15, 22–4, 26, 27–9, 32, 42, 183*n*46
regeneration 37, 78, 135, 154
Reichardt, Kelly: *Meek's Cutoff* (2011) 2
Reinl, Harald: *The Treasure of the Silver Lake* (1962) 21
religion 40–1, 81; *see also* Christianity; Jews
remakes 2, 9, 15, 21, 26–7, 34–5; see also *The Lone Ranger*
reservation life 6, 49, 51, 52, 75; and *Broken Arrow* 56; and *Devil's Doorway* 65
re-temporalization 50
The Revenant (2015, Inarritu) 2
revenge 2, 67; and *Rancho Notorious* 112, 113, 119, 120
Richards, Silvia 109
Rio Grande (1950, Ford) 46, 88
Robertson, Pamela 122, 130
Rocco e i suoi fratelli (1960, Visconti) 17
Rodriguez, Robert: *Once Upon a Time in Mexico* (2003) 1
romance *see* love stories
Rose of Cimarron (1952, Keller) 47
Rousseau, Jean-Jacques 73
Run of the Arrow (1950, Fuller) 51

Salkow, Sidney: *Sitting Bull* (1954) 190*n*37
salvation 67, 70
The Salvation (2014, Levring) 2, 154
samurais *see jidaigeki*
sandal-and-sword epics 18–19, 20, 21
Sanders, Julie 156
Santa Fe Passage (1955, Witney) 47
savages 10, 29, 55, 80–1, 82, 158; *see also* noble savages
science fiction 2, 155
Scorsese, Martin 129

Index

The Searchers (1956, Ford) 8, 46, 66, 175–6
Second World War *see* World War II
Selznick, David O. 109, 137–9, 141, 149, 213n104; and women 146, 147–8
Seraphim Falls (2006, Von Ancken) 1
The Servant of Two Masters (Goldoni) 5, 21, 22, 24–6, 183n47
settlers 64–5, 68, 69–70, 89, 91, 92
The Seven Samurai (1954, Kurosawa) 26–7, 33
sexual liberation 11
sexuality 105–7, 133, 136; and *Duel in the Sun* 138, 142, 145, 146, 147–8
Shakespeare, William: *Macbeth* 26
Shane (1953, Stevens) 7, 8, 89–93
Sherman, George: *The Battle of Apache Pass* (1952) 6, 47, 58–9; *Chief Crazy Horse* (1955) 190n37; *Comanche* (1956) 190n37
Shoshone Indians 59, 61, 64, 65, 191n47
Shugart, Helene 102
Siegel, Don: *Flaming Star* (1960) 47; *Two Mules for Sister Sara* (1970) 43
silent cinema 8, 154
Silverheels, Jay 157, 158, **159**
Silverstein, Elliot: *A Man Called Horse* (1970) 177n5, 195n82
Sioux Indians 81, 82
Sirk, Douglas 48, 110; *Taza, Son of Cochise* (1954) 47, 190n37
Sitting Bull (1954, Salkow) 190n37
The Six-Gun Mystique (1984, Cawelti) 86
Six Guns and Society (1976, Wright) 86
slavery 2
Slotkin, Richard 46, 66, 135, 150
Slow West (2015, Maclean) 2
Smith, Ian Robert 5
Sodom and Gomorrah (1961, Aldrich) 20
Soldati, Mario 19
Soldier Blue (1970, Nelson) 153
sound effects 30–1
soundtrack *see* music
South Asia 2
South Dakota 74
sovereignty 66
space 103, 131–2; *see also* private space; public space
spaghetti Westerns 2, 5, 10; *see also* Leone, Sergio
Spain *see* Almeria
Stagecoach (1939, Ford) 36, 46, 72, 87, 88, 109

The Stalking Moon (1968, Mulligan) 188n24
Stanwyck, Barbara 86
star personas 113–15, 119, 120, 130–1, 163
Steno 19
stereotyping 81–2
Sternberg, Josef von 114, 115
Stevens, George: *Shane* (1953) 7, 8, 89–93
Stewart, James 52–3, 55
Striker, Fran 156–7, 160, 172
Sturges, John: *Last Train from Gun Hill* (1959) 47; *The Magnificent Seven* (1960) 26, 33
submission 89–93
Sukiyaki Western Django (2007, Miike) 2
suspense 98, 160

taboos 136
Tamblyn, Russ 74, **76**
Taradash, Daniel 109
Tarantino, Quentin: *Django Unchained* (2012) 2, 178n8; *The Hateful Eight* (2015) 2–3, 177n1, 178n8
Taylor, Robert 59, 74, **76**, 100, **101**, **104**
Taza, Son of Cochise (1954, Sirk) 47, 190n37
Technicolor 137, 142–3
television 8, 10, 84, 155–60, 170
Termination Act (1950) 6, 50, 65, 66
Tessari, Duccio 20
theatre *see* Goldoni, Carlo
theme songs 116–18, 119, 121, 134
3:10 to Yuma (2007, Mangold) 1, 2
Throne of Blood (1957, Kurosawa) 26
time 119, 120, 166–7, 172–3, 175
Tiomkin, Dimitri 138
titles 121, 127, 135
Tombstone (1993, Cosmatos) 153
Tompkins, Jane 87
Tonto 9, 11; and TV series 157, 158, 159, 160; and 2013 film 161, 162, 163, 165–70, 171, 174–5, 176
town women 93, 96, 102, 125
transformation 100–8
transgression 93–100, 146, 147
transnationalism 4–5, 13–16; and Italy 18–19, 21–2, 182n27; and Kurosawa 26–32
The Treasure of the Silver Lake (1962, Reinl) 21
Trendle, George 156, 158, 172
tribalism 49

Index

Trosper, Guy 62
True Grit (2010, Coen Brothers) 2, 154
Truffaut, François 127
Truman, Harold S. 48
Turner, Frederick Jackson 1, 4, 49, 172
20th Century–Fox 52, 55
Two Mules for Sister Sara (1970, Siegel) 43
Two Rode Together (1961, Ford) 87
Tyrell, Ian: "What Is Transnational History?" 14

Unforgiven (1992, Eastwood) 2, 84, 153
The Unforgiven (1960, Huston) 47
United States of America (USA) 17–18, 33–4, 43, 56, 187n9; and cowboys 153; and minorities 48–50; and Native Americans 65, 66
"unreal women" 115–16

The Vanishing American (1955, Kane) 47
Verbinski, Gore: *Rango* (2011) 2, 164; see also *The Lone Ranger*
Vidor, King 137–8; see also *Duel in the Sun*
Vietnam War 43, 153
violence 2, 7–8, 154; and *Devil's Doorway* 61; and *Johnny Guitar* 134, 135; and *The Last Hunt* 75, 78; and Leone 37, 38–9; and *The Lone Ranger* 162; and melodrama 110; and *Rancho Notorious* 113, 118; and *Shane* 91, 92; and spaghetti Westerns 16; and *Westward the Women* 101, 105–6; and *Yojimbo* 30, 31, 32, 36; see also massacres
Visconti, Luchino: *Rocco e i suoi fratelli* (1960) 17
voice-overs 55, 57, 143, 147, 158
Von Ancken, David: *Seraphim Falls* (2006) 1

Wagner, Robert 57
Walk the Proud Land (1956, Hibbs) 47, 190n37
Walsh, Raoul 19; *Colorado Territory* (1949) 177n1; *The Lawless Breed* (1952) 87
Warren, Charles Marquis: *Arrowhead* (1953) 188n24
The Warrior's Way (2010, Lee) 2
Wayne, John 39, 99, 135, 153
Webb, Robert D.: *White Feather* (1955) 6, 47, 57, 190n37

Welles, Orson 143
Wellman, William A. 201n54; *Across the Wide Missouri* (1951) 47, *Westward the Women* (1951) 7, 100–8
West Germany 21
Westward the Women (1951, Wellman) 7, 100–8
White, Susanna: *Woman Walks Ahead* (2018) 2
white actors 80–2, 83, 190n37
White Feather (1955, Webb) 6, 47, 57, 190n37
The White Squaw (1956, Nazarro) 47
Widmark, Richard **69, 72**
Wild Bill (1995, Hill) 153
The Wild Bunch (1969, Peckinpah) 43, 153, 176
Wildermuth, Mark E.: *Feminism and the Western in Film and Television* 84
wilderness 71–2, 73, 74, 78–9; and *High Noon* 98; and *The Lone Ranger* 173, 174; and *Westward the Women* 103; see also land
Wilkinson, Tom 166
William Tell Overture (Rossini) 158, 162, 165, 174
"Winnetou Westerns" 21
Witney, William: *Santa Fe Passage* (1955) 47
Woman Walks Ahead (2018, White) 2
women 2, 6–8, 10, 84–5, 86–8, 109–10; and *Devil's Doorway* 59, 61, 63–4; and *Duel in the Sun* 140–1, 142, 144–9, 150–1; and *High Noon* 93–100; and *Johnny Guitar* 125, 126–7, 128, 129–33, 135; and *The Last Hunt* 76–7, 78; and Native Americans 51–2, 53–4; and *Rancho Notorious* 113–16, 118–19, 119–20, 121; and *Shane* 89–91; and *Westward the Women* 100–8; see also femininity; love stories
Wood, Robin 146
World War II 45, 48–9, 56, 66
Wright, Will: *Six Guns and Society* (1976) 86
Wyatt Earp (1994, Kasdan) 153
Wyler, William: *Ben-Hur* (1959) 18, 19, 20
Wyoming 111, 112, 123, 128

x-glossia 7, 85, 86, 100–8

Yellowstone Kelly (1959, Douglas) 47
Yojimbo (1961, Kurosawa) 26–32, 39;

241

Index

and Leone 5, 15, 20, 22, 33, 34–7, 40–1, 42, 44
Yordan, Philip 109, 121, 122, 123
Young, Victor 134

Zahler, S. Craig: *Bone Tomahawk* (2015) 2
Zanuck, Darryl F. 52, 187n9
Zeller-Jacques, Martin 164
Zinnemann, Fred: *High Noon* (1952) 7, 93–100, 112; *The Nun's Story* (1959) 19

www.ingramcontent.com/pod-product-compliance
Lightning Source LLC
Chambersburg PA
CBHW021352300426
44114CB00012B/1186